Thomas Kelly Cheyne

Job and Solomon

Or, the wisdom of the Old Testament

Thomas Kelly Cheyne

Job and Solomon
Or, the wisdom of the Old Testament

ISBN/EAN: 9783337316181

Printed in Europe, USA, Canada, Australia, Japan

Cover: Foto ©Lupo / pixelio.de

More available books at **www.hansebooks.com**

JOB AND SOLOMON

OR

THE WISDOM OF THE OLD TESTAMENT

BY THE

REV. T. K. CHEYNE, M.A., D.D.

ORIEL PROFESSOR OF INTERPRETATION AT OXFORD
CANON OF ROCHESTER

NEW YORK
THOMAS WHITTAKER
2 AND 3 BIBLE HOUSE
1889

TO

THE VERY REVEREND

GEORGE GRANVILLE BRADLEY, D.D.

DEAN OF WESTMINSTER

IN HIGH APPRECIATION OF HIS LONG-PROVED INTEREST IN EXEGESIS

AND OF HIS HAPPILY CONCEIVED LECTURES ON ECCLESIASTES

PREFACE.

THE present work is a fragmentary realisation of a plan which has been maturing in my mind for many years. Exegesis and criticism are equally necessary for the full enjoyment of the treasures of the Old Testament, and just as no commentary is complete which does not explain the actual position of critical controversies, so no introduction to the criticism of a book is trustworthy which does not repose, and show the reader that it reposes, on the basis of a thorough exegesis. In this volume I do not pretend to have approached the ideal of such students' manuals as I have described; I have not been sufficiently sure of my public to treat the subject on the scale which I should have liked, and such personal drawbacks as repeated changes of residence, frequent absence from large libraries, and within the last two years a serious eye-trouble, have hindered me in the prosecution of my work. Other tasks now claim my restored strength, and I can no longer withhold my volume from those lovers of the sacred literature who in some degree share the point of view from which I have written.

The Books of Job and Ecclesiastes are treated somewhat more in detail than those of Proverbs and Ecclesiasticus. The latter have a special interest of their own, but to bring this into full view, more excursions into pure philology would have been necessary than I judged it expedient to allow myself. I had intended to make up for this omission so far as Proverbs is concerned at the end of the volume, but have been interrupted in doing so. Perhaps, however, even in the Appendix such detailed treatment of special points might have repelled some readers, and I hope that the Appendix is on the whole not unreadable. The enlarged notes on Proverbs in the forthcoming new edition of Messrs. Eyre and Spottiswoode's Variorum Bible may enable the student to do for himself what I have not done. As for Ecclesiasticus, the light which Prof. Bickell's and Dr. Edersheim's researches are sure to throw on the text may enable me some day to recast the section on this book ; at present, I only offer this as an illustrative sequel to the section on Proverbs. It should be added that the canonicity of Ecclesiasticus is handled in conjunction with that of Ecclesiastes at the close of the part on the latter book.

The interest of Job and Ecclesiastes is of a far deeper and more varied kind. Even from a critical point of view, the study of these books is most refreshing after the incessant and exciting battles of Pentateuch-criticism. But as monuments of the spiritual struggles of a past which is not wholly dead, they have been to me, as doubtless to many others, sources of pure delight. If I appreciate Job more highly than Ecclesiastes, it is not from any want of living sympathy with the philosophic doubter, but because the enjoyment even of Scriptures is dependent on moods and impulses. De Sanctis has pointed out (*Storia della letteratura italiana*, i. 80) how the story of Job became the favourite theme of the early Italian moralists, and everyone knows how the great Latin doctors (Gregory the Great, Bede, Aquinas, Albertus Magnus) delighted to comment on this wonderful book. In our own day, from perfectly intelligible causes, Ecclesiastes has too much drawn off the attention of the educated world, but there are signs that the character-drama of Job will soon reassert its old fascinating power.

In conclusion, will earnest students, whether academical or not, grant me two requests ? The first is, that they will meet me with confidence, and gather any grains of truth they can, even where they cannot yield full assent. The problems of Hebrew literature are complex; herein partly lies their fascination; herein also is a call for mutual tolerance on the part of all who approach them. There is nothing to regret in this complexity; in searching for the solution of these problems, we gain an ever fresh insight into facts and ideas which will never lose their significance. My second request is, that the Appendix, which, short as it is, contains something for different classes of readers, may not be neglected as *only an Appendix*.

I would add that the 'much-desired aid' in the critical use of the Septuagint referred to on p. 114 has already to a large extent been given by Gustav Bickell's essay (see p. 296), which I have now been able to examine. His early treatise (1862) is at length happily supplemented and corrected. We shall know still more when P. Ciasca has completed the publication of the fragments of the Sahidic version. It is clear however that each omission in the pre-Hexaplar Septuagint text (represented by this version) must be judged upon its own merits, nor can I estimate the value of the text of the Septuagint quite as highly as some critics.

It is hoped that the present work may be followed by a volume on the Psalms, the Lamentations, and the Song of Songs.

CONTENTS.

	PAGE
INTRODUCTION	1

THE BOOK OF JOB.

CHAPTER
- I. JOB'S CALAMITY; THE OPENING OF THE DIALOGUES (Chaps. i.-xiv.) 11
- II. THE SECOND CYCLE OF SPEECHES (Chaps. xv.-xxi.) . . 30
- III. THE THIRD CYCLE OF SPEECHES (Chaps. xxii.-xxxi.) . 37
- IV. THE SPEECHES OF ELIHU (Chaps. xxxii.-xxxvii.) . . 42
- V. THE SPEECHES OF JEHOVAH (Chaps. xxxviii.-xlii. 6) . 48
- VI. THE EPILOGUE AND ITS MEANING 58
- VII. THE TRADITIONAL BASIS AND THE PURPOSE OF JOB . 60
- VIII. DATE AND PLACE OF COMPOSITION 71
- IX. ARGUMENT FROM THE USE OF MYTHOLOGY . . . 76
- X. ARGUMENT FROM THE DOCTRINE OF ANGELS . . . 79
- XI. ARGUMENT FROM PARALLEL PASSAGES 83
- XII. ON THE DISPUTED PASSAGES IN THE DIALOGUE PORTION, ESPECIALLY THE SPEECHES OF ELIHU . . 90
- XIII. IS JOB A HEBRÆO-ARABIC POEM? 96
- XIV. THE BOOK FROM A RELIGIOUS POINT OF VIEW . . 102
- XV. THE BOOK FROM A GENERAL AND WESTERN POINT OF VIEW 106
    - *Note* on Job and the Modern Poets . . . 112
    - *Note* on the Text of Job 112
    - *Aids to the Student* 115

THE BOOK OF PROVERBS.

CHAPTER		PAGE
I.	HEBREW WISDOM, ITS NATURE, SCOPE, AND IMPORTANCE	117
II.	THE FORM AND ORIGIN OF THE PROVERBS	125
III.	THE FIRST COLLECTION AND ITS APPENDICES	130
IV.	THE SECOND COLLECTION AND ITS APPENDICES	142
V.	THE PRAISE OF WISDOM	156
VI.	SUPPLEMENTARY ON QUESTIONS OF DATE AND ORIGIN	165
VII.	THE TEXT OF PROVERBS	173
	Note on Prov. xxx. 31	175
VIII.	THE RELIGIOUS VALUE OF THE BOOK OF PROVERBS	176
	Aids to the Student	178

THE WISDOM OF JESUS THE SON OF SIRACH.

I.	THE WISE MAN TURNED SCRIBE. SIRACH'S MORAL TEACHING	179
II.	SIRACH'S TEACHING (continued). HIS PLACE IN THE MOVEMENT OF THOUGHT	188
	Aids to the Student (see also Appendix)	198

THE BOOK OF KOHELETH; OR, ECCLESIASTES.

I.	THE WISE MAN TURNED AUTHOR AND PHILOSOPHER	199
II.	'TRUTH AND FICTION' IN AN AUTOBIOGRAPHY	207
III.	MORE MORALISING, INTERRUPTED BY PROVERBIAL MAXIMS	213
IV.	FACTS OF CONTEMPORARY LIFE	218
V.	THE WISE MAN'S PARTING COUNSELS	222

CONTENTS

CHAPTER		PAGE
VI.	KOHELETH'S 'PORTRAIT OF OLD AGE;' THE EPILOGUE, ITS NATURE AND ORIGIN	229
VII.	ECCLESIASTES AND ITS CRITICS (FROM A PHILOLOGICAL POINT OF VIEW)	236
VIII.	ECCLESIASTES AND ITS CRITICS (FROM A LITERARY AND PSYCHOLOGICAL POINT OF VIEW)	242
IX.	ECCLESIASTES FROM A MORAL AND RELIGIOUS POINT OF VIEW	248
X.	DATE AND PLACE OF COMPOSITION	255
XI.	DOES KOHELETH CONTAIN GREEK WORDS OR IDEAS?	260
XII.	TEXTUAL PROBLEMS OF KOHELETH	273
XIII.	THE CANONICITY OF ECCLESIASTES AND ECCLESIASTICUS	279
	Aids to the Student	285

APPENDIX (*see* Special Table of Contents) . . . 287

INDEX 303

xiv

JOB AND SOLOMON.

INTRODUCTION.

HOW IS OLD TESTAMENT CRITICISM RELATED TO CHRISTIANITY?

THE point of view represented in this volume is still so little recognised and represented in England and America that the author ventures to prefix a short paper delivered as an address at the Church Congress held at Reading in October 1883. It is proverbially more difficult to write a thin book than a thick one, and the labour involved in preparing this twenty minutes' paper, with its large outlook and sedulously understated claims, was such as he would not willingly undertake again for a like purpose. The subject was not an ephemeral one and the attitude of the Churches towards it has not materially altered within the last three years. The present volume is pervaded by the spirit which breathes, as the author trusts, in every line of this paper. It relates, indeed, only to a small section of the Old Testament, but no part of that 'library' (as mediæval writers so well named it) can be studied in complete severance from the rest. And if a high aim is held forward in one of the opening sentences to the Church of which the writer is a son, those who are connected with the other historic communions will easily understand the bittersweet feeling of hope against hope with which those lines were penned.

'My own conviction,' said the late Dr. Pusey, 'has long been that the hope of the Church of England is in mutual tolerance.'[1] That truly great man was not thinking of the new school of Old Testament critics, and yet if the Anglican Church is ever to renovate her theology and to become in any real sense undeniably the Church of the future, she cannot afford to be careless or intolerant of attempts to modernise our methods of criticism and exegesis. It would no doubt be simpler to content ourselves with that criticism and exegesis, and consequently with that theology, which have been fairly adequate to the wants of the past; but are we sure that Jesus Christ would not now lead us a few steps further on towards 'all the truth,' and that one of His preparatory disciplines may not be a method of Biblical criticism which is less tender to the traditions of the scribes, and more in harmony with the renovating process which is going on in all other regions of thought? Why, indeed, should there not be a providence even in the phases of Old Testament criticism, so that where some can see merely the shiftings of arbitrary opinion more enlightened eyes may discern a veritable progress, leading at once to fresh views of history, and to necessary reforms in our theology, making this theology simpler and stronger, deeper and more truly Catholic, by making it more Biblical?

Some one, however, may ask, Does not modern criticism actually claim to have refuted the fundamental facts of Bible history? But which *are* these fundamental facts? Bishop Thirlwall, twenty years ago, told his clergy 'that a great part of the events related in the Old Testament has no more apparent connection with our religion than those of Greek and Roman history.' Put these events for a moment on one side, and how much more conspicuous does that great elementary fact become which stands up as a rock in Israel's history—namely, that a holy God, for the good of the world, chose out this people, isolating it more and more completely for educational purposes from its heathen neighbours, and interposing at various times to teach, to chastise, and to deliver it! It is not necessary to prove that all such recorded interpositions are in the strictest sense historical; it is enough if

---

[1] 'Toleranz sollte eigentlich nur eine vorübergehende Gesinnung sein; sie muss zur Anerkennung führen.'—*Goethe*.

the tradition or the record of some that are so did survive the great literary as well as political catastrophe of the Babylonian captivity. And I have yet to learn that the Exodus, the destruction of Sennacherib's army, the restoration of the Jews to their own land, and the unique phenomenon of spiritual prophecy, are called in question even by the most advanced school of Biblical criticism. One fact, indeed, there is, regarded by some of us as fundamental, which these advanced critics do maintain to be disproved, and that is the giving of the Levitical Law by Moses, or if not by Moses, by persons in the pre-Exile period who had prophetic sanction for giving it. Supposing the theory of Kuenen and Wellhausen to be correct, it will no doubt appear to some minds (1) that the inspiration of the Levitical Law is at any rate weakened in quality thereby, (2) that a glaring inconsistency is introduced into the Divine teaching of Israel, which becomes anti-sacrificial at one time, and sacrificial at another, and (3) that room is given for the supposition that the Levitical system itself was an injurious though politic condescension to popular tastes, and consequently (as Lagarde ventures to hold) that St. Paul, by his doctrine of the Atonement, ruined, so far as he could, the simple Gospel of Jesus Christ.

But I only mention these possible inferences in order to point out how unfair they are. (1) The inspiration (to retain an often misused but indispensable term) of the Levitical Law is only weakened in any bad sense if it be maintained that the law, whenever the main part of it was promulgated, failed to receive the sanction of God's prophetic interpreters, and that it was not, in the time of Ezra, the only effectual instrument for preserving the deposit of spiritual religion. (2) With regard to the inconsistency (assuming the new hypothesis) between the two periods of the Divine teaching of Israel, the feeling of a devout, though advanced critic would be that he was not a fit judge of the providential plan. Inconsistent conclusions on one great subject (that of forgiveness of sins) might in fact be drawn from the language of our Lord Himself at different periods of His ministry, though the parallel may not be altogether complete, since our Lord never used directly anti-sacrificial language. And it might be urged on the side of Kuenen, that neither would the early prophets have used such language—at any rate in the literary version of their discourses—if they had foreseen the canonical character which this would assume, and the immense importance of a sacrificial system in the post-Exile period. (3) The theory that the law involves an injurious condescension is by no means compulsory upon advocates of the new hypothesis. Concessions to popular taste have, indeed, as we know but too well, often almost extinguished the native spirit of a religion; but the fact that some at least of the most spiritual psalms are acknowledged to be post-Exile ought to make us all, critics and non-critics alike, slow to draw too sharp a distinction between the legal and the evangelical. That the law was misused by some, and in course of time became spiritually almost obsolete, would not justify us in depreciating it, even if we thought that the lesser and not the greater Moses, the scribe and not the prophet, was mainly responsible for its promulgation. Finally, the rash statement of Lagarde has been virtually answered by the reference of another radical critic (Keim) to the well-attested words of Christ at the institution of the Eucharist (Matt. xxvi. 28).

I have spoken thus much on the assumption that the hypothesis of Kuenen and Wellhausen may be true. That it will ever become universally prevalent is improbable—the truth may turn out to lie between the two extremes—but that it will go on for some time gaining ground among the younger generation of scholars is, I think, almost certain. No one who has once studied this or any other Old Testament controversy from the inside and with a full view of the evidence can doubt that the traditional accounts of many of the disputed books rest on a very weak basis, and those who crave for definite solutions, and cannot bear to live in twilight, will naturally hail such clear-cut hypotheses as those of Kuenen and Wellhausen, and credit them with an undue finality. Let us be patient with these too sanguine critics, and not think them bad Churchmen, as long as they abstain from drawing those dangerous and unnecessary inferences of which I have spoken. It is the want of an equally intelligent interest which makes the Old Testament a dead letter to so many highly orthodox theologians. If the advanced critics succeed in awakening such an interest more generally, it will be no slight compensation for that 'unsettlement of views' which is so often the temporary consequence of reading their books.

One large part, however, of Kuenen and Wellhausen's critical system is not peculiar to them, but accepted by the great majority of professed Old Testament critics. It is this part which has perhaps a still stronger claim to be considered in its relation to Christian truth, because there is every appearance that it will, in course of time, become traditional among those who have given up the still current traditions of the synagogue. I refer (1) to the analysis of the Pentateuch and the Book of Joshua into several documents, (2) to the view that many of the laws contained in the Pentateuch arose gradually, according to the needs of the people, and that Ezra, or at least contemporaries of Ezra, took a leading part in the revision and completion of the law book, and (3) to the dating of the original documents or compilations at various periods, mostly long subsequent to the time of Moses. Time forbids me to enter into the grounds for the confident assertion that if either exegesis or the Church's representation of religious truth is to make any decided progress, the results of the literary analysis of the Pentateuch must be accepted as facts, and that theologians must in future recognise at least three different sections, and as many different conceptions of Israel's religious development, within the Pentateuch, just as they have long recognised at least three different types of teaching in the Old Testament as a whole. On the question as to the date of these sections, and as to the Mosaic origin of any considerable part of them, the opinions of special scholars within the Church will, for a long time yet, be more or less divided. There is, I know, a belief growing up among us, that Assyrian and Egyptian discoveries are altogether favourable to the ordinary English view of the dates of the historical books, including the Pentateuch. May I be pardoned for expressing the slowly formed conviction that apologists in England (and be it observed that I do not quarrel with the conception of apologetic theology) frequently indulge in general statements as to the bearings of recent discoveries, which are only half true? The opponents of whom they are thinking are long since dead; it is wasting time to fight with the delusions of a past age. No one now thinks the Bible an invention of priestcraft; that which historical critics doubt is the admissibility of any unqualified assertion of the strict historicalness of all the details of all its component parts. This doubt is not removed by recent archæological discoveries, the critical bearings of which are sometimes what neither of the critical schools desired or expected. I refer especially to the bearings of Assyrian discoveries on the date of what are commonly called the Jehovistic narratives in the first nine chapters of Genesis. I will not pursue this subject further, and merely add that we must not too hastily assume that the supplement hypothesis is altogether antiquated.

The results of the anticipated revolution in our way of looking at the Pentateuch strike me as fourfold. (1) Historically. The low religious position of most of the pre-Exile Israelites will be seen to be not the result of a deliberate rebellion against the law of Jehovah, the Levitical laws being at any rate virtually non-existent. By this I mean, that even if any large part of those laws go back to the age of Moses they were never thoroughly put in force, and soon passed out of sight. Otherwise how can we account for this, among other facts, that Deuteronomy, or the main part of it, is known in the reign of Josiah as '*the* law of Moses'? We shall also, perhaps, get a deeper insight into the Divine purpose in raising up that colossal personage who, though 'slow of speech,' was so mighty in deed—I mean Moses—and shall realise those words of a writer specially sanctioned by my own university: 'Should we have an accurate idea of the purpose of God in raising up Moses, if we said, He did it that He might communicate a revelation? Would not this be completely to misunderstand the principal end of the mission of Moses, which was the establishment of the theocracy, and in so far as

God revealed through him the revelation was but as means to this higher end?'[1]

(2) We shall, perhaps, discriminate more between the parts of the Old Testament, some of which will be chiefly valuable to us as bringing into view the gradualness of Israel's education, and as giving that fulness to our conceptions of Biblical truths which can only be got by knowing the history of their outward forms; others will have only that interest which attaches even to the minutest and obscurest details of the history of much-honoured friends or relatives; others, lastly, will rise, in virtue of their intrinsic majesty, to a position scarcely inferior to that of the finest parts of the New Testament itself.

(3) As a result of what has thus been gained, our idea of inspiration will become broader, deeper, and more true to facts.

(4) We shall have to consider our future attitude towards that Kenotic[2] view of the person of Christ which has been accepted in some form by such great exegetical theologians as Hofmann, Oehler, and Delitzsch. Although the Logos, by the very nature of the conception, must be omniscient, the incarnate Logos, we are told, pointed His disciples to a future time, in which they should do greater works than He Himself, and should open the doors to fresh departments of truth. The critical problems of the Old Testament did not then require to be settled by Him, because they had not yet come into existence. Had they emerged into view in our Lord's time, they would have given as great a shock to devout Jews as they have done to devout Christians; and

---

[1] See essay on 'Miracles' in *Christian Remembrancer* (list of works recommended to theological honour-students in Oxford).

[2] The self-humiliation of Christ is described (need I remark?) by St. Paul as a κένωσις (Phil. ii. 7). How far this κένωσις extended is a theological problem which in the sixteenth century, and again in our own, has exercised devout thinkers. For the modern form of the Kenotic view or doctrine the English reader will naturally go to Dorner's *History of the Doctrine of the Person of Christ*, vol. iii., in Clark's *Library*. Dorner's opposition to this view is a weighty but not, of course, a decisive fact. We must be loyal to the facts of Christ's humanity reported in the Gospels. The question as to the extent of the κένωσις is an open one.

our Master would, no doubt, have given them a solution fully adequate to the wants of believers. In that case, a reference to some direction of the law as of Mosaic origin would, in the mouth of Christ, have been decisive ; and the Church would, no doubt, have been guided to make some distinct definition of her doctrine on the subject.

Thus in the very midst of the driest critical researches we can feel that, if we have duly fostered the sense of Divine things, we are on the road to further disclosures of religious as well as historical truth. The day of negative criticism is past, and the day of a cheap ridicule of all critical analysis of ancient texts is, we may hope, nearly past also. In faith and love the critics whose lot I would fain share are at one with many of those who suspect and perhaps ridicule them : in the aspirations of hope their aim is higher. Gladly would I now pass on to a survey of the religious bearings of the critical study of the poetical and prophetical books, which, through differences of race, age, and above all spiritual atmosphere, we find, upon the whole, so much more attractive and congenial than the Levitical legislation. Let me, at least, throw out a few hints. Great as is the division of opinion on points of detail, so much appears to be generally accepted that the number of prophets whose works have partly come down to us is larger than used to be supposed. The analysis of the texts may not be as nearly perfect as that of the Pentateuch, but there is no doubt among those of the younger critics whose voices count (and with the pupils of Delitzsch the case is the same as with those of Ewald) that several of the prophetical books are made up of the works of different writers, and I even notice a tendency among highly orthodox critics to go beyond Ewald himself and analyse the Book of Daniel into portions of different dates. The result is important, and not for literary history alone. It gives us a much firmer hold on the great principle that a prophet's horizon is that of his own time ; that he prophesied, as has been well said, into the future, but not directly to the future. This will, I believe, in no wise affect essential Christian truth, but will obviously modify our exegesis of certain Scripture proofs of Christian doctrine, and is perhaps not without a bearing on the two grave theological subjects referred to already.

Bear with me if, once again in conclusion, I appeal to the Church at large on behalf of those who would fain modernise our criticism and exegesis with a view to a not less distinctively Christian but more progressive Church theology. The age of œcumenical councils may have passed; but if criticism, exegesis, and philosophy are only cultivated in a fearless and reverent spirit, and if the Church at large troubles itself a little more to understand the workers and their work, an approximation to agreement on great religious questions may hereafter be attained. What the informal decisions of the general Christian consciousness will be, it would be impertinent to conjecture. It is St. John's 'all truth' after which we aspire—'all the truth' concerning God, the individual soul, and human society, into which the labours of generations, encouraged by the guiding star, shall by degrees introduce us. But one thing is too clear to be mistaken—viz. that exegesis must decide first of all what essential Christian truth is before a devout philosophy can interpret, expand, and apply it, and Old Testament exegesis, at any rate, cannot be long separated from its natural ally, the higher criticism. A provisional separation may no doubt be necessary, but the ultimate aim of successive generations of students must be a faithful exegesis, enlightened by a seven-times tested criticism.

THE BOOK OF JOB.

CHAPTER I.

JOB'S CALAMITY; THE OPENING OF THE DIALOGUES.

(CHAPS. I.–XIV.)

THE Book of Job is not the earliest monument of Hebrew 'wisdom,' but for various reasons will be treated first in order. The perusal of some of the pages introductory to Proverbs will enable the student to fill out what is here given. The Hebrew 'wisdom' is a product as peculiar as the dialectic of Plato, and not less worthy of admiration; and the author of *Job* is its greatest master. To him are due those great thoughts on a perennial problem, which may be supplemented but can never be superseded, and which, as M. Renan truly says, cause so profound an emotion in their first naïve expression. His wisdom is that of intuition rather than of strict reasoning, but it is as truly based upon the facts of experience as any of our Western philosophies. He did not indeed reach his high position unaided by predecessors. The author of the noble 'Praise of Wisdom' in Prov. i.–ix. taught him much and kindled his ambition. Nor was he in all probability without the stimulus of fellow-thinkers and fellow-poets. The student ought from the outset to be aware of the existence of discussions as to the unity of the book—discussions which have led to one assured and to several probable results—though he ought not to adopt any critical results before he has thoroughly studied the poem itself. The student should also know that the supposed authors of the (as I must believe) inserted passages belong to the same circle as the writer of the main part of the book, and are therefore not to be accused of having made 'interpolations.' I need not here distinguish between passages added by the author himself as afterthoughts (or perhaps *paralipomena* inserted by disciples from his literary remains) and compositions of later poets added to give the poem greater didactic completeness. A passage which does not fall into the plan of the poem is to all intents and purposes the work of another poet. The philosophic Goethe of the second part of *Faust* is not the passion-tossed Goethe of the first.

All the writers who may be concerned in the production of our book are, however, well worthy of reverent study; they were not only inspired by the Spirit of Israel's holy religion, but in their various styles true poets. In some degree we may apply to *Job* the lines of Schiller on the *Iliad* with its different fathers but one only mother—Nature. In fact, Nature, in aspects chiefly familiar, but not therefore less interesting, was an open book to these poets, and 'Look in thine heart and write' was their secret as well as Spenser's for vigorous and effective expression.

I now proceed to give in plain prose the pith and substance of this great poem, which more than any other Old Testament book needs to be brought near to the mind of a Western student. I would entitle it THE BOOK OF THE TRIAL OF THE RIGHTEOUS MAN, AND OF THE JUSTIFICATION OF GOD.

In its present form the Book of Job consists of five parts—

1. The Prologue, written in prose (ch. i.–ii.), the body of the work in the Hebrew being written in at any rate an approach to metre;[1]

2. The Colloquies between Job and his three friends (ch. iii.–xxxi.);

3. The Discourses of Elihu (ch. xxxii.–xxxvii.);

---

[1] Jerome already saw this. He represents the Book of Job as composed mainly in hexameters with a dactylic and spondaic movement (*Præf. in Job*). Does he mean double trimeters?

4. Jehovah's Reply to Job (ch. xxxviii.–xlii. 6);
5. The Epilogue, in prose (ch. xlii. 7–17).

There are some differences in the arrangement which will presently be followed, but these will justify themselves in the course of our study. Let us first of all examine the Prologue, which will bear to be viewed by itself as a striking specimen of Hebrew narrative. The idyllic manners of a patriarchal age are delineated with sympathy—no difficult task to one who knew the early Hebrew traditions—and still more admirable are the very testing scenes from the supernatural world.

It may perhaps seem strange that this should be only a prose poem, but the truth is that narrative poetry was entirely alien to the Hebrew genius, which refused to tolerate the bonds of protracted and continuous versification. Like that other great hero of parallelistic verse, Balaam, Job is a non-Israelite; and in this the unknown author shows a fine tact, for he is thus absolved from the embarrassing necessity of referring to the Law, and so complicating the moral problem under consideration. Job, however, though an Arabian sheich[1] (as one may loosely call him), was a worshipper of Jehovah, who declares before the assembled 'sons of the Elohim' that 'there is none like Job in the earth,' &c. (i. 8). Job's virtue is rewarded by an outward prosperity like that of the patriarchs in Genesis: he was a great Eastern Emeer, and had not only a large family but great possessions. His scrupulous piety, which takes precautions even against heart-sins, is exemplified to us by the atoning sacrifice which he offers as head of his family at some annual feast (i. 4, 5). Then in ver. 6 the scene is abruptly changed from earth to heaven. The spirit of the narrative is not devoid of a de-

[1] Where is the 'Uz' spoken of in Job i. 1? The 'land of *Uzza*' seems to have been not far from the Orontes (Shalmaneser's Obelisk; see Friedr. Delitzsch's *Paradies*, p. 259). Tradition places the home of Job in the fertile volcanic region called the Haurân (see the very full excursus in Delitzsch's *Job*). But the 'land of Uz' *might* be farther south, nearer to Edom, in connection with which it is mentioned, Lam. iv. 21, Gen. xxxvi. 28 (comp. ver. 21). This is supported by the curious note appended to the Book of Job in the Septuagint. It is true that Uz is called a son of Aram (Gen. x. 23), but 'Uz' may have had several branches, or the use of Aramaic may have extended far beyond the limits of Aram proper.

lightful humour. In the midst of the 'sons of the Elohim' —supernatural, Titanic beings, who had once been at strife with Jehovah (if we may illustrate by xxi. 22, xxv. 2), but who now at stated times paid Him their enforced homage —stood one who had not quite lost his original pleasure in working evil, and who was now employed by his Master as a kind of moral and religious censor of the human race. This malicious spirit—'the Satan' or adversary, as he is called— had just returned from a tour of inspection in the world, and Jehovah, who is represented under the disguise of an earthly monarch, boldly and imprudently draws his attention to the meritorious Job. The Satan refuses to give human nature credit for pure goodness, and sarcastically remarks, 'Does Job serve God for nothing?' (i. 9.) Jehovah therefore allows His minister to put Job's piety to as severe a test as possible short of taking his life. One after another Job's flocks, his servants, and his children are destroyed. His wife, however, by a touch of quiet humour, is spared; she seems to be recognised by the Satan as an unconscious ally (ii. 9). The piety of Job stands the trial; he is deeply moved, but maintains his self-control, and the scene closes with a devout ascription of blessing to Jehovah alike for giving and for recalling His gifts.

Before passing on the reader should notice that, according to the poet, the ultimate reason why these sufferings of Job were permitted by the Most High was that Job might set an example of a piety independent of favouring outward circumstances. The poet reveals this to us in the Prologue, that we may not ourselves be staggered in our faith, nor cast down by sympathy with such an unique sufferer; for after the eulogy passed upon Job in the celestial court we cannot doubt that he will stand the test, even if disturbed for a time.

A second time the same high court is held. The first experiment of the Adversary has failed, and this magnified earthly monarch, the Jehovah of the story, begins to suspect that he has allowed a good man to be plagued with no sufficient motive. Admiringly he exclaims, pointing to Job, 'And still he holds fast his integrity, so that thou didst incite

me against him to annihilate him without cause' (ii. 3).
Another sarcastic word from the Adversary ('Touch his bone
and his flesh, and then see . . . .'), and once more he receives
permission to try Job. The affliction this time is elephantiasis, the most loathsome and dangerous form of leprosy. But
Job's piety stands fast. He sits down on the heap of burnt
dung and ashes at the entrance of the village, such as those
where lepers are still wont to congregate, and meets the despairing counsel of his wife (comp. Tobit's wife, Tob. ii. 14) to
renounce a God from whom nothing more is to be hoped but
death with a calm and pious rebuke. So baseless was the
malicious suggestion of the Satan! Meantime many months
pass away (vii. 3), and no friend appears to condole with him.
Travelling is slow in the East, and Job's three friends[1] were
Emeers like himself (the Sept. makes them kings), and their
residences would be at some distance from each other. At
last they come, but they cannot recognise Job's features, distorted by disease (as Isa. lii. 14). Overpowered with surprise
and grief, they sit down with him for seven days and seven
nights (comp. Ezek. iii. 15). Up to this point no fault can
be found with his friends.

> I never yet did hear
> That the bruised heart was pierced through the ear.
>   (*Othello*, act i. scene 3.)

It was their deep, unspoken sympathy which encouraged
him to vent his sorrow in a flood of unpurified emotion
(chap. iii.) The very next thing recorded of Job is that he
'opened his mouth and cursed his day' (i.e. his birthday; see
ver. 3). This may at least be the poet's meaning, though it is
also possible that the prologue and the body of the poem are
not homogeneous. Not to mention other reasons at present,
the tone of Job's speech in chap. iii. (the chapter read by
Swift on his birthday) is entirely different from the stedfast

---

[1] Of the three friends Eliphaz comes from the Edomitish district of Teman, so famous for its wisdom; Bildad from the land of Shuah ('Suḫu' lay, according to the inscriptions, between the mouths of the Belich and the Khabur, confluents of the Euphrates); Zophar from Naamah, some unknown district east of the Jordan. How well these notes of place agree with the Aramaic colouring of the book!

resignation of his reply to his wife, which, as Prof. Davidson has said, 'reveals still greater deeps in Job's reverent piety' than the benediction at the end of chap. i., the latter being called forth not by the infliction of positive evil, but merely by the withdrawal of unguaranteed favours.

How strangely vivid were the sensations of the race to which the author of Job belonged! How great to him must have been the pleasures of existence, and how great the pains! Nothing to him was merely subjectively true: his feelings were infallible, and that which seemed to be was. Time, for instance, had an objective reality: the days of the year had a kind of life of their own (comp. Ps. xix. 2) and paid annually recurring visits to mankind. Hence Job, like Jeremiah (Jer. xx. 14-18), in the violence of his passion [1] can wish to retaliate on the instrument of his misery by 'cursing his day.'

> Perish the day wherein I was born,
> and the night which said, A man has been conceived.
> (iii. 3 ; comp. 6) ;

i.e. let my birthday become a blank in the calendar. Or, if this be too much and the anniversary, so sad to me, must come round, then let magicians cast their spell [2] upon it and make it an unlucky day (such as the Babylonians had in abundance).

> Let them curse it that curse days,
> that are skilful to rouse the leviathan (iii. 8) ;

i.e. the cloud dragon (vii. 12, xxvi. 13, Isaiah li. 9, Jer. li. 34), the enemy of the sun (an allusion to a widely spread solar myth). So fare it with the day which might, by hindering Job's birth, have 'hid sorrow from his eyes!' Even if he must be born, why could he not have died at once and escaped his ill fortune in the quiet phantom world (iii.

---

[1] Bishop Lowth (*Prælect.* xxxiii.) admires the dramatic tact with which the poet makes Job err at first merely by the exaggeration of his complaints, thus inviting censure, which in turn leads to bold misstatements on Job's part.

[2] For a late Egyptian incantation of this class see Ancessi, *Job et le Rédempteur*, pp. 240-1 ; for the dragon myth itself see Cheyne's note in the *Prophecies of Isaiah* (on Isa. xxvii. 1) and in the *Pulpit Comm. on Jeremiah* (on Jer. li. 34).

13–19)? Alas! this melancholy dream does but aggravate Job's mental agony. He broods on the horror of his situation, and even makes a shy allusion to God as the author of his woe—

> Wherefore gives he light to the miserable,
> and life to the bitter in soul? (iii. 20.)

And now Job's friends are shaken out of their composure. They have been meditating on Job's calamity, which is so difficult to reconcile with their previous high opinion of him; for they are the representatives of orthodoxy, of the orthodoxy which received the high sanction of the Deuteronomic *Tōra*, and which connected obedience and prosperity, disobedience and adversity. Still it is not a stiff, extreme orthodoxy which the three friends maintain: calamity, as Eliphaz represents their opinion (v. 17; comp. 27), is not always a punishment, but sometimes a discipline. The question therefore has forced itself upon them, Has the calamity which has befallen our friend a judicial or a disciplinary, educational purpose? At first they may have leaned to the latter alternative; but Job's violent outburst, so unbecoming in a devout man, too clearly pointed in the other direction, and already they are beginning to lose their first hopeful view of his case. One after another they debate the question with Job (Eliphaz as the depositary of a revelation, Bildad as the advocate of tradition, Zophar as the man of common sense)—the question of the cause and meaning of his sufferings, which means further, since Job is not merely an individual but a type,[1] the question of the vast mass of evil in the world. This main part of the work falls into three cycles of dialogue (ch. iv.–xiv., ch. xv.–xxi., ch. xxii.–xxxi.) In each there are three pairs of speeches, belonging respectively to Eliphaz and Job, Bildad and Job, Zophar and Job. Eliphaz opens the debate as being the oldest (xv. 10) and the most experienced of Job's friends. There is much to admire in his speech; if he could only have adopted the tone of a sympathising friend and not of a lecturer—

[1] See Chap. VII. (end of Section 2).

> Behold, this have we searched out ; so it is ;
> hear thou it, and know it for thyself (v. 27)—

he might have been useful to the sufferer. At the very beginning he strikes a wrong key-note, expressing surprise at his friend's utter loss of self-control (*vattibbāhēl*, ver. 4), and couching it in such a form that one would really suppose Job to have broken down at the first taste of trouble. The view of the speaker seems to be that, since Job is really a pious man (for Eliphaz does not as yet presume to doubt this), he ought to feel sure that his trouble would not proceed beyond a certain point. 'Bethink thee now,' says Eliphaz, 'who ever *perished*, being innocent?' (iv. 7.) Some amount of trouble even a good man may fairly expect ; though far from 'ploughing iniquity,' he is too weak not to fall into sins of error, and all sin involves suffering ; or, as Eliphaz puts it concisely—

> Man is born to trouble,
> as the sparks fly upward (v. 7).

Assuming without any reason that Job would question this, Eliphaz enforces the moral imperfection of human nature by an appeal to revelation—not, of course, to Moses and the prophets, but to a vision like those of the patriarchs in Genesis. Of the circumstances of the revelation a most graphic account is given.

> And to myself came an oracle stealthily,
> and mine ear received the whisper thereof,
> in the play of thought from nightly visions,
> when deep sleep falls upon men,
> a shudder came upon me and a trembling,
> and made all my bones to shudder,
> when (see !) a wind sweeps before me,
> the hairs of my body bristle up :
> it stands, but I cannot discern it,
> I gaze, but there is no form,
> before mine eyes (is) . . . .
> and I hear a murmuring voice.[1]

---

[1] The translation follows Bickell's text. The correction in line 2 of ver. 16 is from the Septuagint ; the transposition in line 4 is suggested by 1 Kings xix. 12.

> 'Can human kind be righteous before God?
> can man be pure before his Maker?
> Behold, he trusts not his own servants,
> and imputes error to his angels'[1] (iv. 12-18).

There is no such weird passage in the rest of the Old Testament. It did not escape the attention of Milton, whose description of death alludes to it.

> If shape it could be called that shape had none,
> Distinguishable in member, joint, or limb;
> Or substance might be called that shadow seemed.
> (*Par. Lost*, ii. 266.)

A single phrase ('a murmuring voice,' ver. 16) is borrowed from the theophany of Elijah (1 Kings xix. 12), but the strokes which paint the scene, and which Milton and Blake between them have more than reproduced, are all his own. The supernatural terror, the wind betokening a spiritual visitor, the straining eyes which can discern no form, the whispering voice always associated with oracles[2]—each of these awful experiences we seem to share. Eliphaz himself recalls his impressions so vividly that he involuntarily uses the present tense in describing them.

But why should Eliphaz imagine that because Job had not had a revelation of this kind he is therefore ignorant of the truth? He actually confounds the complaints wrung from Job by his unparalleled mental and bodily sufferings with the 'impatience' of the 'foolish man' and the 'passion' of the 'silly' one, and warns him against the fate which within his own experience befell one such rebellious murmurer against God—an irrelevant remark, unless he has already begun to suspect Job of impiety. Then, as if he feels that he has gone too far, he addresses Job in a more hopeful spirit, and tells him what he would do in his place, viz. turn trustfully to God, whose operations are so unsearchable, but so bene-

---

[1] So xv. 15. M. Lenormant compares Gen. vi. 1-4 (an incomplete fragment). See above on the 'sons of the Elohim' of the prologue, and comp. Chap. X.

[2] Compare the Hebrew *ne'ûm* in a common prophetic formula.

volent. Let Job regard his present affliction as a chastening and he may look forward to even more abundant blessings than he has yet enjoyed.

In these concluding verses Eliphaz certainly does his best to be sympathetic, but the result shows how utterly he has failed. He has neither convinced Job's reason nor calmed the violence of his emotion. It is now Job's turn to reply. He is not, indeed, in a mood to answer Eliphaz point by point. Passing over the ungenerous reference to the fate of the rebellious, which he can hardly believe to be seriously meant, Job first of all justifies the despair which has so astonished Eliphaz.[1] Since the latter is so cool and so critical, let him weigh Job's calamity as well as his words, and see if the extravagance of the latter is not excusable. Are these arrow wounds the fruit of chastisement? Does the Divine love disguise itself as terror? The good man is never allowed to perish, you say; but how much longer can a body of flesh hold out? Why should I not even desire death? God may be my enemy, but I have given Him no cause. And now, if He would be my friend, the only favour I crave is that He would shorten my agony.

> Then should (this) still be my comfort
> (I would leap amidst unsparing pain),
> that I have not denied the words of the Holy One (vi. 10).

Job's demeanour is thus fully accounted for; it is that of his friends which is unnatural and disappointing.

> My brethren have been treacherous as a winter stream,
> as the bed of winter streams which pass away:
> (once) they were turbid with ice,
> and the snow, as it fell, hid itself in them;
> but now that they feel the glow they vanish,
> when it is hot they disappear from their place.
> Caravans bend their course;
> they go up into the desert and perish.
> The caravans of Tema looked;

---

[1] The following lines develope what Job may be supposed to have had in his mind.

the companies of Sheba hoped for them ;[1]
they were abashed because they had been confident ;
when they came thither they were ashamed (vi. 15-20).

And was it a hard thing that Job asked of his friends? No; merely sympathy. And not only have they withheld this; Eliphaz has even insinuated that Job was an open sinner. Surely neither honesty nor wisdom is shown in such captious criticism of Job's expressions.

> How forcible is honest language,
> and how cogent is the censure of a wise man!
> Think ye to censure words,
> and the passionate speech of one who is desperate? (vi. 25, 26.)

With an assertion of his innocence, and a renewed challenge to disprove it, this, the easiest part of Job's first reply, concludes.

And now, having secured his right to complain, Job freely avails himself of his melancholy privilege. A 'desperate' man cares not to choose his words, though the reverence which never ceased to exist deep down in Job's nature prompts him to excuse his delirious words by a reference to his bitter anguish (vii. 11). Another excuse which he might have given lies on the very surface of the poem, which is coloured throughout by the poet's deep sympathy with human misery in general. Job in fact is not merely an individual, but a representative of mankind; and when he asks himself at the beginning of chap. vii.—

> Has not frail man a warfare [hard service] upon earth,
> and are not his days like the days of a hireling?—

it is not merely one of the countless thoughts which are like foam bubbles, but the expression of a serious interest, which raises Job far, very far above the patriarchal prince of the legend in the Prologue. It is the very exaggeration of

---

[1] Thomson has finely but inaccurately paraphrased this, changing the localities :—

> 'In Cairo's crowded streets
> The impatient merchant, wondering, waits in vain,
> And Mecca saddens at the long delay.'
> (*Summer*, 980-2; of the caravan which perished in the storm).

this interest which alone explains why the thought of his fellow-sufferers not only brings no comfort[1] to Job, but fails even to calm his excitement.

> Am I the sea (he says) or the sea monster,
> that thou settest a watch over me? (vii. 12.)

It is an allusion to a myth, based on the continual 'war in heaven' between light and darkness, which we have in these lines. Job asks if he is the leviathan (iii. 8) of that upper ocean above which dwells the invisible God (ix. 8, Ps. civ. 3). He describes Jehovah as being jealous (comp. Gen. iii. 4, 5, 22) and thinking it of importance to subdue Job's wild nature, lest he should thwart the Divine purposes. But here, again, Job rises above himself; the sorrows of all innocent sufferers are as present to him as his own; nay, more, he bears them as a part of his own; he represents mankind with God. In a bitter parody of Ps. viii. 5 he exclaims—

> What is frail man that Thou treatest him as a great one
> and settest Thy mind upon him;
> that Thou scrutinisest him every morning,
> and art every moment testing him? (vii. 17, 18.)

It is only now and then that Job expresses this feeling of sympathetic union with the human race. Generally his secret thought (or that of his poet) translates itself into a self-consciousness which seems morbidly extravagant on any other view of the poem. The descriptions of his physical pains, however, are true to the facts of the disease called elephantiasis, from which he may be supposed to have suffered. His cry for death is justified by his condition—'death rather than (these) my pains'[2] (vii. 15). He has no respite from his

---

[1] Contrast the touchingly natural expressions of an Arabian poet, translated by Rückert (*Hamâsa*, ii. 315):—

> 'Gieng es nicht wie mir vil andern,
> Würd' ich's nicht ertragen;
> Doch wo ich nur will, gibt Antwort
> Klage meinen Klagen.'

The same sentiment is expressed more than once again; comp. Buddha's apologue of the mustard seed.

[2] So Merx and Bickell. Text, 'my bones.'

agony; 'nights of misery,' he says, 'have been allotted to me' (vii. 3), probably because his pains were more severe in the night (xxx. 17). How can it be worth while, he asks, thus to persecute him? Even if Eliphaz be right, and Job has been a sinner, yet how can this affect the Most High?

> (Even) if I have sinned, what do I unto thee,
> O thou watcher of men? (vii. 20.)

What bitter irony again! He admits a vigilance in God, but only the vigilance of 'espionage' (xiii. 27, xiv. 16), not that of friendly guardianship; God only aims at procuring a long catalogue of punishable sins. Why not forgive those sins and relieve Himself from a troublesome task? Soon it will be too late: a pathetic touch revealing a latent belief in God's mercy which no calamity could destroy.

Thus to the blurred vision of the agonised sufferer the moral God whom he used to worship has been transformed into an unreasoning, unpitying Force. Bildad is shocked at this. 'Can God pervert judgment'? (viii. 3.) In his short speech he reaffirms the doctrine of proportionate retribution, and exhorts Job to 'seek earnestly unto God' (viii. 5), thus clearly implying that Job is being punished for his sins.[1] Instead of basing his doctrine on revelation, Bildad supports the side of it relative to the wicked by an appeal to the common consent of mankind previously to the present generation (viii. 8, 9). This common consent, this traditional wisdom, is embodied in proverbial 'dark sayings,' as, for instance—

> Can the papyrus grow up without marsh?
> can the Nile reed shoot up without water?
> While yet in its verdure, uncut,
> it withers before any grass.
> So fares it with all that forget God,
> and the hope of the impious shall perish (viii. 11–13).

It is interesting to see at how early a date the argument in favour of Theism was rested to some extent on tradition. 'We are of yesterday, and know nothing,' says Bildad, 'be-

---
[1] Bildad more than implies that the fate which overtook Job's children was the punishment of iniquity (viii. 4). Wonderful harshness!

cause our days on earth are a shadow' (viii. 9), whereas the wisdom of the past is centuries old, and has a stability to which Job's novelties (or, for this is the poet's meaning, those of the new sceptical school of the Exile) cannot pretend. But Job at least is better than his theories, so Eliphaz and Bildad are still charitable enough to believe, and the closing words of the speech of Bildad clear up any possible doubt with regard to his opinion of erring but still whole-hearted [1] ('perfect') Job.

> Those that hate thee shall be clothed with shame,
> and the tent of the wicked shall be no more (viii. 22).

But Job has much to say in reply. He ironically admits the truth of the saying, 'How can man be righteous with God?' but the sense in which he applies the words is very different from that given to them by his friends. Of course God is righteous ('righteousness' in Semitic languages sometimes means 'victory'), because He is so mighty that no one, however innocent, could plead successfully before Him. This thought suggests a noble description of the stupendous displays of God's might in nature (ix. 5-10). The verse with which it closes is adopted from Eliphaz, in whose first speech to Job it forms the text of a quiet picture of God's everyday miracles of benevolence to man (v. 9). Where Eliphaz sees power, wisdom, and love, Job can see only a force which is terrible in proportion to its wisdom. The predominant quality in this idol of Job's imagination is not love, but anger—capricious, inexorable anger, which long ago 'the helpers of Rahab' (another name for the storm dragon, which fought against the sun) experienced to their cost (ix. 13; comp. xxvi. 12). Job himself is in collision with this force; and how should he venture to defend himself? The tortures he endured would force from him an avowal of untruths (ix. 20). If only God were a man, or if there were an umpire whose authority would be recognised on both sides, how gladly would Job submit his case to adjudication! But, alas! God stands over against him with His rod (ix. 32-34).

---

[1] See viii. 20. Bildad agrees with the statement in the prologue (i. 1).

Bildad had said, 'God will not cast away a perfect man' (viii. 20). But Job's experience is, 'He destroys the perfect and the wicked' (ix. 22). Thus Job has many fellow-sufferers, and one good effect of his trial is that it has opened his eyes to the religious bearings of facts which he had long known but not before now seriously pondered.

At last a milder spirit comes upon the sufferer. He has been in the habit of communion with God, and cannot bear to be condemned without knowing the cause (x. 2). How, he enquires, can God have the heart to torture that which has cost Him so much thought (comp. Isa. lxv. 8, 9)? A man is not a common potter's vessel, but framed with elaborate skill.

> Thy hands fashioned and prepared me;
> afterwards dost thou turn [1] and destroy me?
> Remember now that as clay thou didst prepare me,
> and dost thou turn me into dust again?
> Life and favour dost thou grant me,
> and thine oversight guarded my spirit (x. 8, 9, 12).

God appeared to be kind then; but, since God sees the end from the beginning, it is too clear that He must have done all this simply in order to mature a perfect human sacrifice to His own cruel self-will. Job's milder spirit has evidently fled. He repeats his wish that he had never lived (x. 18, 19), and only craves a few brighter moments before he departs to the land of darkness (x. 20–22).

It was not likely that Zophar would be more capable of rightly advising Job than his elders. Having had no experience to soften him, he pours out a flood of crude dogmatic commonplaces, and in the complaints wrung from a troubled spirit can see nothing but 'a multitude of words' (xi. 2). Yet he only just misses making an important contribution to the settlement of the problem. He has caught a glimpse of a supernatural wisdom, to which the secrets of all hearts are open:—

> But oh that God [Eloah] would speak,
> and open his lips against thee,

---

[1] Following Sept., with Merx and Bickell.

> and show thee the secrets of wisdom,
> for wondrous are they in perfection ! [1]
> Canst thou find the depths of God [Eloah]?
> canst thou reach to the end of Shaddai?
> Heights of heaven ! what canst thou do ?
> deeper than Sheól ! what canst thou know ? (xi. 5–8.)

If Zophar had worked out this idea impartially, he might have given to the discussion a fresh and more profitable turn. He is so taken up with the traditional orthodoxy, however, that he has no room for a deeper view of the problem. His inference is that, in virtue of His perfect knowledge, God can detect sin where man sees none, though that cruellest touch of all with which the Massoretic text [2] burdens the reputation of Zophar is not supported by the more accurate text of the Septuagint, and we should read xi. 6 thus:

> and thou shouldest know that God [Eloah] gives unto thee
> thy deserts [3] for thine iniquity.

But indeed a special revelation ought not to be necessary for Job. His trouble, proceeding as it does from one no less wise than irresistible (xi. 10, 11), ought to dispel his dream of innocence; as Zophar generalises, when God's judgments are abroad—

> (Even) an empty head wins understanding,
> and a wild ass's colt is new-born as a man (xi. 12).

We may pass over the brilliant description of prosperity consequent on a true repentance with which the chapter concludes. It fell quite unheeded on the ears of Job, who was more stung by the irritating speech of Zophar than by those of Eliphaz and Bildad.

The taunt conveyed indirectly by Zophar in xi. 12 is ex-

---

[1] Comp. Isa. xxviii. 29 (Heb.) By a slight error of the ear the copyist whom our Hebrew Bibles follow put a Yōd for an Alef. Hence the Massoretic critics pronounce *kiflayim* 'twofold,' instead of *kifʼlāim* 'like wonders:' following this text, Davidson renders, 'that it is double in (true) understanding.'

[2] Literally '. . . . that God brings into forgetfulness for thee some of thy guilt.'

[3] Following Sept., with Bickell. Comp. the Hebrew of Job xxxiii. 27.

posed in all its futility in the reply of Job. Zophar himself, however, he disdains to argue with; there is the same intolerable assumption of superiority in the speeches of all the three, and this he assails with potent sarcasm.

> No doubt ye are mankind,
> and with you shall wisdom die.
> I too have understanding like you,
> and who knows not the like of this? (xii. 2, 3.)

In what respect, pray, is he inferior to his friends? Has Eliphaz enjoyed a specially unique revelation? Job has had a still better opportunity of learning spiritual truth in communion of the heart with God (xii. 4). Is Bildad an unwearied collector of the wisdom of antiquity? Job too admits the value of tradition, though he will not receive it unproved (xii. 11, 12). In declamation, too, Job can vie with the arrogant Zophar; Job's description of the omnipotence of God forms the counterpart of Zophar's description of His omniscience. But of what account are generalities in face of such a problem as Job's? The question of questions is not, Has God all power and all wisdom, but, Does He use them for moral ends? The three friends refuse to look facts in the face; the *righteous* God (we must understand the words, *if there be one*) will surely chastise them for insincerity and partisanship (xiii. 10).

And now Job refuses to waste any more words on his opponents.

> But as for me, to Shaddai would I speak,
> I crave to reason with God;
> But ye—are plasterers of lies,
> patchers of that which is worthless.
> Your commonplaces are proverbs of ashes;
> your bulwarks are bulwarks of clay (xiii. 3, 4, 12).

He forms a new project, but shudders as he does so, for he feels sure of provoking God thereby to deadly anger. Be it so; a man who has borne till he can bear no longer can even welcome death.

Behold, let him slay me ; I can wait [be patient] no longer ;[1]
still I will defend my ways to his face (xiii. 15).

It is the sublimest of all affirmations of the rights of conscience. Job is confident of the success of his plea: 'This also (guarantees) victory to me, that an impious man cannot come before him' (xiii. 16) with such a good conscience. Thus virtue has an intrinsic value for Job, superior to that of prosperity or even life: moral victory would more than compensate for physical failure. He indulges the thought that God may personally take part in the argument (xiii. 20-22), and in anticipation of this he sums up the chief points of his intended speech (xiii. 23-xiv. 22), such as, 'How many[2] are my sins,' and 'Why chase dry stubble?' (xiii. 23, 25). Sad complaints of the melancholy lot of mankind follow, reminding us again that Job, like Dante in his pilgrimage, is not only an individual but a representative.

> Man that is born of woman,
> short-lived and full of unrest,
> comes up as a flower and fades,
> flies as a shadow and continues not.
> And upon such an one keepest thou thine eye open,
> and me dost thou bring into judgment with thee ! (xiv. 1-3.)

Hard enough is the natural fate of man ; why make it harder by exceptional severity ? An early reader misunderstood this, and thought to strengthen Job's appeal by a reference (in ver. 4) to one of the commonplaces of Eliphaz (iv. 17-21). But ver. 5 shows that the idea which fills the mind of Job is the shortness of human life.[3] A tree, when cut down according to the rules still current in Syria,[4] displays a marvellous vitality ; but man is only like the falling

---

[1] This rendering is based on the reading of the Hebrew margin. The Hebrew text has, 'Behold, should he slay me, for him would I wait,' implying an expectation of a Divine interposition in Job's favour after his death. But this idea is against the connection; besides which the restrictive particle 'only' (nearly = still) agrees better with the other reading and rendering. 'Wait' means 'wait for a change for the better,' as in vi. 11, which occurs in a similar context.

[2] He admits that he is not without sins (comp. ver. 26).

[3] Comp. the well-known lamentation of Moschus (iii. 106-111).

[4] See the notices from Wetzstein in Delitzsch.

leaves of a tree (xiii. 25), or (the figure preferred here) like the canals of Egypt when the dykes and reservoirs are not properly kept up (xiv. 11 ; comp. Isaiah xix. 5, 6). If it were God's will to 'hide' Job in dark Sheól for a time, and then to recall him to the light, how gladly would he 'wait' there, like a soldier on guard (comp. vii. 1), till his 'relief' came (xiv. 14)!—a fascinating thought, on which, baseless though he considers it, Job cannot forbear to dwell. And the beauty of the passage is that the happiness of restoration to conscious life consists for Job in the renewal of loving communion between himself and his God (xiv. 15). Alas! the dim light of Sheól darkens the glorious vision and sends Job back into despair.

CHAPTER II.

THE SECOND CYCLE OF SPEECHES.

(CHAPS. XV.-XXI.)

THE three narrow-minded but well-meaning friends have exhausted their arsenal of arguments. Each with his own favourite receipt has tried to cure Job of his miserable illusion, and failed. Now begins a new cycle of speeches, in which our sympathy is still more with Job than before. His replies to the three friends ought to have shown them the incompleteness of their argument and the necessity of discovering some way of reconciling the elements of truth on both sides. *They* can teach him nothing, but the facts of spiritual experience which *he* has expounded ought to have taught them much. But all that they have learned is the impossibility of bringing Job to self-humiliation by dwelling upon the Divine attributes. No doubt their excuse lies in the irreverence of their friend's manner and expressions. It is a part of the tragedy of Job that the advice which was meant for practical sympathy only resulted in separating Job for a time both from God and from his friends. The narrow views of the latter drove Job to irreverence, and his irreverence deprived him of the lingering respect of his friends and seemed to himself at times to cut off the slender chance of a reconciliation with God. From this point onwards the friends cease to offer their supposed 'Divine consolations' (xv. 11)— such as the gracious purpose of God's ways and the corrective object of affliction (v. 8-27)—and content themselves with frightening Job by lurid pictures of the wicked man's fate, leading up, in the third cycle of speeches, to a direct accusation of Job as a wicked man himself. And yet, strange to say, as the tone of the friends becomes harsher and more cutting, Job meets their vituperation with growing calmness and dignity. Disappointed in his friends, he clings with convulsive energy to that never quite surrendered postulate of his consciousness a God who owns the moral claims of a creature on the Creator. Remarkable indeed is the first distinct expression of this faith of the heart, of which an antiquated orthodoxy sought to deprive him. He has just listened to the personalities, the cruel assumptions, and the shallow commonplaces of Eliphaz (who treats Job as an arrogant pretender and a self-convicted blaspheming sinner), and with a few words of utter contempt he turns his back on his 'tormenting[1] comforters' (xvi. 2). (Soon, however, he will appeal to them for sympathy; so strong is human nature! See xix. 21.) Left to his own melancholy thoughts, he repeats the sad details of his misery and of God's hostility (and again we feel that the poet thinks of suffering humanity in general[2]), and reasserts his innocence in language afterwards used of the suffering Servant of Jehovah (xvi. 17; comp. Isaiah liii. 9). Then in the highest excitement he demands vengeance for his blood. But who is the avenger of blood but God (xix. 25; comp. Ps. ix. 12)—the very Foe who is bringing him to death? And hence the strange but welcome thought that behind the God of pitiless force and undiscriminating severity there must be a God who recognises and returns the love of His servants, or, in the fine words of the Korán, 'that there is no refuge from God but unto Him.'[3] 'Even now,' as he lies on the rubbish-heap—

> Even now, behold, my Witness is in heaven,
> and he that vouches for me is on high.
> My friends (have become) my scorners;
> mine eye sheds tears unto God—
> that he would right a man against God,
> and a son of man against his friend (xvi. 20, 21).

[1] Miss E. Smith's rendering, 'irksome,' Renan's 'insupportable,' are not definite enough. Job means that his would-be comforters do but aggravate his unease.

[2] Notice the expressions in xvi. 10, and comp. Ps. xxii. 7, 12, 13. (Ps. xxii., like the Book of Job, has some features which belong to an individual and some to a collection of sufferers.) Job would never have spoken of his friends in the terms used in xvi. 10, 11.   [3] Sur. ix. 119.

It is a turning-point in the mental struggles of Job. He cannot indeed account for his sufferings, but he ceases to regard God as an unfeeling tyrant. He has a germ of faith in God's goodwill towards him—only a germ, but we are sure, even without the close of the story, that it will grow up and bear the fruit of peace. And now, perhaps, we may qualify the reproach addressed above to Job's friends. It is true that they have driven Job to irreverent speeches respecting God, but they have also made it possible for him to reach the intuition (which the prophetic Eliphaz has missed) of an affinity between the Divine nature and the human. In an earlier speech (ix. 32-35) he has already expressed a longing for an arbiter between himself and God. That longing is now beginning to be gratified by the certitude that, though the God in the world may be against him, the God in heaven is on his side. Not that even God can undo the past; Job requests no interference with the processes of nature. (Did the writer think that Job lived outside the sphere or the age of miracles?) All that he asks is a pledge from God, his Witness, to see his innocence recognised by God, his Persecutor (xvii. 3). So far we are listening to Job the individual. But immediately after we find the speaker exhibiting himself as the type of a class—the class or representative category of innocent sufferers. Job, then, has a dual aspect, like his God.

> And he hath set me for a byword of peoples,
> and I am one in whose face men spit.
> At this the upright are appalled,
> and the innocent stirs himself up against the impious ;
> but the righteous holds on his way,
> and he who has clean hands waxes stronger and stronger
> (xvii. 6, 7, 9).

Here it is difficult not to see that the circumstances of the poet's age are reflected in his words. The whole Jewish nation became 'a byword of peoples' during the exile,[1] and the mutual sympathy of its members was continually taxed.

---

[1] Comp. Ps. xxii. 6, Isa. xlix. 7, Joel ii. 17 (where we should render 'make a byword upon them').

It was a paradox which never lost its strangeness that a 'Servant of Jehovah' should be trampled upon by unbelievers, and the persecutor was rewarded by the silent indignation of all good Jews. That this is the right view is shown by the depression into which Job falls in vv. 11-16, in spite of the elevating passage quoted above.

Bildad's speech, with its barbed allusions to Job's sad history, had a twofold effect. First of all it raised the anguish of Job to its highest point, and, secondly, it threw the sufferer back on that great intuition, already reached by him, of a Divine Witness to his integrity in the heavens. It is a misfortune which can scarcely be appraised too highly that the text of the famous declaration in xix. 25-27 is so uncertain. 'The embarrassment of the English translators,' remarks Prof. Green, of Princeton,[1] 'is shown by the unusual number of italic words, and these of no small importance to the meaning, which are heaped together in these verses.' It is scarcely greater, however, than that of the ancient versions, and we can hardly doubt that the text used by the Septuagint translator was already at least as corrupt as that which has descended to us from the Massoretic critics.[2] This would the more easily be the case since, as Prof. Green says again, 'Job is speaking under strong excitement and in the language of lofty poetry; he uses no superfluous words; he simply indicates his meaning in the most concise manner.' Without now entering on a philological discussion, we have, I think, to choose between these alternatives, one of which involves emending the text, the other does not. Does Job simply repeat what he has said in xvi. 18, 19 (viz. that God will avenge his blood and make reparation, as it were, for his death by testifying to his innocence), without referring to any consequent pleasure of his own, or does he combine with this the delightful thought expressed in xiv. 13-15 of a

[1] *The Argument of the Book of Job* (1881), p. 200.
[2] Dr. Hermann Schultz is an unexceptionable witness, because his tastes lead him more to Biblical and dogmatic theology than to minute textual studies. He is convinced, he says, after each fresh examination, of 'the baffling intricacy and obscurity and the probable corruption of the text' (*Alttestamentliche Theologie*, ed. 2 [1878], pp. 661-2).

conscious renewal of communion with God after death?[1] The context, it seems to me, is best satisfied by the former alternative. Job's mind is at present occupied with the cruelty, not of God (as when he said, 'O that thou wouldst appoint me a term and then remember me,' xiv. 13), but of his friends. His starting-point is, 'How long will ye (my friends) pain my soul?' &c. (xix. 2.) We may admit that the best solution of Job's problem would be 'the beatific vision' in some early and not clearly defined form of that deep idea; but if Job can say that he not merely dreams but *knows* this ('I *know* that .... I shall see God,' xix. 25, 26), the remainder of the colloquies ought surely to pursue a very different course: as a matter of fact, neither Job nor his friends, nor yet Jehovah Himself, refers to this supposed newly-won truth, and the only part of 'Job's deepest saying' which the next speaker fastens upon (xx. 3) is the threatening conclusion (xix. 29). Ewald himself has drawn attention to this, without remarking its adverse bearing on his own interpretation.[2]

Here, side by side, are Dr. A. B. Davidson's and Dr. W. H. Green's translations of the received text of vv. 25-27, and Dr. Bickell's version of his own emended text.

> But I know that my redeemer liveth,
> and in after time he shall stand upon the dust
> and after this my skin is destroyed
> and without my flesh I shall see God:

[1] I agree with Dr. W. H. Green that the third view, which 'conceives Job to be here looking forward, not to a future state, but to the restoration of God's favour and his own deliverance out of all his troubles in the present life,' is to be rejected. I do not follow him in all his reasons, but these two are decisive. 1. Everywhere else Job 'regards himself as on the verge of the grave. ... Every earthly hope is annulled; every temporal prospect has vanished. He invariably repels the idea, whenever his friends present it to him, of any improvement of his condition in this world as plainly impossible.' 2. 'If he here utters his expectation that God will interfere to reward his piety in the present life, he completely abandons his own position and adopts [that of the friends]' (*The Argument of Job*, pp. 204-5).

[2] Job's vindication, thinks Ewald, would be incomplete if at least the spirit of the dead man did not witness it.

[3] The dust beneath which Job lies; comp. 'ye that dwell in dust' (Isa. xxvi. 19).

whom I shall see for myself,
and mine eyes shall behold, and not another—
my reins consume within me!

And I know my redeemer liveth, and last on earth shall he arise; and after my skin, which has been destroyed thus, and out of my flesh [i.e. when my vital spirit shall be separated from my flesh] shall I see God . . . .

> Ich weiss, es lebt mein Retter,
> Wird noch auf meinem Staub stehn;
> Zuletzt wird Gott mein Zeuge,
> Lässt meine Unschuld schauen,
> Die ich allein jetzt schaun kann,
> Mein Auge und kein andres.

Most critics are now agreed that the immediately preceding words (vv. 23, 24) are not an introduction, as if vv. 25–27 composed the rock inscription. Job first of all wishes what he knows to be impossible, and then announces a far better thing of which he is sure. His wish runs thus:

> Would then that they were written down—
> my words—in a book, and engraved
> with a pen of iron, and with lead
> cut out for a witness in the rock.[1]

But whatever view we take of the prospect which gladdened the mind of Job, his remaining speeches contain no further reference to it. Henceforth his thoughts appear to dwell less on his own condition, and more on the general question of God's moral government, and even when the former is spoken of it is without the old bitterness. In his next speech, stirred up by the gross violence of Zophar, Job for the first time meets the assertions of the three friends in this cycle of argument, viz. that the wicked, at any rate, always get their deserts, and, according to Zophar, suddenly and overwhelmingly. He meets them by a direct negative, though in doing so he is as much perturbed as when he

---

[1] On the text see Bickell, Merx, Hitzig; on the use of metal for public notices see Chabas, quoted by Cook in *Speaker's Comm.*, ad loc.

proclaimed his own innocence to God's face. He is familiar now with the thought that the righteous are not always recompensed, but it fills him with horror to think that the Governor of the world even leaves the wicked in undeserved prosperity, as if, in the language of Eliphaz, He could not 'judge through the thick clouds' (xxii. 16).

> Why do the wicked live on,
> become old, yea, are mighty in power?
> Their houses are safe, without fear,
> neither is Eloah's rod upon them.
> They wear away their days in happiness,
> and go down to Sheól in a moment (xxi. 7, 9, 13).

CHAPTER III.

THE THIRD CYCLE OF SPEECHES.

(CHAPS. XXII.-XXXI.)

It is not wonderful that the gulf between Job and his friends should only be widened by such a direct contradiction of the orthodox tenet. The friends, indeed, cannot but feel the force of Job's appeal to experience, as they show by the violence of their invective. But they are neither candid nor, above all, courageous enough to confess the truth; they speak, as the philosopher Kant observes, as if they knew their powerful Client was listening in the background. And so a third cycle of speeches begins (chaps. xxii.-xxxi.), in which the friends grasp the only weapon left them and charge Job directly with being a great sinner. True to his character, however, Eliphaz even here seeks to soften the effect of his accusations by a string of most enticing promises, partly worldly and partly other-worldly in their character, and which in a different context Job would have heartily appreciated (xxii. 21-30).

But Job cares not to reply to those charges of Eliphaz; his mind is still too much absorbed in the painful mystery of his own lot and that of all other righteous sufferers. He longs for God to set up his tribunal, so that Job and his fellows might plead their cause (xxiii. 3-7, xxiv. 1). What most of all disturbs him is that he cannot see God—that is cannot detect the operation of that moral God in whom his heart cannot help believing. 'I may go forward, but he is not there; and backward, but I cannot perceive him' (xxiii. 8). With the ardour of a pessimist he depicts this failure of justice in the darkest colours (chap. xxiv.), and is as powerless as ever to reconcile his deep sense of what God ought to be and must be and the sad realities of life. Upon this Bildad tries to frighten Job into submission by a picture of God's irresistible power, as exhibited not only in heaven and earth, but even beneath the ocean depths in the realm of the shades (xxv., xxvi. 5–14). Not a very comforting speech, but fine in its way (if Bildad may really be credited with all of it), and the speaker frankly allows its inadequacy.

> Lo ! these are the outskirts of his ways,
> and how faintly spoken is that which we hear !
> but the thunder of his power who can understand ? (xxvi. 14.)

In a speech, the first which is described as a *mashal*,[1] Job demolishes his unoriginal and rhetorical opponent, and with dignity reasserts his innocence (xxvi. 1–4, xxvii. 1–7). He may have said more ; if so, it has been lost. But, in fact, all that was argumentative in Bildad's speech was borrowed from Eliphaz, and though Job had the power (see chaps. ix., xii.), he had not the will to compete with his friends in rhetoric. The only speaker who is left is Zophar, and, as it is unlikely that the poet left one of his triads of speeches imperfect, we may conjecture that xxvii. 8–10, 10–23 belongs to the third speech of Zophar.[2] Certainly they are most inappropriate in the mouth of Job, being in direct contradiction to all that he has yet said. If so it seems very probable that besides the introductory formula a few opening verses have dropped out of the text. The verses which now stand at the head of the speech transport us to the disputes of those rival schools of which Job and his friends were only the representatives. Hence the use of the plural in ver. 12, of which an earlier instance occurs in the second speech of Bildad (xviii. 2). What Zophar says is in effect this : Job's condition is desperate, for he is an 'impious' or 'godless' man. It is too late for

---

[1] On this characteristic word for parallelistic poetry, see on Proverbs.

[2] Note that xxvii. 13 is repeated from an earlier speech of Zophar (xx. 29). There it concludes a sketch of the 'impious' man's fate ; here it begins a similar description. Verses 11 and 12 of the same chapter would stand more properly (Bickell and virtually Hirzel) immediately before chap. xxviii. Mr. B. Wright is very near doing the same ; following Eichhorn, he takes vv. 13–23 as a specimen quoted by Job of the friends' 'inconsequential' style of argument (a less natural hypothesis than that adopted here).

any one to attempt to pray when overtaken by a fatal calamity. For how can he feel that 'deep delight' in God which enables a man to pray, with the confidence of being heard, 'in every season' of life, whether prosperous or the reverse? The rest of the speech is substantially a repetition of Zophar's former description of the retribution of the wicked. It was not to be expected that Job should reply to this, and accordingly we find that in continuing his *mashal* (xxix. 1) he utterly ignores his opponents. But unhappily he is almost as far as ever from a solution of his difficulty. His friends, we may suppose, have left him, and he is at liberty to revive those melancholy memories which are all that remain to him of his prosperity.

In chap. xxix. (a fine specimen of flowing, descriptive Hebrew poetry) Job recalls the honour in which he used to be held, and the beneficent acts which he was enabled to perform. Modesty were out of place, for he is already in the state of 'one turned adrift among the dead' (Ps. lxxxviii. 5). The details remind us of many Arabic elegies in the *Hamâsa* (e.g. No. 351 in Rückert's adaptation, vol. i., or 97 in Freytag). In chaps. xxx., xxxi. he laments, with the same pathetic self-contemplation, his ruined credit and the terrible progress of his disease. Then, by a somewhat abrupt transition,[1] he enters upon an elaborate profession of his innocence, which has been compared to the solemn repudiation of the forty-two deadly sins by the departed souls of the good in the Egyptian 'Book of the Dead.' The resemblance, however, must not be pressed too far. Job's morality, even if predominantly 'legal,' has a true 'evangelical' tinge. Not merely the act of adultery, but the glance of lust; not merely unjust gain, but the confidence reposed in it by the heart; not merely outward conformity to idol-worship, but the inclination of the heart to false gods, are in his catalogue of sins. His last words are a reiteration of his

---

[1] It seems clear that chap. xxxi. was not written as the sequel of chap. xxx. Since, however, it bears such a strong impress of originality, one can only suppose that the author placed it here by an afterthought, and omitted to construct a connecting link with the preceding chapter.

deeply cherished desire for an investigation of his case by Shaddai. With what proud self-possession he imagines himself approaching the Divine Judge! In his hands are the accusations of his friends and his own reply. Holding them forth, he exclaims—

> Here is my signature—let Shaddai answer me—
> and the indictment which mine adversary has written.
> Surely upon my shoulder will I carry it,
> and bind it as chaplets about me.
> The number of my steps will I declare unto him;
> as a prince will I come near unto him (xxxi. 35–37).[1]

We must here turn back to a passage which forms one of the most admired portions of the Book of Job as it stands—the *mashal* on Divine Wisdom in chap. xxviii. The first eleven verses are at first sight most inappropriate in this connection. The poet seems to take a delight in working into them all that he knows of the adventurous operations of the miners of his day—probably those carried on for gold in Upper Egypt, and for copper and turquoises in the Sinaitic peninsula (both skilfully introduced by Ebers into his stories of ancient Egypt). How vividly the superiority of reason to instinct is brought out to vary the technical description of the miners' work in vv. 7, 8.

> A path the eagle knows not,
> nor has the eye of the vulture scanned it;
> the sons of pride have not trodden it,
> nor hath the lion passed over it.

No earthly treasures lie too deep for human industry; but —here we see the use of the great literary feat (Prov. i.–ix.) which has gone before—'where can wisdom be found, and where is the place of understanding?' And then follows that fine passage in which language is strained to the uttermost (with another of those pictorial inventories in which poets delight, vv. 15–19) to convey at once the preciousness and the unattainableness of the higher wisdom. The moral of the whole, however, is not revealed till the last verse.

---

[1] These verses have been misplaced in the Massoretic text (as Isa. xxxviii. 21, 22). They clearly ought to stand at the end of the chapter. So Kennicott, Eichhorn, Merx, Delitzsch.

And unto man he said,
'Behold, the fear of the Lord is wisdom,
and to turn aside from evil is understanding' (xxviii. 28).

Thus there is no allusion whatever to Job's problem, and it is only the present position of the *mashal* in the Book of Job which suggests a possible relation for it to that problem.

And now, looking at the passage by itself, is it conceivable that it was originally written to stand where it now does? Is it natural that the solemn contents of chap. xxvii. (even if we allow the first seven verses only to be Job's) should leave Job in a mood for an elaborate poetical study of mining operations, or that after agonising so long over the painful riddles of Divine Providence he should suddenly acquiesce in the narrow limits of human knowledge, soon, however, to relapse into his old inquisitiveness? Is it not, on the other hand, very conceivable (notice the opening word 'For') that it was transferred to its present position from some other work? In a didactic poem on Wisdom (i.e. the plan of the universe), similar to Prov. i.-ix., it would be as much in place as the hymn on Wisdom in Prov. viii. To this great work indeed it presents more than one analogy, both in its subject and its recommendation of religious morality (or moral religion) as the branch of wisdom suitable to man. The only difference is that the writer of Job xxviii. expressly says that this is the only wisdom within human ken, whereas the writer of Prov. viii. does not touch on this point. But, whether an extract from a larger work or written as a supplement to the poem of Job, the passage in its present position is evidently intended to have a reference to Job's problem. The author, or the extractor, regarded the foregoing debates much as Milton regarded those of the fallen angels, who 'found no end, in wandering mazes lost;' in short, he could only solve the problem by pronouncing it insoluble.[1] Verses 11 and 12 of chap. xxvii. have very much the appearance of an artificial bridge inserted by the new author or the extractor.

[1] But for this tendency of the poem one might follow Delitzsch (art. 'Hiob' in *Herzog-Plitt*, vi. 133) and regard chap. xxviii. as inserted by the author of *Job* from his 'portfolio.'

CHAPTER IV.

THE SPEECHES OF ELIHU.

(CHAPS. XXXII.-XXXVII.)

AT a (perhaps) considerably later period than the original work (including chap. xxviii.)—symbolised by the youthfulness of Elihu as compared with the four older friends—the problem of the sufferings of the innocent still beset the minds of the wise men, the attempt of the three friends to 'justify the ways of God' to the intellect having proved, as the wise men thought, a too manifest failure (xxxii. 2, 3). One of their number therefore invented a fourth friend, Elihu (or is this the name of the author himself?[1]), who is described as having been a listener during the preceding debates, and who reduces Job to silence. It is noteworthy that the sudden introduction of Elihu required the insertion of a fresh narrative passage (xxxii. 1-6) as a supplement to the original prologue.

I assume, as the reader will observe, the one assured result of the criticism of Job. To those who follow me in this, the speeches of Elihu will, I think, gain greatly in interest. They mark out a time when, partly through the teaching of history, partly through a deeper inward experience, and partly through the reading of the poem of *Job*, the old difficulties of faith were no longer so acutely felt. Two courses were open to the Epigoni of that age—either to force Job to say what, as it seemed, he ought to have said (this,

---

[1] So M. Derenbourg, who points out that none of the other speakers have a genealogy, and identifies Buz with Boaz, and Ram with an ancestor of David (Ruth iv. 19). The author of chaps. xxxii.-xxxvii. might thus be a descendant of Elihu the brother of David (1 Chr. xxvii. 18).

however, was not so easy as in the case of Ecclesiastes), or to insert fresh speeches in the style of the original, separating the corn from the chaff in the pleadings of the three friends, and adding whatever a more advanced religious thought suggested to the writer. In forms of expression, however, it must be admitted that Elihu does not shine. (True, he does not profess to comfort Job.) For offensiveness the two following verses are not easily matched:

> Where is there a man like Job,
> who drinks [1] scoffing like water? (xxxiv. 7.)
> Would that Job might be tried to the uttermost
> because of his answers in the manner of wicked men (xxxiv. 36).

A 'vulgar braggart' he may not be from an Oriental point of view, nor is he 'the prototype of the Bachelor in *Faust*;' but that he is too positive and dogmatic, and much overrates his own powers, is certain. He represents the dogmatism of a purified orthodoxy, which thinks too much of its minute advances ('one perfect in knowledge is with thee,' xxxvi. 4).

Elihu distributes his matter (of which he says that he is 'full,' xxxii. 18–20) over four speeches. His themes in the first three are: 1, the ground and object of suffering (chaps. xxxii., xxxiii.); 2, the righteousness of God (chap. xxxiv.); and 3, the use of religion (chap. xxxv.), all of which are treated in relation to the questionable or erroneous utterances of Job. Then, in his last and longest effort, Elihu unrolls before Job a picture of the government of God, in its beneficence and righteousness as well as its omnipotence, in the hope of moving Job to self-humiliation (chaps. xxxvi., xxxvii.) Let us remember again that Elihu represents the debates of the 'wise men' of the post-regal period, who were conscious of being in some sense 'inspired' like their prophetic predecessors (xxxii. 8, xxxvi. 4; Ecclus. xxiv. 32–34, l. 28, 29), so that we cannot believe that the *bizarre* impression made by Elihu on some Western critics was intended by the original author. That his portrait suggests certain grave infirmities, may be granted; but these are

---

[1] On 'drinks' see Thomson, *The Land and the Book*, p. 319.

the failings of the circle to which the author belongs: the self-commendation of Elihu in his exordium is hardly excessive from an Oriental point of view, or would at any rate be justifiable in a more original thinker. Indeed, he only commends himself in order to excuse the unusual step of criticising the proceedings of men so much older than himself. After what he thinks sufficient excuse has been offered, Elihu takes up Job's fundamental error, self-righteousness, but prepares the way by examining Job's assertion (xix. 7, xxx. 20) that God took no heed of his complaints.

> Wherefore hast thou contended with Him
> because 'He answers none of my words'?[1] (xxxiii. 13.)

To this Elihu replies that it is a man's own fault if he cannot hear the Divine voice. For God is constantly speaking to man, if man would only regard it ('revelation,' then, is not confined to a class or a succession). Two means of communication are specially mentioned—nightly dreams and visions, and severe sickness. The object of both is to divert men from courses of action which can only lead to destruction. At this point a remarkable intimation is given. In order to produce conversion, and so to 'redeem a man from going down to the pit,' a special angelic agency is necessary—that of a 'mediator' or 'interpreter' (Targ. $p'raqlītā$; comp. παράκλητος, John xiv. 16, 26), whose office it is to 'show unto man his rightness' (i.e. how to conform his life to the right standard, xxxiii. 23).

We must pause here, however, to consider the bearings of this. It seems to show us, first, that inspired minds (see above) were already beginning to refine and elevate the popular notions of the spiritual world. That there were two classes of spirits, the one favourable, the other adverse to man, had long been the belief of the Israelites and their neighbours.[2] The author of the speeches of Elihu now intro-

---

[1] The *text* (which has '*His* words') is generally rendered 'because He gives not account of any of His matters,' i.e. of the details of His government. This is very strained; the Sept. has 'my words,' the Vulgate 'thy words,' either of which readings gives a natural sense.

[2] See 2 Sam. xxiv. 16, and comp. 1 Chr. xxi. 15, Ps. lxxviii. 49, Prov. xvi.

duces one of them among the symbols of a higher stage of religion. In antithesis to the 'destroyers'[1] (ver. 22) he implies that God has thousands of angels (the 'mediator' is 'one among a thousand'), whose business it is to save sinners from destruction by leading them to repentance. Such is the φιλανθρωπία, the friendliness to man, of the angelic world,[1] without which indeed, according to Elihu, the purpose of sickness would be unobserved and a fatal issue inevitable. To students of Christianity, however, it has a deeper interest, if the concluding words, 'I have found a ransom,' be a part of the Old Testament foundation of the doctrine of redemption through Christ. This, however, is questionable, and even its possibility is not recognised by the latest orthodox commentator.[2] In his second speech Elihu returns to the main question of Job's attitude towards God. He begins by imputing to Job language which he had never used, and which from its extreme irreverence Job would certainly have disowned (xxxiv. 5, 9), and maintains that God never acts unjustly, but rewards every man according to his deeds. There is nothing in his treatment of this theme which requires comment except its vagueness and generality, to which, were the speech an integral part of the poem, Job would certainly have taken exception.

The subject of the third speech is handled with more originality. Job had really complained that afflicted persons such as himself appealed to God in vain (xxiv. 12, xxx. 20). Elihu

14, Ezek. ix. 1, x. 7; also Jost, *Gesch. des Judenthums*, i. 304. For Assyria see *Records of the Past*, i. 131-5; iv. 53-60 (the sinner was thought to be given up in displeasure by his God into the hands of the evil spirits). For Arabia see Korán, lxxix. 1, 2 —

'By those (angels) who tear out (souls) with violence,
And by those who joyously release them:'

for the early Christian, Justin M. *Dial. c. Tryph.* 105, τὰ αὐτὰ αἰτῶμεν τὸν θεὸν, τὸν δυνάμενον ἀποστρέψαι πάντα ἀναιδῆ πονηρὸν ἄγγελον μὴ λαβέσθαι ἡμῶν τῆς ψυχῆς: and for the medieval, Dante, *Inferno*, xxvii. 112-123; *Purgatorio*, v. 103-108. Comp. below, Chap. X.

[1] Blake seems to have felt Elihu's strong faith in the angels. The border of his 12th illustration is filled with a stream of delicate angel forms.

[2] Davidson. Ewald explains the 'ransom' partly of the intercession of the angel, partly of the prayer of repentance.

replies to this (xxxv. 9-13) that such persons merely cried from physical pain, and did not really pray. The fourth and last speech, in which he dismisses controversy and expresses his own sublime ideas of the Creator, has the most poetical interest. At the very outset the solemnity of his language prepares the reader to expect something great, and the expectation is not altogether disappointed. 'God,' he says, 'is mighty, but despiseth not any' (xxxvi. 5); He has given proof of this by the trials with which He visits His servants when they have fallen into sin. Might and mercy are the principal attributes of God. The verses in which Elihu applies this doctrine to Job's case are ambiguous and perhaps corrupt, but it appears as if Elihu regarded Job as in danger of missing the disciplinary object of his sufferings. It is in the second part of his speech (xxxvi. 26–xxxvii. 24) that Elihu displays his greatest rhetorical power, and though by no means equal to the speeches of Jehovah, which it appears to imitate, the vividness of its descriptions has obtained the admiration of no less competent a judge than Alexander von Humboldt. The moral is intended to be that, instead of criticising God, Job should humble himself in devout awe at the combined splendour and mystery of the creation.

It is tempting to regard the sketch of the storm in xxxvi. 29–xxxvii. 5 and the appeals which Elihu makes to Job as preparatory to the appearance of Jehovah in xxxviii. 1. 'While Elihu is speaking,' says Mr. Turner, 'the clouds gather, a storm darkens the heavens and sweeps across the landscape, and the thunder utters its voice . . . . out of the whirlwind that passes by Jehovah speaks.'[1] So too Dr. Cox thinks that Job's invisible Opponent 'opens His mouth and answers him out of the tempest which Elihu has so graphically described.'[2] In fact in xxxviii. 1 we may equally well render '*the* tempest' (i.e. that lately mentioned) and '*a* tempest.' The objection is (1) that the storm does not come into the close of Elihu's speech, as it ought to do, and (2) that in His very first words Jehovah distinctly implies that

---
[1] Turner, *Studies Biblical and Oriental*, p. 146.
[2] Cox, *Commentary on the Book of Job*, p. 489.

the last speaker was one who 'darkened counsel by words without knowledge' (xxxviii. 2).

Such are the contributions of Elihu, which gain considerably when considered as a little treatise in themselves. It is, indeed, a strange freak of fancy to regard Elihu as representing the poet himself.[1] Neither æsthetically nor theologically do they reach the same high mark as the remainder of the book. 'The style of Elihu,' as M. Renan remarks, 'is cold, heavy, pretentious. The author loses himself in long descriptions without vivacity. . . . His language is obscure and presents peculiar difficulties. In the other parts of the poem the obscurity comes from our ignorance and our scanty means of comprehending these ancient documents; here the obscurity comes from the style itself, from its *bizarrerie* and affectation.'[2] Theologically it is difficult to discover any important point (but see Chap. XII., below, on Elihu) in which, in spite of his sharp censure of the friends, he distinctly passes beyond them. His arguments have been so largely anticipated by the three friends that, on the whole, we may perhaps best regard chaps. xxxii.–xxxix. as a first theological criticism on the contents of the original work. From this point of view it is interesting that the idea of affliction as correction, which had already occurred to Eliphaz, acquired in the course of years a much deeper hold on thinking minds (see xxxiii. 19–30, xxxvi. 8–10). There is one feature of the earlier speeches which is not imitated by Elihu, and that is the long and terrifying descriptions in each of the three original colloquies of the fate of the impious man, and one of the most considerate of Elihu's Western critics[3] thinks it possible that Elihu, who says in one place—

And the impious in heart cherish wrath,
and supplicate not when he hath bound them (xxxvi. 13)—

considered no calamity whatever as penal in the first instance.

[1] So Lightfoot (see Lowth, *Prælect.* xxxii.).   [2] *Le livre de Job*, p. liv.
[3] Davidson, *The Book of Job*, p. xlv.

CHAPTER V.

THE SPEECHES OF JEHOVAH.

(CHAPS. XXXVIII.-XLII. 6.)

'THE words of Job are ended' (xxxi. 40b), remarks the ancient editor, and amongst the last of these words is an aspiration after a meeting with God. That Job expected such a favour in this life is in the highest degree improbable, whatever view be taken of xix. 25-27. It is true, he sometimes did almost regard a theophany as possible, though he feared it might be granted under conditions which would make it the reverse of a boon (ix. 3, 15, 33-35; xiii. 21, 22). He wished for a fair investigation of his character, and he craved that God would not appear in too awful a form. It seems at first sight as if Jehovah, casting hard questions at Job out of the tempest, and ignoring both the friends' indictment and Job's defence (xxxi. 35-37), were realising Job's worst fears and acting as his enemy. The friends had already sought to humble Job by pointing him to the power and wisdom and goodness of God, and Job had proved conclusively that he was no stranger to these high thoughts. Is the poet consistent with himself, first, in introducing Jehovah at all, and, secondly, in making Him overpower Job by a series of sharp, ironical questions? Several answers may be given if we wish to defend the unity of the poem. Job himself (it may be said) has not continued at the same high level of faith as in xix. 25-27 (assuming Prof. Davidson's view of the passage); he needs the appearance of Jehovah more than he did then. As to the course attributed in xxxviii. 1 to Jehovah, this too (the poet may have felt in adding these speeches) was really the best for Job. Jehovah might no doubt have declared Job to be in the right as against his friends. He might next have soothed the sufferer's mind by revealing the reason why his trials were permitted (*we* know this from the Prologue). But this would not have been for Job's spiritual welfare : there was one lesson he needed to learn or to relearn, one grace of character he needed to gain or to regain—namely, devout and trustful humility towards God. In the heat of debate and under the pressure of pain Job's old religious habit of mind had certainly been weakened—not destroyed, but weakened— and a strong remedy was necessary if he was not to carry his distracted feelings to the grave. And so, as a first joyful surprise, came the theophany : to 'see' God before death *must* have been a joyful surprise ; and if the questioning cast him down, yet it was only to raise him up in the strength of self-distrust. The object of these orations of Jehovah is not to communicate intellectual light, but to give a stronger tone to Job's whole nature. He had long known God to be strong and wise and good, but more as a lesson learned than as personal experience (xlii. 5). And the means first adopted to convey this life-giving 'sight' is not without a touch of that humour which we noticed in the Prologue. Job, who was so full of questions, now has the tables turned upon him. He is put through a catechism which admits of but one very humbling answer, each question being attached to a wonderfully vivid description of some animal or phenomenon. For descriptive power the first speech of Jehovah, at any rate, is without a parallel. The author, as Prof. Davidson remarks, 'knew the great law that sublimity is necessarily also simplicity.' It is true he does but give us isolated features of the natural world : no single scene is represented in its totality. But this is in accordance with the Hebrew genius, to which nature appears, not in her own simple beauty, but bathed in an atmosphere of emotion. The emotion which here animates the poet is mainly a religious one ; it is the love of God, and of God's works for the sake of their Maker. He wishes to cure the murmuring spirits of his own day by giving them wider views of external nature and its mysteries, so wondrously varied and so full of Divine wisdom and goodness. He has this great advantage in doing so, that they, like himself (and Job), are theists; they are not of those who say in their heart, 'There is no God,' but of the 'Zion' who complains, 'Jehovah has forsaken me, and my Lord has forgotten me' (Isaiah xlix. 14). And the remedy which he applies is the same as that of the Babylonian-Jewish prophet, a wider study of the ways of God. Job had said, 'I would tell Him the number of my steps;' Jehovah replies by showing him, in a series of questions, not irritating but persuasive, the footprints of His own larger self-manifestation.

The Divine Speaker is introduced by the poet thus:

> And Jehovah answered Job out of a tempest, and said.

A storm was the usual accompaniment of a Divine appearance: there was no intention of crushing Job with terror. In Blake's thirteenth drawing Job (and his wife!) are represented kneeling and listening, with countenances expressive of thankfulness; in his fourteenth, Job and his four friends kneel rapt and ecstatic, while the 'sons of God,' sweet, vital, heavenly forms, are shouting for joy. In fact, the speeches of Jehovah contain, not accusations (except in xxxviii. 2), but remonstrances, and, though the form of these is chilling to Job's self-love, yet the glorious visions which they evoke are healing to every sorrow of the mind. The text of the speeches is unfortunately not in perfect order. For instance, there are four verses which have, no one can tell how, been deposited in the description of behemoth (xli. 9–12, A. V.) but which most probably at one time or another opened the first speech of Jehovah. Perhaps the author himself removed them, feeling them to be too depressing for Job to hear; or perhaps it was purely by accident that they were transferred, and Merx and Bickell have done well to replace them in their corrected editions of *Job* between xxxi. 37 and xxxviii. 1. As corrected by the former they run thus:—

> Behold, his hope is belied:
> will he fight against mine appearing?

He is not so bold as to stir me up;
who indeed could stand before me?
Who ever attacks me in safety?
all beneath the whole heaven is mine.
I will not take his babbling in silence,
his mighty speech and its comely arrangement.

We must regard this as a soliloquy, after which, directly addressing Job, Jehovah upbraids the 'mighty speaker' with having shut himself out by his 'blind clamour' from a view of the Divine plan of his life.

Who is this that darkens counsel
by words without knowledge? (xxxviii. 2.)

To gain that 'knowledge' which will 'make darkness light before him,' Job must enrich his conception of God. Those striking pictures already referred to have no lower aim than to display the great All-wise God, and the irony of the catechising is only designed to bring home the more forcibly to Job human littleness and ignorance. Modern readers, however, cannot help turning aside to admire the genius of the poet and his sympathetic interest in nature. His scientific ideas may be crude; but he observes as a poet, and not as a naturalist. Earth, sea, and sky successively enchain him, and we can hardly doubt that the natural philosophy of the Chaldæans was superficially at least known to him.[1] In his childlike curiosity and willingness to tell us everything he reminds us of the poet of the *Commedia*.

Has the rain a father?[2]
or who has begotten the dew-drops?
from whose womb came forth the ice,
and the hoar frost of heaven—who engendered it,
(that) the waters close together like a stone,
and the face of the deep hides itself?

---

[1] See Sayce on 'Babylonian Astronomy' (*Transactions of Soc. of Bibl. Archæology*, 1874); Lenormant, *La magie chez les Chaldéens*, and his *Syllabaires cunéiformes* (1876), p. 48.

[2] This is not mere 'patriarchal simplicity' (Renan, p. lvi.), but a contradiction of the mythic view that a nature god like Baal is the 'father' or producer of the rain and the crops (see Cheyne, *Isaiah*, ed. 3, i. 28, 294, ii. 295). Elihu no doubt goes further in his explanations; see xxxvi. 27, 28.

> Dost thou bind the knots of the Pleiades,[1]
> or loose the fetters of Orion?[2]
> Dost thou bring forth the moon's watches at their season,
> and the Bear and her offspring—dost thou guide them?
> Knowest thou the laws of heaven?
> dost thou determine its influence upon the earth?
>
> (xxxviii. 28–33.)

'The laws of heaven!' Can we refuse to observe the first beginnings of a conception of the cosmos, remembering other passages of the Wisdom Literature in which the great world plan is distinctly referred to? Without denying a pre-Exile, native Hebrew tendency (comp. Job xxxviii. 33 with Jer. xxxi. 35, 36) may we not suppose that the physical theology of Babylonia had a large part in determining the form of this conception? Notice the reference to the influence of the sky upon the earth, and especially the Hebraised Babylonian phrase Mazzaroth (i.e. *mazarati*,[3] plural of *mazarta*, a watch), the watches or stations of the moon which marked the progress of the month. But it is not so much the intellectual curiosity manifest in these verses which we would dwell upon now as the poetic vigour of the gallery of zoology, and, we must add, the faith which pervades it, reminding us of a Bedouin prayer quoted by Major Palmer, 'O Thou who providest for the blind hyæna, provide for me!' Ten (or nine) specimens of animal life are given—the lion and (perhaps) the raven,[4] the wild goat and the hind, the wild

---

[1] Heb. *kîma*; comp. Ass. *kimtu*, 'a family.' The word occurs again in ix. 9, Am. v. 8 (but are not this verse and the closely related one in iv. 13 additions by a later editor of Amos in the Exile period?)

[2] Heb. *k'sîl*, the name of the foolhardy giant who strove with Jehovah. The Chaldeo-Assyrian astrology gave the name *kisiluv* to the ninth month, connecting it with the zodiacal sign Sagittarius. But there are valid reasons for attaching the Hebrew popular myth to Orion.

[3] 'He did not watch the stars of heaven, nor the *mazarati*.' So Fox Talbo quotes from a cuneiform tablet (*Transactions of Soc. of Bibl. Archæology*, 1872, p. 341). The above explanation, however, which is that of Delitzsch on *Job*, differs from that of Fox Talbot.

[4] Mr. Bateson Wright's pointing, *lâ'ereb* for *la'ōrēbh*, is plausible. The raven is an insignificant companion to the lion, and the birds of prey are mentioned at the end of Job's picture gallery. Render 'who provides in the evening his food,' &c.; but in this case should not *lâbhî* in ver. 39 be rendered 'lion' rather than 'lioness' (note '*his* young ones')? The root idea is probably voracity. That.

ass, the wild ox,[1] the ostrich, the war horse, the hawk and the eagle. It is to this portion that the student must turn who would fain know the highest attainments of the Hebrew genius in pure poetry, such as Milton would have recognised as poetry. The delighted wonder with which the writer enters into the habits of the animals, and the light and graceful movement of the verse, make the ten descriptions referred to an ever-attractive theme, I will not say for the translator, but for the interpreter. They are ideal, as the Greek sculptures are ideal, and need the pen of that poet-student, faint hints of whose coming have been given us in Herder and Rückert. The finest of them, of course, is that of one of the animals most nearly related in Arabia to man (in Arabia, but not in Judæa), the horse.

> Dost thou give might to the horse?
> Dost thou clothe his neck with waving mane?
> Dost thou make him bound as a locust?
> The peal of his snort is terrible !
> He paws in the valley and rejoices in his strength ;
> he goes forth to meet the weapons ;
> he laughs at fear, and is not dismayed,
> and recoils not from the sword :
> the quiver clangs upon him,
> the flashing lance and the javelin :
> bounding furiously he swallows the ground,
> and cannot stand still at the blast of the trumpet ;
> at every blast he says, ' Aha !'
> and smells the battle from afar,
> the captain's thunder and the cry of battle (xxxix. 19-25).

The terrible element in animal instincts seems indeed to fascinate the mind of our poet ; he closes his gallery with a sketch of the cruel instincts of the glorious eagle. We are

---

lābhī in iv. 11 is the feminine is no objection. Comp. Ps. lvii. 5, and perhaps Hos. xiii. 8. Possibly, however, the 'raven' was inserted here to make up the number ten, by a reminiscence of Ps. cxlvii. 9.

[1] The 'unicorn' of A. V. comes from the Sept. and Vulg.; but in Deut. xxxiii. 17 the *re'ēm* is said to have 'horns.' Schlottmann and Delitzsch identify it with the oryx or antelope, but the oryx was tamable (Wilkinson, *Egyptians*, i. 227), whereas our poet asks, ' Will the *re'ēm* be willing to serve thee?' See Cheyne on Isa. xxxiv. 7.

reminded, perhaps, of the lines of a poet painter inspired by Job—

> Tiger, tiger, burning bright
> In the forests of the night,
> What immortal hand or eye
> Could frame thy fearful symmetry? [1]

And now we might almost think that the object of the theophany has been attained. Never more will Job presume to litigate with Shaddai, or measure the doings of God by his puny intellect. He has learned the lesson expressed in Dante's line—

> State contenti, umana gente, al quia, [2]

but also that higher lesson, so boldly expressed by the same poet, that in all God's works, without exception, three attributes are seen united—

> Fecemi la divina potestate,
> La somma sapienza, e 'l primo amore. [3]

He is silenced, indeed, but only as with the poet of Paradise—

> All' alta fantasia qui mancò possa. [4]

The silence with which both these 'vessels of election' meet the Divine revelation is the silence of satisfaction, even though this be mingled with awe. Job has learned to forget himself in the wondrous creation of which he forms a part, just as Dante when he saw

> La forma universal di questo nodo. [5]

Job cannot, indeed, as yet express his feelings; awe preponderates over satisfaction in the words assigned to him in xl. 4, 5. In fact, he has fallen below his better knowledge, and must be humbled for this. He has known that he is but a part of humanity—a representative of the larger whole, and might, but for his frailty, have comforted himself in that thought. God's power and wisdom and goodness are so wondrously blended in the great human organism that he

---

[1] Blake, *Songs of Experience*.
[3] *Inf.*, iii. 5, 6.
[5] *Parad.*, xxxiii. 91.
[2] *Purg.*, iii. 37.
[4] *Parad.*, xxxiii. 142.

might have rested amidst his personal woes in the certainty of at least an indirect connection with the gentler manifestations of the 'Watcher of mankind' (vii. 20). This thought has proved ineffectual, and so the Divine Instructor tries another order of considerations. And, true enough, nature effects what 'the still, sad music of humanity' has failed to teach. Job, however, needs more than teaching; he needs humiliation for his misjudgment of God's dealings with him personally. Hence in His second short but weighty speech 'out of the tempest' Jehovah begins with the question (xl. 8)—

> Wilt thou make void my justice?
> wilt thou condemn me, that thou mayest be righteous?

This gives the point of view from which Jehovah ironically invites Job, if he thinks (see chap. xxiv.) that he can govern the world—the human as well as the extra-human world—better than the Creator, to make the bold attempt. He bids him array himself with the Divine majesty and carry out that retribution in which Jehovah, according to him, has so completely failed (xl. 11–13). If Job will prove his competence for the office which he claims, then Jehovah Himself will recognise his independence and extol his inherent strength. Did the poet mean to finish the second speech of Jehovah here? It is probable; the subject of the interrogatory hardly admitted of being developed further in poetry. A later writer (or, as Merx thinks, the poet of *Job* himself) seems to have found the speech too short, and therefore appended the two fancy sketches of animals which follow. But in the original draft of the poem xl. 14 must have been followed immediately by Job's retractation, closing with those striking words (see above, p. 49) which so well supplement the less articulate confession of xl. 4, 5—

> I had heard of thee by the hearing of the ear,
> but now mine eye sees thee :[1]
> therefore I retract and repent
> in dust and ashes (xlii. 5, 6).

---

[1] [All his thinkings seemed like hearsay. This, then, was the real God.] So an anonymous writer well expresses it (*Mark Rutherford's Deliverance*, p. 196).

How complete a reversal of the 'princely' anticipations of Job in xxxi. 37! To us, indeed, it may seem somewhat ungracious to Job to give this as the last scene of his pathetic drama. But the poet leaves it open to us to animate Job's repentance with love as well as awe and compunction. With fine feeling Blake in his seventeenth illustration almost fills the margin with passages from the Johannine writings.

The long description of the two Egyptian monsters (xl. 15, xli. 26) is, as we have hinted above, out of place in the second speech of Jehovah. It has indeed been suggested that the writer may have intended it as a development of xl. 14—

> Then will I in return confess unto thee
> that thy right hand can help thee—

which implies that Job has no power to help himself in the government of the world. According to this view, the opening words of the behemoth section will mean, 'Consider, pray, that thou hast fellow-creatures which are far stronger than thou; and how canst thou undertake the management of the universe?' It must, however, be admitted that the emphasis thus laid on the omnipotence of God, apart from His righteousness, introduces an obscurity into the argument which almost compels us to assume that the sketches of behemoth and leviathan are later insertions. At any rate, even if we regard them as the work of the principal writer of Job, we must at least ascribe them to one of those afterthoughts by which poets not unfrequently spoil their best productions. The style of the description, too, is less chastened than that of chaps. xxxviii. xxxix. (so that Bickell can hardly be right in placing xl. 15, &c., immediately after xxxix. 30), and if it relates to the hippopotamus and the crocodile is less true to nature than the other 'animal pieces.'

The truth is that neither behemoth nor leviathan corresponds strictly to any known animal. The tail of a hippopotamus would surely not have been compared to a cedar by a truthful though poetic observer like the author of chaps. xxxviii. xxxix. Moreover that animal was habitually hunted by the Egyptians with lance and harpoon, and was therefore no fit symbol of indomitable pride. The crocodile too was attacked and killed by the Egyptians, though in xli. 26-29 leviathan is said to laugh at his assailants. Seneca in his description of Egypt describes the crocodile as ' fugax animal audaci, audacissimum timido' (*Quæst. Nat.*, iv. 2). Comp. Ezek. xxix. 4, xxxii. 3 ; Herod. ii. 70.

To me, indeed, as well as to M. Chabas, the behemoth and the leviathan seem to claim a kinship with the dragons and other imaginary monsters of the Swiss topographies of the sixteenth century. A still more striking because a nearer parallel is adduced by M. Chabas from the Egyptian monuments, where, side by side with the most accurate pictures from nature, we often find delineations of animals which cannot have existed out of wonderland.[1]

It is remarkable that the elephant should not have been selected as a type of strange and wondrous animal life ; apparently it was not yet known to the Hebrew writers, though of course it might be urged that the poet was accidentally prevented from writing more. Merx has pointed out that the description of behemoth is evidently incomplete. He also thinks that the poet has not yet brought the form of these passages to final perfection : a struggle with the difficulties of expression is observable. He therefore relegates xl. 15-xli. 26 to an appendix with the suggestive title (comp. Goethe's *Faust*) Paralipomena to Job. He thinks that a reader or admirer of the original poem sought to preserve these unfinished sketches by placing them where they now stand. This is probably the most conservative theory (i.e. the nearest to the traditional view) critically admissible.

[1] *Etudes sur l'antiquité historique*, prem. éd., pp. 391-393.

CHAPTER VI.

THE EPILOGUE AND ITS MEANING.

WE now come to the *dénoûment* of the story (xlii. 7-17), against which, from the point of view of internal criticism, much were possible to be said. We shall not, however, here dwell upon the inconsistencies between the epilogue on the one hand and the prologue and the speeches on the other. The main point for us to emphasise is the disappointingness of the events of the epilogue regarded as the final outcome of Job's spiritual discipline. Surely the high thoughts which have now and then visited Job's mind, and which, combined with the personal self-revelation of the Creator, must have brought back the sufferer to a state of childlike resignation, stand in inappropriate companionship with a tame and commonplace renewal of mere earthly prosperity. Would it not have been fitter for the hero on whom so much moral training had been lavished to pass with humble but courageous demeanour through the dark valley, at the issue of which he would 'see God'? It is hardly a sufficient answer that a concession was necessary to the prejudices of the unspiritual multitude; for what was the object of the poem, if not to subvert the dominion of a one-sided retribution theory? The solution probably is that Job in the epilogue is a type of suffering, believing, and glorified Israel. Not only the individual believer, not only all the elect spirits of suffering humanity, but the beloved nation of the poet—Israel, the 'Servant of Jehovah'—must receive a special message of comfort from the great poem. In Isa. lxi. 7 we read that glorified Israel is to 'have double (compensation) instead of its shame;' comp. Zech. ix. 12, Jer. xvi. 14-18. The people of Israel, according to the limited view of the prophets, was bound indissolubly to the Holy Land. The only promise, therefore, which would be consolatory for suffering Israel, the only possible sign of God's restored favour, was a material one including fresh 'children' and many flocks and herds (Isa. liv. 1, lx. 7). Observe in this connection the phrase, xlii. 10, 'Jehovah turned the fortunes of Job' (others, as A. V., 'turned the captivity of Job')—the phrase so well known in passages relating to Israel (e.g. Ps. xiv. 7, Joel iii. 1).

The explanation is perhaps adequate. Some, however, will be haunted by a doubt whether the author of the prologue would not have thrown more energy and enthusiasm into the closing narrative. An early reader, probably of Pharisaic leanings, felt the poverty of the epilogue,[1] and sought to remedy it by the following addition in the Septuagint: 'And Job died, old and full of days; and it is written that he will rise again with those whom the Lord raiseth.'[2] The remainder of the Septuagint appendix testifies only to the love of the later Jews for amplifying Biblical notices (see Chap. VII.) Our own poet painter has also amplified the details of the epilogue, but in how different a way! (Gilchrist's *Life of Blake*, i. 332-3).

[1] Other readers, however, found no difficulty in the close of the story; to such St. James addresses himself in the words, 'Ye have heard of the endurance of Job, and have seen the end of the Lord' (James v. 11), i.e. the blessed end vouchsafed by the Lord to Job. It was also, no doubt, such a reader who composed the beautiful romance of Tobit, to show that, however tried, the righteous man is at last delivered by his God.

[2] Those rabbis who in later times held this view appear to have assumed that Job was of the Israelitish race (Frankl in Grätz's *Monatsschrift*, 1872, p. 311).

CHAPTER VII.

THE TRADITIONAL BASIS AND THE PURPOSE OF JOB.

I.

Did Job really live ?

THIS is widely different, remarks Umbreit,[1] from the question whether Job actually said and did all that is related of him in our book. It is scarcely necessary, he adds, in the present day to disprove the latter, but we have no reason to doubt the former (the theory as to the historical existence of a sort of Arabian king Priam, named Job). In truth, we have no positive evidence either for affirming or denying it, unless the 'holy places,' each reputed to be Job's grave, may be mentioned in this connection. The allusion in Ezek. xiv. 14 to 'Noah, Daniel, and Job,' proves no more than that a tradition of some sort existed respecting the *righteous* Job during the Babylonian Exile: we cannot tell how much Ezekiel knew besides Job's righteousness. In later times, Jewish students do appear to have believed that 'Job existed;' but the force of the argument is weakened by the uncritical character of the times, and the extreme form in which this belief was held by them. How early doubts arose, we know not. The authors of *Tobit* and *Susanna* may very likely have been only half-believers, since they evidently imitate the story of Job in their romantic compositions. At any rate, the often-quoted saying of Rabbi Resh Lakish, איוב לא היה ולא נברא אלא משל היה, 'Job existed not, and was not created, but he is (only) a parable,'[2] shows that even before the Talmud great freedom

[1] *Book of Job* (1836), E. T. i. 7.
[2] *Baba Bathra,* § 15, 1. Comp. Frankl in Grätz's *Monatsschrift,* 1872, pp. 309-310.

CHAP. VII. TRADITIONAL BASIS AND PURPOSE OF JOB 61

of speech prevailed among the Rabbis on such points. In Hai Gaon's time (d. 1037), the saying quoted must have given offence to some, for this Rabbi not only appeals for the historical character of Job to the passage in Ezekiel, but wishes (on traditional authority) to alter the reading of Resh Lakish's words, so as to read איוב לא היה ולא נברא אלא למשל, 'Job existed not, and was not created, except to be a parable.'[1] (See note 7, Appendix.)

The prevailing opinion among the Jews doubtless continued to be that the Book of Job was strictly historical, and Christian scholars (with the exception of Theodore—see Chap. XV.) found no reason to question this till Luther arose, with his genial, though unscientific, insistence on the right of questioning tradition. In his *Tischreden* Luther says, 'Ich halte das Buch Hiob für eine wahre Historia; dass aber alles so sollte geschehen und gehandelt sein, glaube ich nicht, sondern ich halte, dass ein feiner, frommer, gelehrter Mann habe es in solche Ordnung bracht.'[2] Poetically treated history—that is Luther's idea, as it was that of Grotius after him, and in our own country of that morning-star of Biblical criticism, Bishop Lowth.[3] It is acquiesced in by Schlottmann, Delitzsch, and Davidson, and with justice, provided it be clearly understood that no positive opinion can reasonably be held as to the historical origin of the tradition (*Sage*, Ewald) used by the author. I have said nothing of Spinoza and Albert Schultens. The former[4] pronounces most unfavourably on the religious and poetical value of the book which he regards as a heathenish fiction, reminding us somewhat (see elsewhere) of the hasty and ill-advised Theodore of Mopsuestia. The latter[5] actually defends the historical character both of the narratives and of the colloquies of Job in the strictest sense. Hengstenberg, alone perhaps among orthodox theologians, takes a precisely opposite view. Like Reuss and Merx, he regards the poem as entirely a work of

---

[1] Ewald and Dukes, *Beiträge zur Gesch. der ältesten Auslegung*, ii. 166.
[2] *Werke* (Walch), xxii. 2093. [3] *De sacrâ poesi* (1753), Prælect. xxxii.
[4] *Tractatus theologico-politicus*, c. x.
[5] *Liber Jobi* (1737), vol. i., *in fine Præf.*

imagination. We may be thankful for his protest against applying a prosaic standard to the poetical books of the Hebrew Canon. Those who do so, he remarks,[1] 'fail to observe that the book stands, not among historical, but among poetical books, and that it would betray a very low grade of culture, were one to depreciate imaginative as compared with historical writing, and declare it to be unsuitable for sacred Scripture.'

I entirely agree with the eminent scholar, whose unprogressive theology could not entirely extinguish his literary and philological sense. But I see no sufficient reason for adopting what in itself, I admit, would add a fresh laurel to the poet's crown. Merx indeed assures us[2] that the meaning of the name 'Job' is so redolent of allegory that it must be the poet's own invention, especially as the name occurs nowhere else in the Old Testament. He adds that the story of Job is so closely connected with the didactic part of the book that it would be lost labour to separate the legendary from the new material. All was wanted; therefore all is fictitious. This is not, however, the usual course of procedure with poets whether of the East or of the West, whose parsimony in the invention of plots is well known. As for the name Job (*Iyyob*) it may no doubt be explained (from the Arabic) 'he who turns to God,'[3] and in other ways, but there is no evidence that the author thought of any meaning for it. When he does coin names (see Epilogue), there is no room for doubting their significance. Ewald may, certainly, have gone too far in trying to recover the traditional element: how difficult it would be to do so with *Paradise Lost*, if we had not Genesis to help us! But the probability of the existence of a legend akin to the narrative in the Prologue, is shown by the parallels to it which survive, e.g. the touching Indian story

---

[1] *Das Buch Hiob* (1870-75), i. 35.
[2] *Das Buch Hiob*, Vorbemerkungen, p. xxxv.
[3] In Korán, xxxviii. 16, 29, 44, David, Solomon, and Job are all called, one after another, *awwâb*, i.e. not 'penitent,' but 'ever turning to God.' Hitzig remarks that Iyyôb (Arabic *Ayyûb*) will thus be equivalent to the mythic prophet Saleh (= 'pious') in the Korán (*Das Buch Hiob*, Einl., S. x.), on whom see Palmer, *Desert of the Exodus*, p. 50, where he is identified with Moses. This is bold, and, in any case, must not such a name be comparatively modern?

CHAP. VII. TRADITIONAL BASIS AND PURPOSE OF JOB 63

of Harischandra,[1] given by Dr. Muir in vol. i. of his *Sanskrit Texts*. The resemblance may be slight and superficial, but the sudden ruin of a good man's fortunes is common to both stories. Had we more knowledge of Arabic antiquity, we should doubtless find a more valuable parallel.[2]

The story of Job had a special attraction for Mohammed, who enriched it (following the precedent of the Jewish Haggada) with a fresh detail (Korán, xxxviii. 40). To him, as well as to St. James, Job was an example of 'endurance.' The dialogue between Allah and Eblis in Korán, xv. 32-42, may perhaps have been suggested by the Prologue of our poem.

'Did then, Job really live?' That for which we most care comes not from 'Tradition, Time's suspected register,'[3] but from an unnamed poet, who embellished tradition partly from imagination, partly (see next section) from the rich and varied stores of his own experience.

2.

The Autobiographical Element in its Bearing on the Purpose of the Poem.

A German critic (Dillmann), in speaking of *Job*, has well reminded us that 'the idea of a work of art must reveal itself in the development of the piece: it is not to be condensed into a dry formula.' Least of all, surely, is such formulation possible when the work of art is an idealised portraiture of the author himself, and such, I think, to a considerable extent is the Book of Job. Those words of a psalmist,

> Come and hear, all ye that fear God,
> and I will declare what he hath done for my soul
> (Ps. lxvi. 16, R. V.)

might be taken as the motto of *Job*. In short, the author is

---

[1] This was perhaps first pointed out by Schlottmann, in chap. i. of the Introduction to his Commentary.

[2] Nothing can be built upon the occurrence of the name Ayyûb in pre-Islamic times, for Jews and Arabs were in frequent intercourse before Mohammed.

[3] Davenant.

thoroughly 'subjective,' like all the great Hebrew and especially the Arabian poets. 'In the rhythmic swell of Job's passionate complaints, there is an echo of the heart-beats of a great poet and a great sufferer. The cry "Perish the day in which I was born" (iii. 3) is a true expression of the first effects of some unrecorded sorrow. In the life-like description beginning "Oh that I were as in months of old" (xxix. 2), the writer is thinking probably of his own happier days, before misfortune overtook him. Like Job (xxix. 7, 21-25) he had sat in the "broad place" by the gate and solved the doubts of perplexed clients. Like Job, he had maintained his position triumphantly against other wise men. He had a fellow-feeling with Job in the distressful passage through doubt to faith. Like Job (xxi. 16) he had resisted the suggestion of practical atheism, and with the confession of his error (xlii. 2-6) had recovered spiritual peace.'

The man who speaks to us under the mask of Job is not indeed a perfect character; but he does not pretend to be so. How pathetic are his appeals to his friends to remember the weight of his calamity—'therefore have my words been wild' (vi. 3)—and not to 'be captious about words when the speeches of the desperate are but for the wind' (vi. 26). He was no Stoic, and had not practised himself in deadening his sensibility to pain. Strong in his sense of justice, he lacked those higher intuitions which could alone soothe his irritation. But he was throughout loyal to the God whom his conscience revered, and, even in the midst of his wild words, he let God mould him. First of all, he renounced the hope of being understood by men; he ceased to complain of his rather ignorant than unfeeling friends. He exemplified that Arabic proverb which says, 'Perfect patience allows no complaint to be heard against (human creatures).' Then he came by degrees to trust God. There is a kernel of truth in that passage of the Jerusalem Talmud (*Berakhoth*, cix. 5) where, among the seven types of Pharisees, the sixth is described as 'he who is pious from fear, like Job,' and the seventh, as 'he who is pious from love, like Abraham.' Job's religion was at first not entirely but still too much marked by fear; it ended by becoming a religion of trust, justifying the title borne by Job among the Syrians, as if in contradiction to the Talmud, of 'the lover of the Lord.'[1]

So far as the author of *Job* has any direct purpose beyond that of giving a helpful picture of his own troubles, it is no doubt principally a polemical one. He has suffered so deeply from the inveterate error (once indeed a relative truth) so tenaciously maintained by the wisest men that he would fain crush the source of so much heart-breaking misery. But that for which we love the book is its φιλανθρωπία, its brotherly love to all mankind. No doubt the author thinks first of Israel, then (as I suppose) suffering exile; but the care with which the poem is divested of Israelitish peculiarities, seems to show that he looks beyond his own people, just as in his view of God he has broken the bonds of a narrow 'particularism.' 'I can see no other explanation of those apparently hyperbolical complaints, that strange invasion of self-consciousness, and that no less strange 'enthusiasm of humanity'[2] . . . . than the view expressed or implied by Chateaubriand, that Job is a type of righteous men in affliction—not merely in the land of Uz, nor among the Jews in Babylonia, nor yet, on Warburton's theory of the poem, in the Judæa of the time of Nehemiah, but wherever on the wide earth tears are shed and hearts are broken.' This is the truth in the too often exaggerated allegorical view[3] of the poem of *Job*. According to his wont, the author lets us read his meaning by occasional bold inconsistencies. No individual can use such phraseology as we find in xvii. 1, xviii. 2, 3, xix. 11, and perhaps I may add xvi. 10, xxvii. 11, 12. And yet the fact that Job often speaks as the 'type of suffering humanity' no more destroys

---

[1] Hottinger, referred to by Delitzsch, *Iob*, p. 7. In the Peshitto, Heb. xii. 3-11 has for a sub-title, ' In commemoration of Job the righteous.' The choice of the section shows in what sense Job's ' righteousness ' is affirmed—not the Talmudic.

[2] See especially Job vi. 2, 3, vii. 1-3, xiv. 1-3.

[3] This view goes back to the last century (Warburton, Michaelis, &c.) It has been remodelled by Seinecke and Hoekstra, who regard Job, not as the people of Israel in general, but the idealised Israël or ' Servant of Jehovah.' See especially Hoekstra's essay, *Theologisch Tijdschrift*, 1871, p. 1 &c., and Kuenen's reply, *Th. Ti.*, 1873, p. 492 &c.

his claim to be an individual 'than the typical character of Dante in his pilgrimage and of Faust in Goethe's great poem annuls the historical element in those two great poetical figures.'[1]

3.

The Purpose of Job as illustrated by Criticism.

More precise definitions of the purpose of Job depend on the acceptance of a critical analysis of the book. Some suggestions on this subject have been already given to facilitate the due comprehension of the poem. I must now offer the reader a connected sketch of the possible or probable stages of its growth. This, if it bears being tested, will perhaps reveal the special purpose of the several parts, and above all of that most precious portion—the Colloquies of Job and his friends. (Compare below, Chap. XII.)

I. The narrative which forms the Prologue is based upon a traditional story which represented Job as hurled from the height of happiness into an abyss of misery, but preserving a devout serenity in the midst of trouble. It is impossible to feel sure that this Prologue is by the same author as the following Colloquies. It stands in no very close connection with them; 'the Satan' in particular (an omission which struck William Blake[2]) is not heard of again in the book; and there is abundant evidence of the liking of the pre-Exile writers for a tasteful narrative style. It is not a wild conjecture that the first two chapters originally formed the principal part of a prose book of Job, comparable to the 'books' once current of Elijah, and perhaps one may add of Balaam and of Daniel—a book free from any speculations of the 'wise men' and in no sense a *mashal* or gnomic poem, but supplying in its own way a high and adequate solution of

[1] Quoted from Essay ix. in vol. ii. of *The Prophecies of Isaiah*.
[2] Blake's 16th design is devoted to the defeat of Satan. Beneath the enthroned Jehovah and his angels, 'the Evil One falls with tremendous plummet force, Hell naked before his face, and Destruction without a covering.' Another point in which Blake corrects his author is the introduction of Job's wife into the illustrations of the Colloquies.

the great problem of the suffering of the righteous. The writer of this Prologue, whether he also wrote the Colloquies or not, firmly believed that the calamities which sometimes fell on the innocent were both for the glory of God and of human nature. It was possible, he said, to continue in one's integrity, though no earthly advantage accrued from it. If the Prologue once formed part of a distinct prose 'book' of Job, one can hardly suppose that the same author wrote the Epilogue; for while the Colloquies *do* contain hints of Job's typical character (as to some extent a representative of humanity), the Prologue does not, and it is only the typical or allegorical intepretation which makes the Epilogue tolerable. In fact, the Epilogue must, as it seems to me, have been written, if not by the author of the Colloquies, yet by some one who had this work before him. The prose 'book' of Job, if it existed, and if it originated in Judah, cannot have been written before the Chaldæan period. This period and no other explains the moral purpose of the 'book,' precisely as the age of the despotic Louis XIV. is the only one which suits the debate on the disinterested love of God with which the name of Fénelon is inseparably connected. The Chaldæan period, however, we must remember, did not begin with the Captivity, but with the appearance of the Babylonian power on the horizon of Palestine. We must not therefore *too hastily* assume that the Book of Job is a monument of the Babylonian Captivity, true as I myself believe this hypothesis to be.

We are, however, of course not confined to this hypothesis of a prose 'book' of Job. The author of the Colloquies may have been equally fitted to be a writer of narrative, and may have felt that the solution mentioned above, although the highest, was not the only one admissible. We may therefore conceive of him as following up the solution offered in the Prologue by a ventilation of the great moral problem before himself and his fellow 'wise men.' He throws the subject open as it were to general discussion, and invests all the worthiest speculations of his time in the same flowing poetical dress, that no fragment of truth contained in them may be lost. He himself is far from absolutely rejecting any of them;

he only seems to deny that the ideas of the three representative sages can be applied at once, as they apply them, to the case of one like Job.

[Böttcher, however, regards Job as the work of one principal and several subordinate writers. It was occasioned, he thinks, by a conversation on the sufferings of innocent men, at that time so frequent (i.e. in the reign of Manasseh). See his *Aehrenlese*, p. 68.]

II. The completion or publication of the colloquies revealed (or seemed to reveal) sundry imperfections in the original mode of treating the subject. Some other 'wise men,' therefore (or possibly, except in the case of III., the author himself), inserted passages in the poem with the view of qualifying or supplementing its statements. These were merely laid in, without being welded with the rest of the book. The first in order of these additions is chap. xxviii., which cannot be brought into a logical connection with the chapters among which it is placed, in spite of the causal particle 'for' prefixed to it ('*For* there is a vein'). It is possible, indeed, that it has been extracted from some other work. The hypothesis of insertion (or, if used without implying illicit tampering with the text, 'interpolation') is confirmed by the occurrence of 'Adonai' in ver. 28, which is contrary to the custom of the author of Job, and by its highly rhetorical character. If the passage was written with a view to the Book of Job, we must suppose the author to have been dissatisfied with the original argument, and to have sought a solution for the problem in the inscrutableness of the divine wisdom. Zophar, it is true, had originally alluded to this attribute, but with a more confined object. According to him, God, being all-wise, can detect sins invisible to mortal eyes (xi. 6):—it is needless to draw out the wide difference between this slender inference and the large theory which appears to be suggested in chap. xxviii.

III. One of the less progressive 'wise men' was scandalised at the irreverent statements of Job and dissatisfied with the three friends' mode of dealing with them (xxxii. 2, 3). Hence the speeches of Elihu, the most generally recognised

CHAP. VII. TRADITIONAL BASIS AND PURPOSE OF JOB

of all the inserted portions (chaps. xxxii.–xxxvii.) The author partly imitates the speeches of Jehovah.

IV. In another inserted passage (ch. xxxviii.–xl. 14, xlii. 1–6), the Almighty is represented as chastising the presumption of Job, and showing forth the supreme wisdom by contrast with Job's unwisdom. It is clear that the copy in which it was inserted was without the speeches of Elihu, for the opening words of Jehovah (xxxviii. 2) clearly have reference to the last discourse of Job, which they must have been intended to follow. The effect of this fine passage is much impaired by the interposition of the speeches of Elihu.

V. The description of the behémoth and the leviathan (xl. 15–24, xli.) seems also to be a later insertion, and somewhat more recent than the speeches of Jehovah. It is a 'purple patch,' and the appendix last mentioned gains by its removal.

VI. An editor appended the epilogue. He must have had the prologue before him, but took no pains to bring his own work into harmony with it, except in the one point which he could not help adopting, namely the vast riches of his hero. He agreed with Job's friends on the grand question of retribution, though he would not sanction their line of argument. Job's doubts, according to him, contained more faith than their uncharitable dogmatism.

Can we feel grateful to this writer? He has at any rate relieved the strain upon the imagination of the reader, and possibly, if we assume him to be distinct from the author of the Prologue, carried out an unfulfilled intention of that author (note the words in i. 12, 'only upon himself put not forth thy hand'). But he did so in a prosaic spirit, and made a sad concession to a low view of providential dealings. He has also, I think, caused much misunderstanding of the object of the book. Thus we find Dr. Ginsburg saying,[1]

> The Book of Job . . . . only confirms the old opinion that the righteous are visibly rewarded here, inasmuch as it represents their calamities as transitory, and Job himself as restored to double his original wealth and happiness in this life.

Against which I enter a respectful protest.

[1] Art. 'Ecclesiastes,' *Ency. Brit.*, 9th ed.

The view here adopted of the gradual growth of the book seems important for its right comprehension. In its present form, it seems like a very confused theodicy, designed to justify God against the charge of bringing misfortune upon innocent persons. But when the disturbing elements are removed, we see that the book is simply an expression of the conflicting thoughts of an earnest, warm-hearted man on the great question of suffering. He protests, it is true, against the rigour and uncharitableness of the traditional orthodox belief, but is far more aspiring to solve the problem theoretically. This is one chief point in which he differs from his interpolators (if the word may be used), who mostly appear to have had some favourite theory (or partial view of truth) to advocate.

CHAPTER VIII.

DATE AND PLACE OF COMPOSITION.

WE have seen (Chap. VII.) that the unity of authorship of the Book of Job is not beyond dispute, but we shall not at present assume the results of analysis. Let us endeavour to treat of the date and place of composition on the hypothesis that the book is a whole as it stands (on the Elihu-portion however, comp. Chap. XII.) It is at any rate probable that the greater part of it at least proceeds from the same period. Can that period be the patriarchal? The author has sometimes received credit for his faithful picture of this early age. This is at any rate plausible. For instance, he avoids the use of the sacred name Jehovah, revealed to Moses according to Ex. vi. 3. Then, too, the great age ascribed to Job in the Epilogue (xlii. 16) agrees with the notices of the patriarchs. The uncoined piece of silver (Heb. *kesita*) which each kinsman of Job gave him after his recovery (xlii. 11), is only mentioned again in Gen. xxxiii. 19 (Josh. xxiv. 32). The musical instruments referred to in xxi. 12, xxx. 31, are also mentioned in Gen. iv. 21, xxxi. 27. There is no protest against idolatry either in the Book of Job [1] or in Genesis. Job himself offers sacrifices to the one true God, like the patriarchs, and the kind of sacrifice offered is the burnt-offering (i. 5, xlii. 8); there is no mention of guilt- or sin-offerings. The settled life of Job, too, as described in the Prologue is not inconsistent with the story of Jacob's life in the vale of

---

[1] The absence of such a protest is characteristic of the Wisdom-literature in general. The reference to star-worship in Job xxxi. 26 suggests a date subsequent to the origination of the title 'Jehovah (God) of Hosts.' See appendix to Isa. i. in my commentary.

Shechem,[1] though in reality the author probably described it from his observation of settled life in Arabia. But none of these allusions required any special gift of historical imagination. The tone of the few descriptive passages in the Colloquies, and of the reflections throughout, is that of an age long subsequent to the patriarchal. The very idea of wise men meeting together to discuss deep problems (as in the later Arabic *maqāmāt*, compared by Bertholdt and others) is an anachronism in a 'patriarchal' narrative, and (like the religious position of the speeches in general) irresistibly suggests the post-Solomonic period. The Job of the Colloquies is a travelled citizen of the world at an advanced period of history; indeed, he now and then seems expressly to admit this (xxiv. 12, xxix. 7). It is therefore needless to discuss the theory which assigns the book to the Mosaic or pre-Mosaic age,—a theory which is a relic of the cold, literal, unsympathetic method of the critics of the last two centuries. A few scholars of eminence, feeling this, placed the poem in the Solomonic period, a view which is in itself plausible, if we consider the pronounced secular turn of the great king, and his recorded taste for eastern parabolistic 'wisdom,' but which falls with the cognate theory of the authorship of Proverbs. A more advanced stage of society than that of the period referred to, and a greater maturity of the national intellect, are presupposed on every page of the poem. The tone of the book—I refer especially to the Colloquies—suggests a time when the nationalism of the older periods had, in general, ceased to satisfy reflecting minds. The doubters, whom Job and his friends represent, have been so staggered in their belief in Israel's loving God, that they decline to use His revealed name :—[2] once or twice only does it slip in (xii. 9; cf. xxviii. 28), as if to show that the poet himself has fought his

---

[1] Mr. Tomkins compares Job's mode of life with that of Abram before his departure from Kharran (*Studies on the Times of Abraham*, 1878, p. 61).

[2] I cannot go quite so far as Lagarde, who argues from the use of 'Eloah' (instead of 'Elohim' and 'Jehovah') that the doubters have cast off belief in all the supposed various manifestations of divinity in the world, and merely retain a comfortless belief in τὸ θεῖον. 'Numen quoddam esse non negant, sed' &c. *Psalterium Hieronymi*, pp. 155-6 ('Corollarium').

way to a reconciling faith. As is clear from the cognate psalms xxxvii., xlix., lxxiii., the patriarchal theory of prosperity and adversity had been found wanting. Doubts had arisen, most painful in their intensity, from observing the disproportion between character and fortune—doubts which might indeed insinuate themselves at any time, but acquire an abnormal force in a declining community (ix. 24, xii. 4-6, 23, and especially chap. xxi.) Some had even ventured on positive doctrinal heresy. In opposition to these, Eliphaz professes his adhesion to the tradition of the fathers, in whose time religion was untainted by alien influence (xv. 17-19). It is merely an incidental remark of Eliphaz, but it points to a date subsequent to the appearance of Assyria on the horizon of Palestine. For it was the growing influence of that power, which, for good and for evil, modified the character of Israelitish religion both in its higher and in its lower forms.

Precise historical allusions are almost entirely wanting. We may, however, infer with certainty that the book was written subsequently to the 'deportation' of Israel, or of Judah, or at the very least of some neighbouring people (xii. 17-19 ; comp. xv. 19 [1]). For the uprooting of whole peoples from their original homes was peculiar to the Assyrian policy.[2] But which of these forced expatriations is intended?—We are not *compelled* to think of the Babylonian Exile by the reference to the Chaldæans in the Prologue. The Chaldæans might have been known to a well-informed Hebrew writer ever since the ninth century B.C., at which time they became predominant in the southern provinces on the lower Euphrates : we find Isaiah, speaking of the 'land of Chaldæa' (Isa. xxiii. 13) in the eighth century. Still I own that the description of the Chaldæans as *robbers* does appear to me most easily explained by supposing a covert allusion to the invasions of Nebuchadnezzar.[3] The Assyrians are indeed once called 'treacherous

---

[1] Job xv. 19 certainly implies the siege and capture of Jerusalem by some foreign foe. Comp. Joel iii. (Heb. iv.) 17.
[2] Dr. Barth quotes Am. i. 6, ii. 1-3, ix. 11, 15 in proof that 'deportation' also took place in the 'pre-Assyrian' time. But, in fact, Amos is not 'pre-Assyrian.'
[3] It is no sufficient objection that the ravages of the Chaldæans in Job are on a

dealers' by Isaiah (xxxiii. 1), but the Babylonians impressed the Hebrew writers by their rapacity far more than the Assyrians. The 'unrighteous' of the Psalms are, when foreigners are spoken of, not the Assyrians, but either the Babylonians or still later oppressors (e.g. Ps. cxxv. 3); and the description of the Babylonians in the first chapter of Habakkuk strongly reminds us of those complaints of Job, 'The earth is given over into the hand of the unrighteous' (ix. 24), and 'The robbers' tents are in peace, and they that provoke God are secure, they who carry (their) god in their hand' (xii. 6; comp. Hab. i. 11, 16).

The view here propounded might be supported by an argument from linguistic data (see Chap. XIII.) which would lead us into details out of place here. It is that of Umbreit, Knobel, Grätz, and (though he does not exclude the possibility of a later date) the sober and thorough Gesenius. Long after the present writer's results were first committed to paper, he had the rare satisfaction of finding them advocated, so far as the date is concerned, in a commentary by a scholar of our own who has the best right to speak (A. B. Davidson, Introduction to *The Book of Job*, 1884). On the other hand, Stickel, Ewald, Magnus, Bleek, Renan (1860), Kuenen (1865), Hitzig, Reuss, Dillmann, Merx, prefer to place our poem in the period between Isaiah and Jeremiah, and this seems to me the earliest date from which the composition and significance of the book can be at all rightly understood. Reasons enough for this statement of opinion will suggest themselves to those who have followed me hitherto; let me now only add that the pure monotheism of the Book makes an earlier date, on historical principles, hardly conceivable.[1] A later date than the Exile-period is not, I admit, inconceivable (see Vatke, *Die biblische*

---

small scale, nor yet that side by side with them are mentioned the Sabeans, surely not those of S. Arabia (Nöldeke), but those of N. Arabia (Delitzsch), detachments of whom might have encamped on the borders of Edom. Comp. Wetzstein in Delitzsch's *Job*, ed. 2, p. 596 &c.

[1] I write this with deference to the contrary opinion of Delitzsch, who is, however, too prejudiced against late dates, and biassed by his belief in the authenticity of the Song of Hezekiah. If the Book of Job be pre-Hezekian, it is of course natural to throw it back to the age of Solomon.

Theologie, i. 563 &c.), and is now supported by Kuenen.[1] If there were an allusion to the doctrine of the Resurrection, in xix. 26, or if the portraiture of Job were (as Kuenen thinks it is) partly modelled on the Second Isaiah's description of the Servant of Jehovah, I should in fact be driven to accept this view. I have stated above that I cannot find the Resurrection in *Job*, and in *Isaiah*, ii. 267 that the priority of *Job* seems to me to be made out. I need not combat Clericus and Warburton, who ascribe the authorship of *Job* to Ezra. For Jeremiah (Bateson Wright) or the author of Lamentations (i.e. Baruch, according to Bunsen) something might perhaps be said, but—Ezra!

As to the place of composition. Hitzig and Hirzel think of Egypt on account of the numerous allusions to Egypt in the book; and so Ewald with regard to xl. 15–xli. 34. 'Die ganze Umgebung ist egyptisch,' says Hitzig with some exaggeration.[2] More might be said in favour of the theory which places the author in a region where Arabic and Aramaic might both be heard. Stickel, holding the pre-Exile origin of the book, supposed it to have come from the far south-east of Palestine. Nowhere better than in the hill-country of the South could the poet study simple domestic relations, and also make excursions into N. Arabia. He thus accounts[3] for the points of contact between the Book of Job and the prophecy of Amos of Tekoa (see below, Chap. XI.), which include even some phonetic peculiarities (the softening of the gutturals and the interchange of sibilants). To me, the whole question seems well-nigh an idle one. The author (or, if you will, the authors) had travelled much in various lands, and the book is the result. The place where, is of far less importance than the time when it was composed.

[1] *Theologisch Tijdschrift*, 1873, p. 538.
[2] *Das Buch Hiob* (1874), p. xlix.   [3] *Das Buch Hiob* (1842), p. 276.

CHAPTER IX.

ARGUMENT FROM THE USE OF MYTHOLOGY.

ONE of the peculiarities of our poet (which I have elsewhere compared with a similar characteristic in Dante) is his willingness to appropriate mythic forms of expression from heathendom. This willingness was certainly not due to a feeble grasp of his own religion; it was rather due partly to the poet's craving for imaginative ornament, partly to his sympathy with his less developed readers, and a sense that some of these forms were admirably adapted to give reality to the conception of the 'living God.' Several of these points of contact with heathendom have been indicated in my analysis of the poem. I need not again refer to these, but the semi-mythological allusions to supernatural beings who had once been in conflict with Jehovah (xxi. 22, xxv. 2), and the cognate references to the dangerous cloud-dragon (see below) ought not to be overlooked. Both in Egypt and in Assyria and Babylonia, we find these very myths in a fully developed form. The 'leviathan' of iii. 8, the dragon probably of vii. 12 (*tannīn*) and certainly of xxvi. 13 (*nākhāsh*), and the 'rahab' of ix. 13, xxvi. 12, remind us of the evil serpent Apap, whose struggle with the sun-god Ra is described in chap. xxxix. of the Book of the Dead and elsewhere. 'A battle took place,' says M. Maspero, 'between the gods of light and fertility and the "sons of rebellion," the enemies of light and life. The former were victorious, but the monsters were not destroyed. They constantly menace the order of nature, and, in order to resist their destructive action, God must, so to speak, create the world anew every day.'[1] An equally close parallel is

---

[1] Maspero, *Histoire ancienne de l'Orient*, ed. 1, p. 30. Comp. Chabas' translation from the Harris papyrus, *Records of the Past*, x. 142-146.

CHAP. IX. ARGUMENT FROM THE USE OF MYTHOLOGY 77

furnished by the fourth tablet of the Babylonian creation-story, which describes the struggle between the god Marduk (Merodach) and the dragon Tiamat or Tiamtu (a fem. corresponding to the Heb. masc. form *t'hom* 'the deep'), for which see Delitzsch's *Assyrische Lesestücke*, 3rd edition, Smith and Sayce's *Chaldæan Genesis*, p. 107 &c., and Budge in *Proceedings of the Society of Biblical Archæology*, Nov. 6, 1883.

Nor must I forget the 'fool-hardy' giant (K'sīl = Orion) in ix. 9, xxxviii. 31, nor the dim allusion to the sky-reaching mountain of the north, rich in gold (comp. Isa. xiv. 13, and Sayce, *Academy*, Jan. 28, 1882, p. 64), and the myth-derived synonyms for Sheól—Death, Abaddon, and 'the shadow of death' (or, deep gloom), xxvi. 6, xxviii. 22, xxxviii. 17, also the 'king of terrors' (xviii. 14), who like Pluto or Yama rules in the Hebrew Underworld. Observe too the instances in which a primitive myth has died down into a metaphor, e.g. 'the eyelids of the Dawn' (iii. 9, xli. 18), and especially that beautiful passage,

> Hast thou ever in thy life given charge to the Morning,
> and shown its place to the Dawn,
> that it may take hold of the skirts of the earth,
> so that the wicked are shaken out of it,
> and the earth changes as clay under a seal,
> and (all things) stand forth as in a garment,
> and light is withheld from the wicked,
> and the arm lifted up is broken? (xxxviii. 12–15).

How very vivid! The personified Dawn seizes the coverlet under which the earth has slept at its four ends and shakes the evil-doers out of it like flies; upon which form and colour return to the earth, as clay (a Babylonian image) receives a definite form from the seal, and as the sad-coloured night-wrapper is exchanged for the bright, embroidered holiday-robe. Could we only transfer the poet to an earlier stage of mythic consciousness, we should find him expressing the same ideas—that morning-light creates all fair things anew, and discomfits the evil-doer—very much in the style of the Vedic hymns to Ushas (the Dawn), from which I quote the following in Grassmann's translation (Rig Veda, I. 123, 4, 5),—

> Die tageshelle kommt zu jedem Hause
> und jedem Tage gibt sie ihren Namen ;
> zu spenden willig, strahlend naht sie immer
> und theilet aus der Güter allerbestes.
> Als Bhaga's Schwester, Varuna's Verwandte,
> komm her zuerst, o schöne Morgenröthe ;
> Wer frevel übt, der soll dahinter bleiben,
> von uns besiegt sein mit der Uschas Wagen.

(There is also an Egyptian parallel in a hymn to the Sun-god, *Records of the Past*, viii. 131, 'He fells the wicked in his season.') How far the poet of Job believed in the myths which he has preserved, e.g. in the existence of potentates or potencies corresponding to the 'dragon' of which he speaks, we cannot certainly tell. Mr. Budge has suggested that Tiamat, the sky-dragon of the Babylonians, conveyed a distinct symbolic meaning. However this may have been, the 'leviathan' of Job was probably to the poet a 'survival' from a superstition of his childhood, and little if anything more than the emblem of all evil and disorder.

And now for the bearing of the above on criticism. It is a remarkable fact that there are mythological allusions, very similar to some of those in Job, in the later portions of the Book of Isaiah (Isa. xxiv. 21, xxvii. 1, li. 9). This evidently suggests a date for the Book of Job not earlier than the Exile. It is not necessary to assume that the authors of these books borrowed either from Egypt or from Babylonia. They drew from the unexhausted store of Jewish popular beliefs. They wrote for a larger public than the older poets and prophets could command, and adapted themselves more completely to the average culture of their people.

CHAPTER X.

ARGUMENT FROM THE DOCTRINE OF ANGELS.

THE facts on which our argument is based are mainly the passages in *Job* which refer to 'sons of Elohim' (or better, as Davidson, 'of the Elohim'), to 'the Satan,' and to the *mal'akim*. The first of these three phrases means probably *inferior* members of the class of beings called Elohim (i.e. 'superhuman powers'); the second, 'the adversary (or opposer);' the third, 'envoys or messengers' (ἄγγελοι). We may at once draw an inference from the expression 'the Satan,' the full importance of which will be seen later on. 'The Satan' being an appellative, the book in which it occurs was probably written before Chronicles, where we find 'Satan' without the article, almost[1] as if a proper name; and being applied to a minister and not an opponent of Jehovah, the Book of Job is probably earlier than the prophecies of Zechariah and the Books of Chronicles; see Zech. iii. 1, 2 (where observe that Jehovah's only true representative gives a severe reproof to 'the Satan'), 1 Chron. xxi. 1 (where 'Satan,' uncommissioned, 'entices' David to an act displeasing to Jehovah[2]). The difference between the notices of the Satan (or Satan) may not seem great to an unpractised student, but no one who has followed the development of any single doctrine will undervalue such traces of a growing refinement in the conceptions of good and evil. Whether or no the ideas of the Chronicler

---

[1] It is not likely that Satan was ever used entirely as a proper name; but being frequently in men's mouths, it naturally lost the article. At last the name Sammael was invented for the arch-Satan (see above).

[2] In 2 Sam. xxiv. 1, the temptation is ascribed to Jehovah; the Chronicler is at any rate on the road to James i. 13. Contrast the stationariness of Mohammed ('God misleadeth whom He will,' Korán, xxxv. 9).

and his age had been modified by hearing of the Persian Ahriman, may be questioned; but a similar supposition cannot be allowed in the case of the author of *Job*. The Satan of the Prologue is, in theory at least, simply Jehovah's agent, though he certainly betrays a malicious pleasure in his invidious function of trying or sifting the righteous. It is not impossible that the author of the Prologue was the first to use the term Satan in this sense. At any rate, it is a pure Hebrew term, unlike the Ashmedai or Asmodæus of the Book of Tobit. [Ashmedai, in later Judaism, is the head of the Shedim—demons who were never angels of God, just as Sammael is the 'head of all Satans,' i.e. the prince of the fallen angels. Weber, *System der altsynagog. Palästin. Theologie*, pp. 243-5.]

Next, turning to the *mal'akim*, observe that the word occurs very rarely in *Job*, viz. once in the original Colloquies (iv. 18), and once (virtually) in the first speech of Elihu (xxxiii. 23). We find, however, a kindred phrase 'the $q'd\bar{o}sh\bar{i}m$,' or 'holy ones,' i.e. superhuman, heavenly beings, separate from the world of the senses[1] (v. 1, xv. 15), and comparing v. 1 with iv. 18 we cannot doubt that the same class of beings is intended. We nowhere meet with the *Mal'ak Yahvè*, so familiar to us in certain Old Testament narratives; Elihu's *mal'ak mēlîç* (xxxiii. 23) is not synonymous with the older expression (see account of Elihu). In fact, the thousands of *mal'akim* known at the period of the writers of Job have made the one great *mal'ak* unnecessary, just as, but for the influence of Persian ideas, the multitudinous 'hurtful angels' (Ps. lxxviii. 49) might sooner or later have entirely supplanted the single Satan. And yet even an ordinary *mal'ak*, when he appears, is more awful than the great *mal'ak Yahvè*; the angel who appears to Eliphaz (Job iv. 15, 16) is as unrecognisable as the 'face' of Jehovah himself. This is an indication, though but a slight one, of a somewhat advanced age, when the gulf between God and man was more acutely felt, and religious thought was more specially directed to filling it up.

The title 'holy ones'(v. 1) enables us to identify the 'angels'

---

[1] So rightly Baudissin, *Studien*, ii. 125.

with the 'sons of the Elohim.' Separateness from human weakness, though not mediatorial ability[1] is equally, predicated of both. But neither the poet of *Job*, nor any of the psalmists, identifies the phrases in express terms;[2] a virtual identification (see above, and Ps. lxxxix. 7, 8) is all that they venture upon. There was a good reason for this—viz. their recollection of the physical and mythological origin of the phrase, 'the sons of the Elohim.' 'Angels' and 'sons of the Elohim' are indeed alike 'holy' and 'servants' of the supreme God, but not always so, according to Hebrew tradition, were the 'sons of the Elohim.' In support of this, we may refer, not only to Gen. vi. 4 (which the author of *Job* need not have known), but to the allusions in his poem (see above) to a war among the inhabitants of heaven. This war, I think, stands in connection not merely with the physical phenomena of light and darkness, but also with speculations of pious Jehovists, or worshippers of Jehovah, as to the basis and value of 'heathen' religions. According to Deut. xxxii. 8,[3] each of the nations of the world was allotted by the Most High (*Elyōn*) to some one of the 'sons of El' (the simplest name for God); of course we are to suppose that these 'sons of El' and their worshippers were meant to recognise the

---

[1] Eliphaz apparently assumes that the 'holy ones' might plead for Job with Eloah (comp. xxxiii. 23). There is an analogy for this in Arabian religion. The Koreish (Qurais) tribe were willing to join Mohammed, if he would only admit their three idol-gods to be mediators with the supreme God, and 'for a time he consented. See Palmer's Korán, Introd., p. xxvii. This was equivalent to recognising these heathen deities as *b'nê Elōhīm* and also (Eliphaz would say) as *Q'dōshīm* or 'holy ones.'

[2] The Elohistic narrator in Gen. xxviii. 12, 17, xxxii. 2, 3 even appears to identify the terms 'angels of Elohim' (= God) and 'Elohim' (= divine powers). *Beth 'elōhīm* and *makhanê 'elōhīm* are more naturally rendered 'place, host, of divine powers' than 'place, host of God.'

[3] The 'Song of Moses' is placed by Ewald and Kamphausen in the Assyrian period of Israel's history. Ver. 8 runs, in a corrected version,

'When Elyōn gave the nations as inheritances, when he parted out the sons of men, he set the bounds of the peoples according to the number of the sons of El;' comp. ver. 9, 'For Jehovah is the portion of his people, Jacob is the lot of his inheritance.' (With many recent critics, I follow the reading of the Septuagint. A scribe, offended by the no longer intelligible statement in ver. 8, inserted an I before ΗΛ, and so formed the usual abbreviation of Ἰσραήλ.) This passage explains Sirach xvii. 17.

supremacy of the 'God of Gods'—Jehovah. But (so we may suppose the train of thought of the Jehovists to have run) the nations and their deities formed the vain dream of independence. The result of the struggle between Jehovah and the inferior Elohim is referred to in *Job*: the Elohim renounced their dream of independent sovereignty and were admitted into Jehovah's service. Henceforth they were no longer *shēdīm*, i.e. 'lords' (?), Deut. xxxii. 17, but *mal'akīm* 'messengers.' But the 'heathen' nations go on worshipping the Elohim, ignorant that their divinities have been dispossessed of their misused lordship.[1] Instead of Him who alone henceforth is 'enthroned in the heavens' (Ps. ii. 4), they honour 'that which is not God' (Deut. xxxii. 21), phantom-divinities whom they localise, like Jehovah, in the sky. Thus, except as to the region of the divine habitation, they differ radically from Jehovists like the author of *Job*. In that one point he agrees with them: the stars and the 'sons of Elohim' he still pictures to himself as closely conjoined (xxxviii. 6). Thus, the old and the new are fermenting in his brain, and on the ground of their angelology we can safely date the authors of *Job* somewhere in the great literary period which opens with the 'Captivity.'

[1] There is a singular reference to a still future deposition of the patron spirits of the nations in Isa. xxiv. 21 (post-Exile), with which comp. Ps. lviii., lxxxii. In lxxxii. 6 the title *'elōhīm* is interchanged with *b'nē 'elyōn* 'sons of the Most High.'

CHAPTER XI.

ARGUMENT FROM PARALLEL PASSAGES.

THE new phase into which the controversy as to the early Christian work on the *Teaching of the Apostles* has passed excuses me from justifying the importance (in spite of its difficulty) of the study of parallel passages. A great point has been gained in one's critical and exegetical training when one has learned so to compare parallel passages as to distinguish true from apparent resemblances, and to estimate the degree of probability of imitation. In Essay viii. of vol. ii. of *The Prophecies of Isaiah*, I endeavoured to help the student to do this for himself within the field of the Book of Isaiah. I shall not attempt this with the same thoroughness for the Book of Job. It is a sign of the consummate skill of the writer that he is an artist even in his imitations. As Luther says, 'Die Rede dieses Buches ist so reisig und prächtig als freilich keines Buches in der ganzen Schrift.' The author retains the parallelistic distich, but is no longer content with a bare synonymous or antithetic bifurcation of his material, and dwells on the decoration of an idea with a freedom which sometimes obscures his meaning; hence too the germinal phrase or word suggested by an earlier book may easily escape notice. I shall confine my attention to the most defensible points of contact, referring for the rest, without pledging myself to agreement, to Dr. J. Barth's *Beiträge zur Erklärung des Buches Job* (Leipzig, s.a.), pp. 1-17.

The influence of *Job* on the works which all admit to be of post-Exile origin need not detain us here. There is but one undoubted reference to Job in Ecclesiastes (v. 14; comp. Job i. 21)—we should perhaps have expected more. But

Sirach with a true instinct detected an affinity between his own ideas and Job xxviii. (comp. this chapter with Ecclus. i. 3, 5, &c.), though he neglects the rest, and does not include our poet among the 'famous men' and the 'fathers that begot us.' Passing upwards, we shall, if historical criticism be our guide, make our first pause at the undeniably later psalms and at the later portions of Isaiah. In the former compare (as specimens),

Ps. ciii.	16	with Job	vii.	12
— cvii.	40	— —	xii.	21, 24
— —	41	— —	xxi.	11
— —	42	— —	xxii.	19, v. 16
— cxix.	28	— —	xvi.	20
— —	50	— —	vi.	10
— —	69	— —	xiii.	4
— —	103	— —	vi.	25.

There is, I think, no question that these psalm-passages were inspired by the parallels in Job. In Isa. xl.–lxvi. there are, as I have pointed out (*Isaiah*, ed. 3, ii. 250), at least twenty-one parallels to passages in our poem. I do not, however, think that we can venture to describe either set of passages *en bloc* as imitations. But there are at least two clear cases of imitation, and here the original is not the prophet but the poet (comp. Isa. li. 9*b*, 10*a*, with Job xxvi. 12, 13, and Isa. liii. 9 with Job xvi. 17). With regard to the book (II. Isaiah) as a whole, or at least the greater part of it, we may say that there is a parallelism of idea running through it and the Book of Job, which may to a large extent account for parallelisms of expression. This does not, however, apply everywhere, least of all to the great prophetic dirge on the 'despised and rejected' one, which presents stylistic phenomena so unlike that of its context that we seem bound to assign the substratum of Isa. lii. 13–liii. to a time of persecution previous to the Exile.[1] How the poet of Job became acquainted with this striking passage, we know not. Did it form part of some prophetic anthology similar to the poetic

[1] See Cheyne, *The Prophecies of Isaiah*, ed. 3, ii. 39; art. 'Isaiah,' *Encyclopædia Britannica*, xi. 380.

Golden Treasury called 'The Book of the Righteous'? or shall we follow those bolder critics who suppose the author of Job to have lived in the post-Exile times, when he may easily have had access to both parts of our Book of Isaiah? These are questions not to be evaded on account of their difficulty, but not to be decided here.

Our next halt may be made at the Book of Proverbs, the three concluding sections of which composite work belong at the earliest to the last century of the Jewish state. Among the clearest literary allusions in *Job* are those to this book, and some of these are especially important with regard to the disputed question of the relation between our poem and the introduction to the Book of Proverbs (Prov. i.-ix.) That the latter work is the earlier seems to me clear from a comparison of the general positions indicated by the following passages from Prov. i.-ix. and the Book of Job. Compare—

Prov.	i.	7	with Job	xxviii. 28
—	iii.	11	— —	v. 17
—	iii. 14, 15	}	— —	xxviii. 15-19
—	viii. 10, 11			
—	iii. 19, 20		— —	xxviii. 26, 27
—	viii. 22, 25		— —	xv. 7, 8
—	viii.	29	—	— xxxviii. 10.

It will be seen by any one who will compare these passages that the case here is different from that of the parallelisms in *Job* and the second part of Isaiah. The latter do not perhaps allow us to determine with confidence which of the two books is the earlier. But, as Prof. Davidson has amply shown,[1] the stage of intellectual development represented by *Job* is more advanced than that in the 'Praise of Wisdom.' The general subjects may be the same, but in Job they have entered upon a new phase.—We now pass to the earliest of the proverbial anthologies (Prov. x.-xxii. 16). Here of course the relation is reversed: the proverbs are the originals to which the author of Job alludes. Compare—

Prov.	xiii. 19	}	with Job	xviii. 5, 6, xxi. 17
—	xxiv. 20			
—	xv. 11		— —	xxvi. 6
—	xvi. 15		— —	xxix. 23, 24.

[1] *The Book of Job* (1884), pp. lx.-lxii.

We may infer from this group of parallels that the author of *Job* not only studied venerated ' Solomonic ' models, but even ventured directly to controvert their leading doctrine; see especially Job xxi. 17. In our next comparison the relation seems reversed. The author of Prov. xxx. 1-4 not improbably alludes sarcastically to the theophany in Job xxxviii.-xlii. 6. Note in passing the occurrence of Eloah for ' God ' in Prov. xxx. 5 (comp. the speeches in *Job*).

There are several parallels in the Book of Lamentations ; I restrict myself to those in the third elegy, which differs in several points from the others, especially in its poetic feebleness. It is easier to believe that the author of the elegy was dependent on *Job* than to take the reverse view. A poem, the hero of which was obviously the typical righteous man, naturally suggested features in the description of the representative Israelite. Compare, then, Lam. iii. 7, 9 with Job xix. 8 ; iii. 8 with Job xxx. 20 ; iii. 10 with Job. x. 16 ; iii. 12, 13 with Job vii. 20, xvi. 12, 13 ; iii. 14, 63 with Job xxx. 9.

Parallels to *Job* also occur in Jeremiah. It is often, indeed, not easy to say on which side is the originality. But in one of the most important instances we may pronounce decidedly in favour of *Job* (comp. Jer. xx. 14-18 with Job iii. 3-10). The despairing utterance referred to is an exaggeration in the mouth of Job, but suitable enough in Jeremiah's. In Job, l.c., we seem to recognise the slightly artificial turn which the author loves to give to the ideas and phrases of his predecessors ; while the cutting irony of the words ' making him very glad ' (Jer. xx. 15) as clearly betokens the hand of the original writer. Compare also Job vi. 15 with Jer. xv. 18 ; ix. 19 with Jer. xlix. 19 ; x. 18-22 with Jer. xx. 14-18 ; xii. 4, xix. 7 with Jer. xx. 7, 8 ; xii. 6, xxi. 7 with Jer. xii. 1 ; xix. 24 with Jer. xvii. 1 ; xxxviii. 33 with Jer. xxxi. 35, 36.

There are two plausible points of contact in *Job* with Deuteronomy (comp. Job xxiv. 2, Deut. xix. 14 [removing landmarks]; Job xxxi. 9, 11, Deut. xxii. 22), but only one worth mentioning with Genesis (xxii. 16 ; comp Gen. vi. &c.),

and here observe that the word for A.V.'s 'flood' (Job, l.c.) is not *mabbūl* but *nāhār*.[1] Hitzig and Delitzsch find another in xxxi. 33. But *ādām* in Job always means 'men :' in xv. 7, 8, where the first man is referred to, he is not named. The reference in xxxi. 33 is not to hiding sins from God, but from man. I think, however, that the Prologue implies a general acquaintance with some current descriptions of the patriarchal period—the 'golden age' to men of a more advanced civilisation.

It is remarkable, what interesting parallels are afforded by the prophets of the Assyrian period. Isaiah, as might be expected, contains the largest number (see *The Prophecies of Isaiah*, ed. 3, ii. 243) ; but Hosea follows close after. Compare especially—

Isa. xix. 5 (certainly the original of Job, l.c., where the special reference to the sea-like Nile is dropped) } with { Job xiv. 11 ('the waters fail from the sea,' i.e. any inland body of water)

Isa. xxviii. 29 . . . } — { Job xi. 6 (God's wisdom marvellous; see Merx, and *Isaiah*, ii. 154)

Hos. x. 13 (combined with Prov. xxii. 8) } — { Job iv. 8 ('ploughing iniquity,' &c.)

Hos. vi. 1 (or Deut. xxxii. 39) } — { Job v. 18 ('he maketh sore and bindeth up,' &c.)

Hos. v. 14, xiii. 7, 8 } — { Job x. 16 (God compared to a lion)

Hos. xiii. 12 (or Deut. xxxii. 34) } — { Job xiv. 17 ('transgression sealed up,' &c.)

Am. iv. 13, v. 8 (the comparison suggests that v. 8, 9 stood immediately after iv. 13 when Job was written, and that 'the sea,' i.e. the upper ocean, stood for 'the earth') } — { Job ix. 8, 9 ('that treadeth upon the heights of the sea; that maketh the Bear, Orion, and the Pleiades')

Comp. also Am. v. 8, ix. 6 with Job xii. 15 ; Am. ii. 9 with Job xviii. 16.

[1] According to Ewald, the reference is to Sodom and Gomorrah, the story f which, we know, was familiar as early as Hosea's time (Hos. xi. 8).

I say nothing here of the parallels in the Song of Hezekiah (Isa. xxxviii. 10–20). I have shown reason in *Isaiah*, i. 228, for believing that the Song is a highly imitative work, and largely based on Job, such a work in fact as can only be accounted for in the Exile or post-Exile period.

There still remains the great body of psalms of disputed date. The parallelisms in Ps. xxxvii.[1] are too general to be mentioned here, striking as they are; but we may venture to compare Ps. viii. 5 with Job vii. 17; Ps. xxxix. 12*b* with Job iv. 19*b*; ib. 14*a* with Job vii. 19*a*, x. 20; ib. 14*b* with Job x. 21, 22; Ps. lxxii. 12 with Job xxix. 12; ib. 16 with Job v. 25*b*; Ps. lxxxviii. 16*b* with Job xx. 25 (the rare word *'ēmīm*); ib. 17 with Job vi. 4 (*bi'ūthīm*); ib. 19 (lxix. 9) with Job xix. 14; and note throughout this psalm the same correspondence of extreme inward and outward suffering which we find in Job. Then, turning to the psalms of different tenor, comp. lxxii. 12 with Job xxix. 12; ib. 16 with Job v. 25*b*. I have selected these instances precisely because they allow us to draw an inference as to priority. Ps. lxxxviii. is clearly imitative, and no doubt there is more imitation of the great poem in other psalms. Psalms viii., xxxix., and (probably) lxxii. were however known to and imitated by the authors of *Job*. The parallel in Ps. viii. is specially important. That this psalm is not earlier than the Exile is disputed, but extremely probable; the bitter 'parody' in Job vii. 17 must in this case be of the same or a later period.

And now to sum up the results of our comparisons. The Colloquies in *Job* are of later origin than Deuteronomy, Jeremiah, Lamentations, and most of Proverbs, but possibly nearly contemporaneous with much in the second part of Isaiah, except that Isa. liii. not improbably lay before the author of *Job*; also that Ps. viii., a work of the Exile period, was well known to him. We are thus insensibly led on to date the Book of Job (the speeches, at any rate) during the

---

[1] See Bateson Wright's *The Book of Job*, Appendix. The author concludes that the poet of *Job* 'selects the main threads from the complete treatise of Ps. xxxvii. and interweaves them into the highly poetical discourse of Eliphaz.'

Exile. This will account for the large amount of imitation to which the book gave rise. Men felt respecting the author that he was the first and greatest exponent of the ideas and feelings, not of a long-past age, but of their own; that he 'sat chief, and dwelt as a king in the army, as one that comforteth the mourners' (Job xxix. 25).

CHAPTER XII.

ON THE DISPUTED PASSAGES IN THE DIALOGUE-PORTION, ESPECIALLY THE SPEECHES OF ELIHU.

A DETAILED exegetical study would alone enable the reader to do justice to the controversies here referred to. But I may at least ask that, even upon the ground of the slender analysis which I have given, he should recognise the difficulties at the root of these controversies. In comparison with his possession of a 'seeing eye,' it is of little moment to me whether he adopts my explanations or not. Poets, like painters, have different periods. It is therefore conceivable that the author of *Job* changed in course of time, and criticised his own work, these afterthoughts of his being embodied in the 'disputed passages.' It is indeed also conceivable that the phenomena which puzzle us are to be explained by the plurality of authorship. In the remarks which follow I wish to supplement the sketch of the possible or probable growth of the Book offered in section 3 of Chap. VII., chiefly with regard to the speeches of Elihu.

Keil has spoken of 'the persistently repeated assaults upon the genuineness' of these discourses. I must however protest against the use of the word 'genuineness' in this connection. Even if not by the author of the poem of *Job*, the speeches of Elihu are as 'genuine' a monument of Israel's religious 'wisdom' as the work of the earlier writer. No critic worthy of the name thinks of 'assaulting' them, though divines no less orthodox than Gregory the Great and the Venerable Bede have uncritically enough set the example. The speeches of Elihu only seem poor by comparison with the original work; they are not without true and beautiful passages, which, with all their faults of expression, would in any other book have commanded universal admiration. The grounds on which chaps. xxxii.–xxxvii. are denied to the original writer may be summed up thus.

(1) Elihu puts forward a theory of the sufferings of the righteous which does not essentially differ from that of the three friends (see especially xxxiii. 25–28 ; xxxiv. 9, 11, 12, 36, 37 ; xxxv. 9–16 ; xxxvi. 5–7, 21–25 ; xxxvii. 23, 24). No doubt he improves the theory, by laying more stress upon the chastening character of the righteous man's afflictions (xxxiii. 14–30 ; xxxvi. 8–12, 15, 16, and comp. Eliphaz in v. 18, 19), and to many disciples of the New Covenant his form of the theory may recommend itself as true. But, even apart from the appendix or epilogue (see xlii. 7–9), it is clear from the whole plan of the poem, particularly if the discourses of Jehovah be taken in, that this was not, in the writer's mind, an adequate solution of the problem, especially in the case of the God-fearing and innocent Job.

(2) These speeches interrupt the connection between the 'words of Job' and those of Jehovah, and seem to render the latter superfluous. Whether the 'words of Job' (to borrow the phrase of some editor of the book) should end at xxxvii. 37 or at ver. 40, it is difficult not to believe that xxxviii. 1, 2, 'And Jehovah answered Job out of the storm, and said, Who then is darkening counsel by words without knowledge?' was meant to follow immediately upon them. The force of this seems to some to be weakened by taking Elihu's description of the storm (xxxvii. 2–5) as preparatory to the appearance of Jehovah in chap. xxxviii. But, evidently, to make this an argument, the storm ought to be at the end of the speech.

(3) There is no mention of Elihu in the Prologue, nor is any divine judgment passed upon him in the Epilogue. It is not enough to reply with Stickel that Jehovah himself is not mentioned in the Prologue as the umpire in the great controversy ; why should he be ?—and that the absence of any condemnation of Elihu on the part of Jehovah, and the harmony (?) between Elihu's and Jehovah's discourses, sufficiently indicate the good opinion of the Divine Judge.

(4) Elihu's style is prolix and laboured; his phrases often very obscure, even where the words separately are familiar. As Davidson remarks, there are not only unknown words (these we meet with elsewhere in the book), but an unknown use of known words. There is also a deeper colouring of Aramaic (see Appendix), which F. C. Cook, following Stickel, explains by the supposed Aramæan origin of the speaker; in this case, it would be a refinement of art which adds a fresh laurel to the crown of the poet. But the statement in xxxii. 2 is that Elihu was 'the son of Barakel the Buzite, of the kindred of Ram.' That Ram = Aram is unproved; while Buz, as Jer. xxv. 23 shows, is the name of a genuine Arabian people. It would be better to explain the increased Aramaism by the lapse of a long interval in the writer's life. This explanation is, to me, equivalent to assigning these speeches to a different writer (as I have remarked elsewhere, comparing Goethe's *Faust*). Those who will may adopt it; but my own respect for the poet of *Job* will not allow me to believe that his taste had so much declined as to insert this inferior poem into his masterpiece.

(5) Elihu's allusions to passages in the rest of the book (comp. xxxiii. 15 with iv. 13; xxxiv. 3 with xii. 11; xxxv. 5 with xxii. 12; xxxv. 8 with xxii. 2; xxxvii. 8 with xxxviii. 40) and his minute reproductions of sayings of Job (see xxxiii. 8, 9; xxxiv. 5, 6; xxxv. 2, 3) point to an author who had the book before him, so far as then known, as a whole.

(6) Elihu's somewhat scrupulous piety, or shall I call it his advance in reverential, contrite devoutness? compared with the three friends, suggests that the poet of Elihu was the child of a later and more sombre generation which found the original book in some respects disappointing.

Putting all this together, if the main part of the Book of Job belongs to the Exile, the Elihu-portion may well belong to the post-Exile period.

To this view, it is no objection that, on the one hand, Elihu not merely (to express oneself shortly) criticises the position of the three friends, but, by ignoring it, criticises the view of Job's afflictions taken in the Prologue, and, on the other, has much in common with the rest of the book in orthographic, grammatical, and lexical respects. The idea that God permits affliction simply to try the disinterestedness of a good man, is one which might easily shock the feelings of one only too conscious that he was not good; and the linguistic points which 'Elihu' and the rest of the book have in common are such as we should expect to find in works proceeding from the same class of writers. If Jeremiah wrote all the pieces which contain Jeremian phraseology, or Isaiah all the prophecies which remind one at all of the great prophet, or the same 'wise man' wrote Proverbs and Ecclesiastes, then we may perhaps believe that the author of *Job* also wrote the speeches of Elihu and perhaps one or two of the didactic psalms.

Professor Briggs, the author of that excellent work *Biblical Study*, takes up a different position, which, though not new, acquires some authority from his respected name. He does not see any literary or theological merit in Elihu's speeches, and yet regards them as 'an important part of the original work.' The author designed to pourtray Elihu as a young and inexperienced man, and uses these ambitious failures 'as a literary foil . . . to prepare the way for the divine interposition, to quiet and soothe by their tediousness the agitated spirits of Job and his friends.'[1] To me, this view of the intention of the speeches lowers the character of the original writer. So reverent and devout a speaker as Elihu is ill rewarded by being treated as a literary and theological foil. Artistically, the value of this part may be *comparatively* slight, but theologically it enriches the Old Testament with a monument of a truly Christian consciousness of sin. Had the original writer equalled him in this, we should perhaps have missed a splendid anticipation of the life of Christ, who 'did no sin, neither was guile found in his mouth.' But the Elihu-section expresses in Old Testament language the great truth announced by St. Paul in 1 Cor. xi. 32.[2]

[1] *Presbyterian Review*, 1885, p. 353.
[2] Delitzsch, art. 'Hiob,' Herzog-Plitt's *Realencyklopädie*, vi. 132.

On the other 'disputed passages' I have little to add.

(*a*) To me, the picture of the behémoth and the leviathan (xl. 15–xli.) seems but little less probably a later insertion than the speeches of Elihu; this view of the case has the authority of Ewald. That cautious critic, Dr. Davidson, remarks that this passage has a very different kind of movement from that of the light and graceful sketches in chaps. xxxviii., xxxix., and that the poetic inventory which it contains reminds us more of an Arab poet's description of his camel or his horse (*Job*, p. liv.)

(*b*) I cannot speak so positively as to the speeches of Jehovah. From a purely æsthetic point of view, I am often as unwilling as any one to believe that they were 'inserted.' At other times I ask myself, Can the inconsistencies of this portion as compared with the Colloquies be explained as mere oversights? The appearance of the Almighty upon the scene is in itself strange. Job had no doubt expressed a wish for this, but did not suppose that it could be realised,[1] at any rate in his own lifetime. It is still stranger that the Almighty should appear, not in the gentle manner which Job had desired (ix. 34, 35), not with the object of a judicial investigation of the case, but in the whirlwind, and with a foregone conclusion on Job's deserts. For in fact that splendid series of ironical questions which occupies chaps. xxxviii., xxxix., and which Job had by anticipation deprecated (ix. 3), is nothing less than a long drawn-out condemnation of Job. The indictment and the defendant's reply, to which Job has referred with such proud self-confidence (xxxi. 35, 36), are wholly ignored; and the result is that which Job has unconsciously predicted in the words,—

> To whom, though innocent, I would not reply,
> but would make supplication unto my Judge (ix. 15).

(*c*) Great difficulties have been found in xxvii. 8 (or 11)–23, xxviii. First of all, Is there an inner connection between these passages? Dr. Green seeks to establish one. 'While continuing,' he says, 'to insist upon his own integrity, notwith-

---

[1] Since this wish cannot be realised, Job pleads his cause against an invisible God with the same earnestness as if he stood before His face.

standing the afflictions sent upon him, he freely admits, and this in language as emphatic as their own, the reality of God's providential government, and that punishment does overtake the ungodly. Nevertheless there is a mystery enveloping the divine administration, which is quite impenetrable to the human understanding' (*The Book of Job*, p. 233). This is very unnatural.[1] How can Job suddenly adopt the language of the friends without conceding that he has himself hitherto been completely in error? And what right have we to force such a subtle connection between chaps. xxvii. and xxviii.? Looking at the latter by itself, one cannot help suspecting that it once formed part of a didactic treatise similar to the Introduction to the Book of Proverbs (see end of Chap. III). For a careful exegetical study of chaps. xxvii., xxviii., see Giesebrecht (see 'Aids to the Student,' after Chap. XV.), with whom Dr. Green seems to accord, but who fails to convince me. See also Budde in his *Beiträge*, and Grätz, 'Die Integrität der Kap. 27 und 28 im Hiob,' *Monatsschrift*, 1872, p. 241 &c.

[1] It is a pleasure to quote the forcible summing-up of Mr. Froude. 'A difficulty,' he remarks, 'now arises which, at first sight, appears insurmountable. As the chapters are at present printed, the entire of the 27th is assigned to Job, and the paragraph from the 11th to the 23rd verses is in direct contradiction to all which he has maintained before—is, in fact, a concession of having been wrong from the beginning. Ewald, who, as we said above, himself refuses to allow the truth of Job's last and highest position, supposes that he is here receding from it, and confessing what an over-precipitate passion had betrayed him into denying. For many reasons, principally because we are satisfied that Job said then no more than the real fact, we cannot think Ewald right; and the concessions are too large and too inconsistent to be reconciled even with his own general theory of the poem' (*Short Studies*, vol. i.) He then proceeds to mention with cautious approbation the theory of Kennicott (see note on Text at end of Chap. XV.)

CHAPTER XIII.

IS JOB A HEBRÆO-ARABIC POEM?

THAT the Book of Job is not as deeply penetrated with the spirit of revelation, nor even as distinctly Israelitish a production, as most of the Old Testament writings, requires no argument. May we venture to go further, and infer from various phenomena that, not merely the artistic form of the *māshāl*, but the thoughts and even the language of *Job* came in a greater or less degree from a foreign source? The question has been answered in the affirmative (as in the case of the words of Agur in Prov. xxx., and those of Lemuel in chap. xxxi.) by some early as well as some more modern writers. This view has been supposed to be implied in the Greek postscript to the Septuagint version [1] (strongly redolent of Jewish Midrash), which contains the statement, οὗτος ἑρμηνεύεται ἐκ τῆς Συριακῆς βίβλου, but though Origen appears so to have understood,[2] it is more probable that οὗτος merely refers to the postscript (Zunz; Frankl). Ibn Ezra, however, on independent grounds does express the opinion (commenting on Job ii. 11) that the Book of Job is a translation; he ascribes to the translator the words in xxxviii. 1

---

[1] There is a doubt whether the Septuagint postscript or the statement of the Egyptian Jew (?) Aristeas (as given by Eusebius from Alexander Polyhistor in *Præf. Evang.* l. ix.) be the earlier. The ordinary view is that Aristeas had the Septuagint *Job* before him; Freudenthal, however, infers from the strange description of Eliphaz, Bildad, and Zophar in Sept. Job ii. 11 (taken verbally from Aristeas) that the reverse was the case, and that the fragment of Aristeas is only a condensed extract from the prologue and epilogue of the Book of Job (Freudenthal, *Hellenistische Studien*, 139, 140; Grätz, *Monatsschrift*, 1877, p. 91). This inference in turn suggests Grätz' hypothesis that the Septuagint Job is a work of the first century A.D. (see note at end of Chap. XV.)

[2] *Opera*, Delarue, ii. 851, *ap.* Delitzsch, *Iob*, p. 603.

containing the sacred name Jehovah. The increased study of Arabic in the 17th century led several theologians of eminence to the same conclusion. Spanheim, for instance, thought that Job and his friends wrote down the history and the colloquies in Arabic, after the happy turn in the fortunes of the sufferer, and that some inspired Israelitish writer, in the age of Solomon, gave this work a Hebrew dress. Albert Schultens, in the preface to his *Liber Jobi* (1737), is at the pains to discuss this theory, which he rejects on two main grounds, (1) the disparagement to our magnificent Book of Job involved in calling it a translation, and (2) that in those primitive and, according to him, pre-Mosaic times, the Hebrew and Arabic languages cannot have been so different (!) as Spanheim from his point of view imagines. Elsewhere he expresses his own opinion shortly thus, [1] 'Linguam quâ liber Jobi conscriptus est, genuinum illius temporis Arabismum esse.' He actually imagines that Job and his friends extemporised the Colloquies we have before us, referring to the amazing faculty of improvisation still possessed by the Arabs—a view scarcely worthier than that of Spanheim, for, as Martineau remarks in another connection, Who ever improvised a great poem or a great sermon? Both these great scholars have fallen into the error of confounding the poet with his hero and the use of poetic and didactic fiction with deliberate fraud. One cannot be severe upon this error, for it has survived among ourselves in Prof. S. Lee's great work (1837), where our Book of Job is actually traced back through Jethro to Job himself. The only form however in which a critic of our day could discuss the question mentioned above would be this, Is it in some degree probable that the author of *Job* was a Hebrew who had passed some time with the Arabic- and Aramaic-speaking peoples bordering on the land of Israel?

On grounds independent of Eichhorn and Dean Plumptre, the former of whom combines his theory with that of a pre-Mosaic, and the latter with that of a Solomonic date of *Job*,

[1] *Opera minora* (Lugd. Bat. 1769), p. 497.

I think that we may venture to reply in the affirmative. These grounds have reference (1) to the ideas of *Job*, (2) to its vocabulary.

(1) I am well aware that the argument from the ideas of *Job* cannot claim a strong degree of cogency. It is possible to account for the conceptions of the author from the natural progress of the (divinely-guided) moral and religious history of Israel, and those who believe (I do not myself) that Psalms xvii., xxxvii., xlix., lxxiii., are Palestinian works of earlier date than *Job* will have a ready argument in favour of a purely native origin of the latter book. Still it seems to me that we can still better account for the author's point of view by supposing that he was in sympathy with an intellectual movement going on outside Israel. The doctrine of retribution in the present life, which he finds inadequate, is common to the friends and to the religion which has in all ages been that of the genuine Arab—the so-called *dīn Ibrāhīm* (or 'religion of Abraham'). The Eloah and the Shaddai of Job are the irresponsible Allah who has all power in heaven and on earth, and before whom, when mysteries occur in human life which the retribution-doctrine cannot solve, the Arab and every true Moslem bows his head with settled, sad resignation. The morality alike of the *dīn Ibrāhīm*, and of the religion of Mohammed (who professed to restore it in its purity), is faulty precisely as the religion of the three friends (and originally of Job himself) is faulty. The same conflict which arose in the heart of Job arose in the midst of the Moslem world. I refer to the dispute between the claimants of orthodoxy and the sect of the Mo'tazilites (8th and 9th centuries); the latter, who were worsted in the strife, viewed God as the absolutely Good, the former as a despotic and revengeful tyrant.[1] May not this conflict have been foreshadowed at an earlier time? Is not the difficulty which led to it a constantly recurring one, so soon as reflection acquires a certain degree of maturity? It may well have been felt among the Jews, especially in the decline of the

---

[1] Kremer, *Herrschende Ideen des Islams*, p. 27 &c.; Kuenen, *Hibbert Lectures*, p. 48 &c.

state, but it must also have been felt among their neighbours, and freedom of speech has always, in historical times, been an Arab characteristic. Putting aside the anachronism of placing Job in the patriarchal age, does not the poet himself appear to hint that it was so felt by the names and tribal origins of the speakers in the great religious discussion?

(2) As to the Arabisms and Aramaisms of the language of *Job* (see Appendix). Jerome already says that his own translation follows none of the ancients, but reproduces, now the words, now the sense, and now both, 'ex ipso hebraico arabicoque sermone et interdum syro.' In the 17th and 18th centuries, De Dieu, Bochart, and above all Schultens made it a first principle in the study of *Job* to illustrate it from Aramaic and especially Arabic. Schultens even describes the language as not so much Hebrew, as Hebræo-Arabic, and says that it breathes the true and unmixed genius of Arabia. This is every way an exaggeration, and yet, after all reasonable deductions, our poem will stand out from the Old Testament volume by its foreign linguistic affinities. It is not enough to say that the Arabisms and Aramaisms have from the first formed part of the Hebrew vocabulary, and were previously employed only because the subjects of the other books did not call for their use. Unless a more thorough study of Assyrian should prove that the Arabism (for of these I am chiefly thinking) belonged to northern as well as to southern Semitic, it will surely be more natural to suppose that the author of *Job* replenished his vocabulary from Arabic sources. There is not a little in the phraseology of *Job* which is still as obscure as in the days of Ibn Ezra, but which receives, or may yet receive, illustration from the stores of written and spoken Arabic.[1]

May we not, in short, conjecture that the poem of Job is a grand attempt to renovate and enrich the Hebrew language?[2]

---

[1] Prof. Socin once observed to me how useful spoken Arabic would be found for this purpose.

[2] Arabic literary history presents an example of literary experimenting which will at once occur to the mind—the 'Maqamas' or Sessions of Hariri.

If so, the experiment can hardly have been made before the great subversion of Hebrew traditions at the Babylonian captivity. Residence in a foreign land produces a marked effect on one's language. Recollect too that our author was a literary man. Internal evidence converges to show that Job belonged to that great literary movement among the wise men, philosophers, or humanists, to which we shall have to refer Prov. i.–ix., the Wisdom of Sirach, and the Book of Ecclesiastes.

Before leaving this subject, let us notice the parallels to descriptions in the speeches of Jehovah in the Arabian poets, who show the same attention to the striking phenomena of earth and sky as the author of these speeches. The Arabian tone and colouring of the descriptions of animals in *Job* has been already remarked upon by Alfred von Kremer in vol. ii. of his *Culturgeschichte des Orients*. Is it possible to conceive that those sketches of the wild goat, the wild ass, and the horse, were not written by one who was familiar with the sight? Or that the author had not observed the habits of the ostrich, when he penned his lines on the ostrich's neglect of her eggs? Or that his interest in astronomy was not deepened by the spectacle of a night-sky in Arabia? Or that personal experience of caravan life did not inspire the touching figure in vi. 15–20? And observation of the mines in the Sinaitic peninsula [1] the fine description of xxviii. 1–10? It is possible that some of these passages may be due to other travelled 'wise men;' but this only increases the probability that the Hebrew movement was strengthened by contact with similar movements abroad. The 'wise men' had certainly travelled far and wide among Arabic-speaking populations, though nowhere perhaps were they so much at home as in Idumæa and its neighbourhood. As M. Derenbourg remarks, 'Les riantes oasis, au milieu des contrées désolées, environnant la mer Morte, étaient la demeure des

---

[1] On the mining passage see further p. 40. Stickel, however, though inclining to the above view, thinks that it is still not quite impossible that Palestinian mines are meant, comparing Edrisi's statements on the iron-mines of Phœnicia and the words of the Deuteronomist in Deut. viii. 9. *Das Buch Hiob*, pp. 265-6.

sages et des rêveurs. Bien des siècles après l'auteur de Job, les Esséniens et les Thérapeutes se plongeaient là dans la vie contemplative, ou bien ils se livraient à une vie simple, active et dégagée de tout souci mondain. Encore un peu plus tard cette contrée devint probablement le berceau de la kabbale ou du mysticisme juif.'

CHAPTER XIV.

THE BOOK FROM A RELIGIOUS POINT OF VIEW.

Motto: 'Jedem nämlich wollte ich dienen, der hinlänglich Sinn hat in die grosse Frage tiefer einzugehen, welche das ernste Leben einmal gewiss an Jeden heranbringt, nach der Gerechtigkeit der göttlichen Waltung in den menschlichen Geschicken.'—STICKEL (*Das Buch Hiob*, Einl. S. vi.)

THERE was a period, not so long since, when a Biblical writing was valued according to its supposed services to orthodox theology. From this point of view, the Book of Job was regarded partly as a typical description of the sufferings of our Saviour,[1] partly as a repository of text-proofs of Christian doctrines, which though few in number acquired special importance from the immense antiquity assigned to the poem. We must not, in our reaction from the exclusively theological estimate of the Old Testament, shut our eyes to the significance of each of its parts in the history of the higher religion. The Book of Job *is* theological, though the theology of its writer, being that of a poet, is less logical than that of an apostle, less definite even than that of a prophet, in so far as the prophet obtained (or seemed to obtain) his convictions by a message or revelation from without. Being a poet, moreover, the writer of *Job* can even less than a prophet have had clear conceptions of the historical Messiah and His period. Moral and spiritual truths—these were his appointed

[1] 'The Church in all ages has regarded the one as a type of the other,' Turner, *Studies Biblical and Oriental*, p. 150. But Del. has already dissuaded from insisting too much on the historic character of the story of Job. 'The endurance of Job' (James v. 11) is equally instructive whether the story be real (*wirklich*) or only ideally true (*wahr*); and if by the phrase 'the end of the Lord' St. James refers to the Passion of Jesus (to me, however, this appears doubtful), he can be claimed with as much reason for the view of Job here adopted as for the older theory advocated by Turner]

province, not the secret counsels of God, nor those exceptional facts or truths which orthodoxy still perhaps regards as among the postulates of the faith of the Hebrew prophets. Nor can the hero of the poem be considered a strict and proper type of the Christ, for this reason among others, that Job is to all intents and purposes a creation of the fancy, whether of the unconsciously working fancy of the people, or of the rich and potent imagination of a poet. In what sense, then, may the Book of Job still claim a theological significance, and be allowed to fill a not unimportant place in the *Vorgeschichte* of Christianity?

I. The hero of the poem (I exclude from consideration the speeches of Elihu [1]) is, not indeed a type, but in some sense prophetic of the Christ, inasmuch as the very conception of a righteous man enduring vast calamities, not so much for his own sake as for the world's, is a bold hypothesis which could only in the Christ be made good. The poet does more than merely personify the invisible Church of righteous and believing sufferers; he idealises this Church in doing so, and this idealising is a venture of faith. Job is an altogether exceptional figure: he is imperfect, no doubt, if viewed as a symbol of the Christ, but this does not diminish the reality and the grandeur of the presentiment which he embodies. To a religious mind, this remarkable creation will always appear stamped by the hand of Providence. Job is not indeed a Saviour, but the imagination of such a figure prepares the way for a Saviour. In the words of Dr. Mozley, 'If the Jew was to accept a Messiah who was to lead a life of sorrow and abasement, and to be crucified between thieves, it was necessary that it should be somewhere or other distinctly taught that virtue was not always rewarded here, and that therefore no argument could be drawn from affliction and ignominy against the person who suffered it.' [2]

II. This then is the grandest of the elements in the Book of Job which helped to prepare the noblest minds among the Jews for the reception of primitive Christianity—

---

[1] On the Elihu-section, see Chap. XII.
[2] Mozley, *Essays*, ii. 227; comp. Turner, *Studies*, p. 149.

viz. the idea of a righteous man suffering simply because (as was said of One parallel in many respects to Job) 'it pleased Jehovah (for a wise purpose) to bruise him.' The second element is the idea of a supra-mundane justice, which will one day manifest itself in favour of the righteous sufferer, not only in this world (xvi. 18, 19, xix. 25, xlii.), so that all men may recognise their innocence, but also beyond the grave, the sufferers themselves being in some undefined manner brought back to life in the conscious enjoyment of God's favour (xiv. 13-15, xix. 26, 27?) There may be only suggestions of these ideas, but suggestions were enough when interpreted by sympathetic readers. Let me add that by 'sympathetic,' I mean in sympathy with the conception of God formed by the author of *Job*. Nothing is more out of sympathy with this conception than the saying of the Jewish scholar, S. D. Luzzatto, 'The God of Job is not the God of Israel, the Gracious One; He is the Almighty and the Righteous, but not the Kind and Faithful One.' No; the God of Job would be less than infinitely righteous if He were not also kind (comp. Ps. lxii. 12). And of this enlarged conception of God, faith in the continuance of the human spirit is a consequence. Justice to those with whom God is in covenant requires that He should not after a few years hurl them back into non-existence (comp. Job x. 8-13). But I can only skirt the fringe of the great religious problems opened by this wonderful book.

In conclusion, and in the spirit of my motto, let me invite the reader's attention (even if he be no theologian) to the spectacle of a powerful mind dashing itself against perennial problems too mighty for it to solve. The author of our poem missed the only adequate and possible solution, and hence he has been erroneously regarded by several moderns as the representative of a mental attitude akin to their own. Heine, for instance, can term this book 'the Song of Songs of scepticism.' No doubt those who are at sea on religious matters can find sayings in *Job* which may seem as if spoken by themselves; but in truth these only enhance the significance of the counteracting elements in the poem. It is the logical incompleteness of *Job* which at once exposes the book to misjudgment, and gives it an eternal fascination. As Quinet has said, 'Ce qui fait la grandeur de ce livre, c'est qu'en dépassant la mesure de l'Ancien Testament il appelle, il provoque nécessairement des cieux nouveaux . . . . Le christianisme vit au fond de ce blasphème.' We need a second part of *Job*, or at least a third speech of Jehovah, which could however only be given by some Hebrew poet who had drunk at the fountains of the Fourth Gospel. Failing these, the reader must supply what is necessary for himself,—a better compensation to Job for his agony than the Epilogue provides, and a more touching and not less divine theophany (comp. Job ix. 32, 33). This Christianity will enable him to do. Intellectually, the problem of Job's life may remain, but to the Christian heart the cloud is luminous.

>The Infinite remains unknown,
> Too vast for man to understand :
>In Him, the 'Woman's Seed,' alone
> We trace God's footprint in the sand.[1]

[1] Aubrey De Vere. Need I guard myself on the subject of Gen. iii. 15, referred to in a recent memorable debate in the *Nineteenth Century*? A strict Messianic interpretation is, since Calvin's time, impossible to the exegete, but the application of the words to Jesus Christ is dear to the Christian heart, and perfectly consistent with a sincere exegesis. M. Réville would, I think, concede this to Mr. Gladstone.

CHAPTER XV.

THE BOOK OF JOB FROM A GENERAL AND WESTERN POINT OF VIEW.

THE Book of Job is even less translatable than the Psalter. And why? Because there is more nature in it. 'He would be a poet,' says Thoreau, 'who could impress the winds and streams into his service to speak for him.' They do speak for the poet of *Job*; the 'still sad music of humanity' is continually relieved by snatches from the grand symphonies of external nature. And hence the words of *Job* are 'so true and natural that they would appear to expand like the buds at the approach of spring.' It is only a feeble light which the Authorised Version sheds upon this poem; and even the best prose translation must for several reasons be inadequate. Perhaps, though English has no longer its early strength, a true poet might yet achieve some worthy result. Rarely has the attempt been made. George Sandys was said by Richard Baxter to have 'restored Job to his original glory,' but he lived before the great era of Semitic studies. The poetical translator of *Job* must not disdain to consult critical interpreters, and yet by his own unassisted skill could he bring this Eastern masterpiece home to the Western reader? I doubt it. Even more than most imaginative poems the Book of Job needs the help of the painter. It is not surprising therefore that a scholar of Giotto should have detected the pictorial beauties of the story of Job. Though only two of the six Job-frescoes remain entire, the Campo Santo of Pisa will be impoverished when time and the sea-air effect the destruction of these. I know not whether any modern painter besides William Blake has illustrated Job. He, a 'seer' born out of due time, understood this wonderful book as no modern before him had done. The student will get more help of a certain kind from the illustrations thus reproduced in the second volume of Gilchrist's *Life of William Blake*, compared with the sympathetic descriptions by Blake's biographer (vol. i. pp. 330-333), than from any of the commentaries old or new.

In every respect the poem of *Job* stands in a class by itself. More than any other book in the Hebrew canon it needs bringing near to the modern reader, untrained as he is in Oriental and especially in Semitic modes of thought and imagination. Such a reader's first question will probably relate to the poetic form of the book. Is it, for instance, a drama ? Theodore of Mopsuestia (died 428) answered in the affirmative, though he was censured for this by the Council of Constantinople. The author of Job, he says, wronged the grand and illustrious story by imitating the manner of the pagan tragedians. ' Inde et illas plasmationes fecit, in quibus certamen ad Deum fecit diabolus, et voces sicut voluit circumposuit, alias quidem justo, alias vero amicis.'[1]

Bishop Lowth devotes two lectures of his *Sacred Poetry* to the same question. He replies in the negative, after comparing Job with the two Œdipi of Sophocles (dramas with kindred subjects), on the ground that action is of the essence of a drama and the Book of Job contains not even the simplest action. Afterwards indeed he admits that Job has at least one point in common with a regular drama, viz. the vivid presentation of several distinct characters in a tragic situation. The view that it is an epic, held in recent times by Dr. Mason Good and M. Godet, found favour with one no less than John Milton, who speaks, as he who knows, of 'that epic form, whereof the two poems of Homer and those other two of Virgil and Tasso are a diffuse, and the Book of Job a brief model.'[2] Something is to be said for this opinion if *Paradise Regained* be a true epic. Dialogue with the addition of a certain amount of narrative is, roughly speak-

---

[1] Migne, *Synes. et Theod.*, col. 698. Comp. Kihn, *Theodor von Mopsuestia*, p. 68 &c. [2] *The Reason of Church Government*, Book II.

ing, the literary form of the Book of Job as well as of the unequally great English poem, and Coleridge is probably right in representing Milton as indebted to the former for his plan. It is however open to us to doubt not only whether *Paradise Regained* is a true epic poem, but whether any section of the Book of Job except the Prologue partakes of the nature of an epic. The Prologue certainly does; it is more than a mere introduction to the subsequent speeches; it is an independent poetical narrative,[1] if not a narrative poem; nor is there wanting a strong infusion of that supernatural element which tradition regards as essential to the epic. True, it is a torso, but this does not interfere with its genuinely poetic character: it is, as Milton says, a 'brief model' or miniature of an epic poem. The Colloquies on the other hand are as undoubtedly a germinal character-drama, as the Song of Songs is a germinal stage-drama. The work belongs to the same class as Goethe's *Iphigenie* and *Tasso*; only there is much more passion in it than in these great but distinctively modern poems. Some one has said that 'there is no action and reaction between the speakers' [in the Colloquies]. This is an over-statement. Not only is each speaker consistent with his type of character, but the passionate excitement of Job, and his able though fragmentary confutation of his opponents, do produce an effect upon the latter, do force them to take up a new position, though not indeed to recall their original thesis.[2]

But in order to bring the Book of Job nearer to the modern Western mind, we must not only study it from the point of view of form, but also compare its scope and range with those of the loftiest modern Western poems of similar import; only then shall we discover the points in which it is distinctively ancient, Oriental, Semitic.—The greatest English work of kindred moral and religious import is *Paradise Lost*. Like *Job*, it is a theodicy, though of a more complex character, and aims

[1] Comp. Bateson Wright, *The Book of Job*, pp. 29-31.

[2] Bunsen observes, not badly, 'Hiob ist ein semitisches Drama aus der Zeit der Gefangenschaft. Das Dramatische windet sich aber erst aus dem Epos heraus, ohne eine selbststständige Gestalt zu gewinnen.' *Gott in der Geschichte*, i. 291.

>   . . . . (to) assert eternal Providence,
>   And justify the ways of God to man.

And the author of *Paradise Lost*, though not to be equalled with the founders of Biblical religion, is still distinguished from all modern poets (except Dante and Bunyan) by his singularly intense faith in the operations of the Divine Spirit. That prayer of his, beginning 'And chiefly Thou, O Spirit,' and a well-known parallel passage in his *Reason of Church Government*, prove conclusively that he held no contracted views as to the limits of Inspiration. This, in addition to his natural gifts, explains the overpowering impression of reality produced by the visions of Milton, and perhaps in a still greater degree by those of our Puritan prose-poet, John Bunyan. A similar faith in the divine Spirit, but more original and less affected by logical theories, was one great characteristic of the author of *Job*. He felt, like all the religious 'wise men' (of whom more presently), that true wisdom was beyond mortal ken, and could only be obtained by an influence from above. In the strength of this confidence he ventured, like Milton, on untrodden paths, and presumed to chronicle, in symbolic form, transactions of the spiritual world. Whether or not he believed in the Satan of the Prologue, as a Sunday School child might, we need not decide; that he used popular beliefs in a wide, symbolic sense, has been pointed out elsewhere. Probably both Milton and he, if questioned on the subject, would have replied in the spirit of those words of our Lord, 'If ye will receive it,' and 'All men cannot receive this saying.' It is not to be forgotten that the author of *Job* distinctly places the Satan in a somewhat humorous light, and though Milton is far from doing the same, yet we know from *Comus* that the conception of a symbol was as familiar to him as to Lord Bacon. Notice, in conclusion, that Milton's Satan, though unlike the Satan of his predecessor in some points,[1] resembles him in this striking particular, that he is not yet (in spite of Milton's attempt to represent him as such) the absolutely evil being.

---

[1] Compare Satan after his overthrow with Tasso's Soldan (*Gerus. Lib.*, c. ix., st. 98.

Faust has in some respects a better right to be compared with *Job* than *Paradise Lost*. Not so much indeed in the Prologue, though Goethe deserves credit for detecting the humorous element in the Hebrew poet's Satan, an element which he has transferred, though with much exaggeration, to his own Mephistopheles. Neither the Satan nor Mephistopheles (a remote descendant of the Hebrew [1] *mastema*, from the root *satam=satan*) is the Origin of Evil in a personal form,[2] but the Hebrew poet would never have accepted the description in *Faust* of the peculiar work of the 'denying spirit.' But in the body of the poem there is this marked similarity to the Book of Job—that the problem treated of is a purely moral and spiritual one; the hero first loses and then recovers his peace of mind; it is the counterpart in pantheistic humanism of what St. Paul terms working out one's own salvation. Still there are great and most instructive divergences between the two writers. Observe, first, the complete want of sympathy with positive religion—with the religion from which Faust wanders—on the part of the modern poet. Next, a striking difference in the characteristics of Job and Faust respectively. Faust succumbs to his boundless love of knowledge, alternating with an unbridled sensual lust; Job is on the verge of spiritual ruin through his demand for such an absolute correspondence of circumstances to character as can only be realised in another world. The greatness of Faust lies in his intellect; that of Job (who in chap. xxviii. directly discourages speculation) in his virtue. Hence, finally, Faust requires (even from a pantheistic point of view) to be pardoned, while Job stands so high in the divine favour that others are pardoned on his account.

A third great poem which deserves to be compared with

---

[1] Mr. Sutherland Edwards (*Fortnightly Review*, Nov. 1885, p. 687) states that Hebrew etymologies have proved failures. But the steps of the change from *mastema* to Mephistopheles are all proved, beginning with the name Mastiphat, for the prince of the demons, in the chronographers Syncellus and Georg. Cedrenus (comp. Μαστιφάτ = Mastema in the Book of Jubilees). Comp. Diez, *Roman. Wörterbuch*, i. pp. xxv., xxvi.

[2] Turner and Morshead, *Faust* (1882), pp. 307-8.

Job is the *Divina Commedia*. Dante has the same purpose of edification as the author of *Job* and even of *Faust*, though he has not been able to fuse the didactic and narrative elements with such complete success as Goethe. Nor is he so intensely autobiographical as either Goethe or the author of *Job*; his own story is almost inextricably interlaced with the fictions which he frames as the representative of the human race. He allows us to see that he has had doubts (*Parad.* iv. 129), and that they have yielded to the convincing power of Christianity (*Purgat.* iii. 34–39), but it was not a part of his plan to disclose, like the author of *Job*, the vicissitudes of his mental history. In two points, however— the width of his religious sympathies (which even permits him to borrow from the rich legendary material of heathendom [1]) and the morning freshness of his descriptions of nature—he comes nearer to the author of *Job* than either Goethe or Milton, while in the absoluteness and fervour of his faith Milton is in modern times his only rival.

The preceding comparison will, it is hoped, leave the reader with a sense of our great literary as well as religious debt to the author of *Job*. His gifts were varied, but in one department his originality is nothing less than Homeric; his Colloquies are the fountain-head from which the great river of philosophic poetry took its origin. He is the first of those poet-theologians from whom we English have learned so much, and who are all the more impressive as teachers because the truths which they teach are steeped in emotion, and have for their background a comprehensive view of the complex and many-coloured universe.

---

[1] On the parallel phenomena in Job, see Chap. IX.

NOTE ON JOB AND THE MODERN POETS.

JOB, like Spenser, should be the poet of poets; but though Goethe has imitated him in royal fashion, and here and there other poets such as Dante may offer allusions, yet Milton is the only poet who seems to have absorbed Job. *Paradise Regained* is in both form and contents a free imitation of the Book of Job, the story of which is described, in i. 368-370, 424-6, iii. 64-67. The following are the principal allusions in *Paradise Lost* :—i. 63, comp. Job x. 22; ii. 266, comp. Job iv. 16; ii. 603, comp. Job xxiv. 19 Vulg.; iv. 999 comp. Job xxviii. 25; vii. 253-4 (Hymn on the Nativity, st. 12), comp. Job xxxviii. 4-7; vii. 373-5, comp. Job xxxviii. 31; vii. 102, comp. Job xxxviii. 5. Shelley, too, is said to have delighted in Job; I must leave others to trace this in his works. I conclude with Thomas Carlyle. The words—'Was Man with his Experience present at the Creation, then, to see how it all went on? System of Nature! To the wisest man, wide as is his vision, Nature remains of quite *infinite* depth, of quite infinite expansion'[1]—are at once a paraphrase of the questions of Eliphaz, 'Art thou the first man that was born?... Didst thou hearken in the council of Eloah?' (xv. 7, 8), and a suggestive statement of the problem of *Job* as a challenge to limited human 'experience' to prove its capacity for criticising God's ways.

NOTE ON THE TEXT OF JOB.

THAT the received text of our Hebrew Bible has a long history behind it, is generally recognised; and few will deny that its worst corruptions arose in the pre-Massoretic and pre-Talmudic periods (comp. *The Prophecies of Isaiah*, vol. ii., Essay vii.) The popularity of the Book of Job may not have been equal to that of many other books, but we have seen reason to suppose that within the circles of the 'wise men' it was eagerly studied and imitated. In those early

---

[1] *Sartor Resartus* ('Natural Supernaturalism').

times such popularity was a source of danger to the text, and hasty copyists left their mark on many a corrupt passage. Is there any remedy for this?

Dr. Merx's book, *Das Gedicht von Hiob* (1871), has the merits and defects of pioneering works, but his introduction should by all means be studied. Two points in it have to be examined, (1) the relative position given by Merx to the chief ancient versions, and (2) the use which he makes of his own strophic arrangement for detecting interpolations or gaps in the text. More, I think, is to be gained from his discussion of the use of the versions than from his strophic arrangement; and yet before quite so much importance is attached to the text of the Septuagint, ought we not to be surer than we are of the antiquity and of the critical value of the Septuagint *Job*? That version may not be of as recent origin [1] as Grätz would have it, but can hardly be much earlier than the second century B.C. Before this date the text of *Job* had time to suffer much from the usual causes of corruption. Besides this, there are special reasons for distrusting the literal accuracy of the translator. He seems to have been in his own way an artist, and to have sought to reproduce poetry in poetical language. In this respect his vocabulary differs from that of all the other Septuagint translators; he thinks more of his Greek readers than of his Hebrew original. Had he been more mechanical in his method, the critical value of his work would have been greater. I agree therefore with H. Schultz that even where the Septuagint and the Peshitto are united against the Massoretic reading, the decisive arguments for the reading of the former will be, not the external one of testimony, but the internal one (if so be it exists) of suitableness.

Mr. Bateson Wright, goes almost farther than Dr. Merx in his opinion of the corruptness of the received text. His work on *Job* (1883), however unripe, shows remarkable independence, and contains, among many rash, a few striking emendations. That he does not restrict himself to corrections suggested by the versions, is not in the least a defect; the single drawback to his work is that he has not pondered long enough before writing. Purely conjectural emendation was doubtless often resorted to by the old translators themselves; it was and still is perfectly justified, though to succeed in its use requires a singular combination of caution and boldness which even older critics have not always attained. Special attention is devoted by Mr. Wright to the poetical features of the speeches in *Job*. Dr. Merx had already observed that most of the στίχοι contain eight

---

[1] 'A child of the first Christian century,' Grätz's *Monatsschrift*, p. 91. Nöldeke dates this version about 150 B.C. (*Gött. gel. Anzeigen*, 1865, p. 575).

syllables, to read which, however, it is often needful to dispense with Metheg and with the Chateph vowels, and contract the dual terminations. Mr. Wright, building upon Dr. Merx's foundation, offers a more elaborate scheme, which cannot be discussed here. It was a misfortune for him that he had not before him the ambitious metrical transliteration of *Job* by G. Bickell, in his *Carmina Vet. Test. metricè*, of which I would rather say nothing here than too little.

Subsequent editors of the text of *Job* will have one advantage, which will affect their critical use of the Septuagint. It is well known that the Alexandrine version was largely interpolated from that of Theodotion. The early Septuagint text itself can however now be reconstructed, through a manuscript of the Sahidic or Thebaic version from Upper Egypt. (Comp. Lagarde, *Mittheilungen*, pp. 203-5 ; Agapios Bsciai, art. in *Moniteur de Rome*, Oct. 26, 1883.) Dr. Merx was well aware of the necessity of expurgating the Septuagint, and would have hailed this much-desired aid in the work (see p. lxxi. of his introduction).

So much must suffice in my present limits on the subject of metre and textual emendation. I need not thus qualify the list which follows of gaps and misplacements of text in our Book of Job. Observe (1) that Bildad's third speech (chap. xxv.) is too short. Probably, as Mr. Elzas has suggested,[1] the continuation of it has been wrongly placed as xxvi. 5-14 ; the affinity of this passage to chap. xxv. is obvious. Probably the close of Bildad's speech is wanting. If so (2), something must have dropped out of Job's reply, since xxvi. 4 has no connection with xxvii. 2. (3) Zophar's third speech appears to be wanting, but may really be contained in chap. xxvii. (ver. 8 to end). The student should not fail to observe that xxvii. 13 is a repetition of xx. 29. As the text stands, Job is made to recant his statements in chaps. xxi., xxiv., and to assert that there is (not merely ought to be) a just and exact retribution. The tone, moreover, of xxvii. 9, 10 is not in accordance with Job's previous speeches. If this view be correct, an introductory formula ('And Zophar answered and said') must have fallen out at the beginning of ver. 7, and probably one or more introductory verses.[2] (4) The verses which originally introduced chap. xxviii. must (on account of the causal particle 'for' in ver. 1) either have dropped out, or else have been neglected by the person who inserted the chapter in the Book of Job. (5) The passage xxxi. 38-40 has at any rate been

---

[1] Elzas, *The Book of Job* (1872), p. 83 ; Grätz inclines to a similar view.

[2] A similar view has been propounded by Kennicott, and also more recently by Grätz (*Monatsschrift*, 1872, p. 247). But Kennicott regarded chap. xxviii. as Job's reply to Zophar, while Grätz would include it in the speech of Zophar.

misplaced (Delitzsch), and probably, as Merx has pointed out, should be inserted between ver. 32 and ver. 33. Thus verses 35-37 will furnish an appropriate and impressive close to the chapter. (6) xxxvi. 31 should probably go after ver. 28 (not ver. 29, as Dillmann misstates the conjecture) ; verses 30, 32 have a natural connection (Olshausen). (7) The passage xli. 9-12 destroys the connection, and should probably be placed immediately before chap. xxxviii. 1, as an introductory speech of Jehovah. In that case, we must, with Merx, supply the words, 'And Jehovah said,' before ver. 9.

AIDS TO THE STUDENT.

THERE are many books and articles of importance besides the commentaries. Among these are Hupfeld, *Commentatio in quosdam Jobeïdos locos* (1855) ; Bickell, *De indole ac ratione versionis Alexandrinæ in interpretando libro Iobi* (1862) ; G. Baur, 'Das Buch Hiob und Dante's Göttliche Comödie,' *Theol. Studien und Kritiken* (1856), p. 583 &c. (with which may be grouped Quinet's splendid chapter, in his early work on religions, entitled 'Comparaison du scepticisme oriental et du scepticisme occidental ') ; Seinecke, *Der Grundgedanke des Buches Hiob* (1863) ; Froude, 'The Book of Job,' *Short Studies*, Series 1 (1867), p. 266 &c.; Reuss, *Das Buch Hiob* (1869) ; Plumptre, 'The Authorship of the Book of Job,' *Biblical Studies* (1870), p. 173 &c. ; C. Taylor, 'A Theory of Job xix. 25-27,' *Journal of Philology* (1871), pp. 128-152 ; Godet, 'Le livre de Job,' *Etudes bibliques*, prem. partie (1873), p. 185 &c. ; Turner, 'The History of Job, and its Place in the Scheme of Redemption,' *Studies Biblical and Oriental* (1876), p. 133 &c. ; Grätz, chapter on Job in *Geschichte der Juden*, Bd. iii. ; Studer, 'Ueber die Integrität des Buches Hiob,' *Jahrbücher für protestant. Theologie* (1875), p. 688 &c., comp. 1877, p. 540 &c. ; Budde, *Beiträge zur Kritik des Buches Hiob* (1876), reviewed by Smend in *Studien u. Kritiken* (1878), pp. 153-173 ; Giesebrecht, *Der Wendepunkt des Buches Hiob* (1879) ; Derenbourg, 'Réflexions détachées sur le livre de Job,' *Revue des études juives* (1880), pp. 1-8 ; Claussen, 'Das Verhältniss der Lehre des Elihu zu derjenigen der drei Freunde,' *Zeitschr. f. kirchl. Wissenschaft und Leben* (1884), pp. 393 &c., 449 &c., 505 &c. ; W. H. Green, *The Argument of the Book of Job Unfolded* (1881) ; Cheyne, 'Job and the Second Part of Isaiah,' *Isaiah*, ii. 259 &c., with which compare the very full essay of Kuenen, 'Job en de lijdende knecht van Jahveh,' *Theologisch Tijdschrift* (1873), p. 492 &c. ; Delitzsch, art. 'Hiob,' Herzog-Plitt's *Realencyclopädie*, bd. vi. (1880).

THE BOOK OF PROVERBS.

CHAPTER I.

HEBREW WISDOM, ITS NATURE, SCOPE, AND IMPORTANCE.

WE have studied the masterpiece of Hebrew wisdom before examining the nature of the intellectual product which the Israelites themselves graced with this title. The Book of Job is in fact much more than a didactic treatise like Ecclesiastes or a collection of pointed moral sayings like the Books of Proverbs and Ecclesiasticus. Its authors were more than thinkers, they were poets, 'makers,' great imaginative artists. But we must not be unjust to those who were primarily thinkers, and only in the second degree poets. The phase of Hebrew thought called 'wisdom' (*khokma*) can be studied even better in Proverbs and Ecclesiastes than in the poetry of Job. Let us then enquire at this point, What is this Hebrew wisdom? First of all, it is the link between the more exceptional revelations of Old Testament prophecy and the best moral and intellectual attainments of other nations than the Jews. 'Wisdom' claims inspiration (as we have seen already), but never identifies itself with the contents of oracular communications.[1] Nor yet does it pretend to be confined to a chosen race. Job himself was a non-Israelite (the Rabbis were even uncertain as to his part in the world to come); and the wisdom of the 'wise king' is declared to have been different in degree alone from that of the neighbouring peoples [2]

[1] The heading 'the oracle' &c. in xxx. 1 is exceptional; so also is the oracle of Eliphaz (Job iv. 12-21).

[2] The author of *Baruch* (iii. 22, 23), however, expressly denies that the ordinary Semitic 'wisdom' was akin to that of Israel. This represents the Judaism of the Maccabean period.

(1 Kings iv. 30, 31; comp. Jer. xlix. 7, Obad. 8). It is to be observed next, that the range of enquiry of this 'wisdom' is equally wide, according to the Biblical use of the term.[1] 'Wisdom,' as Sirach tells us, 'rains forth skill' of every kind; 'the first man knew her not perfectly: no more shall the last trace her out' (Ecclus. i. 19, xxiv. 28). Nothing is too high, nothing too low for Wisdom 'fitly' to 'order' (Wisd. viii. 1). Law and government (Prov. viii. 15, 16), and even the precepts of husbandry (Isa. xxviii. 23-29) are equally her productions with those moral observations which constitute in the main the three books of the Hebrew *Khokma*. The fact that the subject of practical ethics ultimately appropriated the technical name of 'wisdom' ought not to blind us to the larger connotation of the same word, which throws so much light on the deeply religious view of life prevalent among the Israelites. For religious this view of wisdom is, though it may seem to be so thoroughly secular. The versatility of the mind of man is but an image of the versatility of its archetype. 'The spirit of man is a lamp of Jehovah,' says one of the 'wise men' (Prov. xx. 27), by an anticipation of John i. 9. 'Surely it is the spirit in man,' says another (Job xxxii. 8), 'and the breath of Shaddai which gives them understanding.' Isaiah, too, says that the 'spirit of wisdom' is one of the three chief manifestations of the 'Spirit of Jehovah' (Isa. xi. 2), and the introductory treatise, which gives the editor's view of the original Book of Proverbs, expressly declares that the 'wise men' are but the messengers of divine Wisdom (ix. 3).

The sages, whose collected wisdom we are about to study, are very different from those antique sages who like Balaam could be hired to curse a hostile people. A new kind of wisdom grew up both in Israel and in the neighbouring countries, as unlike its spurious counterpart as the spiritual lyric poetry both of Israel and of Babylonia is unlike the incantations which in Babylonia coexisted with it. Israel, never slow to adopt, received the higher wisdom, and assimilated it.

---

[1] Observe that 'wisdom' is called *khokmōth* (plural form) in Prov. i. 20, ix. 11, all the forms of wisdom being viewed as one in their origin. So too Wisdom adorns her house with seven pillars (Prov. ix. 1).

The earthly elements can still be traced in it; the 'wise men' are not prophets but philosophers; indeed, the Seven Wise Men of Greece arose at precisely the same stage of culture as the Hebrew sages. It is true, the latter never (in pre-Talmudic times) attempted logic and metaphysics; they contentedly remained within the sphere of practical ethics. If a modern equivalent must be found, it would be best to call them the humanists, to indicate their freedom from national prejudice (the word 'Israel' does not occur once, the word *ādām* 'man' thirty-three times in the Book of Proverbs), and their tendency to base a sound morality on its adaptation to human nature. We might also venture to call them realists in contradistinction to the idealists of the prophethood; they held out no prospect of a Messianic age, and 'meddled not with them that were given to change.'[1] The sages whose 'wisdom' is handed down to us were not however opposed to the spiritual prophets. It is only 'the fool' (or, to employ a synonym from the proverbs, the 'scorner' or 'mocker') who 'saith in his heart, There is no God.' A mocking poet of a late period may demand the Creator's name (Prov. xxx. 4), but the writer who (if I may anticipate) has perpetuated this strange poem indicates his own very different mental attitude; and though religious proverbs are less abundant than secular in the early anthologies, such as we do find are pure and elevated in tone. For instance,

(1) Who can say, I have made my heart clean,
    I am pure from my sin? (xx. 9.)
(2) The eyes of Jehovah are in every place,
    observing the evil and the good (xv. 3).
(3) Sheól and Abaddon[2] are before Jehovah,
    how much more then the hearts of the sons of men!
    (xv. 11.)
(4) The hearing ear and the seeing eye,
    Jehovah has made them both (xx. 12).
(5) A man's steps are from Jehovah,
    and man—how can he understand his way? (xx. 24.)

One point in which the wise men agreed with Amos and

---

[1] xxiv. 21 A.V.   [2] I.e. Perdition; a synonym for Sheól.

Isaiah was the inferiority of a ceremonial system [1] to prayer and faithful obedience (xv. 8, xxi. 3, 27, xvi. 6), and the importance which one of the proverb-writers attached to prophecy is strikingly expressed (if only the text be sound) in the saying,

When there is no prophecy (lit., vision) people become disorderly, but he that observes precept, happy is he (xxix. 18).

The prophets seem to have returned the friendly feeling of the sages. In tone and phraseology they are sometimes evidently influenced by their fellow-teachers (see e.g. Isa. xxviii. 23-29, xxix. 24, xxxiii. 11), and if they do not often refer to the wise men,[2] yet they do not denounce them, as they denounce the priests and the lower prophets. It may perhaps be inferred from this that there was in the early times no opposition-party of sceptical wise men, such as Ewald supposes,[3] and such as not improbably did exist in later times (see below on xxx. 1-4); and I notice that Ewald himself does not attempt to strengthen his view by appealing to the phrase 'men of scorn' in Isa. xxviii. 14, which some, following Rashi and Aben Ezra, explain of wise men who misused their talent by making mischievous proverbs.[4] The

[1] The author of the Introduction however writes, 'Honour Jehovah with thy substance,' i.e. by dedicating a part of it to the sanctuary (iii. 9), which the Septuagint translator carefully limits to substance lawfully gained (Deut. xxiii. 19).

[2] As perhaps they do in Am. v. 10, Isa. xxix. 21 ('him that rebuketh in the gate'). Observe again in this connection that the endowments of the Messiah include the spirit of wisdom as well as that of might (Isa. xi. 2), and that the wisdom of Jehovah is emphasised in Isa. xxxi. 2 ; comp. xxviii. 29.

[3] *Die dichter des alten bundes*, ii. 12. Ewald refers to xiii. 1, xiv. 6, and other passages in which 'scorners' are referred to. But it is not clear that 'a powerful school' of wise men is here intended ; the title may be given to 'those who opposed or despised the counsels of the wise men, and broke through the restraints of law and religion ; comp. Prov. xv. 12, xxi. 24' (*The Prophecies of Isaiah*, ed. 3, i. 165). Among such persons were the politicians of Isaiah's day, so far as they opposed the warnings of the prophet ; they were popularly considered 'wise men' (xxix. 14 ; comp. Jer. viii. 9), but not in the technical sense with which our present enquiries are concerned.

[4] Luzzatto renders, 'o voi uomini insipienti, *poeti* di questo popolo,' taking *mōshĕlīm* in the same sense as in Num. xxi. 27 (similarly Barth, in his tract on Isaiah, p. 23, following Rashi and Aben Ezra), a view which receives some support from the parable offered by Isaiah in xxviii. 23-29 as if in opposition to the false parables of unsound teachers. But in Isa. xxix. 20 'scorner' is clearly used, not as a class-name for certain wise men, but in a moral sense.

inference mentioned just now commends itself to me as sound; but I admit that the saying on prophecy in Prov. xxix. 18 (already quoted) is isolated, and that the tone of the religious proverbs falls far short of enthusiasm. This is probably all that M. Renan means in a too French sentence of his work on Ecclesiastes. Religion, according to the wise men, was a necessary element in a worthy character, was even (I should say) the principal element, but the religion of these practical moralists has nothing of that delighted *abandon* which we find in the more distinctly religious Scriptures. 'Happy the man who dreadeth continually,' says one characteristic proverb (xxviii. 14; contrast the 'not caring' of the 'fool' in xiv. 16). Later on, a more devout moralist writes that 'the fear of Jehovah is the beginning of wisdom' (i. 7), and though 'fear' need not exclude 'love' yet there is nothing here to suggest their combination. The proverb of the Egyptian prince Ptahhotep,[1] 'To obey is to love God; not to obey is to hate God,' has no parallel, at any rate in the early anthologies; much less does the great saying in Ps. lxxiii. 25 strike a note congenial to any of the Hebrew sages. And yet it remains true that the wise men happily supplemented the more spiritual teaching of psalmists and prophets.

There is still another important point on which both prophets and 'wise men' were agreed. Whatever their inward religion may have been, they (like the Egyptian moralists) were outwardly utilitarians; i.e., they invite men to practise righteousness, not because righteousness is the secret of blessedness, but because of its outward rewards both for the man himself and for his posterity (Prov. xi. 21, xx. 7; comp. Jer. xxxii. 18). The form in which the doctrine of proportionate retribution is expressed in xi. 4 would have been completely acceptable to the prophets, whose conception of the 'day of Jehovah' (i.e., not the last great *dies iræ*, but any providential crisis in the world's history) is adopted in it,—

> Wealth is of no profit in the day of wrath,
> but righteousness delivers from death.

Proverbs expressing this idea in various forms abound in the

[1] Brugsch, *Religion und Mythologie der alten Aegypter*, p. 91.

first anthology. Not a hint is given that retribution loiters on the road ; at most a warning not to envy the (temporary) prosperity of the wicked (xxiii. 17, xxiv. 1, 19 ; with regard to xxiii. 18 see above).

This was the 'certitude of the golden age,' to use Mr. Matthew Arnold's expression ; it is just what we might expect in a simple and stationary condition of society. The strange thing is that it should have lasted on when oppression within or hostile attacks from without had brought manifold causes of sorrow upon both good and bad.[1] That the teachers of the people should have held up the doctrine of earthly retribution—

> Behold, the righteous hath a reward upon earth ;
> much more the ungodly and the sinner (xi. 31)—

as long as it could reasonably be defended, was natural. But that shortly before the Maccabean rising a 'wise man '[2] should still be found to write—

> The gift of the Lord remains with the godly,
> and his favour brings prosperity for ever (Ecclus. xi. 17),

seems to contradict the usual correspondence between the received moral theory and the outward circumstances of society. All that we can say is that such inconsistencies are found to exist ; old forms of doctrine do not, as a rule, ' melt like frosty rime.' There must have been circles of Jewish moralists averse to speculation, who would continue to repeat the older view of the providential government even at a time when the social state had completely exposed its shallowness.

Dean Plumptre, indeed, following Ewald, credits the 'wise men' of pre-Exile times with deeper views. According to him, certain proverbs, e.g. x. 25, xi. 4, xiv. 32, xxiii. 18 (Ewald adds xii. 28) imply the hope of immortality. None of these passages however can be held conclusive. x. 25, xi. 4 simply say that the righteous shall be unhurt in a day of judgment ; in xiv. 32 the antithesis is between the ruin which follows upon wickedness and the safe refuge of integrity (read *b'thummō* with the

---

[1] Yet in Prov. iii. 11, 12 there is distinct evidence of deepened experience and progress of moral thought.
[2] On the orthodoxy of Ecclesiasticus, see later on.

Sept.); in xxiii. 18, 'there is a future,' the reference is perfectly vague—it is natural to explain by comparing Job xlii. 12. xii. 28, no doubt, on Ewald's view of the passage, seems conclusive,
> In the way of righteousness is life,
> and the way of its path is immortality.

But this great word 'immortality' is unparalleled before the Book of Wisdom, and cannot fairly be extracted from the Hebrew.[1] The Septuagint has a different view of the pronunciation of the text, and renders ὁδοὶ δὲ μνησικάκων εἰς θάνατον. The easiest plan is to correct *n'thībhāh* into *nith'ābh*, with Levy, and render,
> but an abominable way (comp. xv. 9) leads unto death.

I do not deny that the idea of eternal life may have been conceived at the time of these proverbs. This may plausibly be inferred from the occurrence of the phrase 'a tree of life' in iii. 18, xi. 30, xiii. 12, xv. 4, and 'a fountain of life' in x. 11, xiii. 14, xiv. 27, xvi. 22,—phrases certainly borrowed from some traditional story of Paradise analogous to that in Gen. ii.[2] It is a singular fact however that in all these passages (even, I think, in iii. 18) these expressions are simply figurative synonyms for 'refreshment,' which suggests that the proverb-writers shrank from using them in their literal sense of the individual righteous man.

The importance of the 'wise men' as a class is too seldom recognised. To the hasty reader they are overshadowed by the prophets, between whom and the rude masses they seem to have occupied a middle position. Their popular style and genial manners attracted probably a large number of disciples; at any rate, in the time of Jeremiah the 'counsel' of the 'wise men' was valued as highly as the 'direction' (*tōra*) of the priests and the 'word' of the prophets (Jer. xviii. 18). By constantly working on suitable individuals, they produced a moral sympathy with the prophets, without which those

---

[1] The Vulg. has, *iter autem devium ducit ad mortem* (but this pregnant sense of *iter devium* is too bold).

[2] Analogous only, because apparently it had both a tree and a fountain of life, like a New Zealand myth mentioned by Schirren.

heroic men would have laboured in vain. Thus that friendly relation must have sprung up between the prophets and the 'wise men,' of which I have spoken already, and which reminds us of the sanction said to have been given to the Seven Sages of Greece by the oracle of Delphi.[1]

It is a misfortune that our sources for the history of Israelitish 'philosophy' are so scanty. Were there 'wise men' in N. Israel? and if so, have any of their proverbs come down to us, besides the *mashal* or fable of Jotham? Did they confine their activity to the capital city or cities, or did they also, like the 'scribes,' settle or itinerate in the provinces? (Matt. ix. 3, Targ. of Judg. v. 9.) Did their public instructions assume anything like the form of the proverbs of our anthologies? Did they teach without fee or reward?[2] At any rate, a post-Exile proverb-writer tells us with retrospective glance where the 'wise men' awaited their disciples—not in the quietude of the chamber, but either within the massive city-gates, or in the adjacent squares or 'broad places' on which the streets converged (i. 20, 21 ; comp. Job xxix. 7). No doubt they had a large stock of sayings in their memory, such as had been tested by the experience of past generations. Sometimes they would modify old proverbs, sometimes they would frame new ones, so that when their disciples gathered round them, they would 'bring out of their treasure things new and old.' From time to time they would commit their 'wisdom' to writing in a more perfect form, and such records must have formed the basis of the proverbial collections in the Old Testament.

[1] Curtius, *History of Greece*, ii. 52.
[2] Ewald infers from xvii. 16 that even in early times it was customary to fee the 'wise men' for their advice (comp. Saul and Samuel). At a later time Sirach says, 'Buy (instruction) for yourselves without money' (Ecclus. li. 25, but comp. 28). The Rabbis were not allowed to receive fees from their pupils. R. Zadok said, 'Make not (the Tora) a crown to glory in, nor an axe to live by' (*Pirke Aboth*, iv. 9). So the Moslem teachers at the great Cairo 'university' (el Azhar).

CHAPTER II.

THE FORM AND ORIGIN OF THE PROVERBS.

IN one of the opening verses of the Book of Proverbs (i. 6) three technical names for varieties of proverbs are put together:—(1) *māshāl*, a short, pointed saying with reference to some striking feature in the life of an individual, or in human life generally, often clothed in figurative language (whence, according to many, the name *māshāl*, as if 'similitude;' comp. παραβολή), (2) *m'lîça*, perhaps a 'bent,' 'oblique' or (as Sept.) 'dark' saying, (3) *khîda*, a 'knotty' or intricate saying, especially a riddle. Each of these words has a variety of applications; for instance (1) is used in Num. xxiii., xxiv., for a parallelistic poem, (1) and (2) sometimes mean a 'taunting speech' (see below, and comp. Hab. ii. 6, Isa. xiv. 4, Mic. ii. 4), and (3) can be used, not merely of true riddles with a moral meaning, such as we find here and there in Prov. xxx., but also of didactic statements upon subjects as difficult as riddles (see Ps. xlix. 5, A.V. 4, lxxviii. 2). We have no collection of popular proverbs, such as exists in Arabic; the proverbs in the canonical collection show great technical elaboration, though some may be based on the naïve 'wisdom' of the people. A very few specimens of the popular proverb have indeed been preserved in the canonical literature.[1] 'Is Saul also among the prophets?'(1 Sam. x. 12, xix. 24) preserves the memory of a humorous fact in the story of that king. 'Wickedness proceeds from the wicked' (1 Sam. xxiv. 13) is, unlike the former, a generalisation, and means that a man's character is shown by his actions (comp.

---

[1] In the Midrash-literature, proverbs are often quoted with an express statement that they are from the lips of the people.

Isa. xxxii. 6). 'As is the mother, so is the daughter' (Ezek. xvi. 44) is also an induction from common experience. 'The fathers have eaten sour grapes, and the children's teeth are set on edge' (Jer. xxxi. 29, Ezek. xviii. 2), words applied no doubt, as Lowth says, profanely, but not originally meant so, is a figurative way of saying that the sins of the fathers are visited upon the children. We have one specimen of the riddle (strictly so called)—that well-known one of Samson's,

> From the eater came forth food,
> and from the strong one came forth sweetness (Judges xiv. 14).

The parable, too, was doubtless called *mashal*, and of this we have three Old Testament examples, which will at once occur to the reader (2 Sam. xii. 1-6, xiv. 4-9, 1 Kings xx. 39, 40); but it is more important to draw the reader's attention to the rare specimens of the fable. Some may think it bold to refer in this connection to a portion of a narrative which seems at first sight to be historical (Num. xxi. 22-35). The strange episode of the speaking ass is, however, most difficult to understand, except as a sportive quasi-historical version of a popular *mashal* or fable (compare the four Babylonian animal-fables discovered among the fragments of King Assurbanipal's library).[1] The passage being evidently distinct from the rest of the story of Balaam, in passing this judgment upon it, we are not committed as a matter of course to a denial of all historical character to the rest of the narrative. The fables of Jotham (Judg. ix. 8-15) and Joash (2 Kings xiv. 9), in which the trees are introduced speaking, have also their parallels in Babylonian literature. One of them indeed has a claim to be called a *mashal* on a second account; the tree-fable of Joash is a taunt of the keenest edge, and one of the secondary meanings of *mashal* is 'taunting speech' (see Isa. xiv. 4, A.V.). It is true the 'taunting speeches' expressly

---

[1] See Smith and Sayce's *Chaldæan Genesis*, pp. 140-154. For the Egyptian animal-fables, which may be the originals of those of Æsop, see Mahaffy, *Prolegomena to Anc. Hist.*, p. 390; for the Indian, see the apologues of the Pancha-tantra by Benfey or Lancereau, and the Buddhist Birth-Stories—'the oldest, most complete, and most important collection of folk-lore extant'—translated by Rhys Davids, vol. i.

called *mashals*—not only those in the prophetic writings (see above), but the verses ascribed to 'those that speak in *mashals*' in Num. xxi. 27-30—are poetical in form, but this is because the Hebrew writers never conceived the idea of a narrative poem; even the prologue of the Book of Job is in prose.

These are the principal specimens of the *mashal* apart from those in the three Books of Old Testament Wisdom. They are but the 'two or three berries' left after the beating of the tree (Isa. xvii. 6), and excite a longing for more which cannot be gratified. We may be sure that in Israel's prime the telling of proverbs was almost as popular as the recital of stories, and became a test of ability. For—

> The legs of a lame man hang loose,
> so is a proverb in the mouth of fools (xxvi. 7);

and though Sirach says of the labouring class, 'They shall not be found where parables are spoken' (Ecclus. xxxviii. 33), it is reasonable to account for this by the aristocratic pride of the students of Scripture in the later Jewish community. At any rate, as I have said already, some at least of the early literary proverbs are very possibly based on popular sayings; these would naturally embody a plain, bourgeois experience such as marks not a few of the proverbs in our book. Dr. Oort conjectures[1] that *some of our proverbs were originally current among the people as riddles*, such for instance as, 'What is sweet as honey?—Pleasant discourse, for it is sweet to the soul and a medicine to the bones' (xvi. 24); 'What is worse than meeting a bear?—Meeting a fool in a fit of folly' (xvii. 12); 'What is sweet at first, and then like sand in the mouth?—Stolen food' (xx. 17). Certainly the introduction to the 'proverbs of Solomon' may seem to imply (i. 6) that the collection which follows contains specimens of the riddle, but probably all the writer means is that the 'words of the wise' are often 'knotty' because epigrammatic. We may indeed reasonably hold that, like their prototype Solomon,[2] the 'wise men' were accustomed to sharpen their intellects upon enig-

[1] *The Bible for Young People*, E. T., iii. 105-6.
[2] 1 Kings x. 1; comp. Menander's account in Josephus, *Antiq.* viii. 5, 3.

mas (such as lie at the root of the so-called 'numerical proverbs' in xxx. 15, 18, 21, 24, 29; comp. vi. 16); but a still more important discipline than the battle of wits was the habit of keen observation. We cannot reduce all the proverbs involving comparison to the form of riddles, any more than we can do this with the following Buddhist sayings, equal to the more refined specimens of the Hebrew proverb:—[1]

As rain breaks through an ill-thatched house, so passion will break through an unreflecting mind.
Like a beautiful flower, full of colour, but without scent, are the fine but fruitless words of him who does not act accordingly.
A tamed elephant they lead to battle; the king mounts a tamed elephant; the tamed is the best among men, he who silently endures abuse.
Well-makers lead the water; fletchers bend the arrow; carpenters bend a log of wood; wise people fashion themselves.

Another plausible hypothesis similar to that of Dr. Oort is that some of our proverbs are based on popular fables, as is the case according to Dr. Back with many of the proverbs in the Talmud and Midrash.[2] The Jewish scholar referred to applies this key to Prov. vi. 6-11 (comp. the Aramaic fable of the ant and the grasshopper—see Delitzsch's note), to the numerical proverbs in chap. xxx. ('skeletons of fables' he calls them), and to Eccles. ix. 4 and x. 11. Both proverbs and fables indeed are common in later Jewish literature. Fables, especially animal fables, were not perhaps appropriate vehicles of moral instruction according to the O.T. writers. But the later Jewish teachers do not seem to have felt this objection. Rabbi Meir (2nd cent. A.D.) was the writer of animal fables *par excellence*; Rabbi Hillel (B.C. 30), however, so noted for his versatility, was also a copious fabulist.[3]

---

[1] From Max Müller's translation of the Dhammapada, or 'Path of Virtue' (1870)
[2] Dr. Back gives a list of these in Grätz's *Monatsschrift*, 1884, pp. 265-7.
[3] In the Talmudic treatise *Soferim* xvi. 9, a list of Hillel's acquirements is given, including the conversations of the mountains, the trees, the animals, the demons &c. On the Jewish fable literature, the wealth of which seems unparalleled, see Back, *Die Fabel in Talmud und Midrash*, in Grätz's *Monatsschrift*, 1875-1884. Curiously enough the two oldest Jewish fables are similar in character to those of the Old Test.

This popular origin of some at least of the proverbs sufficiently accounts for their comparatively trite and commonplace character. They were not trite and commonplace to those who first used them, and successive generations loved them because of their antiquity (Job viii. 8-10). Even to us they are not so commonplace as the far less popular and piquant Egyptian proverbs,[1] though I confess that they will hardly compare with the relics of Indian gnomology,[2] still less with the singularly rich and pointed proverbs of the Chinese.[3] The practice of writing antithetic sentences on paper or silk to suspend in houses (contrast Deut. vi. 9) gave an edge to the shrewd earthly wisdom of the countrymen of Confucius. The Jewish intellect developed but slowly into the acuteness of the later periods which produced fables, proverbs, and riddles which can safely challenge comparison.[4]

[1] Comp. Renouf, *Hibbert Lectures*, pp. 75, 76, 100-103; Mahaffy, *Prolegomena to Ancient History*, pp. 273-291; Brugsch, *Religion und Mythologie der alten Aegypter*, p. 91; *Records of the Past*, viii. 157-160.
[2] Comp. Weber, *Indische Literaturgeschichte*, p. 227.
[3] See Scarborough, *Collection of Chinese Proverbs* (1875). The Chinese proverbs have no known authors.
[4] On the riddles referred to, see Wünsche, *Die Räthselweisheit bei den Hebräern* (1883). Comp. them with the later Arabic proverbs (see Hariri, and comp. Freytag, *Proverbia arabica*).

K

CHAPTER III.

THE FIRST COLLECTION AND ITS APPENDICES.

UPON entering what Dante in the *De Monarchiâ* so well calls 'the forest' of the canonical proverbs, we are soon struck by differences of age and growth. The central portion of the book, and in some respects the most interesting, is comprised in x. 1–xxii. 16. To this, which is indeed the original Book of Proverbs, the first nine chapters were intended to serve as the introduction. It is the oldest Hebrew proverbial anthology extant. Probably from its compiler it received the name 'Proverbs of Solomon,' and from this title has sprung the tradition accepted by so many subsequent ages and indeed by the editor of the whole book (Prov. i. 1) of Solomon's authorship of the Proverbs. The title however cannot be historically correct. Those maxims in this anthology which refer to the true God under the name Jehovah (*Yahvè*) are too monotheistic and inculcate too pure a morality to be the work of the Solomon of the Book of Kings. That great despot's 'wisdom,' so far as we can judge both from his character and from the traditional notices, cannot have had a distinctively religious character. Listen to these proverbs,—

> Better a little with the fear of Jehovah
> than great treasure and turmoil therewith (xv. 16).
> The horse is prepared against the day of battle,
> but victory is Jehovah's (xxi. 31).
> The mouth of strange women is a deep pit;
> he with whom Jehovah is wroth falleth therein (xxii. 14).
> A wise son (loveth) his father's correction,
> but a scorner heareth not rebuke (xiii. 1),—

and for a commentary read 1 Kings iv. 26, xi. 1, 4, 14–40, xii. 14, 15. Nor is the moral tone of the 'Solomonic' proverbs in its plain bourgeois simplicity any more suitable to the name they bear than the religious. Unless Solomon was like Haroun al-Rashid, and made himself privately acquainted with the ways and thoughts of the citizens, it is difficult to see how he can have written so completely as one of them would have done.

The truth is that both David and Solomon were idealised by later generations. The heroes of a grander if not better age, they towered far above the petty figures of their successors. Favoured by the contemporary depression of Egypt and Assyria, they had been enabled to rear and to retain a powerful empire, comparable to those which afflicted and oppressed the divided people of the later Israelites. Solomon in particular is represented in tradition as not only the most fortunate but the wisest of kings, not in the sense in which it is said that religion is the best part of wisdom (Prov. i. 7), but in that in which the 'children of the east' were accustomed to use the word. This is clear from the language of the Hebrew narrator:—

'And God gave Solomon wisdom and understanding exceeding much, and largeness of heart even as the sand on the sea-shore. And Solomon's wisdom excelled the wisdom of all the children of the east country, and all the wisdom of Egypt. For he was wiser than all men; than Ethan the Ezrahite [read, perhaps, 'the native,' i.e. the Israelite], and Heman, and Calcol, and Darda, the sons of Mahol [probably a foreigner] : and his fame was in all the nations round about. And he spoke three thousand proverbs [or, similitudes], and his songs were a thousand and five. And he spoke of trees, from the cedar in Lebanon unto the hyssop that springeth out of the wall : he spoke also of beasts, and of birds, and of creeping things, and of fishes. And there came of all peoples to hear the wisdom of Solomon, from all kings of the earth, who had heard of his wisdom.' (1 Kings iv. 29–34.)

I see no reason for not accepting the substance of this tradition. The principal point in it is the ascription to Solomon of a power of apophthegmatic composition which the author, as a devout theist, could not but trace to a divine gift, just as the author of Ex. xxxvi. ascribes the skill of the artisans of the tabernacle to the direct operation of Jehovah.

But we are also informed that the talents of Solomon were neither peculiar to him, nor exercised on different subjects from those of foreign sages. The precise meaning of the Hebrew *m'shālīm* in 1 Kings iv. 32 is suggested by ver. 33. The word seems to mean moralising similitudes[1] derived partly from the animal, partly from the vegetable kingdom (for Lord Bacon's view,[2] hinted in the *New Atlantis*, is more plausible than sound). Was I not right in saying that the traditional notices of Solomon's wisdom do not agree with the title of our anthology? I wish that it were otherwise. How gladly one would see a few of Solomon's genuine utterances (whether proverbs, or similitudes, or fables) incorporated into one or another of the Hebrew Scriptures!

I think however that it is unfair both to the compiler and to the editor who repeats his statement (i. 1) to take the ascription of these proverbs to Solomon literally. Accuracy in the details of literary history was not a qualification which would seem important to an Israelite. The name of Solomon was attached (for dogmatism here seems permissible) to these choice specimens of Hebrew proverbiology simply from a very characteristic hero-worship. Solomon had in fact become the symbol of plain ethical 'wisdom' just as David had become the representative of religious lyric poetry. We may see this from the alternative title of the Book of Proverbs in both Jewish and Christian writings—' Book of Wisdom ;'[3] still more from the fiction of Solomon's authorship of Ecclesiastes, and

---

[1] Dr. Grätz is of opinion that Solomon was a fabulist like Jotham; in the text I have followed Josephus (*Ant.* vii. 2, 5). Legend related how the wise king, like the early men in African folk-lore (Max Müller, *Hibbert Lectures*, p. 116), talked *with* (not merely *of*) beasts, birds, and fishes, but delighted most in the birds.

[2] This was also the opinion of Ewald (*History*, iii. 281). It might now be urged in its favour that Assurbanipal's library contained bilingual lists of animals, vegetables, and minerals. But remember that the Assyrians were incomparably more civilised than the Israelites, and had both a lexicographical and a scientific interest in making these lists, and above all that Solomon is not stated to have written, but only to have *spoken*.

[3] See the *Tosefoth* to the Talmudic treatise *Baba bathra*, 14*b*, where the name is given both to Proverbs and to Ecclesiastes. It is however more commonly found in Christian than in Jewish literature, often under the fuller form ἡ πανάρετος σοφία (see especially Eusebius, *H. E.*, iv. 22).

from the Targumic paraphrase of Jer. ix. 23, 'Let not *Solomon the son of David*, the wise man, glory in his wisdom.' Of course, the real names of the authors of the proverbs had been as irrecoverably lost as those of our early ballad-writers.

But though we must deny the Solomonic authorship a far-off influence of the Solomonic age may perhaps be admitted; at least, there are grounds for the opinion that some of the proverbs are as old as the ninth century. (1) The second collection of so-called Solomonic proverbs was compiled according to a credible tradition (xxv. 1) in the reign of Hezekiah; this of itself throws the earlier collection a considerable way back into the eighth century. (2) Upon examining the first anthology we find that some of the proverbs already have a history. For instance, (*a*) the solemn generalisation in xiv. 12 occurs in exactly the same form in xvi. 25, (*b*) eight other proverbs are repeated with slight changes in expression (x. 1 = xv. 20, x. 2 = xi. 4, xiii. 14 ≒ xiv. 27, xiv. 20 = xix. 4, xvi. 2 = xxi. 2, xix. 5 = xix. 9, xx. 10 = xx. 23, xxi. 9 = xxi. 19), but except in the case of xi. 4, xiv. 27 no change in thought, (*c*) ten are repeated, at least so far as one line goes, either exactly or with but slight differences (x. 15 = xviii. 11, x. 6^1 = x. 11, x. 8 = x. 10,^{2} xv. 33 = xviii. 12, xi. 13 = xx. 19, xi. 21 = xvi. 5, xii. 14 = xiii. 2, xiv. 31 = xvii. 5, xvi. 18 = xviii. 12, xix. 12 = xx. 2). It is probable that some time would elapse before a proverb attained such notoriety as to be circulated in varying forms. (3) The originality of the diction (*a*) and the careful observance of technical rules of composition (*b*) favour an early date. (*a*) For instance, 'steersmanship'^{3} (xi. 14, xii. 5, xx. 18), as a term for practical wisdom or counsels, evidently springs from a fresh enthusiasm for commerce; a long list of striking expressions might be added from any chapter of the collection. (*b*) Nor is technical precision at all less conspicuous in this early anthology. Each proverb is a distich, i.e.

---

[1] The second line however seems to have intruded from ver. 11, and thus to have supplanted the original.

[2] Here again the second line is evidently an intruder (from ver. 8). We should doubtless read with Sept., 'but he that reproves produces welfare.'

[3] This word (*takhbūlōth*) also occurs in xxiv. 6, i. 5, Job xxxvii. 12.

consists of two lines, as a rule three-toned, and in most cases antithetically parallel. It is true, xix. 7 in its present form is a tristich, i.e. consists of three members, but this proverb undoubtedly arose out of two, the second of which is mutilated in the Hebrew text, but is found in a complete though not entirely correct form in the Septuagint. The incomprehensible third line of xix. 7 given in versions based upon the Hebrew now becomes the distich,

> He that does much evil perfects mischief;
> he that provokes[1] with words shall not escape.

According to Ewald, the collection is divided into five parts by the recurrence at intervals of a proverb exhorting the young to receive instruction; see x. 1, xiii. 1, xv. 20, xvii. 25, xix. 20. If this division is intentional it may be compared with the equally mechanical triple division found by some in Isa. xl.–lxvi. Of arrangement by subject there is but little trace; here and there two or more verses come in succession dealing with the same theme. Observe too the recurrence of 'Jehovah,' xv. 33, xvi. 1–9, 11, and of the word 'king' in xvi. 10, 12–15, which shows that one principle of arrangement was simply the recurrence of certain catchwords. Bickell thinks that another principle was the occurrence of the same initial letter (see xi. 9–12, xx. 7–9, xx. 24–26, xxii. 2–4).

Altogether, it is abundantly clear that we have before us works of art, and not the simple maxims handed down in Israel from father to son. There may sometimes be a traditional basis, but no more. The anthology contrasts, therefore, as Ewald remarks, with the collections of Arabic proverbs due to Abu-Obaida, Maidani[2] and others. But whether we may go on to assert with the same great critic that we have here the wise men's applications of the truths of religion to the infinite cases and contingencies of the secular life, seems doubtful. It is not clear to me that these wise

---

[1] For *m'raddēf* read *m'gaddēf*.
[2] Landberg denies that Maidani's proverbs were ever really popular, but A. Müller judges that this view is extravagant (*Zeitschrift für Völkerpsychologie*, xii. 441).

men were preoccupied by religion. There are indeed not a few fine religious proverbs, but it cannot be shown that those who wrote the secular proverbs also wrote the religious. It is possible and even probable that some of the religious proverbs are the work of the author of the introductory chapters; without dogmatising, I may refer to xiv. 34 (comp. viii. 15, 16), xv. 33, xvi. 1-7, and perhaps to xix. 27, which is quite in the parental tone of chaps. i.-ix. The tone of the secular proverbs is not, from a Christian point of view (of which more later on), an elevated one. The ethical principle is prudential. Virtue or 'wisdom' is rewarded, and vice or 'folly' punished in this life. It is indeed nowhere expressly said that every trouble is a punishment; but there is nothing like xxiv. 16 in this anthology to prevent the reader from inferring it. At any rate, the writers are clearly not in the van of religious thought: no 'obstinate questionings' have yet disturbed their tranquillity.

We need not pause here to demonstrate what no one probably will dispute, that the origin of this first anthology is impersonal. The fact that it is so may well give us the more confidence in the accuracy of the social picture which it contains. This is certainly a pleasing one, and points to a comparatively early period in the history of Judah. Commerce and its attendant luxury have not made such progress as at the time when the introduction was written; poverty is only too well known, but there seems to be a middle class with a sound moral sense, to which the writers of proverbs can appeal. It is true, says one of these, that in daily life 'rich and poor meet together,' but for all that 'Jehovah is the maker of them all' (xxii. 2), and 'he that oppresses the poor reproaches his maker' (xiv. 31). And if it is true on the one hand that 'the poor is hated even of his neighbour' (xiv. 20), and that 'the destruction of the wretched is their poverty' (x. 15), it is equally so on the other that 'he that trusts in his riches shall fall' (xi. 28), and that

> Better is the poor man who walks in his blamelessness,
> than he who is perverse in his ways and is rich [1] (xix. 1).

[1] The text has 'than he who is perverse in his lips and is a fool.' With Grätz, I follow the Peshitto and (partly) the Vulgate.

The strength of the land still consists in the number of small proprietors tilling their own ground. Two proverbs express an interest in these, e.g.

> The poor man's newly ploughed field gives food in abundance,
> but there is that is cut off by injustice (xiii. 23).
> Better is a mean man that tills for himself[1]
> than he that glorifies himself and has no bread (xii. 9).

All the farmers however were not so diligent as those indicated in these passages. One of the numerous proverbs against laziness (then as now a prevalent vice in this part of the East[2]) brings before us a land-owner who is too lazy to give the order for ploughing at the right time, and so when he looks for the harvest, there is none.

> When autumn comes the sluggard ploughs not;
> so if he asks at harvest-time, there is nothing (xx. 4).

The right use of the gift of speech is another very favourite subject in this anthology. The charm of suitable words is best described in a Hezekian proverb (xxv. 11), but it is well said in xv. 4 that 'a gentle tongue is a tree of life,' and elsewhere that

> There is that babbles like the thrusts of a sword,
> but the tongue of the wise is gentleness (xii. 18).

The wonderful power of language could hardly at that age have been better expressed than by the saying,

> The words of a man's mouth are deep waters,
> a gushing torrent, a wellspring of wisdom (xviii. 4).

The standard of family morals is high ; a good wife is described as God's best gift (xii. 4, xviii. 22, xix. 14), and the restraints of home are commended to the young (xix. 18, xxii. 6, 15), as in the Egyptian proverbs. Monogamy is throughout presupposed, and a want of respect for *either* parent is condemned (xiii. 1, xv. 5, xix. 26). The king too is repeatedly held up to reverence (xiv. 35, xvi. 10, 12–15, xix.

---

[1] Pointing *ōbhēd*, with Hitzig, Ewald, and Bickell ; comp. ver. 11. Dijserinck ingeniously emends *çōbhēr* ' heaps up ' (i.e. saves).

[2] Comp. Thomson, *The Land and the Book*, pp. 336–8.

12, xx. 2, 8, 26, 28, xxii. 11) ; it is not so in the Hezekian collection. The king however is not identified with the Deity, as in Egypt; we are told that the will of the monarch is pliable in the hand of Jehovah (xxi. 1), and the true glory of a nation is, not in the prowess of its king, but in righteousness (xiv. 34). And even if we must confess that the spirit of the more secular proverbs is utilitarian, the utilitarianism is sometimes a very refined one, as for instance where the refreshing character of a quiet, contented mind is contrasted with the dull reaction which follows on an outburst of passion (xiv. 30). In conclusion, I will quote a few proverbs interesting chiefly as characteristic of their age, and then a few more of the gems of the collection.

(a) The poor is hated even by his neighbour,
    but the rich has many friends (xiv. 20).
Whoso withholds corn, him the people curse,
    but blessing is on the head of him who sells it (xi. 26).
The beginning of strife is as when one lets out water,
    so leave off quarrelling before the teeth be shown (xvii. 14).
The gift of a man makes a free space for him,
    and brings him before the great (xviii. 16).
'Bad, bad,' says the purchaser,
    but when he goes away, he boasts (xx. 14).

(b) The righteous regards the life of his cattle,[1]
    but the heart of the wicked is cruel (xii. 10).
The heart knows its own bitterness,
    and a stranger cannot intermeddle with its joy (xiv. 10).
He that covers transgression helps forward love,
    but he that repeats a matter separates best friends (xvii. 9).
There are friends (good enough) acting their part,[2]
    and there is a loving friend who sticks closer than a brother
                        (xviii. 24 ; comp. xvii. 17).
Who can say, I have made my heart clean,
    I am pure from my sin? (xx. 9.)
Say not, I will recompense evil ;
    wait for Jehovah, and he will deliver thee (xx. 22).

[1] The word is *behēma* (Seneca's 'muta animalia'). Schopenhauer, thinking perhaps of the Levitical sacrifices, accuses the Old Testament of cruelty to animals. But see, besides this passage, Gen. i. 27-29, Num. xxii. 28, Jon. iv. 11.
[2] With Hitzig and others, taking '*ĭsh* as a softened form of *yēsh* (comp. 2 Sam. xiv. 19, Mic. vi. 10); the *yōd* is kept as in Aramaic. So Targ., Pesh.

The first appendix to the original Book (appended possibly *before* the composition of the Introduction) is a small collection of proverbial sayings called 'words of the wise' (xxii. 17–xxiv. 22). Virtually the same phrase occurs again in xxiv. 23 at the head of a still shorter work, compiled or composed evidently about the same time by another ' wise man ' (perhaps the whole work has not come down to us). In the introductory verses the compiler's object in writing down these proverbs is said to have been that his disciple might learn virtue and religion, and might become qualified to teach others. There is one very difficult passage in it, but this has been corrected in a masterly way by Bickell :—[1]

That thy confidence may be in Jehovah,
to make known unto thee thy ways.
Now, yea before now, have I written unto thee,
long before, with counsels and knowledge,
That thou mayest know the rightness of true words,
that thou mayest answer in true words to those that ask thee
(xxii. 19–21).

The construction of ver. 20*b* and ver. 21 in the Hebrew thus becomes more idiomatic (comp. $\chi\theta\acute{\epsilon}\varsigma\ \tau\epsilon\ \kappa\alpha\grave{\iota}\ \pi\rho\acute{\omega}\eta\nu$), though not free from ambiguity. The words may mean either that the compiler took long over his work, or that this was not the first occasion of his writing. On the latter explanation the passage may imply that the compiler of this anthology also wrote chaps. i.–ix. (comp. i. 6*b*). His hortatory style and predilection for grouping verses may seem to plead for this view. There are however no important points of contact in phraseology between the work before us and Prov. i.–ix.,[2] and certainly the appendix falls far below the standard of the Introduction.

---

[1] At the end of ver. 19 Bickell nearly follows Sept. Cod. Vat., τὴν ὁδόν σου (A.C.S. αὑτοῦ). But as this takes the place of *hayyōm*, it would seem that Bickell ought to begin ver. 20 with *af ethmōl*. This however would not suit his metrical theory.

[2] The phraseological resemblance of xxiii. 19*b* to iv. 14*b* is incomplete. As for *khokmōth* in xxiv. 7, it means simply 'wisdom' (as in xiv. 1, where *khakmōth* is wrong); the parallelism with i. 20, ix. 1 is not of critical importance. Any real points of contact (such as xxiii. 23*a*; comp. iv. 5, 7) can be accounted for by imitation, and one could easily bring together points of difference.

At any rate, it is undoubted that these 'words of the wise' appeared long after the 'Solomonic' proverbs. The peculiarities of style referred to show this, and also the imitation of some of the 'Solomonic' proverbs in the 'words of the wise;' (comp. xi. 14 with xxiv. 5, 6; xiii. 9 with xxiv. 19, 20; xxii. 14*a* with xxiii. 27).

There is no occasion to suppose that all these proverbs come from one period; but the hand of a compiler is more conspicuous here than in the first anthology. He has not indeed removed repetitions (see xxii. 28*a*, xxiii. 10*a*; xxiii. 17*a*, xxiv. 1*a*; xxiii. 18, xxiv. 14), but the personal element preponderates so much that he might fairly have prefixed his own name as the author. Artistically, he may perhaps be found wanting. He has left one tristich (i.e. a proverb of three lines), viz. xxii. 29; two pentastichs (i.e. proverbs of five lines), viz. xxiii. 4, 5, xxiv. 13, 14; and one heptastich (i.e. a proverb of seven lines), viz. xxiii. 6–8. Unsymmetrical as these may be, it seems hazardous, unless there be any specially doubtful passage, to restore symmetry (i.e. to convert tristichs into tetrastichs, and so on) by inserting words conjecturally. There are a few distichs (xxii. 28, xxiii. 9, xxiv. 7, 8, 9, 10), thus affording a slight point of contact with the first anthology; more tetrastichs (xxii. 22, 23; 24, 25; 26, 27; xxiii. 10, 11; 15, 16; 17, 18; xxiv. 1, 2; 3, 4; 5, 6; 15, 16; 17, 18; 19, 20; 21, 22), and hexastichs (xxiii. 1–3; 12–14; 19–21; 26–28; xxiv. 11, 12). One octastich occurs (xxiii. 22–25), and one long poem, in the main a group of distichs, referred to again below (xxiii. 29–35).

Beautiful in form, the proverbs of this collection certainly are not; one cannot apply to the author the saying in xxiv. 26, 'He kisses the lips who answers in suitable words.' The contents however are not without points of interest. In xxiii. 1–3 we have a picture of a man of the middle class admitted to the table of a governor. Being unused to 'dainties,' he is tempted to excess; as a restraint, the 'wise man' bids him consider the capriciousness of princely favour (comp. Ecclus. ix. 13). The abuse of luxuries such as wine and meat was in fact a sore evil in the eyes of this writer (see the caution in xxiii. 20, 21 in the Septuagint version, which reminds one of vii. 14). He has even left us a poem on the evils of drunkenness (xxiii. 29–35) which contains several striking details from its satirical opening, 'Who hath *oi*, who hath *aboi*?' (interjections expressing pain), to the picturesque comparison of the drunkard to a man 'that lieth upon the top of a mast,'[1] which shows incidentally that sea-life was by this time a familiar experience. Another interesting passage, though marred by its obscurity, is that in xxiv. 11, 12. The innocent victims of a miscarriage of justice are about to be dragged away to execution; the pupil of the wise is exhorted to 'deliver' them, by intervening with resistless energy, like the St. Ives of a favourite Breton legend, and testifying to the innocence of the sufferers (see xxxi. 8). He may of course refuse, thinking to pretend afterwards that he had not heard of the case; but God knows all, and will requite falsehood, not perhaps at once, but at a future time, when 'the lamp of the wicked shall be put out' (xxiv. 20). The wise men, as we have seen, clung firmly to the doctrine of retribution in some one of its various forms. We are not therefore surprised that a book of proverbs should conclude with a dissuasion from consorting with lawless persons, and an earnest advice to 'fear Jehovah and the king' (xxiv. 21).

Much need not be said of the second appendix (xxiv. 23–34). 'These also are by wise men,' writes the collector, implying that he is to be distinguished from the editor of the preceding collection. The proverbs are all[2] either in two, four, or six lines, except ver. 27, where however it is possible that some words have dropped out.[3] At the end comes a parable or apologue professedly drawn from the writer's experience (reminding us in this of vii. 6–23, but still more of Job v. 3–5). The scene is laid in a vineyard which has run to waste and become a wilderness from the carelessness of its

---

[1] The word for 'mast' is a ἄπ. λεγ. The Septuagint and Peshitto have 'as a steersman (or seaman) in great breakers.'

[2] xxiv. 23*b* is no exception; it is merely the first line of a hexastich.

[3] For 'and afterwards' the Hebrew has 'afterwards and thou shalt build.' 'And' may mean 'then,' marking out the perfect as consecutive, but it may also have been intended to join two parts of a sentence.

owner (comp. xx. 4). The *mashal* (xxiv. 30–32) has been lengthened by the addition of two verses from vi. 9, 10, originally no doubt a marginal note. It was needless; the story (if story it can be called) is more vivid in its brevity, and forms a fitting close to this section of proverbial wisdom.

CHAPTER IV.

THE SECOND COLLECTION AND ITS APPENDICES.

THE next proverbial anthology (xxv.–xxix.) like its chief predecessor is described in the heading as ' Proverbs of Solomon.'[1] The social state however presupposed in many of them is so different from that of the Solomonic age that we may at once reject the theory of the wise king's authorship. Another name with which in xxv. 1 the work is connected is that of Hezekiah, who has been suggestively called 'the Pisistratus of Judah.' The comparison halts, no doubt; for Pisistratus and his 'companions' meant to collect the whole of the Homeric poems, whereas completeness can hardly have been the object of those 'friends (or counsellors) of Hezekiah' who 'collected'[2] the 'Proverbs of Solomon' in xxv. 2–xxix. 27 ; at least, we know that there was much proverbial wisdom in circulation which had as good or as bad a claim to be called 'Solomonic' as the sayings which they have admitted into their anthology. It may indeed well be doubted whether the compilers had any thought of collecting the relics (now already

---

[1] 'These *also*' suggests that what follows is a last gleaning of Solomonic proverbs. And in fact xxv. 24, xxvi. 13, 15, 22, xxvii. 12, 13, 21*a*, seem to be taken from *the* 'Solomonic' collection. Hitzig however rejects this view. Why did not the collectors combine all the Solomonic proverbs they could find in one work ? So he supposes this new collection to have been made 'aus dem Volksmunde,' and remarks that a commission would be specially appropriate for this task. To me this seems an anachronism. The proverbs of the Hezekian collection are moreover as artistic as those of the first 'Solomonic.'

[2] So virtually the Septuagint (ἐξεγράψαντο), followed by the Peshitto and the Targum ; Aquila, μετῆραν. The Greek, curiously enough, inserts an epithet for the proverbs, viz. αἱ ἀδιάκριτοι, i.e. either impossible to distinguish, miscellaneous (so Sophocles, *Lexicon*), or better, difficult to interpret. Symmachus has ἀδιάκριτος for *bōhū*, Gen. i. 2. The Peshitto and Targum render the Greek of our passage by 'deep proverbs,' i.e. enigmatical ones (so too Aquila and Theodotion in the Syro-hexapla).

more than 200 years old) of the wise king. The style of these proverbs makes such a hypothesis even more improbable than in the case of x. 1–xxii. 16. The words with which the heading begins are of course not decisive, especially as the whole verse appears to be due, not to the royal officials who are spoken of, but to the author of the heading in xxiv. 23*a* (both headings begin with 'these also'). That Hezekiah was the instigator of the compilation, need not however be disputed. Even if not himself an author,[1] he may well have shared his friend Isaiah's interest in literature; and besides, it was at that time one of the glories of a great king to be the founder of a library.[2] The word used in describing the activity of his commissioners means literally 'transferred' (from one place to another), and will equally well apply to the noting down of oral traditions and to the making extracts from existing collections. Among the latter, the 'Proverbs of Solomon' in x. 1–xxii. 16 are of course to be included, though it is not quite certain whether the compilers of the later anthology had the book before them. It is true that nine proverbs are the same in the two books either absolutely (xxv. 24=xxi. 9, xxvi. 22=xviii. 8, xxvii. 12=xxii. 3, xxvii. 13=xx. 16) or virtually (xxvi. 13=xxii. 13, xxvi. 15 =xix. 24, xxviii. 6=xix. 1, xxviii. 19=xii. 11, xxix. 13 =xxii. 2), besides two which agree in one line (xxvii. 21 =xvii. 3, xxix. 22=xv. 18; comp. also xxvii. 15, xix. 13). But there still remains the question, Why the collectors took so little and left so much of manifest antiquity, and to this question we cannot expect to find an answer. All that we can say is that their compilation has striking characteristics of its own. In technicalities they admit a greater variety than those of the first anthology. They allow not only distichs but tristichs (xxv. 8, 13, 20, xxvii. 10, 22, xxviii. 10), tetrastichs (xxv. 4, 5, xxv. 9, 10, xxv. 21, 22, xxvi. 18, 19, xxvi. 24, 25, xxvii. 15, 16), and in one case a pentastich[3] (xxv. 6, 7), agreeing in this

[1] Cheyne, *The Prophecies of Isaiah*, i. 228-9 (on Isa. xxxviii. 9).
[2] Sayce's ed. of Smith's *Chaldean Genesis*, pp. 15, 26, 27.
[3] Sept., Symm., Pesh., Vulg., however, attach the last line of ver. 7 to ver. 8 ('Quæ viderunt oculi tui, ne proferas in jurgio cito'), which makes ver. 7 a distich and ver. 8 a tetrastich.

respect with the two appendices of the first anthology. There is also a long *mashal*, analogous to some we have had already, which can only with some laxity be called a proverb, and which extends over ten distichs (xxvii. 23-27). With regard to parallelism, the antithetic kind, which predominates in the first 'Solomonic' anthology, is rare in this collection, except in chaps. xxviii., xxix.; sometimes indeed there is no parallelism at all (see xxv. 8, 9, 10, 21, 22, xxvi. 18, 19, xxvii. 1, xxix. 12). As a compensation, similitudes abound in the three first chapters of the collection. Sometimes the comparison is expressed, e.g.

> As the cold of snow in the heat [1] of harvest
> is a faithful messenger to those that send him:
> he refreshes the soul of his master (xxv. 13);

at other times it is implied by the juxtaposition of the two objects, e.g.

> Apples of gold in chased work of silver,
> a word smoothly spoken [2] (xxv. 11).

Let us pause on this favourite proverb of Goethe's. The Hebrew 'wise men' would not have agreed to a later sage's depreciation of speech.[3] 'A word in due season, how good is it' (xv. 23); but when not only seasonable but set off by charms of style, how much better is it! The 'apples of gold' in xxv. 11 are probably oranges; the 'chased work of silver' means either baskets of silver filagree, or, as I should like to think with Mr. Neil, the brilliant white blossoms among which the golden fruit is seen peeping out. If the 'gold' is figurative, why not also the 'silver'? We are reminded of Andrew Marvell's lines in the 'Emigrants' Song,'

> He hangs in shades the orange bright,
> Like golden lamps in a green night,

---

[1] Reading *b'khōm* for *b'yōm* with Sept.

[2] Literally, 'a word spoken (or, perhaps, driven, or sent home) on its wheels,' i.e. smoothly and elegantly ('ore rotundo'). So Schultens, who sees a reference to the tropes and figures of elegant Oriental style. Comp. Neil, *Palestine Explored*, p. 197. The interpretation is an attractive one, though uncertain. Ewald has a slightly different view (see *History*, ii. p. 14, n. 6).

[3] Carlyle however borrows an Arabic proverb (Freytag, *Prov. Ar.*, iii. 92).

though Marvell forgot what Addison (*Spectator*, No. 455) well knew, that flowers as well as fruit and leaves continue on the orange-tree for the best part of the year.

But to return to our anthology. It would almost seem as if two editors with different tastes had been concerned in it, the one responsible for chaps. xxv.–xxvii., and the other for chaps. xxviii, xxix. According to Ewald, the proverbs in the latter section are mostly somewhat older than those in the former. This is perhaps an impression rather than a judgment; and few will deny that some at least of the parabolic proverbs in the first section may be as old as those of the same class in x. 1–xxii. 16.

It is difficult to suppose that many of the proverbs in either part of the book go back to a remote date. The cheerfulness of Israel's 'golden prime' is gone; society seems to have changed, not altogether for the better, even since the first great anthology was made. The king is still looked up to with awe; the book begins with a group of four sentences on the true glory of a monarch, followed by two on the right behaviour for a subject (xxv. 2–7). The king is described (surely with a touch of idealism) as inquisitive in the best sense; his 'heart,' or understanding, is unsearchable. But this happy view of monarchy passes away. There are several proverbs complaining of the wickedness of kings, which are almost without a parallel in the earlier collection. Ungodly rulers have made the people 'sigh' (xxix. 2); they have been like 'roaring lions and ravenous bears' to the 'poor folk' (xxviii. 15, 16), and have completely destroyed the freedom of social intercourse (xxviii. 12, 28). Sometimes, as in the northern kingdom after the death of Jeroboam II.,[1] the crown has become the object of competition to a crowd of pretenders (xxviii. 2). The misery of the people has been heightened by the greed of petty tyrants, according to the forcible saying,—

---

[1] It is of course possible that xxviii. 2 may be of northern origin, but why should not a wise man in Judah have watched with sympathy the course of events in Israel?

A man who is rich[1] and oppresses the poor
(is) a rain which sweeps away and gives no bread (xxviii. 3).

What kind of oppression is meant we may learn from Micah (ii. 3),—

And they covet lands and take them by violence;
houses, and take them away;
and they oppress the owner and his house,
a man and his inheritance.

It is in short the same unscrupulous accumulation of landed property to which Isaiah devotes one of his solemn 'woes' in his earliest prophecy, and which is one of the causes of the threatened captivity (Isa. v. 8–10 13). Exile has indeed become a familiar idea to those who admitted xxvii. 8 into the anthology, if, as most think, in the pathetic words of xxvii. 8 we may hear an echo of the march of Assyrian armies, 'to wander' being an euphemism for going into banishment.

As a bird that wanders from her nest,
so is a man that wanders[2] from his home (xxvii. 8).

As a rule, however, the proverbs relate to ordinary bourgeois life. Religious proverbs occur but rarely.[3] 'Folly' too is not so often mentioned as in the first collection, and the censure which it has to bear is mostly indirect and more or less satirical; see e.g. the proverb—

Though thou shouldest beat a fool in a mortar
in the midst of bruised corn with a pestle,
his folly would not depart from him (xxvii. 22),

and especially the paradoxical exhibition of the two sides of a truth—

Answer not the stupid man according to his folly,
lest thou thyself also become like unto him:
Answer the stupid man according to his folly,
lest he regard himself as wise (xxvi. 4, 5),

where the first distich dissuades from retaliating on a fool by a word or an action on his own low moral plane, while the

---

[1] Reading, with Grätz, '*āshīr* for *rāsh* 'poor,' which makes no sense.
[2] Sept. well ἀποξενωθῇ.
[3] Notice however the remarkable saying, already quoted, in xxix.

second recommends giving his folly the exposure or the sharp answer which it so richly deserves.¹ The wide meaning of 'folly' in this pair of proverbs may be illustrated by xvii. 12, where it evidently means a paroxysm of passion Next to this noisy passionate 'folly,' if we may judge from the arrangement of chap. xxvi., comes the vice of idleness (xxvi. 13–16). How dangerous this was felt to be we have seen already, and the exhortation to agricultural industry in xxvii. 23–27 forms a counterpart to the meditation on the 'field of the slothful' in xxiv. 30–32. If the motives urged for this and other duties are not lofty, the standard is at least an easily attainable one.

Sometimes, indeed, the eye sharpened by a regard to prudence discerns moral points of some refinement.² This proverb, for instance, strikes one as delicate, in spite of the prudential motive attached to it in the next verse,—

> Conduct thy quarrel with thy neighbour,
> but expose not the secret of another (xxv. 9);

and the well-known precept on showing kindness to one's enemies, though partly supported by the prospect of a reward (comp. xxiv. 17, 18), is so nobly expressed that an apostle can adopt it without change (Rom. xii. 20),—

> If one that hates thee hunger, give him bread to eat,
> and if he thirst, give him water to drink,
> for thou heapest coals of fire thereby
> upon his head, and Jehovah shall recompense thee (xxv. 21, 22).

Let us pause a moment on this proverb, which contrasts so strongly with the advice on the treatment of enemies given by Sirach. 'Coals of fire on the head' is probably here a metaphorical expression for what St. Augustine calls 'urentes conscientiæ gemitus' (*De doctr. Christ.*, l. iii., c. 16). The appositeness of the phrase will be heightened if we suppose the enemy spoken of to be one who has never heard

---

[1] The proverbs xxvi. 1, 3–12, form a string of satirical attacks on the 'fool' or stupid man.
[2] One of these points however is noticed in the earliest part of the Law. The love of one's enemy is taught in Ex. xxiii. 4, 5.

of the wise man's rule—a man of rude, uncultured nature, and perhaps of alien race. To such a one, the being fed by the very man whom he 'hated' would give first of all a shock of surprise, and then a pang of intolerable remorse for his own unworthiness.[1] I wish one could be sure that this pang was referred to as purifying as well as painful to the sufferer. A parallel passage would be a great boon. Of course we can *apply* the passage in the same sense as St. Paul when he followed his quotation with the words, 'Be not overcome of evil, but overcome evil with good.'

But we should wrong our 'wise men' by treating them as pure utilitarians; they are often sympathetic observers of character and circumstance. For instance,—

> Vinegar falling upon a wound,[2]
> and he who sings songs to a heavy heart (xxv. 20).
> Silver dross spread over an earthen vessel—
> fervent lips[3] and a bad heart (xxvi. 23).
> Let another man praise thee, and not thine own mouth;
> a stranger, and not thine own lips (xxvii. 2).
> Faithful are the wounds of one who loves,
> but the kisses of a hater are profuse[4] (xxvii. 6).
> Thine own friend, and thy father's friend, forsake not;
> and go not to thy brother's house in the day of thy calamity:
> better is a near neighbour than a far off brother[5] (xxvii. 10).
> He who blesses his friend with a loud voice, rising early in the morning,
> it is reckoned to him for a curse[6] (xxvii. 14).
> Iron is sharpened by iron,
> and a man sharpens the face (or edge) of his friend (xxvii. 17).

---

[1] See however Mr. Yonge in *The Expositor*, Aug. 1885, pp. 158-9.

[2] The received text has 'vinegar upon nitre;' but this would be rather an emblem for anger. The correction is Bickell's, and is partly founded on Sept. (ὥσπερ ὄξος ἕλκει ἀσύμφορον). The opening words of the verse in rec. text arise from the repetition in a corrupt form of the four last words of the preceding verse (Lagarde and Bickell).

[3] The Septuagint has 'smooth lips.'

[4] To have added 'but perfidious,' would have made the line too long.

[5] This seems a combination of two distinct proverbs. The one says that a friend can give more sympathy than a relative; the other, that a neighbour, being on the spot, can give more help than a relative at a distance.

[6] A humorous picture! Such ostentatious and inopportune salutations are execrable flattery.

The three appendices to the Hezekian collection (xxx., xxxi. 1–9, xxxi. 10–31) are, to take the most conservative position possible, obviously not earlier than the closing century of the Jewish state. The art of proverb-writing has declined ever since the compilation of the previous anthology. The marks of simplicity and naturalness are wanting; the enigmatical and artificial seem to be sought for. Each part of these two chapters has moreover something of its own pointing in the direction of a late origin. The two first appendices are very possibly even later than the return of the Jews from Babylon.

The first appendix begins—'The words of Agur the son of Jakeh, the prophecy' (or, divine utterance)[1] (comp. xxxi. 1). The heading is enigmatical; in what sense are the 'words' 'a prophecy,' and who are the persons spoken of? The latter question we have no means of answering. The names are not found elsewhere, and have been thought to be pseudonyms (Agur might mean 'collector' and Jakeh 'obedient,' i.e. 'religious').[2] As to the title 'the prophecy,' it must be admitted that it is not by any means an appropriate one. It is too bold to accuse the proverb-writer of claiming prophetic inspiration. (And why should the article be prefixed?) The only alternative to this is to read, with Prof. Grätz, (for *hammassā* 'the prophecy') *hammōshēl* 'the proverb-writer.' After the heading comes a group of four verses complete in itself.

> The oracle of the man 'I have wearied [3] myself about God' (?),
> I have wearied myself about God and have not prevailed.[4]
> For I am too stupid for a man,
> and am without human reason;
> I have not learned wisdom,
> nor have I knowledge of the All-holy.[5]
> Who has gone up to heaven and come down?

[1] On the conjectural reading, 'the man of Massa' ('Massa,' instead of 'the prophecy'), see Chap. VI.

[2] This was the view of St. Jerome, derived of course from his Jewish teacher.

[3] Pointing *lāīthī*.

[4] Reading with Bickell *v'lō ūkāl*. Another correction of the text is, *v'ēkel* 'and have pined away.'

[5] *Q'dōshīm*, a word formed on the analogy of *elōhīm*; comp. ix. 10, Hos. xii. 1.

who has gathered the wind in his fists?
who has bound up the waters in a garment?
who has established all the ends of the earth?
what is his name, and what is his son's name, if thou knowest?

It is not easy to interpret this little passage. Evidently the speaker is a 'wise man,' who, according to some critics, inculcates a reverent humility by reporting the fruitlessness of his own theological speculations. After long brooding over the problems of the divine nature (so they explain), the Hebrew sage was compelled to desist with the feeling of his utter incapacity. Like Israel the patriarch he strove with God, but unlike Israel he did not prevail. He knows indeed what God has done and is continually doing; He is the Omnipresent One, the Lord of wind and flood, the Author of the boundaries of the earth. But what is this great Being's name, and (to know Him intimately) what is His son's name? On this view of its meaning, the passage reminds one of the words of Goethe's Faust, 'Who can name Him, or who confess, I believe Him? Who can feel, and can be bold to say, I believe Him not?' Or perhaps we may still better compare Max Letteris' masterly Hebrew translation or adaptation, in which the mediæval doctor has been transformed into Ben Abuyah (or Acher אַחֵר), the famous apostate from Judaism in the second century of our era. The passage with which we are concerned as illustrative of the passage before us is on page 164, and begins מִי יַפְּיְרֵהוּ וּמִי יְכַנֵּהוּ. Notice the delicate tact in the choice of the second verb, 'Who can give Him an honourable surname?' (comp. Isa. xliv. 5, xlv. 4.) Later on, after other names suggested by the German original, the modern Hebrew poet continues, אוֹ בְּיָהּ שְׁמוֹ כִּי נִשְׂגָּב הַצְפִירוּ, and in a note refers to a parallel passage in a Hebrew poem by Ibn Gabirol.

I must make bold to doubt the correctness of this explanation. (1) Because it does not sufficiently account for the language of ver. 2. (2) Because upon this view of the questions of ver. 4, an Israelite's answer would simply be, Jehovah (comp. Job xxxviii. 5, Isa. xl. 12). (3) Because it is so difficult to see why the poet should have asked further,

What is His son's name? Is not the passage rather a philosophic fragment from a school of 'wise men,' not so much unbelieving as critical? The speaker declares, soberly enough, that he has tried in vain by thinking to find out God. Then comes in a piece of irony. No doubt it is his own stupidity; grand theologians, such as the writer of Isa. xl. 12 &c., Job xxxviii., Prov. viii. 22 &c., may well look down upon the dullard, who has not passed through their school! 'But who is it that is ever and anon coming down [1] to earth, and that performed all these creative works of which you delight to speak? I have never seen him; tell me his name and his son's name since you are so learned.' The latter phrase may be an allusion, either (anticipating Philo, who calls Wisdom God's Son) to the 'I was brought forth' in viii. 24, or more probably [2] the primeval man (who might be called a 'son of God' in the sense of Luke iii. 38) spoken of in Job xv. 7, who was the embodiment of all wisdom and sat in the council of Elohim.[3] The satirical turn of this secularistic 'wise man' is even perhaps traceable in the heading of his poem. He calls his work an 'oracle,' taking up a favourite word of the disciples of the prophets, and flinging it back to them with a laugh. Obviously too the name of the writer, if genuine, is best explained as an assumed name. [But the emphatic *haggebher* is very difficult. I cannot believe, with Ewald, that *haggebher* is said ironically, as if 'the mighty one in his own conceit;' comp. Isa. xxii. 17 (?), Ps. lii. 3. The analogy of Num. xxiv. 3, 15, 2 Sam. xxiii. 1, suggests that there is a corruption in the text, and that *haggebher*, 'the man,' was originally followed by words descriptive of the person referred to. Grätz boldly corrects (*haggebher*) *lō-khayil* 'the man without strength.]

Are we surprised at this? But a strikingly parallel con-

---

[1] It may be objected that 'hath gone up and come down' does not suit this explanation, and that, to refer to God, it should run 'hath come down and gone up.' But we have 'angels of Elohim ascending and descending' in Gen. xxviii. 12; usage, in Hebrew as in English, forbids the phrase 'to go down and up.'

[2] 'More probably;' because the name of the speaker in viii. 24 has been told.

[3] Comp. Ewald, *Die Lehre der Bibel von Gott*, iii. 2, pp. 81, 82.

fession of honest scepticism is found in the Rig Veda (x. 129), though I would not of course identify the opinions of the Sanskrit and the Hebrew poet,

Who knows, who here can declare, whence has sprung—whence, this creation? .... From what this creation arose; and whether [any one] made it, or not,—he who in the highest heaven is its ruler, he verily knows, or [even] he does not know.[1]

The poet who 'takes up his parable' after Laithi-el calmly and uncontroversially indicates his own very different religious position. He earnestly prays that he may not 'become a liar and ask, Who is Jehovah?' (xxx. 9); for him the divine revelations (the outward form of which is already sacred) are amply sufficient. 'Every utterance of God [*Eloah*, the sing. form, as in Job] is free from alloy (xxx. 5; see the commentators on Ps. xviii. 31); the divine 'name' declared in Ex. xxxiv. 6, should satisfy the wisest of men. Thus, like the editors of Ecclesiastes, this later writer neutralises the doubtful expressions of the poem which he has saved from perishing.

Can we avoid the impression that both these poets lived in an age of advanced religious reflection and of Scripture-study? The one is more of a philosopher, the other of a Biblical theologian; both would be at home only in the Exile or in the post-Exile period, when doubt and even scepticism lifted their heads side by side with Biblical study. Our second more believing poet seems to be thinking of Ps. xviii. 30; but the portion of that verse which he adopts assumes another colour through the warning which follows, derived from Deut. iv. 1, xiii. 1. It is no longer the 'promise of God' which is 'tried' or 'pure,' but the revelation of which the Jewish Church is gradually finding itself the possessor.

The poet's prayer for himself (vv. 7-9) is followed by eight groups of proverbs, each of which describes some quality or character which is either commended or warned against, and (with the exception of the first) contains a similitude. In most of these the number four is conspicuous generally as the climax after 'three' (vv. 15, 18, 21, 29).

[1] Muir, *Original Sanskrit Texts*, v. 356; comp. Max Müller, *Hibbert Lectures*, p. 316.

The fact that similar 'numerical proverbs' were popular in the early Rabbinical period,[1] gives a certain support to the view that this collection is of late origin. The groups referred to are—

The four marks of an evil generation	vv. 11–14
The four insatiable things	— 15, 16
The fate of the disobedient son	— 17
The four incomprehensible things	— 18–20
— — intolerable things	— 21–23
— — wise animals	— 24–28
— — comely in going (see p. 175)	— 29–31
A warning against strife	— 32, 33.

One of these (vv. 15, 16) has probably suffered a slight mutilation, which has been thus remedied by Bickell,—

> The leech has two [three [2]] daughters,
> they say continually, 'Give, give:'
> there are three things which are never satisfied,
> four which never say, 'Abundance.'
> Sheól is never satisfied with dead,
> and the closing of the womb is never satisfied with men,
> the earth is never satisfied with water,
> and fire never says, 'Abundance.'[3]

'Daughters of the leech' is a quasi-mythical expression, which no one could misunderstand (comp. 'upon a hill the son of oil,' Isa. v. 1). We find a similar group of four insatiables in the Sanskrit Hitopadesa.[4]

> Fire is never satisfied with fuel; nor the ocean with rivers; nor death with all creatures; nor bright-eyed women with men.

The verses are of course older than the trumpery story of the cowherd's wife which they serve to illustrate. The coincidence with the Hebrew, being obviously accidental, is worth remembering in other connections. The two parallels, present in

---

[1] See above, p. 128, and comp. Wünsche, *Midrasch Kohelet*, p. xiii.

[2] Sept., followed by Pesh., reads 'three' for 'two.' Accepting this reading, the second half of the verse becomes an explanation of the first.

[3] Bickell's reconstruction of the text makes the proverbs symmetrical with the rest. In lines 5, 6 he makes an ingenious parallelism with *mēthīm* 'dead' and *m'thīm* 'men' (i.e. children).

[4] F. Johnson's translation (1848), chap. ii., fable 7; comp. Fritze's metrical version (Leipz. 1884).

the Hebrew but not in this Sanskrit quaternion, are given in a quatrain of a Vedic hymn to Varuna—

> The path of ships across the sea,
> The soaring eagle's flight he knows.[1]

The second appendix (xxxi. 1-9) consists of a single group of sayings, described as 'the words of Lemuel, a king, the prophecy [better the proverb, reading *māshāl*] with which his mother instructed him.' Possibly, as Ewald suggests, Lemuel (or rather, Lemoel, as the word is pointed in ver. 4) is an imaginary name, descriptive of the character of an ideal monarch ('God's own;' comp. Lael, Num. iii. 24). It is not necessary to suppose that the poet himself lived under a native king; he may, like the author of Koheleth, have thrown himself back in imagination to Israel's golden prime. His own period was late, judging from the unclassical Hebrew (notice the Aramaisms in vv. 2, 3, and the strange expressions in vv. 5, 8). The form of the heading suggests that these 'words of Lemuel' formed part of the same collection as the 'words of Agur;' and there is at least nothing in the contents to forbid this view. The warnings of this queen-mother [2] (whose relation to Lemuel reminds us of that of Bathsheba to Solomon) are very homely and practical; one is against sensuality, another against drunkenness; upon which follows an admonition to defend the cause of the poor. Even if there were no native king at the time, the advice would be appropriate for all members of the upper class of society.

The third appendix (xxxi. 10-31) contains the praise of the virtuous woman. In style it is quite unlike the two preceding sections; it must come therefore from another source. It is an alphabetic poem; each distich begins with a letter of the Hebrew alphabet. This, combined with the position of the work at the close of the various collections of proverbs, of itself suggests a date not far removed on the one side or the other from the Exile-period, when Hebrew literature became undoubtedly more artificial and technical. From

---

[1] Muir, *Metrical Translations* (1879), p. 160.

[2] On the early importance of the queen-mother, see Cheyne's *Isaiah*, i. 47, note 1 (on Isa. vii. 13).

xxxi. 23 ('the elders of the land') we may perhaps infer that it was written in Palestine. It is very interesting to see the ideal of womanhood formed by a late Hebrew poet. Activity appears to him the one great feminine virtue—not however the activity which is entirely devoted to trifling details, for the ideal woman 'is like the ships of the merchant; from far she brings her food' (ver. 14). Nor is she a stranger to sympathetic impulses; 'she holds out her hand (with something in it) to the afflicted; and stretches forth her hands to the needy [to bring them in],' ver. 20. Nor must we forget 'one of the most beautiful features in the portrait' (Delitzsch): 'she opens her mouth with wisdom, and a law of kindness is on her tongue' (ver. 26). But for this verse, indeed, it would read almost like satire that 'far above pearls is her value' (ver. 10), since no higher estimate than this has been offered for God's choicest blessing, 'Wisdom.'[1]

The poet does not say that he has found such a woman (comp. Eccles. vii. 28). The picture is perhaps too brightly coloured to be drawn from reality, unless with Hitzig we bring down the composition of the poem as late as the Greek period. Most probably, it is idealistic.

[1] This hardly recommends the view of Castelli, that this poem is properly the conclusion of the introductory treatise (i.-ix.)

CHAPTER V.

THE PRAISE OF WISDOM.

'THOU hast kept the good wine until now,' for 'good wine' well describes the glorious little treatise at the head of our Book of Proverbs (i. 7–ix. 18). I do not think it is right to infer from the heading in i. 1 that its unknown author assumed the mask of Solomon. In itself such a hypothesis would not be incredible. We have the analogy of the Egyptian scribe who represents Amenemhat I. 'rising up like a god' and addressing to his son some instructions on the royal art of governing.[1] But it is more natural to explain the heading as a repetition of the formula in x. 1, for the 'Praise of Wisdom' (to coin another title) is in fact the introduction to the following anthology,[2] together with which and its appendices it forms the 'older book of Proverbs.' If we ask why an introduction was prefixed, the answer must be that the writer wished to recommend his own inspiring view of practical ethics as a branch of divine wisdom ; in other words, to counteract the sometimes commonplace morality of the earlier proverbs by enveloping the reader in a purer and more ethereal atmosphere. The key-note of the anthology is nothing but Experience ; that of the introductory treatise is Divine Teaching. It is a sign of moral progress that the editor of an anthology of Experience should have thought his work only half-done till he had prefixed the 'Praise of Wisdom.' As a wise teacher of our own time [3] has observed, ' It would not be untrue to say that in all essential points Experience is the teacher

---

[1] (Maspero) *Records of the Past*, ii. 9–16.
[2] Its close relation to the first of the two great anthologies is shown by the linguistic points of contact between the two works (see Chap. VI.)
[3] Rev. J. H. Thorn.

only of fools, of those who have gone astray through turning a deaf ear to the voice of a prior and more legitimate teacher.' The nature of the wisdom so earnestly commended by this self-forgetting writer, we will consider presently; and our study will probably convince us that such a writer can only have arisen at an advanced period of Israel's history. The class or circle to which he belonged, and its characteristics, can easily be determined; but the precise period only with some degree of hesitation. Without anticipating the discussion which will be given at another point, I think it may safely be laid down that each of those kindred poems—the 'Praise of Wisdom' and 'Job'—must have arisen at one of three periods, marked respectively by the composition of Deuteronomy, by the Captivity, and by the Restoration. The progress of the higher Israelitish wisdom was so gradual that it does not perhaps, to the exegete as distinguished from the historian, greatly matter which of these periods we select. For my own part, however, I incline to connect at any rate the former of these works with the age of Deuteronomy. Apart from the details to be mentioned elsewhere, it is clear (I speak now of Prov. i.–ix.) that the tone of the exhortations, and the view of religion as ' having the promise of the life that now is,' correspond to similar characteristics of the Book of Deuteronomy. And if we turn from the contents to the form of this choice little book, the same hypothesis seems equally suitable. The prophets had long since seen the necessity of increasing their influence by committing the main points of their discourses to writing; some rhetorical passages indeed were evidently composed to be read and not to be heard. It was natural that the moralists should follow this example, not only (as in the anthologies) by remodelling their wise sayings for publication, but also by venturing on long and animated quasi-oratorical recommendations of great moral truths.

Such a recommendation, addressed especially to the young and impressionable (i. 4), lies before us in chaps. i.–ix. In grave but harmonious accents the opening verses (which refer chiefly to i. 7–ix. 18, but not without a secondary reference to the anthology which follows) describe its object and character.

Then follows a motto, the first line of which occurs again near the close of the book in ix. 10 (Job xxviii. 28, Ps. cxi. 10), and which stamps the author as belonging to a new and more religious class of 'wise men' (see p. 121),—

The fear of Jehovah is the beginning of wisdom,

i.e. the foundation of true wisdom (its 'root,' Ecclus. i. 20) is reverence. The disciple is to begin by taking this upon trust, but when further advanced he will see that it is the shortest way to his goal, true wisdom having an objective existence in the unseen world. At present he is simply to follow the 'direction' of those wiser than himself:—our moralist is as zealous for a *tōra* as the author of Deuteronomy. But though serious and authoritative, he is never stern; indeed, to enforce his appeal he breaks through a Hebrew writer's usual veil of reticence and describes his own home-life (iv. 3, 4). He can enter into the feelings of the young, for he too has 'borne the yoke in his youth' (Lam. iii. 27), and learned to prefer it to 'unchartered freedom.' The whole of chap. iv. is devoted to a summary of the wise doctrine which he received from his father; indeed, throughout the book he shows a wonderful appreciation of the parental and the filial relations, and, according to Ewald's arrangement (see below), begins each section with an exhortation to listen to parental instruction. He himself feels like a father to his young disciples (iv. 1).

The errors to which his hearers are specially tempted are highway robbery (i. 11-18, iv. 16, 17) and unchastity (ii. 16, v. 3-20, vi. 24-35, vii. 5-27, ix. 13-18). From the time that the simplicity of the ancient life began to give way to the inroads of luxury, we meet in the Biblical writings with complaints of acts of violence leading to murder (see, for instance, in the prophecies, Isa. i. 15, v. 7, xxxiii. 15, Mic. iii. 10, Jer. ii. 34, xxii. 17, Isa. lix. 3, 7, and in a collection of proverbs contemporary with our book, Prov. xxiv. 15, 16). 'At no time,' as Dean Plumptre well remarks, 'has Palestine ever risen to the security of a well-ordered police-system;' even down to the fall of Jerusalem, bands of robbers defied the authority of the central government. The remarkable thing is that young men in the higher circles of society (for such our moralist appears to address) should be thought capable of joining the banditti, at a time when 'bandit' could not be synonymous with 'patriot.' Our moralist contents himself with dissuading his disciple from doing so, on the ground of the retribution which will follow (i. 18, 19). The exhortation to industry, with its slow but sure profits, comes later, and in a less appropriate place (vi. 6-8). But the other besetting sin of youth is still more earnestly denounced as the most glaring specimen of 'folly.' Once indeed the 'strange, or alien, woman,' i.e. the adulteress, is introduced dramatically as 'Madam Folly' (ix. 13). The picture is remarkable, and forms a designed contrast to that at the beginning of the chapter. She sits at the door of her house, counterfeiting her great rival Wisdom (comp. ver. 14 with ver. 3, and ver. 16 with ver. 4), like Dante's Siren; but the disciple of the 'wise man' knows

. . . . that phantoms are there,
and that her guests are in the depths of Sheól
(ix. 18; comp. ii. 18, xxi. 16).

'Wherewithal shall a young man cleanse his way?' is the problem for our moralist to solve. He does so by insisting on an education conducted in reliance on divine Wisdom. The reward of diligent attention to the earlier lessons (for each chapter is a lesson, and its repetitions have a pedagogic justification) is the famous portrait of Wisdom in viii. 22-31. She (for Wisdom, *khokma*, is a feminine word) has indeed been mentioned before (i. 20, iii. 13-20, iv. 5-9), but from viii. 1 to ix. 6 the poet is absorbed in his grand personification. Wisdom is now presented to us, in the familiar dialect of poetry, as the firstborn Child of the Creator. There is but one Wisdom; though her forms are many, in her origin she is one. The Wisdom who presided over the 'birth' of nature is the same who by her messengers (the 'wise men') calls mankind to turn aside from evil (ix. 3). There can therefore be no real disharmony between nature and morality; the picture leaves no room for an Ahriman, in this and other respects resembling the Cosmogony in Gen. i. and portions of the striking descriptions in Job xxvi., xxviii., xxxviii. There is also no time when we can say that 'Wisdom was not.' Faith declares that even in that primitive Chaos of which our reason has a horror divine Wisdom reigned supreme. The heavenly ocean, the ancient hills, the combination of countless delicate atoms to form the ground, the fixing of the vault of heaven on the world-encircling ocean, the separation of sea and dry land [1]—all these were later works of God than the Architect through whom He made them. And how did the Architect work? By a 'divine improvisation' which allowed no sense of effort or fatigue, and which still continues with unabated freshness. But though her sportive path [2] can still be traced in the processes of nature, her highest delight is in the regeneration of the moral life of humanity. The passage runs thus—

> Jehovah produced [3] me as the beginning of his way,
> as the first of his works, long since.
> From of old I received my place,
> from the beginning, from the first times of the earth.
> When there were no floods, I was brought forth,
> when there were no fountains rich in water.
> Before the mountains were settled,
> before the hills was I brought forth;
> While as yet he had not made the earth with (its) fields,
> and the atoms of dust which form the ground.
> When he established the heaven, I was there,
> when he marked a circle upon the face of the flood, [4]

[1] The poet, we can see, has not arranged the creative works as carefully as the cosmogonist in Genesis.

[2]   Pleaseth him, the Eternal Child,
    To play his sweet will, glad and wild.—Emerson, *Wood Notes*.

[3] 'Produced' seems the best rendering (Sept., ἔκτισε), in the sense of 'creating,' not (as Del.) of 'revealing,' for which there is no authority. The secondary meaning 'possessed' (Aquila &c. ἐκτήσατο, Vulg. *possedit*; comp. Ecclus. xxiv. 6) is less agreeable to the context (see Hitzig's note). There is the same diversity of rendering in Gen. xiv. 19-22. On the patristic expositions of this passage, see Dean Goode, *The Divine Rule of Faith and Practice*, ed. 1, i. 299. The ante-Nicene Fathers mostly apply it to the divine generation of the Son, the post-Nicene to the generation of the human nature of Christ. Basil and Epiphanius are exceptions. The former applies the passage to 'that wisdom which the apostle mentions' (in 1 Cor. i. 21); the latter expresses a strong opinion that 'it does not at all speak concerning the Son of God.'

[4] Comp. Milton's noble conception of the Creator's golden compasses (*Par. Lost*, vii. 225, 6).

When he made firm the sky above,
when he strengthened the fountains of the flood,
When he appointed to the sea his bound,
that the waters should not transgress his command,
when he fixed the foundations of the earth,
Then was I beside him as architect,
and was daily full of delight,
sporting [1] before him at all times,
I who (still) have sport with his fruitful earth,
and have my delight with the sons of men.

The bold originality of this passage requires no proof. It cuts away at a blow the old mythical conception of the world as the work of God's hands, and of an arbitrary omnipotence. 'God,' as Hooker says, 'is a law both to himself and to all things beside;' 'his wisdom hath stinted the effects of his power.' 'Nor is the freedom of the will of God any whit abated, let, or hindered, by means of this; because the imposition of this law upon himself is his own free and voluntary act' ('Jehovah produced me'). The idea, then, of the world as a Cosmos was not adopted by the Jews from the Greeks; it arose of itself as soon as religious men pondered over the phenomena of nature. The author of *Job* took up the idea, and reexpressed it worthily in xxviii. 12–28, the chief difference between him and his predecessor being that he denies the attainableness for man of wisdom in the larger sense, while the author of the 'Praise of Wisdom' does not raise the question whether the higher department of wisdom is open to human enquiry.

At the subsequent history of the conception of Wisdom we can barely glance.[2] The cosmogonist in Gen. i., a sublime

---

[1] Comp. Delitzsch, *System der christlichen Apologetik*, § 16, where the history of this conception in Jewish literature is traced in connection with that of the Logos-idea; also Ewald, *Die Lehre der Bibel von Gott*, iii. 74–77.

[2] In Wisd. vii. 22 &c. the language appears to some to rise above poetical personification, and to imply a conscious hypostatising of Wisdom. Dante, a good judge on this point, certainly thought otherwise (*Convito*, iii. 15); he evidently holds that the Sophia of the Book of Wisdom is precisely analogous to his own very strong personification of divine Philosophy. Still such language may have partly prepared the way for the well-known Gnostic myth of Achamoth or Sophia (comp. Baur, *Three First Centuries*, E. T., i. 207). It was well, as Plumptre remarks, that Philo adopted Logos rather than Sophia as the name of

M

thinker, but addressing untutored minds, preferred to convey truth in forms borrowed from mythology. The moralists however saw the poetical and religious importance of the personification of Wisdom, and repeatedly introduced it into their didactic works (see Ecclus. i., xxiv., Wisd. vi.–ix.,[1] and comp. Bar. iii. 29-37). Sirach even takes a step in advance of his original, and at least for a moment identifies Wisdom with the Law of Moses.[2] It became indeed a tradition of Jewish exegesis (see *Pirke Aboth*, vi. 10) to interpret the absolute Khokma of the Tora, either in opposition to Hellenistic views of the higher wisdom, or from a practical instinct such as Wordsworth followed when in praise of Duty he employed figures which had occurred long before in the 'Praise of Wisdom,' or (a closer parallel) Richard Hooker, when he described the Scripture as one embodiment of that divine Law which he so splendidly eulogises at the close of his first book. That Jewish legalism degenerated into a mechanical formalism, should not blind us to the practical instinct in which it originated.

The title 'The Praise of Wisdom' has now, I hope, been justified. The passage quoted above forms the high-water mark of this elevated poetry, and points the way to the grand things in the poem of Job. Regularity of structure is not a merit of our treatise, but the repetitions are not feeble, and are perhaps deliberately made. The author is a *didactic* poet, and only after he can presume that his lessons have been assimilated will he venture on his highest flights. Does Ewald bear this in mind when he divides the book into three sections, I. a general exhortation to wisdom, in which the

the creative energy. A system in which Sophia had been the dominant word might have led to an earlier development of Mariolatry (Introduction to Proverbs in the *Speaker's Commentary*).

[1] Ecclus. xxiv. 23. (Comp. a sublime passage of E. Irving, identifying the contents of the 'sacred volume' with 'the primeval divinity of revealed Wisdom,' *Miscellanies*, p. 380 &c.) According to late Jewish theology, the Law is one of the seven things produced before the creation of the world. The alphabet-fables in Talmud and Midrash, in which letters of the alphabet converse with God, pre-suppose the same view (comp. the Mohammedan view of the Korán).

[2] So Milton (a Hebraist), *Paradise Lost*, vii. 10 ('didst play'), and again in *Tetrachordon* ('God himself conceals not his own recreations,' &c.)

whole of the truth is touched upon, but no part is completely unfolded (i. 8–iii. 35); II. an exhaustive treatment of a few details (iv. 1–vi. 19); III. a gradual rise to the highest and most universal truth, closing in almost lyric enthusiasm (vi. 20–ix. 18)? Or Hitzig, when, to suit an artificial arrangement, he omits as later additions iii. 22–26, vi. 1–19, viii. 4–12, 14–16, ix. 7–10? These are the two extremes of critical theory; their failure may be taken as a proof that the only possible division is one like that of Delitzsch into fifteen poems, rather loosely connected together, but presenting the same peculiarities of style and diction. *Mashals* we can only term them in a wide sense of the word; not condensation but expansion is the characteristic of this book; the discourse flows on till the subject has been exhausted, and then, after a brief pause, it gushes forth anew. One of the chapters (ii.) actually forms a single carefully elaborated sentence. Now and then the matter is more broken up; we meet with some small groups of detached sentences (e.g. iii. 27–35, vi. 1–11, 12–19), which introduce some variety into the style, and suggest that the author revised his work with the view of making it an ethical manual, as well as an introduction to the anthology. In one of these groups we find the interesting similitude of the ant, which the Septuagint has supplemented by one of purely Greek origin (see Hitzig and Lagarde) on the bee.

The author has the pen of a ready writer, and his work shows that he has studied the literature of his time. He was familiar [1] with the phraseology of the 'Solomonic' proverbs, though he struck out a style of his own, in harmony with the altered conditions of the teaching office. He addresses those who have time to listen, and taste to appreciate his flowing rhetoric. He implies throughout that his audience belongs to the wealthier class, and his favourite images are drawn from the life of the merchant.[2] Clearly too he has a strong hold upon the doctrine that prosperity and adversity are indicative of moral character. Thus, speaking of ethical Wisdom, he says,

---

[1] The proof of this cannot be given here.
[2] See ii. 4, iii. 13–15, iv. 7, vii. 16, 17, 19, 20 (especially), viii. 10, 18–21.

> Length of days is in her (Wisdom's) right hand,
> in her left riches and honour (iii. 16).[1]

And yet there is evidence, even in Prov. i.–ix., of a nascent scepticism on this point, originating probably in some recent event, such as the captivity of the Ten Tribes. In words which remind us of Psalms xxxvii. and lxxiii. the writer exclaims—

> Envy thou not the man of violence,
> and have thou pleasure in none of his ways . . .
> The curse of Jehovah is in the house of the ungodly,
> but the habitation of the righteous he blesses (iii. 31, 33);

and to furnish his disciples with an answer to the sceptic—

> Truly, whom Jehovah loves, he corrects,
> and as a father the son in whom he delights
> (iii. 12 ; comp. Job v. 17).

With this sweet saying I take leave for the present of this beautiful work. How true it is that the doubts of a believer are the stepping-stones to higher attainments of faith!

[1] Comp. i. 32, 33, ii. 21, 22, iii. 1–10, ix. 11, 12, 18.

CHAPTER VI.

SUPPLEMENTARY ON QUESTIONS OF DATE AND ORIGIN.

THERE are two extreme views on the date of the Book of Proverbs, between which are the theories of the mass of moderate critics. The one is that represented by Keil in his Introduction and Bishop Ellicott's Commentary, that the whole book except chaps. xxx., xxxi., and perhaps the heading i. 1-6, is in substance of Solomonic origin;[1] the other is that of Vatke and Reuss (the precursors of Kuenen and Wellhausen) that our proverbs as a collection come from the post-Exile period. Much need not be said on the first of these extreme views. It has been pointed out already that the ethical and religious character even of the earliest proverbial collection stands far removed from that of the historical Solomon. It is indeed a pure hypothesis that any Solomonic element survives in the Book of Proverbs. I doubt not that many bright and witty *sayings* of Solomon came into circulation, and some of them might conceivably have been gathered up and included in the anthologies. But have we any adequate means of deciding which these are? It would appear from 1 Kings iv. 33 that the wisdom of the historical Solomon expressed itself in *spoken* fables or moralisations about animals and trees. A few, a very few, of the proverbs in our book may perhaps satisfy the test thus obtained, and be plausibly represented as a Solomonic element. But why Solomon should be singled out as the author, it would tax one's ingenuity to say, and the judgment of Hitzig (in such matters a conservative critic) must be maintained that the survival of Solomonic proverbs is no more than a possibility.[2]

[1] Keil qualifies this however by admitting that Solomon may have incorporated many sayings of other wise men.   [2] *Die Sprüche Salomo's*, p. xvii.

The other extreme view requires some little explanation. Vatke does not deny that Solomon composed proverbs, but only that his proverbs can have resembled those in the canonical book. Putting aside some sayings of earlier date Vatke holds that the stamp of the post-Exile period (and more particularly of the fifth century) is as marked in the Book of Proverbs as it is, according to him, in that of Job; in short, that both works imply, equally with the still later Ecclesiastes, a long and earnest struggle between the principles represented respectively by the higher prophets and by the priests. The result of this struggle has become to the authors of these books an objective truth which it is henceforth their business to realise as true subjectively.[1] The existence of a free-minded school of thought in the post-Exile period is very plausibly defended both by Vatke and by Kuenen,[2] and if our only choice lay between the extreme alternatives mentioned above, we should be shut up to the acceptance of the latter.

I shall not however discuss here the post-Exile origin of the Book of Proverbs as a whole, but only that part of the hypothesis which relates to the very interesting section designated by Ewald the 'Praise of Wisdom.' If this portion is not of Exile or post-Exile origin, I do not see how it can be maintained that any other part of the book is so, except indeed the sayings of Agur and Lemuel (xxx. 1–xxxi. 9).

The following are some of the leading arguments for the late origin of Prov. i.–ix. I. These chapters are said to contain a few parallels to passages in works belonging probably to the Exile or post-Exile period (II. Isaiah,[3] Job). I lay no stress on the occurrence of Prov. i. 16 (with the addition of 'innocent') in Isa. lix. 7a, because this verse is not in the rhythm of the rest of Prov. i.–ix., and is not found in the Septuagint. There may however be a parallelism between Prov. ii. 15 and Isa. lix. 8; the prophet is, at any rate, influenced by some proverbial work similar to Prov. i.–ix.

---

[1] *Die biblische Theologie*, i. 563.   [2] *The Religion of Israel*, ii. 242.

[3] The passages in II. Isaiah referred to in this paragraph belong to sections most probably of post-Exile origin. (See art. 'Isaiah' in *Encyclopædia Britannica*, new ed.)

There may also be one between Prov. i. 24, 26, 27 and Isa. lxv. 12, lxvi. 4. More striking are the affinities already pointed out between Prov. i.–ix. and the Book of Job, which may be taken to prove that these works proceeded from the same circle of 'wise men,' but not necessarily that they are of the same period (see above, p. 85).

II. As to the religious ideas of these chapters. (*a*) The Theism expressed is both pure und broad. Polytheism is not even worthy to be the subject of controversy; the tone is throughout positive. Jehovah's vast creative activity fills the writer's mind, and begins to stimulate speculative curiosity; from this point of view comp. Prov viii. 22-31 with Job xv. 7, 8,[1] xxxviii. 4–11, and Gen. i. (The affinities with the cosmogony are only general,[2] but perhaps gain in importance when taken together with the possible allusion to Gen. ii. in Prov. iii. 18, 'She is a tree of life' &c.) (*b*) It is no objection to the Exile or post-Exile date that the doctrine of invariable retribution is presupposed in this treatise. We find this doctrine both in the speeches of Elihu (Job. xxxii.–xxxvii., a separate work in its origin) and in the Wisdom of Sirach. There is some weight in these arguments. But it can, I think, be shown that the age of Jeremiah contained the germs of various mental products which only matured in the later periods, and Reuss seems to me singularly wilful in assuming that the personification of Wisdom of itself proves the late date of Prov. i.–ix.

III. The luxurious living implied in Prov i.–ix. would suit the Exile and post-Exile period. As soon as the Jews had the chance of participating in the world's good things, they eagerly availed themselves of it. The prominence of the retribution doctrine in these nine chapters might possibly be accounted for by the prosperity of many of the dispersed Jews. To me however the expression 'peace-offerings' (vii. 14) points away

---

[1] We should perhaps read here *v'thigga'* for *v'thigra'*, following Sept.'s εἰς δέ σε ἀφίκετο σοφία ; so Merx and Bickell.

[2] Were the affinities with Gen. i. more definite, critics of Wellhausen's school would naturally derive from them an argument for the post-Exile origin of Prov. i.–ix. I do not myself attach much weight to these slight parallelisms.

from Babylon, just as the expression 'yarn of Egypt' in vii. 16 points away from Egypt.

IV. The phraseology of these chapters (as well as of the rest of the book) is said by Hartmann[1] to be late. His instances of late and Aramaising words and forms require testing ; an argument of this sort (except in more extreme cases) is not conclusive as to date. Reuss appears to base his linguistic argument rather on the clearness of the style, which ' betrays this section to be the latest part of the book.'[2] Nöldeke however more soberly infers, from the 'flowingness and facility of the language,' that the author lived subsequently to Isaiah.[3]

On the whole, I am compelled to reject the hypothesis of either the Exile or the post-Exile origin of Prov. i.-ix. The Exile-date seems to be excluded by Prov. vii. 14, which implies the sacrificial system ; the post-Exile by the want of any sufficient reason for descending so late in the course of history. The fifth century in particular, to which Vatke refers the whole Book of Proverbs, seems to me out of the question for this section of the book. Before the time of Sirach, I cannot find a period in the post-Exile history in which the life of Jerusalem can have much resembled the picture given of it in Prov. i.-ix. But Sirach's evident imitation of the ' Praise of Wisdom ' (we shall come back to this in studying Ecclesiasticus) seems of itself to suggest that Prov. i.-ix. is the monument of an earlier age, and this is confirmed by Sirach's different attitude towards ceremonial religion.

There remains the hypothesis that the treatise, Prov. i.-ix., was written towards the close of the kingdom of Judah. There seems to me no sufficient argument against this view, which agrees with the result above attained on the relation of Prov. i.-ix. to the Book of Job (p. 85). The collapse of the state was sudden, and for some time after the composition or at least promulgation of the Deuteronomic *Tōra* the Jews ap-

---

[1] *Die enge Verbindung des A. T. mit dem Neuen*, pp. 148-9.
[2] *Geschichte der heiligen Schriften Alten Testaments*, p. 494.
[3] *Die alttestamentliche Literatur* (1868), p. 159.

peared to be in the enjoyment of national prosperity. Now the author of Prov. i.–ix. depicts a state of outward prosperity and is evidently familiar with the exhortations of Deuteronomy. Who, as Delitzsch remarks, can fail to hear in Prov. i. 7–ix. an echo of the *Shemà* ('hear'), Deut. vi. 4–9 (comp. xi. 18–21)? This is quite consistent with the opinion that Prov. i.–ix. is later than the proverbs in the two principal collections of our book, an opinion which commends itself to most [1] especially on account of the higher moral standard of Prov. i.–ix., and its advance in the treatment of literary form.

I have said 'the composition or at least promulgation' of Deuteronomy. If Deuteronomy was written (which is at least possible) as early as the reign of Hezekiah,[2] we may perhaps follow Ewald, who places the 'Praise of Wisdom' in the period of relative prosperity which, he thinks, closed the reign of Manasseh.[3] It is noteworthy that Mic. vi., which Ewald plausibly assigns to the period of Manasseh's persecution, also presents some points of contact with Deuteronomy.[4] And yet it seems to me safer to date the book in the reign of Josiah, when, as we know from history and prophecy, the discourses of Deuteronomy first became generally known.

Next, as to the body of the work. That the collection in x. 1–xxii. 16 is the earliest part of the book is admitted by most critics. The fact that chaps. i.–ix. present linguistic points of contact with it, does not prove the two parts to be of the same date, for the opening chapters also display peculiarities quite unlike those of the 'Solomonic' anthology.[5] I have already set forth my own view on this and on other critical points, and will now only register the results of Ewald

---

[1] Hitzig, however, almost alone among recent critics, regards the opening chapters as the oldest part of the book.

[2] This seems to me the earliest probable date, but does not exclude the possibility that early traditional material has been worked into the book.

[3] *History of Israel*, iv. 219. It should be mentioned however that Ewald places Job (except the Elihu-portion), Prov. i.–ix., and, last in order, Deuteronomy *all in the reign of Manasseh*. He fails to recognise the influence of Deuteronom on the 'Praise of Wisdom.'

[4] See *Micah* in the Cambridge School and College Bible.

[5] Delitzsch, *Proverbs*, i. 33; Kuenen, *Onderzoek*, iii. 75.

and of Delitzsch. Both are agreed that the older Book of Proverbs extends from i. 1 to xxiv. 22, i. 1-6 (or 7) being the descriptive heading of the work, and i. 7 (or 8) -ix. 18 a hortatory treatise, by the author, more or less introductory to the sayings which follow. The date of the collection of the latter Ewald places at the beginning of the eighth century; that of the heading and introduction in the middle of the seventh. Towards the end of the seventh century the three appendices (xxii. 17-xxiv. 22, xxiv. 23-35, xxv. 1-xxix. 27) were added; the contents of the two former were derived from two popular proverbial collections, while the latter was a great and officially sanctioned anthology dating from the end of the eighth century. The remaining parts of the book (xxx. 1-xxxi. 9, and xxxi. 10-31) Ewald assigns to the seventh century. Delitzsch (whose view is perhaps the most conservative one still tenable) dates the publication of the first Book of Proverbs as early as the reign of Jehoshaphat (referring to 2 Chr. xvii. 7-9). To its editor he ascribes not only the authorship of i. 1-ix. 18 but the conclusion of the 'older book' by the words of the wise, xxii. 17-xxiv. 22, while a later editor is responsible both for the supplementary sayings of the wise, xxiv. 22-34, and for the great Hezekian collection, of which he thus ensured the preservation. The same person probably appended the obscure sayings of Agur (xxx.) and of Lemuel (xxxi. 1-9), possibly too the closing alphabetic poem (xxxi. 10-31), which is assigned by Delitzsch to the pre-Hezekian period. Both Ewald and Delitzsch are substantially agreed as to the existence of a genuine Solomonic element in both the great anthologies (especially in the first), but upon very conjectural grounds.

One point only remains to be considered, however briefly. The Book of Job has already furnished an example of the poetical fiction of the non-Israelitish authorship of a Hebrew poem. It is possible enough that this and the similar instance of the Balaam-oracles were not alone in Hebrew literature. Nor are they so, if a view of the first words of the headings in Prov. xxx. 1, xxxi. 1, which has found many friends, be correct, and we may render in the one case, 'The words of Agur the son of Jakeh, of (the country of) Massa,' reading either *mim-massā* (or, as Delitzsch proposes, *mimmēshā*) or *hammassā'ī* [1]) ; and in the other, 'The words of Lemuel the king of Massa.' Mühlau in his monograph on 'Agur' and 'Lemuel' thinks that both the contents and the language of the sayings of Agur 'almost necessarily point to a region bordering on the Syro-Arabian wastes, but his theory of an Israelitish colony in a certain Massa in the Hauran (comp. 1 Chr. v. 10), like a somewhat similar theory of Hitzig's (he places 'Massa ' in N. Arabia, comparing 1 Chr. iv. 42, 43, where the Simeonites are said to have settled in *Mount Seir*, and Isa. xxi. 11, 12 [2]), is too conjectural to be readily accepted. There is however much force in a part of the arguments of Mühlau, especially in his first and second (referring to xxxi. 1), 'The word *melek* in apposition to Lemuel cannot go without the article,' [3] and '*Massā* "utterance" is never used elsewhere except of (prophetic) oracles.' If any one therefore likes to adopt the above renderings, taking Massa as the name of a country (comp. Gen. xxv. 14, 1 Chr. i. 30), I have no strong objection. Ziegler's view cited by Mühlau,[4] that Lemuel was an Emeer of an Arabian tribe in the east of Jordan, and that an Israelitish wise man translated the Emeer's sayings into Hebrew, is perhaps not as untenable as Mühlau thinks, provided that 'translation' be taken to include recasting in accordance with the spirit of the Old Testament religion. For my own part, however, I prefer the

---

[1] In the version known as the *Græcus Venetus* (14th or 15th cent.) xxx. 1*a* runs thus, Λόγοι ἀγούρου υἱέως Ἰακέως τοῦ μασάου (Jakeh the Massaite). Delitzsch's view, given above, is taken from his art. on 'Proverbs' in Herzog-Plitt's Encyclopædia ; he refers to Friedrich Delitzsch's *Paradies*, p. 303 ; comp. 243.

[2] On Isa. xxi. 11, 12, see *The Prophecies of Isaiah*, i. 129, ii. 152. Hitzig's theory, originally stated in Zeller's *Theol. Jahrbücher*, 1844, pp. 269-305, will be found in the well-known short commentary (*Kurzgefasstes exeg. Handbuch*, 1847) by Bertheau, who substantially accepts it.

[3] This is a little too strong. We should certainly have expected *melek Lemuel* (or *Lemoel*) rather than *Lemuel melek*, on the analogy of *melek Yārēb*, Hos. v. 13, x. 6. As it stands in the text, *melek* (after *Lemuel*, and without the article) can only be a definition of class. The Lemuel spoken of was quite unknown to the reader, and therefore the editor appends the descriptive title 'king.' Comp. Ex. xxxiii. 11, where Joshua, son of Nun, being introduced for the first time, is described as *na'ar* 'a squire.'

[4] Referring to *Neue Uebersetzung der Denksprüche Salomo's*, 1791, p. 29.

simpler explanation given already in considering chaps. xxx., xxxi. 1-9. I account for the Aramaisms, Arabisms, and other peculiarities of these sections by their post-Exile origin, with which the character of the contents of the most striking portion, xxx. 1-6, appears to me to harmonise (notice e.g. the strong faith in the words of revelation in xxx. 5). But I am not writing a commentary, and can only draw the reader's attention to some of the most important exegetical phenomena. Let me refer in conclusion to a critical note on p. 175, which has a bearing on the question raised by some whether Job and this part of Proverbs may fitly be called Hebræo-Arabic works. It is strange that Hitzig should have renounced the support for his theory (see p. 171) to be obtained from Prov. xxx. 31.

CHAPTER VII.

THE TEXT OF PROVERBS.

THE sense of proverbs is naturally most difficult to catch when there has been no attempt to group them by subjects. Hence the textual difficulties of so large a part of the earliest anthology. Grätz has made some valuable among many too arbitrary corrections; but a systematic use of the ancient versions is still a desideratum. Lagarde, Oort, Bickell, and others have led the way; but much yet remains to be done. My space only allows me to give some preliminary hints, which may at least stimulate further inquiry, on the relation of the Hebrew text to the versions, especially the Septuagint version (if I should not rather speak of 'versions'). How comes it, we may ask first of all, that the Septuagint contains so many passages not found in the Hebrew? One answer is that in a foreign land, with a new language and a new circle of ideas, explanation was as necessary to the Hellenistic Jews as translation. Hence the tendency of the Septuagint translators to introduce glosses. But the form of the Book of Proverbs specially favoured interpolations. Sometimes only a few words were inserted to make the text more distinct (e.g. i. 22, xii. 25, xxiv. 23); at other times explanatory or suggested remarks were added, at first perhaps in the margin. Of course, it is perfectly conceivable that the received Hebrew text itself may contain similar additions; the analogy of other books, in which such interpolations occur, even favours this idea. One such insertion is patent; there can be no doubt that i. 16 was added in the Hebrew, to the detriment of the connection, from Isa. lix. 7. As this passage is wanting in the best MSS. of the Septuagint, we might be tempted to use this version as a means of detecting other interpolations in the Hebrew. This however would lead us into researches of too much complexity.

Some of the Septuagint additions are also found in the Vulgate, some again also in the Peshitto ; and where a Septuagint addition is not found in the Vulgate we may, at least in some cases, assume that the Septuagint text did not in St. Jerome's time contain the additional matter. Among the most interesting passages from a text-critical point of view peculiar to the Septuagint are those found at iii. 15, iv. 27, vi. 8, 11, vii. 2, ix. 12,[1] 18, xi. 16, xii. 13, xv. 18, xvi. 5, xix. 7, xxvi. 11, xxvii. 20, 21, xxviii. 10. Most of these can be rendered back into Hebrew, though this is difficult with vi. 11*b* as it stands, and impossible with vi. 8 ('the bee'). In any case the Hebrew origin of a proverb does not prove that it was inserted by the original collector or collectors. With regard to the Targum and its deviations from the Hebrew text, it is to be observed that this version has the same relation to the Peshitto as the Vulgate to the old Latin version on which it is based. The Peshitto translates from a Hebrew text substantially the same as our own ; though the translator has consulted the Septuagint (according to Hitzig) in the portion of the book beginning at vii. 23.

There are also some remarkable transpositions in the Septuagint Proverbs, reminding us of those in the Septuagint Jeremiah. The three appendices to the Hezekian collection are given in a very different order from that of the Hebrew. The first fourteen verses of chap. xxx. are inserted between ver. 22 and ver. 23 of chap. xxiv., and all the remainder, together with xxxi. 1-9, is placed before chap. xxv. The treatment of the headings in the Septuagint is also remarkable, and seems arbitrary ; e.g. it looks as if the translator had expunged all those peculiarities in the superscriptions which suggested a variety of authorship. The proper names in chaps. xxx., xxxi. have been explained away, and the heading in x. 1, which limits the Solomonic authorship too much for the translator, has been actually omitted.

---

[1] The addition here is very poetical, and may, as Ewald says, have been extracted from an ancient anthology. But it disturbs the connection.

On the Septuagint additions to Proverbs, comp. Deane in *Expositor*, 1884, pp. 297-301 ; on the larger subject of the Greek and the Hebrew text, see introduction to Hitzig's commentary, Lagarde's *Anmerkungen &c.*, and a series of papers, thorough but less masterly than Hitzig's or Lagarde's work, by Heidenheim (title in ' Aids to the Student,' below).

NOTE ON PROVERBS XXX. 31.

SOME assume here a corruption of the text, but the margin of the Revised Version gives an appropriate sense. It implies indeed the admission of a downright Arabism, but there are parallels for this in vv. 15, 16, 17, and *alqūm* for the Arabic *al-qaum* is (see Gesenius) like *elgābhīsh* (Ezek. xiii. 11, 13, xxxviii. 22) and *almōdād* (Gen. x. 26). 'The king when his army is with him' may very fitly be adduced as a specimen of the 'comely in going.' M. Halévy indeed has suggested that *qūm* in *alqūm* may be the *Qāvam* or *Qājam* often mentioned in the Sinaitic inscriptions (*Bulletin* No. 28 of the Société de Linguistique ; see *Academy*, March 27, 1886). But the former view is still the more plausible one. Why should a king with whom is 'God Qavam' be described as specially 'comely in going'? Wetzstein too has stated that *alqaum* is still pronounced *al-qōm* by the Bedawins. Comp. Blau, *Zeitschr. d. deutschen morg. Ges.*, xxv. 539.

CHAPTER VIII.

THE RELIGIOUS VALUE OF THE BOOK OF PROVERBS.

IT is only in modern times that the Book of Proverbs has been disparaged; the early Christian Fathers considered it to be of much ethico-religious value. Hence the sounding title, first used by Clement of Rome (*Cor.*, c. 57), ἡ πανάρετος σοφία. From our point of view, indeed, the value of the book is different in its several parts, but no part is without its use. Can any Christian help seeing the poetic foregleams of Christ in the great monologue of Wisdom in chap. viii.? Dorner may be right in maintaining that the idea of the Incarnation cannot have been evolved from Hebraism or Judaism, and yet the description of Wisdom, 'sporting with Jehovah's world' and 'having her delights with the sons of men' (viii. 31), cannot but remind us of the sympathetic, divine-human Teacher, who 'took the form of a servant.' How deeply this great section has affected the theology of the past, I need not here relate. Will it ever lose its value as a symbolic picture of the combined transcendence and immanence of the Divine Being?

Turning to the other parts of the book, do they not furnish abundant justification of that type of Christianity which accepts but does not dwell on forms, so bent is it upon moral applications of the religious principle? Do they not show that the 'fear of the Lord' is quite compatible with a deep interest in average human life and human nature? The Book of Proverbs, taken as a whole, seems to supply the necessary counterweight to the psalms and the prophecies. ·The psalmists love God more than aught else; but must every one say, 'Possessing this, I have pleasure in nothing upon earth' (Ps. lxxiii. 26)? Would it be good to be always in this mood? Is there not something more satisfactory in the Pauline saying, 'All things are yours, and ye are Christ's'? And as for the prophets—do they not (we may conjecture and perhaps partly prove this) depreciate too much the morality and religion of their neighbours? The Book of Proverbs gives us only average morality and religion; yet, if we judge it fairly, how pleasing on the whole is the picture! Taking it as equally authoritative with the psalms and prophecies, shall we not rise to a more comprehensive religion than a mere pupil of psalmists or prophets knew—to one that charges us, not to love God less, but our neighbour more? It would no doubt be easy to criticise the Book from a New Testament point of view. But the New Testament itself has absorbed much that is best in it, and quotations from it occur not unfrequently, especially in the Epistles. Nor can any teacher of the people afford to neglect its stores of happily expressed practical wisdom. We must not even despise its 'utilitarianism.' The awful declarations of 'Wisdom' in Prov. i. 24-32 are simply the voice of the personified laws of God [1] warning men that the consequences of their acts, even if they may be overruled for good, yet cannot by any cunning be escaped. Does the New Testament quite supersede this form of teaching? And does not the Hebrew sage once at least give a suggestion of that very overruling love of God which is among the characteristic ideas of Christian lore (see Prov. iii. 11)?

---

[1] So we may venture to paraphrase 'Wisdom' in this connection.

AIDS TO THE STUDENT.

THE 'aids' here mentioned are such as might otherwise escape notice. W. Nowack, *Die Sprüche Salomo's u.s.w.* (a recast of Bertheau's commentary in the *Kurzgefasstes Exeg. Handbuch*), 1883; H. Deutsch, *Die Sprüche Salomo's nach der Auffassung im Talmud und Midrasch dargestellt und kritisch untersucht* (erster Theil, 1885); Bickell, 'Exegetisch-kritische Nachlese: Proverbien und Job,' in *Zeitschr. fur kathol. Theologie*, 1886, pp. 205-208; Aben Ezra's commentary on Proverbs, edited by Chaim M. Horowitz, 1884; Loewenstein, *Die Proverbien Salomo's, mit Benutzung älterer und neuerer Manuskripte*, 1837 (text and commentary in Hebrew, with German metrical version; contains valuable contributions to a more critical Massoretic text from the papers of W. Heidenheim); M. Heidenheim, 'Zur Textkritik der Proverbien,' in his *Vierteljahresschrift* for 1865 and 1866; Lagarde, *Anmerkungen zur griechischen Uebersetzung der Proverbien*, 1863; Grätz, 'Exegetische Studien zu den Salomonischen Sprüchen,' in his *Monatsschrift*, 1884; Dijserinck, 'Kritische Scholien,' in *Theologisch Tijdschrift*, 1883, p. 577 &c.; Oort, 'Spreuken I.-IX.,' in same periodical, 1885, p. 379 &c.; Böttcher, *Aehrenlese*, part iii., 1865 (contains 39 pages on Proverbs); Mühlau, *De proverbiorum Agur et Lemuel origine*, 1869; Bruch, *Weisheitslehre der Hebräer*, 1851; Hooykaas, *Gesch. van de beoefening der Wisheid onder de Hebreën*, 1862; Dukes, *Rabbinische Blumenlese*, 1844 (includes Talmudic proverbs; comp. the older works of Drusius, 1590-1, and Brüll's supplement in his *Jahrbücher*, 1885); Delitzsch, art. 'Sprüche Salomo's,' in Herzog-Plitt's *Real-Encyklopädie*, ed. 2, vol. xiv.; and the works of Oehler and Schultz on Old Testament Theology (the former in Clark's Library).

THE WISDOM OF JESUS THE SON OF SIRACH.

CHAPTER I.

THE WISE MAN TURNED SCRIBE. SIRACH'S MORAL TEACHING.

THE inclusion of Sirach within our range of study, as an appendix and counterpart to the canonical Book of Proverbs, requires no long justification. The so-called 'Wisdom of Solomon' is in form and colouring almost as much Greek as Hebrew, and has no place in a survey of the wisdom of Palestine. But the 'Wisdom' more modestly ascribed to the son of Sirach is a truly Israelitish production, though as yet none but the masters of our subject have recognised its intrinsic importance. Whence comes this prevalent neglect of a work still known as 'Ecclesiasticus' or a 'church-book'? Doubtless it has fallen in estimation from being combined with books more difficult to appraise fairly and consequently regarded with suspicion. The objection which some Jewish doctors entertained to recommending parts of the Hagiographa has been felt by many moderns with regard to the Apocrypha. The objection is too strong and general not to have some foundation, but it implies an unhistorical habit of mind. Granted that the Apocryphal writings of the Old Testament belong in the main to a period of outer and inner decadence (though the noble Maccabean days may qualify this); yet periods of decadence are often also periods of transition to some new and better thing, which cannot be understood or appreciated without them. Ewald has suggested the title of 'intermediate writings' (*Zwischenschriften*[1]) as a substitute for Apocrypha, to indicate that transitional character which gives these books so high a value for the student of both Testaments.

The book now before us—the largest and most comprehensive in the Wisdom-literature—is one of these 'intermediate writings,' but in what sense beyond the most superficial one remains to be seen. It is mentioned here first of all because of the proof which it gives of the great literary force of the canonical Book of Proverbs. But no product of literature could maintain itself as Sirach has done if it were a mere imitation; Sirach, not less than the Wisdom-books of the Old Testament proper, is at least a partial reflection of the life of the times. Its date indeed has been disputed. Suffice it to say here that the author was, beyond reasonable doubt,[2] a contemporary of 'Simon the high priest, the son of Onias.' Now there were five high priests who bore the name of Simon or Simeon, two of whom, Simon I. (B.C. 310-290) and Simon II. (B.C. 219-199), have by different critics been thought of. The weight of argument is in favour of the second of the name, who was certainly the more important of the two, and who is referred to in the Talmud under the name of Simeon the Righteous.[3] This is in accordance with the Greek translator's statement in his preface that he was the grandson of the author, and we may conjecturally fix the composition of the book at about 180 B.C. The translator himself came into Egypt, as he tells us, in the 38th year of king Euergetes[4] (comp. Luke xxii. 25). Now Euergetes II. Physkon, who must be here intended, began to reign jointly with his brother

---

[1] *Revelation*, p. 365; *Die Lehre der Bibel von Gott*, i. 378.

[2] Note the phrase in l. 1, 'who *in his life* repaired the house,' implying 'now indeed he is dead.' Grätz in fact is the only scholar who doubts the author's contemporaneousness with Simon (*Monatsschrift*, 1872, p. 114).

[3] See, besides the well-known passage in *Pirke Aboth* (i. 2), the legendary extracts from (*Bab.*) *Yoma*, 39*b*, translated by Wünsche, *Der bab. Talmud*, i. 1, pp. 368-9; and comp. Derenbourg, *Hist. de la Palestine*, i. 44 &c.

[4] So we must paraphrase ἐν τῷ ὀγδόῳ καὶ τριακοστῷ ἔτει ἐπὶ τοῦ Εὐεργέτου βασιλέως. See Stanley's note in *Jewish Church*, iii. 235, and Abbot's note in the American edition of Smith's *Bible Dict.* (I am indebted to Bissell for the latter reference). Comp. Wright, *The Book of Koheleth*, p. 34 n.

Philometor B.C. 170; his brother died B.C. 145, and he reigned alone for twenty-five years longer (till B.C. 116). Hence the translator's arrival in Egypt and possibly the translation itself fall within the year 132. The object of his work, we gather from the preface, was to correct the inequalities of moral and religious culture (παιδεία) among the Jews of Egypt by setting before them a standard and a lesson-book of true religious wisdom.

Let us pause a little over these dates. It has been well observed by Mommsen that the foundation of Alexandria was as great an event in the history of the people of Israel as the conquest of Jerusalem. It must indeed have seemed to many Israelites more fraught with danger than with hope. Never before had Paganism presented itself to their nation in so attractive a guise. Would their religion exhibit sufficient power of resistance on a foreign soil? The fears, however, were groundless; at any rate, for a considerable time. The forms of Egyptian-Jewish literature might be foreign, but its themes were wholly national. Even in that highly original synthesis of Jewish, Platonic, and Stoic elements—the Book of Wisdom—the Jewish spirit is manifestly predominant. In Palestine there was also a Hellenic movement, though less vigorous and all-absorbing than in Egypt. Without a spontaneous manifestation of Jewish sympathy, Antiochus Epiphanes would never have made his abortive attempt to Hellenise Judæa. Girt round by a Greek population, the Palestinian Jews, in spite of Ezra's admirable organisation, could not entirely resist the assaults of Hellenism. It is probable that not merely Greek language, but Greek philosophy, exerted a charm on some of the clearest Jewish intellects. But we are within the bounds of acknowledged fact in asserting that the ardour of Judæan piety, at least in the highest class, greatly cooled in the age subsequent to Ezra's, and in ascribing this to Greek influences. The high priest Simeon II.,[1] surnamed the Righteous (i.e. the strict

---

[1] The Mishna (*Pirke Aboth*, i. 2) ascribes this saying to Simeon the Righteous: 'On three things the world stands—revelation (*tōra*), worship, and the bestowal of kindnesses.'

observer of the Law), of whom so glowing an account is given by Sirach (chap. l.), is the chief exception to this degeneracy; yet he was powerless to stem the revolutionary current even within his own family. His cousin Joseph was the notorious farmer of the taxes of Palestine, who by his public and private immorality[1] sapped the very foundations of Jewish life, while two of Simeon's sons, Jason and Menelaus, became the traitorous high priests who promoted the paganising movement under Antiochus. It is well known that many critics refer the Book of Ecclesiastes to the period immediately preceding this great movement. The deep and almost philosophical character of the unknown author's meditations seems to be in harmony with this date. On the other hand, there is the well-ascertained fact that the Book of Sirach shows no trace of really philosophical thought: it is little more than a new version of the ordinary proverbial morality. It is to this book, the 'Doppelgänger des kanonischen Spruchbuchs,' as Schürer calls it, the work, as a Greek writer puts it, of an attendant (ὀπαδός) of Solomon, that these pages are devoted. Nothing is more remarkable (and it ought to make us very deliberate in determining dates upon internal evidence) than the appearance of such a book at such a time.

The name of the author in full is Joshua (Jesus) ben Sira (Sirach),[2] but he may be called Sirach for shortness, this being the form of his family-name in the Greek translation. He tells us himself that he was of Jerusalem; that from his youth up his desire was for wisdom; that he laboured earnestly in searching for her; and that the Lord gave him a tongue for his reward (l. 27; li.) Sirach, in fact, is one of those 'wise men' to whom was entrusted so large a part of the religious education of the Jewish people. The remarkable fact that 'wise men' exist so long after the time of their prototype Solomon, proves that their activity was an integral part of the Jewish national life. The better class of 'wise

---

[1] See Jos., *Ant.*, xii. 4.
[2] On the identity of the Ben Sira of the Talmud and our Sirach, see Horowitz in Frankel's *Monatsschrift*, 1865, p. 181 &c. The *ch* in the form Sirach may be due to an old error in the Greek text.

men' gave an independent support to the nobler class of prophets. With their peremptory style, the prophets would never have succeeded in implanting a really vigorous religion, had not the 'wise men,' with their more conciliatory and individualising manner of teaching, supplemented their endeavours. The Babylonian Exile introduced a change into the habits of the 'wise men,' who, though some of them used the pen before the overthrow of the state, became thenceforward predominantly, if not entirely, writers on practical moral philosophy. Such was Sirach. He is not indeed a strictly original writer, nor does he lay claim to this. This is how he describes the nature of his work (xxxiii. 16)—

> I too, as the last, bestowed zeal,
> and as one who gleans after the vintage;
> By the blessing of the Lord I was the foremost,
> and as a grape-gatherer did I fill the winepress.

Sirach, then, was first of all a collector of proverbs, and he found that most of the current wise sayings had been already gathered. It is not likely that up to xxxvi. 22 he merely combined two older books of proverbs (as Ewald supposed[1]), though it is more than probable that older proverbs do really lie imbedded in his work. But whether old proverbs or new, Sirach has this special characteristic, that he loves to arrange his material by subjects. This was already noticed by the early scribes,[2] and is well brought out by Holtzmann in Bunsen's *Bibelwerk*, and I will merely refer to chap. xxii. 1-6, 'On good and bad children;' 7-18, 'The character of the fool;' 19-26, 'On friendship,' 27-xxiii. 6, 'Prayer and warning against sins of the tongue and lusts of the flesh;' 7-15, 'The discipline of the mouth;' 16-27, 'On adultery;' xxix. 1-20, 'On suretyship;' 21-28, 'An independent mode of life.'[3] The plan of grouping his material is not indeed thoroughly carried out, but even the attempt marks a progress in the

---

[1] *Hist. of Israel*, v. 263-4. Ewald includes xxxix. 12-35 in the portion belonging to the second (supposed) collection.
[2] See the headings at certain points of the Greek version.
[3] With vv. 21, 23 comp. St. Paul, Phil. iv. 11, 12.

literary art. This is one of the points in which Sirach differs from his canonical predecessors.

In other respects his indebtedness is manifest. Night and day he must have studied his revered models to have attained such insight into the secrets of style. But, so far from affecting originality, he delights in allusions to the older proverbialists. Many parallelisms occur in the sayings on Wisdom (comp. Sir. i. 4, Prov. viii. 22; Sir. i. 14, Prov. i. 4, ix. 10; Sir. iv. 12, 13, Prov. iv. 7, 8; Sir. xxiv. 1, 2, Prov. viii. 1, 2; Sir. xxiv. 3, Prov. ii. 6; Sir. xxiv. 5, Prov. viii. 27). This we might expect; for Wisdom in a large sense is more persistently the object of Sirach than it was at any rate of the earlier writers in Proverbs. But, besides this, points of contact abound in very ordinary sayings. Thus compare, among many others which might be given,

(*a*) Better a mean man that tills for himself
than he that glorifies himself and has no bread
(Prov. xii. 9, Sept. &c.)
Better he that labours and abounds in all things
than he that glorifies himself and has no bread
(Sir. x. 27, Fritzsche).

(*b*) A merry heart makes a cheerful face,
but with sorrow of heart is a crushed spirit (Prov. xv. 13).
The heart of a man alters his face,
as well for good cheer as for bad;
A merry face betokens a heart in good case (Sir. xiii. 25, 26*a*).

(*c*) A passionate man stirs up strife,
and one that is slow to anger allays contention (Prov. xv. 18).
Abstain from strife, and thou shalt diminish thy sins,
for a passionate man will kindle strife (Sir. xxviii. 8).

(*d*) An intelligent servant rules over the son that causes shame
(Prov. xvii. 2).
Unto the wise servant shall free men do service (Sir. x. 25).

(*e*) Death and life are in the power of the tongue (Prov. xviii. 21).
Good and evil, life and death;
and the tongue rules over them continually (Sir. xxxvii. 18).

(*f*) Golden apples in silver salvers;
a word smoothly spoken (Prov. xxv. 11).
Golden pillars upon a silver pediment;
fair feet upon firm soles (Sir. xxvi. 18, Fritzsche).

(g) He who digs a pit shall fall therein,
and he who rolls a stone, upon himself it shall return
(Prov. xxvi. 27).
He who casts a stone on high, casts it on his own head;
He who digs a pit shall fall therein (Sir. xxvii. 25a, 26a).
(h) The crucible for silver, and the furnace for gold,
and a man is tried by his praise (Prov. xxvii. 21).
The furnace proves the potter's vessels,
the trial of a man is in his discourse (Sir. xxviii. 5).

It will be seen from these examples that, though Sirach adapted and imitated, he did so with much originality. His style has colour, variety, and vivacity, and though Hengstenberg accuses the author of too uniform a mode of treatment, yet a fairer judgment will recognise the skill with which the style is proportioned to the subject; now dithyrambic in his soaring flight, now modestly skimming the ground, the author of the πανάρετος σοφία (for so Sirach, no less than Proverbs, was called[1]) is never feeble and rarely trivial. 'Its general tone,' says Stanley, 'is worthy of that first contact between the two great civilisations of the ancient world.' 'Nothing is too high, nor too mean,' says Schürer, 'to be drawn within the circle of Sirach's reflections and admonitions.' I have elsewhere spoken of his comprehensiveness. This quality he partly owes to his being so steeped in the Scriptures. One result of this is that he is more historical than his predecessors, and connects his wisdom with those narratives of early times, which were either but little known to or valued by the proverb-writers of antiquity. The earlier psalmists and prophets indeed show the same neglect of the traditions of the past: they lived before the editing and gradual completion of any roll of 'Scriptures.' Sirach on the other hand (see his preface) had 'the Law and the Prophets, and the rest of the books,' the latter collection being a kind of appendix, still open to additions. He was a true 'scribe,' and gloried in the name (xxxviii. 24), not in the New Testament sense, but in one not unworthy of a religious philosopher; he gave his mind to the wisdom both

[1] See St. Jerome, *Præf. ad Libros Salomonis*, and comp. Lightfoot's *Clement of Rome*, p. 164 &c.

of the Scriptures and of 'all renowned men,' and travelled through strange countries, trying the good and evil among men. If parts at least of the Book of Job probably contain an autobiographical element, it is still more certain that the chapter (xxxix.) which closes the book before us expresses the ideal of the author's life. And if he *does* sometimes take delight in his own attainments, yet why is this to be censured as mere 'böse Selbstgefälligkeit'?[1] A deep consciousness of moral imperfection is not equally to be expected in the Old Testament and in the New, nor should the philosophic writings in the former be appealed to for striking anticipations of fundamental Gospel ideas. Sirach does no doubt in some sense claim inspiration (xxiv. 32-34, l. 28, 29), and place his own work in a line with the prophecies (xxiv. 33), but why should this be set down to arrogant inflation? Lowth, with more charity, quotes similar language of Elihu (Job xxxii. 8, xxxvi. 4) in proof of the speaker's *modesty* (*Prælect.* xxxiv.) It was probably a characteristic of the later 'wise men' so to account for their wisdom (see above, p. 43), and surely in that wide sense recognised by the Anglican Prayerbook he *was* 'inspired,' he *was* a 'son of the prophets.' I am only sorry that he forgot the lesson of Ex. xxxi. 2 when he wrote so disparagingly of trades (xxxviii. 25 &c.), and agree with Dr. Edersheim[2] that the Jewish teachers of the time of Christ and afterwards were more advanced on this point than the son of Sirach.

It is true enough that there are sayings in this book which offend the Christian sentiment, and which serve to show how great was the spiritual distress which the Gospel alone could relieve. For instance,

(*a*) He who honours his father shall make atonement for sins (iii. 3).
Water will quench a flaming fire,
and alms make atonement for sin (iii. 30).
Brethren and help are against time of trouble;
but alms deliver more than both (xl. 24).

Here is one of those 'false beacon lights' of which Prof. Bissell speaks (*Apocrypha*, p. 282). But in arrest of judgment

---

[1] Keerl, *Die Apokryphenfrage* (1855), p. 214.
[2] *Sketches of Jewish Social Life*, p. 189.

remember that long discipline in the duties spoken of has produced some of the finest qualities in the Jewish character.

(*b*) Happy the man who has not offended in his speech,
and is not pricked with grief for sins (xiv. 1).
(*c*) Gain credit with thy neighbour in his poverty,
that thou mayest rejoice in his prosperity ;
abide stedfast unto him in the time of his affliction,
that thou mayest be heir with him in his heritage (xxii. 23).
(*d*) Nine things I in my heart pronounce happy, ...
and he that lives to see the fall of enemies
(xxiv. 7 ; comp also xii. 10-12, xxx. 6).
(*e*) Who will praise the Most High in Hades,
instead of those who live and give praise? (xvii. 27.)
For man cannot do everything,
because the son of man is not immortal (xvii. 30).

With the latter saying, contrast Wisd. of Sol. ii. 23, 'For God created man for immortality.'

(*f*) (Give me) any plague but the plague of the heart,
and any wickedness but the wickedness of a woman &c.
(xxv. 13-26).

This opening verse might perhaps be otherwise rendered,

Any wound but a wound in the heart,
and any evil but evil in a wife.

The misfortune of having a bad wife is often touched upon in the Talmud. Ewald's sentence is however just, that Sirach's 'estimate of women, and sharp summary counsel concerning divorce [see ver. 26], place [him] far below the height of the Hebrew Bible.'[1]

I admit the imperfection of these moral statements ; but can they not several of them be paralleled from the Psalms, Proverbs, and Ecclesiastes ? And can we not find as many more anticipations of the moral teaching of the Synoptic Gospels and St. James (e.g. iv. 10, vii. 11, 14, xi. 18, 19, xv. 14, xvii. 15, xxiii. 4, 11, 18) ? Do not let us undervalue any foregleams of the coming dawn.

[1] Ewald, *Revelation*, p. 364 n.

CHAPTER II.

SIRACH'S TEACHING (*continued*). HIS PLACE IN THE MOVEMENT OF THOUGHT.

PASSING now from Sirach's moral statements to those which are concerned with doctrine, an honest critic must admit that the author is here even less progressive. The Messianic hope, in the strict sense of the word, has faded away.[1] In xlv. 25 (comp. xlviii. 15) the 'covenant with David' is described as being 'that the inheritance of the king should be only from father to son;' similarly in xlvii. 22 the 'root of David' denotes Rehoboam and his descendants. But this want of a definite Messianic hope is characteristic of the age; it is no special defect of Sirach. But what shall we say of another charge brought against our author, viz. that he has unbiblical conceptions of the Divine nature? One of these (xi. 16; see A.V.) may be dismissed at once, the passage having insufficient critical authority. Another—

> We may speak much and not attain;
> indeed to sum up, He is all (xliii. 27)—

has been misapprehended. The *Bereshith Rabba* says (c. 68), 'Why is the Holy One also called *Mākōm* (place)? Because He is the place of the world; His world is not His place.' This is all that Sirach means, and Philo, too, who uses similar words, accused by Keerl of heresy, and adds, ἅτε εἰς καὶ τὸ πᾶν αὐτὸς ὤν.

The doctrines of the Satan and the Resurrection, which Sirach probably regarded somewhat as we regard the 'develop-

---

[1] Ewald (*History*, v. 263, n. 3) refers to iv. 15, x. 13-17, xi. 5 sq., xxxii. 17-19, xxxiii. 1-12, xxxvi. 11-17, xxxvii. 25, xxxix. 23, xlviii. 10 sq., but only for a *vague* Messianism (in the last passage the Greek seems to be interpolated). I would add xxxv. 17-19, xxxvi. 1-10.

ments' of the Papal Church, he appears studiously to ignore [1] —more especially the latter—and he thereby puts himself into direct opposition to the newer popular orthodoxy. For though not the invention (as M. Renan regards it) of the Maccabean period, there can be no doubt that the doctrine of the Resurrection became then for the first time an article of the popular creed. Instead of the 'awakening to everlasting life' (Dan. xii. 2), it is the peaceful but hopeless life of the spirits in Sheól to which he resignedly looks forward.

> Weep for the dead, for he hath lost the light,
> and weep for the fool, for he wanteth understanding:
> make little weeping for the dead, for he is at rest,
> but the life of the fool is worse than death.[2]

This, however orthodox (as former generations had counted orthodoxy), was rank Sadduceanism, and hence (for how otherwise to interpret the glosses of the Greek and Syriac versions of xlviii. 11b[3] it is difficult to see) very early readers of Sirach, especially perhaps well-meaning but unscrupulous Christian readers, effected an entrance for their cherished beliefs by violence.

Another point on which Sirach is equally—shall we say orthodox, or reactionary?—is the connection between piety and temporal prosperity. He really seems to be no more troubled by doubts on this ancient doctrine than the author of the beautiful, but in this respect naïvely simple, introduction to the Book of Proverbs. This perhaps was strange under Sirach's circumstances. How striking and even pain-

---

[1] True, the Greek version of Sirach has, at xxi. 27, the words, 'When the ungodly curseth the Satan, he curseth his own soul;' but 'the Satan' may here be synonymous with the depraved will, the *yēçer rā'* (this seems to have Talmudic authority; see Weber, *System der altsynag. pal. Theol.*, pp. 228-9). In *Baba bathra*, 15a, Satan is not distinguished from the *yēçer rā'*. See Appendix.

[2] Chap. xxii. 11. Comp. xiv. 11-19 (correcting by the help of the Syriac), xvii. 27, 28, 30. Contrast the glowing language of the 'Wisdom of Solomon,' iii. 1-4.

[3] The Syriac has, 'Nevertheless he dieth not, but liveth indeed.' The Greek version I have quoted farther on. Also the Latin, which probably corresponds most to the original. See Geiger, *Zeitschr. d. d. morg. Ges.*, xii. 536. The false reading κεκοιμημένοι, adopted by A.V., for κεκοσμημένοι, in xlviii. 11a, is due to the same theological motive.

ful is the contrast between Josephus' vivid and truthful comparison of Judæa at this period to 'a ship in a storm, tossed by the waves on both sides,'[1] and that proverb of Sirach, worthy, considering the times, of the 'miserable comforters' of Job—

> The gift of the Lord remains with the godly,
> and his favour brings prosperity for ever.[2]

In short, Sirach represents the reconciliation between the practical ethics of the inspired 'wise men' of old and the all-embracing demands of the Law. Himself only in a comparatively low sense inspired—for we should not hastily reject his claim to a 'tongue' from above—he did nothing, on the ethical side, but repeat the old truths in their old forms, though one gladly admits that he shows a genuine and unassumed interest in the varieties of human character. But on the religious side he is really in a certain sense original, in so far as he combines the traditional 'wisdom' with a heartfelt regard for the established forms of religion, such as the older 'wise men' scarcely possessed. On the latter point he would sympathise with the author of Ps. cxix. Unlike the older proverb-writers, he recommends the punctual observance of rites and ceremonies. These however are to be penetrated by a moral spirit; hence he says,

> Do not [seek to] corrupt [the Lord] with gifts, for he receives them not;
> and trust not to unrighteous sacrifices.
> He who serves acceptably shall be received,
> and his prayer shall reach unto the clouds (xxxv. 12, 16).

By Greek philosophy Sirach, as far as we can see, was wholly uninfluenced.

And yet Sirach cannot have been entirely unacquainted with Greek culture, in the more general sense of the word. One striking proof of this is his attitude towards medical science,[3] which is exactly the opposite of the Chronicler's (2

---

[1] *Antiquities*, xii. 3, 3.

[2] Ch. xi. 17; comp. ii. 7 &c.; xvi. 6 &c.; xl. 13, 14. There are, however, passages in which Sirach betrays some little feeling of the practical difficulties of the older form of the doctrine of retribution; see xxxv. 18 [xxxii. 18].

[3] See Dukes, *Rabbinische Blumenlese*, pp. 29, 30; Grätz, *Schir ha-schirim*, p. 86. Grotius even supposed the author to be a physician.

Chr. xvi. 12). It seems as if the older generation were offended by human interference with the course of nature, appealing perhaps to Ex. xv. 26; a curious Talmudic tradition ascribes a similar view to Hezekiah and his wise men. Sirach, however, appealing to the passage preceding that referred to above (see Ex. xv. 23-25), seeks to reconcile the opposing parties (xxxviii. 1-15). No doubt he had learned this at Alexandria: he tells us himself that he had travelled and learned many things (xxxiv. 9-11), and from xxxix. 4 we may even infer that he had appeared at court, where probably his life was endangered by calumnious accusations (li. 6). There, perhaps, he acquired his taste for the Greek style of banquet, with its airy talk and accompaniment of music, a taste which seems to have inspired a piquant piece of advice to the killjoys of his time, who insisted on talking business out of season (xxxii. 3-5)—

> Speak, O elder, with accurate knowledge, for it beseemeth thee,
> but be not a hindrance to music.[1]
> When playing is going on, do not pour out talk;
> and show not thyself inopportunely wise.
> A seal-ring of carbuncle set in gold,
> [such is] a concert at a banquet of wine.

In a similar mood he writes (xiv. 14)—

> Defraud not thyself of a joyous day,
> and let not a share of a lawful pleasure escape thee.

But his tone is commonly more serious. Though no ascetic, he cautions his readers against the unrestrained manners which had invaded Judæa, especially against consorting with the singing and dancing girls ($\mu\epsilon\tau\grave{a}$ $\psi a\lambda\lambda o\acute{u}\sigma\eta s$, ix. 4, includes both; Vulg. *cum saltatrice*), and draws a picture of the daughters of Israel (xlii. 9, 10) which forms a melancholy contrast with the Old Testament ideal. His prayer to be guarded from the infection of lust (xxiii. 4, 5) finds its commentary in the story already mentioned of Joseph the tax-farmer. He notes with

---

[1] $\kappa a\grave{\iota}$ $\mu\grave{\eta}$ $\dot{\epsilon}\mu\pi o\delta\acute{\iota}\sigma\eta s$ $\mu o v\sigma\iota\kappa\acute{a}$. So xlix. 1, $\dot{\omega}s$ $\mu o v\sigma\iota\kappa\grave{a}$ $\dot{\epsilon}\nu$ $\sigma v\mu\pi o\sigma\acute{\iota}\psi$ $o\check{\iota}\nu o v$; comp. Ex. xxxii. 18 Sept. That Greek music was known in Palestine *very shortly afterwards* may be inferred from the Greek names of musical instruments in the Book of Daniel.

observant eye the strife of classes. What bitter sighs must have prompted a saying like this (xiii. 2, 3)—

> A burden that is too heavy for thee take not up,
> and have no fellowship with one that is stronger and richer than thyself:
> For what fellowship hath the kettle with the earthen pot?
> this will smite, and that will be broken.
> The rich man doth wrong, and *he* snorteth with anger,
> the poor man is wronged, and *he* entreateth withal.

And again (xiii. 18)—

> What peace hath the hyæna with the dog?
> and what peace hath the rich man with the poor?

He is painfully conscious of the deserved humiliation of his country, and the only reason which he can urge why God should interpose is the assured prophetic word (xxxvi. 15, 16=20, 21). Elsewhere he ascribes all the evil of his time to the neglect of the Law (xli. 8), which, by a strong hyperbole, he almost identifies with personified Divine Wisdom (xxiv. 23; see above on Prov. viii.) Not however without a noble introduction leading up to and justifying this identification. In the true *māshāl*-style he describes how Wisdom wandered through the world seeking a restingplace,—

> Then the Creator of all gave me a commandment,
> and he that made me caused my tent to rest,
> and said, Let thy dwelling be in Jacob,
> and thine inheritance in Israel (xxiv. 8).

And after a series of wondrous images, all glorifying the Wisdom enthroned in Jerusalem, he declares—

> All this [is made good in] the book of the covenant of the Most High God,
> the Law which Moses commanded us
> as a heritage unto the congregations of Jacob (xxiv. 23).

This remarkable chapter deserves to be studied by itself; it is most carefully composed in 72 στίχοι. Lowth and Wessely[1] have with unequal success retranslated it into Hebrew. I

---

[1] Wessely was one of the most eminent fellow-workers of the great Moses Mendelssohn. See Wogue, *Histoire de la Bible et de l'exégèse biblique* (1881), pp. 334-337.

have already spoken (on Proverbs) of its interest for the student of doctrine; it has indeed been thought to show clear traces of Alexandrinism, but this is improbable and unproved.

It remains to notice the author's interest in nature and history. The hymn of praise for the works of creation (xlii. 15–xliii. 32) is only poor if compared with parts of the Book of Job. But perhaps more interesting is the panegyric of 'famous men' (xliv.–l.), from Enoch the patriarch to Simeon the Righteous, whose imposing appearance and beneficent rule are described with the enthusiasm of a contemporary.[1] It is worth the student's while to examine the contents of this roll of honour. A few corrections of the text may be noticed as a preliminary. At xlviii. 11*b*, the Greek has 'for we shall surely live (again).' But the Latin has, 'nam nos vitâ vivimus tantum, post mortem autem non erit tale nomen nostrum.' There is good reason in this instance, as we shall see presently, to prefer the reading of the Latin to that of the Greek. At l. 1, after 'son of Onias,' it is well to remove the abruptness of the transition by inserting from the Syriac, 'was the greatest of his brethren and the crown of his people.' At l. 26 (27), for 'Samaria' we should probably read 'Seir' (else how will there be three nations?), and for 'foolish,' 'Amoritish' (with the Ethiopic version and Ewald, comp. Ezek. xvi. 3). Turning to the names of the heroes commemorated, it is startling to find no mention made of Ezra, the second founder of Jewish religion. Aaron, on the other hand, is celebrated in no fewer than seventeen verses. This cannot be a mere accident, for the veneration of the later Jews for Ezra was hardly less than that which they entertained for Moses. Notice, however, that Moses himself is only praised in five verses. It seems as if Aaron better than Moses symbolised those ritual observances in which Sirach perhaps took a special delight. The name of Ezra, too, may have had its

---

[1] The Mussaph prayer in the liturgy of the Day of Atonement (German ritual) contains a striking imitation of Sirach's eloquent description of the high priest (see Delitzsch, *Gesch. der jüd. Poesie*, p. 21), every verse of which closes with the refrain *mar'eh kōhēn* 'the appearance of the priest;' Meshullam bar-Kleonymos is known to be the author.

symbolic meaning to the author. He may have had deficient sympathy with those elaborators of minute legal precepts, who took Ezra as their pattern. Not that he disbelieved in the continuity of inspiration—for in some sense he claims it for himself (e.g. xxiv. 33), but that he did not fully recognise the workings of the spirit in the 'fence about the Law.' Other names which he passes over in silence are Daniel and Mordecai. Does this mean that he was unacquainted with the Books of Daniel and Esther? Whatever be the date of these books, so much as this is at least a probable inference.

The panegyric seems to have originally closed with the ancient liturgical formula in verses 22-24. But the writer could not resist the temptation of giving a side-blow to the hated Samaritans (those 'half-Jews,' as Josephus the historian calls them), called forth perhaps by the dispute respecting the rival temples held at Alexandria before Ptolemy Philometor.[1] The last chapter of all (chap. li.) contains the aged author's final leave-taking. It is a prayer of touching sincerity and much biographical interest. The immediateness of the religious sentiment is certainly greater in this late 'gatherer' than in many of the earlier proverb-writers.

Enough has been said of the contents of the book to give a general idea of its moral and religious position. Let us now consider its outward form. The work, as we have seen, was originally written in Hebrew. This indeed was to have been expected. For although the influence of the Seleucidæ had greatly strengthened the hold of Aramaic on the Jewish population of Palestine, Hebrew was still, and for a long time afterwards remained, the language of scholars and *littérateurs*. The author of the 'Wisdom of Sirach' was both. He was thoroughly penetrated with the spirit and style of the Scriptures, especially of those of the *Khokma*, and he would have thought it as much a descent to lavish his great powers on Aramaic as Dante did at first to write in Italian. Is this Hebrew original still extant? Alas! no; Hebrew literature, so scantily represented for this period, has to mourn this great loss. A page of fragments, gathered from the Talmud and

[1] Jos., *Ant.*, xiii. 3, 4.

the Midrāshīm,[1] is all that we can, with some occasional hesitation, plausibly regard as genuine. There is indeed a small work, called the Alphabet of Ben Sira, consisting of two series of proverbs, one in Aramaic, and one in Hebrew. But no significance can be attached to this. The genuineness of many of the Hebrew proverbs is guaranteed by their occurrence in the Talmud, but the form in which the alphabetist quotes them is often evidently less authentic than that in the Talmud. The original work must have been lost since the time of Jerome, if we may trust his assurance[2] that he had found it in Hebrew, and that it bore the name 'Parables' (*m'shālīm*). Of the ancient versions, the Syriac and the Old Latin are (after the Greek) the most important; the former is from the Hebrew, the latter from a very early form of the Greek text. Neither of them is always in accordance with the Greek as we have it, but such differences are often of use in restoring the original text. All the versions appear to contain alterations of the text, dictated by a too anxious orthodoxy, and in these the one may be a check upon the other. Bickell indeed goes further than this, and states that an accurate text of Sirach can only be had by combining the data of the Greek and the Syriac. Lowth, in his 24th Lecture, strongly urges the retranslation of Sirach into Hebrew. Such an undertaking would be premature, if Bickell's judgment be correct that the book consists of seven-syllabled verses or στίχοι, grouped in distichs,[3] except in the alphabetic poem on wisdom (li. 13-20). The latter, consisting of 22 στίχοι, he has translated into German from his own corrected text, dividing it into four-lined strophes, as also the preceding, 'alphabetising' poem, con-

---

[1] See Zunz, *Gottesdienstliche Vorträge*, p. 102; Delitzsch, *Zur Gesch. der jüdischen Poesie*, p. 204 (comp. p. 20, note 5); Dukes, *Rabbinische Blumenlese*, p. 67 &c. It should be noticed that among these Talmudic *m'shālīm* there are some, and even long ones, which do not occur in the Greek Sirach.

[2] *Præf. in libr. Sal.* 'Fertur et πανάρετος Jesu filii Sirach liber et alius ψευδεπίγραφος liber . . . Quorum priorem Hebraicum reperi, non Ecclesiasticum, ut apud Latinos, sed *parabolas* prænotatum, cui juncti erant Ecclesiastes et Canticum canticorum.' Nowhere since has Sirach been found in this position, nor with this title.

[3] But is not a strophic division sometimes visible, e.g. ii. 7-17? See Seligmann, *Das Buch der Weisheit des J. S.*, &c., p. 34.

sisting of 22 distichs (li. 1–12), in the *Zeitschrift für katholische Theologie*, 1882, pp. 326–332.

We must reserve our opinion on Bickell's theory till the appearance of a complete edition from his pen. Meantime three passages (xxiv. 27, xxv. 15, xlvi. 18) may be referred to as giving striking proof of the Hebrew original of the work. In xxiv. 27 the translator seems to have found in his Hebrew copy כאר, i.e. properly כְּיְאֹר 'as the Nile' (the weak letter' being elided in pronunciation as in כאר, Am. viii. 8), but as he supposed כָּאוֹר 'as the light.' In xxv. 15, he found ראש, which in the context can only mean 'poison,' but which he inappropriately rendered 'head.' In xlvi. 18, the Hebrew had צרים, i.e. צָרִים 'enemies,' but, according to the translator, צֹרִים 'Tyrians.' Compare also in this connection the allusions to the meanings of Hebrew words in vi. 22 ('wisdom') and xliii. 8 ('the month'). There are still questions to be decided which can only be adverted to briefly here. Did the translator make use of the Septuagint, and more particularly of the portion containing the prophets? He certainly refers to a translation of the Scriptures in his preface, but Frankel thinks that a Targum may be meant, and even doubts the genuineness of the passage; he explains the points of contact with the Septuagint which are sometimes so interesting[1] in the Greek version of Sirach by *Ueberarbeitung*, i.e. the 'working over' of the version by later hands.[2] This seems to me a forced view. It is more probable that a Greek version is meant, or perhaps we may say Greek *versions*; no special honour is given to any one translation. Next, as to the position accorded to the Wisdom of Sirach. It is often cited in the Talmud with formulæ which belong elsewhere to the Scriptures, and was therefore certainly regarded by many as worthy to be canonical (see Appendix). In strict theory, this was wrong. According to the *Tosephta Yadayim*, c. 2, the book of Ben Sira, though much esteemed, stood on the border between the canonical and extraneous or non-canonical books. Such books might be read cursorily, but were not to

---

[1] See especially xlvi. 19, with which comp. the Septuagint of 1 Sam. xii. 3.
[2] *Vorstudien zu der Septuaginta* (1841), p. 21, note *w*.

be studied too much.¹ Sirach neither claimed the authorship of a hero of antiquity, nor was it, according to the rising Pharisaic school, orthodox; thus perhaps we may best account for the fact that a work, regarded in itself, in no way inferior to the Book of Proverbs, was left outside the sacred canon.

No certain allusions to our book are traceable in the New Testament; the nearest approach to a quotation is James i. 19; comp. Ecclus. v. 13. Clement of Alexandria is the first Christian writer who quotes directly from Sirach. From its large use in the services of the Church the book received the name Ecclesiasticus, to distinguish it perhaps from the canonical book which was also often called 'Wisdom.' In later times, it half attracted, but—owing to the corrupt state of the text—half repelled, the great Hellenist Camerarius, the friend of Melancthon, who published a separate edition of Sirach (the first) at Basle in 1551. It appears from his preface that it was highly valued by the reformers from an educational point of view. Bullinger proposes it as a less dangerous text book of moral philosophy than the works of Plato and Aristotle, and Luther admits it to be a good household book, admired however too much by the world, which 'sleepily passes by the great majestic word of Christ concerning the victory over death, sin, and hell.'

No impartial critic will place the Wisdom of Jesus the son of Sirach on the same literary eminence with the so-called Wisdom of Solomon. It is only from its greater fidelity to the Old Testament standard, or at least to a portion of this standard, that it can claim a qualified superiority. A few noble passages of continuous rhetoric it no doubt contains, especially the noble Hymn of Praise on the works of creation (xxxix. 16-xliii. 33); and a few small but exquisite gems especially the sayings on friendship (counterbalanced, I admit by those on the treatment of one's enemies, xii. 10-12, xxv. 7, xxx. 6), e.g.—

¹ Wright, *Koheleth*, p. 48 n.; Strack, art. 'Kanon des A. T.' in Herzog-Plitt, *Realencyclopädie*, vii. 430, 431; Grätz, *Kohélet*, p. 48.

Forsake not an old friend,
for the new is not comparable to him.
A new friend is as new wine,
when it is old, thou wilt drink it with pleasure (ix. 10),

with which we may bracket the noble passage on the treatment of a friend's trespass (xix. 13-17). One of the fine religious passages has been quoted already (xliii. 27; comp. Job xxvi. 14); we may couple this [1] with it—

As a drop from the sea, and a grain of sand,
so are a few years in the day of eternity (xviii. 9).

Still the chief value of the book is, historically, to fill out the picture of a little known period, and doctrinally, to show the inadequacy of the old forms of religious belief, and the moral distress from which the Christ was a deliverer.

AIDS TO THE STUDENT.

BESIDES the commentaries of Bretschneider (1806), Fritzsche (1859), and Bissell (in the American edition of Lange), see Gfrörer, *Philo*, ii. (1831), pp. 18-52; Dähne, *Geschichtliche Darstellung der jüdisch-alexandrin. Religionsphilosophie*, ii. (1834), pp. 126-150; Zunz, *Die gottesdienstl. Vorträge der Juden* (1832), pp. 100-105; Ewald, *Jahrbücher der bibl. Wissenschaft*, iii. (1851), pp. 125-140; *History of Israel*, v. 262 &c.; Jost, *Gesch. des Judenthums*, i. (1857), p. 310 &c.; Herzfeld, *Gesch. des Volkes Jisrael*, iii. (1863), see Index; Horowitz, *Das Buch Jesus Sirach* (1865); Dyserinck, *De Spreuken van Jesus den zoon van Sirach vertaald* (1870); Grätz, *Monatsschrift* for 1872, pp. 49 &c., 97 &c.; Seligmann, *Das Buch der Weisheit des Jesus Sirach* (1883); Fritzsche, art. in Schenkel's *Bibellexikon*, iii. 252 &c.; Stanley, *Jewish Church*, vol. iii. (see Index); Westcott, art. 'Ecclesiasticus' in Smith's *Bible Dictionary*; Deane, 'The Book of Ecclesiasticus: its Contents and Character,' *The Expositor*, Nov. 1883; Wright, *The Book of Koheleth*, 1883, chap. ii. (decides, perhaps, too hastily that Sirach in many passages imitates Koheleth).

---

[1] Bishop Butler, who is fond of Sirach, quotes this saying in his 4th sermon.

THE BOOK OF KOHELETH;
OR, ECCLESIASTES.

CHAPTER I.

THE WISE MAN TURNED AUTHOR AND PHILOSOPHER.

.... Il mondo invecchia,
E invecchiando intristisce.—TASSO, *Aminta*.

IN passing from the book of Ecclesiasticus to that of Ecclesiastes, we are conscious of breathing an entirely different intellectual atmosphere. 'Seek not out the things that are too hard for thee,' said Sirach, 'for thou hast no need of the secret things' (iii. 21, 22), but the book now before us is the record of a thinker, disappointed it is true, but too much in earnest to give up thinking. Of meditative minds there was no lack in this period of Israel's history. The writers of the 119th and several other Psalms, as well as Jesus the son of Sirach, had pondered over the ideal life, but our author (the only remaining representative of a school of writers [1]) was meditative in a different sense from any of these. He could not have said with the latter, 'I prayed for wisdom before the temple' (Ecclus. li. 14), nor with the former, 'Thy commandment is exceeding broad' (Ps. cxix. 96). The idea of the religious primacy of Israel awakened in his mind no responsive enthusiasm. We cannot exactly say that he conceals the place of his residence,[2] but he has certainly no overpowering interest in

---

[1] The 'many books' spoken of in xii. 12 were probably less orthodox than Ecclesiastes, but in so far as Ecclesiastes, especially in its uncorrected state, is sceptical, it may be grouped with them.

[2] In common with most interpreters, I regard Ecclesiastes as a Judæan work.

the scene of his life's troublesome drama. In this feature he resembles to a considerable extent the humanists of an earlier date (see p. 119), but in others, and those the most characteristic, he differs as widely from them as the old man from the child. They believed that virtue was crowned by prosperity; even the writer of *Job*, as some think, had not wholly cast off the consecrated dogma; but the austere and lonely thinker who has left us Ecclesiastes finds himself utterly unable to harmonise such a theory with facts (viii. 14). To him, living during one of the dreariest parts of the post-Exile period, it seemed as if the past aspirations of Israel had turned out a gigantic mistake. That home-sickness which impelled, if not the Second Isaiah himself, yet many who were stirred by his eloquence, to exchange a life of ease and luxury for one of struggle and privation—in what had it issued? In 'vanity and pursuit of wind' (comp. Isa. xxvi. 18). To quote a great Persian poet, who in some of his moods resembles Koheleth (see end of Chap. IX.),

> The Revelations of Devout and Learn'd,
> Who rose before us and as Prophets burn'd,
>   Are all but Stories, which, arose from Sleep,
> They told their fellows, and to Sleep return'd.

Such thoughts as these made the history of Israel an aid to scepticism rather than to faith; added to which it is probable that society in Koheleth's [1] time seemed to him too corrupt to admit of an idealistic theory of life. For an individual to seek to put in practice such a theory would expose him to hopeless failure and misery. Therefore, 'be not righteous overmuch,'[2] neither pretend to be exceedingly wise; why wilt thou ruin (lit. desolate) thyself?' (vii. 16). Some, no doubt, as the Soferim or Scripturists, had tried it, but they had only succeeded in making their lives 'desolate,' without any compensating advantage. Nor can we say that Ecclesiastes had given up theistic religion. He does not indeed

---

[1] Following the precedent of the Epilogue (xii. 9), I designate the author by the name which he has invented for his hero.
[2] There is a touch of humour in the expression, which can perhaps best be reproduced in our northern Doric, 'Be not unco' guid.'

believe in immortality and a future judgment, and is thus partly an exception to the rule of Lucretius,

> . . . nam si certam finem esse viderent
> Aerumnarum homines, aliqua ratione valerent
> Religionibus atque mineis obsistere vatum.
> (*De rerum naturâ*, i. 108–110.)

He mentions God twenty-seven times, but under the name Elohim, which belonged to Him as the Creator, not under that of Yahveh, which an Israelite was privileged to use ; and his one-sided supernaturalism obscured the sense of personal communion with God. He accepts only the first part of the great proclamation concerning the dwelling place of God in Isa. lxvii. 15 (see Eccles. v. 2). It is no doubt God who 'worketh all' (xi. 5), but there are nearer and almost more formidable potentates, an oppressive hierarchy of officials ranging from the taxgatherer to the king, 'a high one watching above the high, and high ones over both' (v. 8). True, our author seems to admit—at least if the text be sound (iii. 17 ; comp. viii. 12, 13)—that ' God will judge the righteous and the wicked ' (i.e. in this life, for he does not believe in another), but the comfort of this thought is dashed with bitterness by an unspoken but distinctly implied complaint, which may perhaps be well expressed in the language of Job (xxiv. 1), 'Why are judgments laid up (so long) by the Almighty,[1] and (why) do they that know him not see his days?' or in other words, Why is divine retribution so tardy? It is, in fact, this extreme tardiness of God's judicial interpositions which our author considers one of the chief causes of the prevalence of wickedness ;—

'Because sentence against the work of wickedness is not speedily executed, therefore the heart of the sons of men is fully set in them to do evil' (viii. 11).

On the whole, we may say that the older humanists were sincere optimists, while Koheleth, though theoretically perhaps an optimist (iii. 11), constantly relapses into a more congenial 'malism.' I use this word designedly. Koheleth can only be

---

[1] I follow Sept. and Dr. Merx. The received reading is very harsh.

called a pessimist loosely. Bad as things are, he does not believe that the world is getting worse and worse and hasting to its ruin. He believes in revolutions, some for evil, some for good, some for 'rending' or 'breaking down,' others for 'sewing' or 'building up.' He believes, in other words, that God brings about recurrent changes in human circumstances. But (like another wise man, Prov. xxv. 21) he does not trust revolutions of human origin ('evil matters' he calls them, viii. 3); he is no *carbonaro* (x. 20). And so for the present he is a 'malist,' and having no imaginative faculty he cannot sympathise with the 'Utopian' prospects for the future contained in the prophetic visions.

Yet, in spite of appearances, Koheleth builds upon a true Israelitish foundation. It is already something that he cannot bear to plunge into open infidelity, that he is still (as we have seen) a theist, though his theism gives him but little light and no comforting warmth. Now and then he alludes to the religious system of his people (see v. 1-5, 17, viii. 10). A stronger proof of his Israelitish sympathies is his choice of Solomon as the representative of humanity; I say, of humanity, because the author evidently declines to place himself upon the pedestal of Israelitish privilege. (Perhaps, too, as Herzfeld thinks,[1] he would console his people by showing them that they have companions in misfortune everywhere 'under the sun;' and we have already seen Job snatch a brief alleviation of pain from the thought of suffering humanity.) Koheleth is not only a Jew, but a man of culture. He cannot perhaps entirely defend himself from the subtle influence of the Greek view of life, and is even willing to associate from time to time with the ministers of alien sovereigns. True, he has noted with bitter irony the absurd and capricious changes in the government of Palestine (x. 5-7), but he has no spark of the spirit of the Maccabees, unless indeed in viii. 2-5, x. 4, 20, beneath the garb of servile prudence we may (with Dr. Plumptre) detect the irony of indignation. To the simple-minded reader at any rate he appears to counsel passive obedience, and a cautious crouching

[1] *Geschichte des Volkes Jisrael*, iii. 30.

attitude towards those in power. I suspect myself that either the advice is but provisional, or else Koheleth still feels the power of the prophetic Utopia : *ce peuple rêve toujours quelque chose d'international.*[1] Nay ; shall we not carry our generosity even farther ? That 'last word,' which he would have spoken had he lived longer, may possibly not have been that which the Soferim have forced upon him. Not a future judgment, but a return of prosperity to a wiser though sadder Israel, may have been his silent hope, and in this prosperity we may be sure that a wider and more philosophic culture would form a principal ingredient. This is by no means an absurd fancy. Koheleth firmly believed in recurrent historical cycles, and if there was 'a time to break down,' there was also 'a time to build up' (iii. 3). Sirach knows no future life and no Messiah ; but he believes in the eternity of Israel ; why, on the ground of his fragmentary remains, deny the same consolation to Koheleth? Much as I should prefer to imagine a far more satisfactory close for his troubled life (see Chap. IX.), I think we ought to admit the possibility of this hypothesis.

As an author, the characteristics of Koheleth are in the main Hebraic, though not without vague affinities to the Greek philosophic spirit. His work is without a model, but the dramatic element in it reminds us somewhat of the Book of Job. Just as the writer of that great poem delineates his own spiritual struggles—not of course without poetic amplification—under the assumed name of Job, so our author, with a similar poetical license, ascribes his difficulties to the imaginary personage Koheleth (or Ecclesiastes). There are also passages in which, like Job, he adopts the tone, style and rhythm [2] of gnomic poetry, though far from reaching the literary perfection of Job or of the proverbial collections. The attempt of Köster and Vaihinger to make him out an artist in the management of strophes is a sport of fancy. Unity and consistency in literary form were beyond the reach, if not of his powers, yet certainly of his opportunities ; even his phraseology, as a rule, is in the highest degree rough

[1] Renan, *L'Antéchrist*, p. 228.
[2] On the rhythm, comp. Bickell, *Der Prediger* (1884), pp. 27, 46-53.

and unpolished. This is the more striking by contrast with the elegant workmanship of Sirach. But the unknown author has very strong excuses. Thus, first, the negative tone of his mind must have destroyed the cheerful composure necessary to the artist. 'The burden of the mystery' pressed too heavily for him to think much of form and beauty. His harp, if he ever had one, he had long since hung up upon the willows. Next, it is highly probable that he was interrupted in the midst of his literary preparations. Nöldeke has remarked [1] that his object was not to produce 'ein literarisches Schaustück.' That is perfectly true ; his primary object was 'to scatter the doubts of his own mind.' But he did not despise the literary craft ; he was well aware that even 'the literature of power' may increase its influence by some attention to form. It seems to me that the 'labour of the file' has brought the first two chapters to a considerable degree of perfection ; but the rest of the book, upon the whole, is so rough and so disjointed, that I can only suppose it to be based on certain loose notes or *adversaria*, written solely with the object of dispersing his doubts and mitigating his pains by giving them expression. The thread of thought seems to break every few verses, and attempts to restore it fail to carry conviction to the unbiassed mind. The feelings and opinions embodied in the book are often mutually inconsistent ; in Ibn Ezra's time, and long before that, the Jewish students of the book were puzzled by this phenomenon, so strange in a canonical Scripture. Not a few scattered remarks have absolutely no connection with the subject. The style, too, is rarely easy and natural, and sometimes (especially in viii. 16, 17) we meet with a sentence which would certainly not have passed an author's final revision. The most obvious hypothesis surely is that from chap. iii. onwards we have before us the imperfectly worked-up meditations of an otherwise unknown writer, found after his death in proximity to a highly finished fragment which apparently professed to be the work of king Solomon. The meditations and the fragment were circulated in combination (for which there was much excuse, especially as some parts of

[1] *Die alttestamentliche Literatur*, p. 173.

the notes seemed to be in the narrative and even autobiographic style), and were received with much favour by the students of 'wisdom,' more, I should think, owing to the intrinsic interest of the book than to the literary fiction of Solomonic authorship. If this hypothesis be correct, we need not be surprised either at the author's inconsistencies in opinion, or at the general roughness of his style. The book may not even be all one man's work. Luther has already brought Ecclesiastes into connection with the Talmud.[1] Now the proverbial sayings which interrupt our thinker's self-questionings on 'vanity of vanities' are like the Haggadic passages which gush forth like fountains in the weary waste of hair-splitting Talmudic dialectics. No one has ever maintained the unity of the Talmud, and no one should be thought unreasonable for doubting the absolute freedom of Ecclesiastes from interpolations.[2]

The third and last excuse which I have to offer is that the meditations of Koheleth partake of the nature of an experiment. He may indeed (as I have remarked) be a member of a school of writers, but his strikingly original manner compels us to regard him as a master rather than a disciple. No such purely reflective work had, so far as we know, as yet been produced in Hebrew literature. Similar moral difficulties to those which preoccupied our author had no doubt occurred to some of the prophets and poets, but they had not been sounded to their depths. Even in the Book of Job the reflective spirit has very imperfect scope. The speeches soon pass into a lyric strain, and Jehovah Himself closes the discussion by imposing silence. But the author of Ecclesiastes was a thinker, not a lyrist, and was compelled to form his own vehicle of thought. He 'sought,' indeed, 'to find out pleasant words' (xii. 10), but had to strain the powers of an unpliant language to the uttermost, to coin (presumably) new words, and apply old ones in fresh senses, till he might well have complained (to apply Lucretius) 'propter

---

[1] 'Dazu so ist's wie ein Talmud aus vielen Büchern zusammengezogen.' Luther's *Tischreden*, quoted in Ginsburg, p. 113.
[2] See Supplementary Chapter.

egestatem linguae et rerum novitatem.'[1] He deserves great praise for his measure of success; Luzzatto in his early work failed to do him justice. He is not ambitious; as a rule, he abstains from fine writing. Once indeed he attempts it, but, as I venture to think, with but ill success—I refer to the closing description of old age (xii. 4-9), which has a touch of the extravagant euphuism of late Arabic literature.[2] From a poetical point of view, the prelude (i. 4-8) is alone worthy to be mentioned, though not included either by Renan or by Bickell among the passages poetical in form (for a list of which see below [3]). Let us mark this fine passage, that we may return to it again in another connection.

[1] *De rerum naturâ*, i. 140 (appositely quoted by Mr. Tyler).

[2] See the passage quoted from Chenery's translation of Hariri by Dr. Taylor (*Dirge of Coheleth*, p. 55); comp. Rückert's rhyming translation (*Hariri*, i. 104-5).

[3] Renan's list is i. 15, 18; ii. 2, 14; iii. 2-8, iv. 5, 14; v. 2; vii. 1-6; 7, 8; 9b; 13b; 24; viii. 1, 4; ix. 16, 17; x. 2, 12, 18; xi. 4, 7; xii. 3-5; 10; 11, 12. Bickell's, i. 7, 8; 15; 18; ii. 2; v. 9; vi. 7; iv. 5; ii. 14; viii. 8; ix. 16-x. 1; vii. 1-6, vi. 9, vii. 7-9; vii. 11, 12; vii. 20; v. 2; x. 16-20; xi. 6; xi. 4; viii. 1-4, x. 2, 3; x. 6, 7; x. 10-15; ix. 7; xi. 9, 10, xii. 1a; xii. 1b-5; 6. (The order of these passages arises out of Bickell's critical theory; on which see Chap. XII.)

CHAPTER II.

'TRUTH AND FICTION' IN AN AUTOBIOGRAPHY.

LET us now take a general survey of this strange book, regarding it as a record of the conflicting moods and experiences of a thoughtful man of the world. The author is too modest to appear in his own person (at least in i. 1–ii. 12), but, like Cicero in his dialogues, selects a mouthpiece from the heroic past. His choice could not be doubtful. Who so fit as the wisest of his age, the founder and patron of gnomic poetry, king Solomon (1 Kings iv. 30–32)? After the preluding verses, from which a quotation has been given above, Ecclesiastes continues thus :—

I Koheleth have been[1] king over Israel in Jerusalem ; and I gave my mind to making search and exploration, by wisdom, concerning all that is done under heaven ; that is a sore trouble which God hath given to the sons of men to trouble themselves therewith ! I saw all the works which are done under the sun ; and behold, all is vanity and pursuit of wind.

> That which is crooked cannot be straightened,
> and a deficiency cannot be reckoned (i. 12–15).

The name or title 'Koheleth' is obscure. According to the Epilogue ' Koheleth was a wise man ' (xii. 9)—a statement which confirms the explanation of the name as meaning 'one who calls an assembly.'[2] The 'wise men' of Israel

---

[1] See the fantastic legend to account for the past tense in *Midrash Koheleth* (transl. Wünsche), or Ginsburg (p. 268 ; comp. p. 38).

[2] Dean Plumptre thinks Koheleth (like ἐκκλησιαστής), which is rendered by him 'the Debater,' means rather a member of an assembly, than a teacher or preacher, and compares Ecclus. xxxviii. 33, where the son of Sirach says of labourers and artisans that they 'shall not sit high in the congregation,' i.e. in the *ecclesia* or academy of sages. But judging from the parallel line the 'congregation' is rather that of the people in general (comp. Ecclus. xv. 5). The Dean's

gathered their disciples together, and such an able teacher as Koheleth would fain gather all who have ears to hear around his seat. But Koheleth is also Solomon (though only for a short time—the author did not, I suppose, live long enough thoroughly to fuse the conceptions of king and philosopher [1]). The wise king is to be imagined standing on the brink of the grave, and casting the clear-sighted glance of a dying man on past life, somewhat as Moses in parts of Deuteronomy or David in 2 Sam. xxii., xxiii. 1–7. A subtle and poetic view of Solomon's career is thus opened before us. He is not here represented in his political relation, but as a specimen of the highest type of human being, with a boundless appetite for pleasure and every means of gratifying it. But even such a man's deliberate verdict on all forms of pleasure is that they are utterly unsubstantial, mere vanity (lit. a vapour—Aquila, ἀτμίς; comp. James iv. 14). Neither pure speculation (i. 13–18), nor riotous mirth (ii. 1, 2), nor even the refined voluptuousness consistent with the free play of the intellect [2] (ii. 3), could satisfy his longing, or enable him, with Goethe's Faust, to say to the flying moment, 'Ah! linger yet, thou art so fair.' It is true that wisdom is after all better than folly; Solomon from his 'specular mount' could 'see' this to be a truth (ii. 13); but in the end he found it as resultless as 'the walking in darkness' of the fool.

'And I myself perceived that one fate befalleth them all. And I said in my heart, As the fate of the fool will be the fate which shall befall me, even me; and why have I then been exceeding wise? and

view that the book embodies the inward debates of a Jewish philosopher may be to a great extent true, but for all that Koheleth is throughout represented as speaking alone and with authority. On the philological explanation of the word, see Appendix.

[1] This seems a reasonable view. Bickell boldly maintains that i. 1, 12, 16, ii. 7, 8, 9 [12] are interpolations (made presumably to facilitate the recognition of the book as canonical). Observe however that the (fictitious) author is nowhere declared to be Solomon, but only ben-David (i. 1). He claims attention merely as a private person, as an interpreter of the complaints of humanity. Though he does once expressly refer to his royal state (i. 12), it is only to suggest to his readers what ample opportunities he has enjoyed of learning the vanity of earthly grandeur. So, very plausibly, Bloch (*Ursprung des Kohelet*, p. 17).

[2] The passage indeed is obscure and possibly corrupt (so Bickell), but the above words probably do justice to the mood described.

I said in my heart that this also is vanity' (ii. 14*b*, 15), i.e. that this undiscriminating fate is a fresh proof of the delusiveness of all things.

And in this strain Koheleth runs on to nearly the end of the chapter, with an added touch of bitterness at the thought of the doubtful character of his successor (ii. 18, 19). Then occurs one of those abrupt transitions which so often puzzle the student of Ecclesiastes. In ii. 1–11 Koheleth has rejected the life of sensuous pleasure, even when wisely regulated, as 'vanity.' He now returns to the subject, and declares this to be, not of course the ideally highest good, but the highest good open to man, if it were only in his power to secure it. But he has seen that both sensuous enjoyment and the wisdom which regulates it come from God, who grants these blessings to the man who is good in his sight, while profitless trouble is the portion of the sinner. He repeats therefore that even wisdom and knowledge and joy, the highest attainable goods, are, by reason of their uncertainty, 'vanity and pursuit of wind' (ii. 26).

At the end of this long speech of Koheleth, we naturally ask how far it can be regarded as autobiographical. Only, I think, in a qualified sense. Its psychological depth points to similar experiences on the part of the author, but to experiences which have been deepened in their imaginative reproduction. It is truth mingled with fiction—*Wahrheit und Dichtung*—which we meet with in the first two chapters. A more strictly biographical narrative appears to begin in chap. iii., from which point the allusions to Solomon cease, and are replaced by scattered references to contemporary history. The confidences of the author are introduced by a passage (iii. 1–8) in the gnomic style, containing a catalogue of the various actions, emotions, and states of feeling which make up human life. Each of these, we are told, has its own allotted season in the fixed order of nature, but as this is beyond the ken and influence of man, the question arises, 'What profit hath he that worketh in that wherewith he wearieth himself?' (iii. 9.) Thus, the 'wearisome trouble' of the 'sons of men' has no permanent result. All that you can do is to accustom yourself to acquiesce in destiny: you will then see that every act and every state in your ever-shifting life is truly beautiful or seemly (iii. 11), even if not profitable to the individual (iii. 9). More than this, man has been endowed with the faculty of understanding this kaleidoscopic world, with the drawback that he cannot possibly embrace it all in one view :—[1]

Also he hath put the world into their heart (i.e. mind), except that man cannot find out from beginning to end the work which God hath made (iii. 11).

In fact, to quote Lord Bacon's words in the *Advancement of Learning*, 'God has framed the mind like a glass, capable of the image of the universe, and desirous to receive it, as the eye to receive the light.' But here a dark mood interrupts the course of our author's meditations; or perhaps it is the record of a later period which is but awkwardly attached to the previous passages. 'To rejoice and to fare well'—sensual (or, let us say, sensuous) pleasure, in short—is now represented as the only good for man, and even that is not to be

---

[1] Among the many other interpretations of this difficult passage, two may be mentioned here. (1) 'He has also set worldliness in their heart, without which man cannot understand the work that God does, from beginning to end.' So Kalisch (*Path and Goal*, frequently). This is an improvement upon the translation of Gesenius and others, who render, not 'without which' &c., but 'so that man may not' &c. The objection to the latter rendering is that it gives 'worldliness' a New Testament sense (comp. 1 John ii. 15). Kalisch, however, in full accord with the spirit of Judaism, makes Koheleth frankly accept 'worldliness' as a good, understanding by 'worldliness' a sense of worldly duties and enjoyments. Had this however been Koheleth's meaning, would he not have coined another of his favourite abstract terms (comp. the Peshitto's '*olmoyuthō* = αἰών in Eph. ii. 2)? (2) 'Also he has put eternity into their heart, but so that man cannot' &c. So Ginsburg and Delitzsch (*desiderium æternitatis*, taking 'eternity' in a metaphysical sense = 'that which is beyond time'); so also Nowack (taking it in the popular sense of years following upon years without apparent limit). Ginsburg's view is against the context, in which the continuance of the human spirit is doubted; but Nowack's explanation is not unacceptable. Man has been enabled to form the idea of Time (for the popular view of 'eternity' comes practically to this), and has divided this long space into longer and shorter periods; what happens in one period or season, he can compare with what happens in another, thus finding all well-adapted and 'beautiful.' But he cannot grasp the whole of Time in one view. But I still prefer the explanation given in the text, as being simpler, in spite of the fact that '*ōlām* nowhere else occurs in the sense of 'world' (or the present order of things), so common in later Hebrew.

too absolutely reckoned upon, for 'it is the gift of God' (iii. 12, 13, 22; comp. ii. 24). Certainly our author at any rate did not succeed in drowning care in the wine-cup: he is no vulgar sensualist. His merriment is spoiled by the thought of the misery of others, and he can find nothing 'under the sun' (a passionate generalisation from life in Palestine) but violence and oppression. In utter despair he pronounces the dead happier than the living (iv. 1, 2). In fact, he says, neither in life nor in death has man any superiority over the other animals, which are under no providential order, and have no principle of continuance. Such is the cynical theory which tempts Koheleth; and yet he seems to have hesitated before accepting it, unless we may venture with Bickell to strike out iii. 17, as the work of a later editor who believed in retributions hereafter (like xi. 9b, xii. 7, 13, 14). I confess that consistency seems to me to require this step; the verse is in fact well fitted to be an antidote to the following verse, which seems to have suggested the opening phrase. This is how the text runs at present:—

I said in my heart, The righteous and the wicked shall God judge; for there is a time for every purpose and for every work *there* (emphatically for 'in the other world;' or read, hath he appointed). I said in my heart, (It happens) on account of the sons of men, that God may test them, and that they may see that they are but beasts. For the sons of men are a chance (comp. Herod. i. 32), and beasts are a chance; yea, all have one chance: as the one dies, so dies the other; yea, they all have one spirit; and advantage of the one over the other there is none, for all is vanity. All go unto one place; all are of the dust, and all turn to dust again. Who knows whether the spirit of man goes upward, and whether the spirit of the beast goes downward to the earth?[1] (iii. 17-21.)

---

[1] This is the rendering of the four principal versions and of all the best critics, including Mercier, Ewald, Ginsburg, Grätz and Delitzsch; it agrees with the general tendency of Koheleth, and in particular with xii. 5, where the grave is called man's 'eternal home' (see below). It is no doubt opposed by the vowel-points, which are followed in King James's Bible. But it is more than probable (considering other parallel phenomena) that the authors of the points were directed by a theological and therefore uncritical motive, that, namely, of effacing as far as possible a trace of Koheleth's opposition to the doctrine, by that time recognised as orthodox, of the immortality of the soul.

Our author's abiding conviction is that 'the spirit does but mean the breath' (*In Memoriam*, lvi.), so that man and the lower animals have 'one spirit' and alike end in dust. '*Pulvis et umbra sumus*.' It is true, some of his contemporaries hold the new doctrine of Immortality, but Koheleth, in his cool scepticism, hesitates to accept it. Which indeed of its enthusiastic advocates can claim to 'know' that which he asserts; or can prove to Koheleth's satisfaction that God (as a psalmist in Ps. xlix. 15 puts it) will 'receive' the spirit of man, in spite of the fact that the vital principle of beasts loses itself in the dust of death? It is no doubt an awkward construction which Koheleth adopts: he *seems* to express an uncertainty as to the fate of the lower animals. To convey the meaning which I have given, the construction ought to have been disjunctive, as in this line from a noble modern poem,

Friend, who knows if death indeed have life, or life have death for goal?[1]

But there is, or rather there ought to be, no doubt as to Koheleth's meaning. Dean Plumptre frankly admits that 'it is not till nearly the close of the book, with all its many wanderings of thought, that the seeker rests in that measure of the hope of immortality which we find' [but this is open to considerable doubt] 'in xii. 7.'

[1] Swinburne, *On the Verge*.

CHAPTER III.

MORE MORALISING, INTERRUPTED BY PROVERBIAL MAXIMS.

LET us now resume the thread of Koheleth's moralising. Violence and oppression were two of the chief evils which struck an attentive observer of Palestinian life. But there were two others equally worthy of a place in the sad picture—the evils of rivalry and isolation. First, with regard to rivalry (iv. 4-6). What is 'skilful work,' or art, but an 'envious surpassing of the one by the other'? This also is 'pursuit of wind;' it gives no permanent satisfaction. True, indolence is self-destruction: but on the other hand a little true rest is better than the labour of windy effort, urged on by rivalry yielding no rest' (Delitzsch). Such at least is the most probable connection, supposing that vv. 5 and 6 are not rather interpolated or misplaced. If however it be objected (here Koheleth passes to a second great evil—that of isolation) that a man may labour for his child or his brother, yet who, pray, is benefited by the money-getting toils of one who has no near relative, and stands alone in the world? A pitiable sight is such unprofitable toil! The fourth chapter closes with maxims on the blessings of companionship (iv. 9-12), followed by a vivid description of the sudden fall of an old and foolish king (iv. 13-16), who had not cared to appropriate one of the chief of these blessings, viz. good advice. There is much that is enigmatical in the last four verses. We should expect the writer to be alluding to some fact in contemporary history, but no plausible parallel has yet been indicated.[1] Ver. 16 is certainly either cor-

[1] Hitzig in his commentary refers to the history of the high priest Onias and his nephew Joseph. Afterwards he recalled this opinion; but we may be thankful to him for directing attention to this curious and instructive historical episode.

rupt or mutilated. Bickell thinks that it must originally have run somewhat as follows :—

There was no end of all the people, even of all those who [applauded him and cast reproaches on the old king. For because he had despised the counsel of the prudent, to rule foolishly and to oppress the people, therefore they hated him, even as those had hated him] who were before them ; they also that came afterwards did not rejoice in him.

At this point the ideal autobiography of Koheleth is interrupted. From v. 1 (=iv. 17 in the Hebrew) to vii. 14 we are presented with a mixture of proverbial sayings (such perhaps as Koheleth was continually framing and depositing in his note-books) and records of the wise man's personal experience. Notice especially the reappearance of the old Israelitish instinctive sympathy with husbandmen (or, shall I say, with yeomen) in ver. 9. Both proverbs and personal records are the offspring of different moods, and therefore not always consistent. Thus at one time our author repeats his preference of sensuous enjoyment to any other mode of passing one's life.

For (then) he will not think much on the (few) days of his life, because God responds to the joy of his heart (v. 20).

But the writer is too pessimistic to rest long in this thought. It is a 'common evil among men' to have riches without the full enjoyment of them : 'better an untimely birth,' he cries, than to be in such a case (vi. 3). Note here in passing the fondness of our author for using a comparison in expressing an emphatic judgment (comp. iv. 9-16, vii. 1-8). Better, he continues, is a momentary experience of real happiness than to let the desire wander after unattainable ends. 'There are many things that increase vanity ;' with the reserve of good taste, he understates his meaning, for what human object, according to Koheleth, is not futile? That gift which to the Christian is so wondrously fair— the gift of life—to him becomes 'the numbered days of his life of vanity ;' and 'who knows what is good for man in life, which he spends as a shadow? For who can tell a man what shall be after him under the sun?' (vi. 12.) Koheleth, we see, has no faith in his nation, nor in humanity.

I do not feel sure that we may say with Dean Bradley that 'out of this very gloom and sadness come forth in the next chapter thoughts that have gone, some of them, the round of the world.' No doubt there is more than a mere tinge of the same midnight gloom in some of these proverbial sayings. But surely there is a complete break in the thread of thought of vi. 12, and a fresh collection of looser notes has found a place at the head of chap. vii. At any rate, these sayings supply a convincing proof that Koheleth was not a mere hedonist or Epicurean. He recalls in vii. 2 his former commendation of feasting, and declares,

> It is better to go into the house of mourning than to go into the house of feasting,
> inasmuch as that is the end of all men, and the living can lay it to his heart (vii. 2).

I said that Koheleth was too pessimistic to remain long under the influence of hedonism. I might have said that he was too thoughtful: a rational man could not, without the anticipations of faith, close his mind to the suggestions of pessimism in the circumstances of Koheleth's age. Better – thoughtful misery than thoughtless mirth, is the keynote of the triad of maxims (vii. 2-6) on the compensations of misery which follows the dreary sentence praising death, in vii. 1.[1] Resignation is the secret of inward peace; 'with a sad face the heart may be cheerful.' Not only in view of the great problem of existence, but in your everyday concerns, restrain your natural impulses whether to towering passion or to brooding vexation at the wrongness or the slowness of the course of human affairs (vii. 8, 9). Above all, do not give way to an ignorant idealism. It is unwise to ask 'How is it that

---

[1] The mechanical juxtaposition of the two halves of ver. 1 is obvious. The proverb gains considerably, if read with Bickell's very plausible supplements,
> 'Better is a good name than precious ointment,
> [but wisdom is still better than fame;
> better is not-being than being]
> and the day of death than the day of one's birth.'
The 'wisdom' meant will be that of resignation and renunciation.

the former days were better than these?' (vii. 10.) The former time, so bright and happy, and the present, with its predominant gloom, were alike ordained by God (vii. 13 should follow vii. 10); and as a last consolation for cool and rational thinkers, be sure that there is nought to fear after death; there are no torments of Gehenna. This in fact is the reason why God ordains evil; there being no second life, man must learn whatever he can from calamity in this life.

On a good day be of good cheer, and on an evil day consider (this): God hath also made this (viz. good) equally with that (evil), on the ground that man is to experience nothing at all hereafter[1] (vii. 14; comp. ix. 10).

Thus, not only ' be not righteous over much ' (vii. 16), but 'do not believe over much' is the teaching of our rationalist-thinker. There is neither good nor evil after death. But is there no *present* judgment? Yes; but this is not a thought of life and hope. It is a true 'religion' to him; it binds him in his words as well as his actions. But although Hooker so admired the saying in v. 2 ('God is in heaven, and thou upon earth, therefore let thy words be few') as to quote it in one of his finest passages,[2] yet the context of v. 2 sufficiently shows how different was the quality of the reverence of the two writers. Be careful to pay thy vows, says Koheleth, lest when thou invokest God's name, His angel should appear, and call thee to account.

Suffer not thy mouth to bring punishment upon thy body; and say not before the angel, It was an oversight;[3] wherefore should God be angry at thy voice, and destroy the work of thy hands?' (v. 6.)

[1] 'Hereafter' is, literally, 'after him' (for the meaning of which see iii. 22, vi. 12); 'experience,' literally 'find' (comp. Prov. vi. 33). For other views, see Wright, who objects to the above explanation that it 'is opposed to the teaching of Koheleth respecting a future judgment.' But the question is, Did Koheleth believe in a future judgment?

[2] *Eccles. Polity*, i. 2, § 3.

[3] There is a touch of humour here; comp. the wretch in the fable who called Death to his aid, but refused him when he came. Klostermann has done well in reviving this interpretation, which, in Germany at least, had been generally abandoned. (Delitzsch thinks the 'angel' is the priest whom the man who has vowed approaches with a request to be released from his vow. This is supported by

To Koheleth the mention of the divine name is a possible source of danger; to Hooker God is One 'whom to know is life, and joy to make mention of his name.' Koheleth has only fear for God's holy name—a fear which is not indeed ineffectual but very pale and cheerless; Hooker, a 'perpetual fear and love,' and the love gives a new quality and a new efficacy to the fear.

Mal. ii. 7, where the priest is called 'the messenger of Jehovah Sabáoth;' but see the notes of Ginsburg and Kingsbury. Renan renders, *à l'envoyé des prêtres*.) The angel is the destroying angel, whose action is discerned by faith in the judicial calamities which, sometimes at least, overtake the wrong-doer. (So the Targum, but postponing the appearance of the angel to the *future* judgment.)

CHAPTER IV.

FACTS OF CONTEMPORARY LIFE.

AT vii. 15 a new section begins, consisting almost entirely of the author's personal experiences, very loosely connected; it continues as far as ix. 12. A curious passage at the outset appears to describe virtue as residing in the mean between two extremes (vii. 15-18). The appearance however is deceptive: it is as much out of place to quote Aristotle's famous definition of virtue ($\mu\epsilon\sigma\acute{o}\tau\eta s$ $\delta\acute{u}o$ $\kappa\alpha\kappa\iota\hat{\omega}\nu$), as Buddha's counsel to him who would attain perfection to 'exercise himself in the medium course of discipline.' Koheleth merely offers practical advice how to steer one's ship between the rocks. Do not, he says, make your life a burden by excessive legalism. But on the other hand, do not earn the reputation of caring nothing for the precepts of the law. That were folly, and would bring you to an early death.[1] Koheleth expresses this sharply and enigmatically; do not be too 'righteous,' and do not be too 'wicked.' 'Righteous' and 'wicked' are both to be taken in the common acceptation of those terms in the religious world: the words are used ironically. Our author's only theory of virtue is that no theory is possible. The 'wisdom' which both gives 'defence' and 'preserves life' (vii. 12) is the practical wisdom of resignation and moderation. Of essential wisdom (or philosophy as we should call it[2]) he says, alluding to Job xxviii. 12-23, that it is 'far off, and exceeding deep; who can find it out?' (vii. 24.) The old theory,

---
[1] As Plumptre well remarks, the vices thought of and the end to which they lead are those of sensual license (comp. Prov. vii. 25-27).

[2] In Koheleth's phrase, 'that which is;' comp. Wisd. vii. 17-21, where 'the infallible knowledge of the things that are' is equivalent to a perfect natural science. Here a similar phrase means rather philosophy.

which claimed to give the secret of history, and which even afterwards satisfied some wise men (e.g. Sirach)—the theory that the good are rewarded and the bad punished in this world —is not borne out by Koheleth's experience,—

There is (many) a righteous man who perishes in spite of his righteousness, and there is (many) an ungodly man who lives long in spite of his wickedness (vii. 15 ; contrast the interpolated passage viii. 12, 13).

But though Koheleth, like Job, despairs of essential wisdom, he 'turns' with hope to the wide field of wisdom—or, as he calls it, 'wisdom and reasoning,' i.e. moral inquiries pursued on the inductive method. And what is the result of his inquiry? He gives it with much deliberateness, stating that he (viz. '*the* Koheleth,' see on xii. 8) has put one fact to another in order to form a conclusion (ver. 27) and it is that women-tempters are more pernicious than Death (man's great enemy personified, as so often). Or, putting it in other words, which I am forced to paraphrase to bring out their meaning—words to which the well-known poem of Simonides is chivalry itself— 'A few rare specimens of uncorrupted human nature I have found, so rare that one may reckon them as one among a thousand ; but not one of these truly human creatures was a woman.'[1] The latter statement is the stronger, and shows that our author agrees with Ecclus. xxv. 19, that 'all wickedness is but little to the wickedness of a woman.' And so much in earnest is he, that he even tries a third mode of expressing his conclusion. Carefully limiting himself he says, ' Lo! this only have I found ; that God made mankind upright, but they have sought out many contrivances' (ver. 29) ; that is, men and women are both born good, but are too soon sophisticated by civilisation (and the leaders in this downward process, we may infer from the context, are the women). Koheleth scarcely means to imply that civilisation is bad in

---

[1] So Klostermann. The ordinary interpretation is, ' One man among a thousand (men) I have found, but a woman among all these I have not found ;' i.e. I have tested a thousand men and a thousand women ; I have found one true man, but not one true woman. The objection is that *'ādām* elsewhere (e.g. ver. 29) means human beings without distinction of sex.

itself; if he does, the few good men he has met must apparently have been hermits! But though not essentially immoral, the inventive or contriving faculty (so wonderful to Sophocles) seems to Koheleth the chief source of moral danger.

But are these the only results of Koheleth's wide induction from the facts of contemporary life? Yes; a time such as this 'when man rules over man to his hurt' (viii. 9) suggests, not only prudential maxims, but this sad conclusion, already (vii. 15) mentioned by anticipation, that the fate proper to the wicked falls upon the righteous, and that proper to the righteous on the wicked (viii. 14), or to express this in the concrete,

And in accordance with this I have seen ungodly men honoured, and that too in the holy place (i.e. the temple; comp. Isa. xviii. 7); but those who had acted rightly had to depart and were forgotten in the city. This too is vanity [1] (viii. 10).

No wonder that wickedness is rampant! It requires singular courage to do right when Nemesis delays her visit; or, as Koheleth puts it, in language which sorely displeased a later editor,

Because sentence against a wicked work is not executed speedily, therefore men have abundant courage to do evil. For I know that it even happens that a sinner does evil for a long time, and yet lives long, whilst he who fears before God is short-lived as a shadow [1] (viii. 12, 13).

Koheleth does not, of course, include himself among the reckless evil-doers. He acquiesces in the painful inconsistencies of the world, and seems to comfort himself with the relatively best good—'to eat and drink and be merry' (viii. 15). Charity may perhaps suggest that this is not said without bitter irony.

Then follows a clumsy but affecting passage (viii. 16, 17) on the uselessness of brooding (as the author had so long

---

[1] Following Bickell. In viii. 10 it is the linguistic form, and in viii. 12, 13 the contents of the Massoretic text which excite suspicion. The former verse is thus rendered by Delitzsch, 'And then I have seen the wicked buried, and they entered into (their 'perpetual house,' the grave); but they that had done right had to depart (into exile) from the holy place (Jerusalem; cf. 11. Isa. xlviii. 2), and were forgotten out of the city: this too is vanity.'

done) over the mysteries of human life, which introduces the concluding part of the section (ix. 1-12). These twelve verses are full of a restrained passion. Such being the unfree condition of man that he cannot even govern his sympathies and antipathies, and so regardless of moral distinctions the course of destiny, and there being no hereafter,[1] what remains but to take such pleasure as life—especially wedded life—can offer, and to carry out one's plans with energy? Yet, alas! it is only too true that neither success nor freedom of action can be reckoned upon, for 'the race is not to the swift,' and men are 'snared' like the fishes and the birds.

The section which begins at ix. 13 is of still more varied contents. It begins with a striking little story about the 'poor wise man,' a Themistocles in common life, 'who by his wisdom delivered the city, and no one remembered that poor man' (ix. 14, 15). Surely here (as in iv. 13, 14, viii. 10) we catch the echo of contemporary history. It is not a generalisation (comp. Prov. xxi. 22), but a fact which the author gives us, and it may plausibly be conjectured that he was the 'poor wise man' himself. The rest of the section (down to x. 15) contains proverbs on wisdom and folly, and some bitterly ironical remarks on the exaltation of servants and burden-bearers [2] above the rich and the princely.

[1] The view expressed in ix. 10 is, I hope, very far from being the private belief of the many preachers who are accustomed to quote it. See the chapter on Ecclesiastes from a religious point of view.
[2] Correcting the text in x. 6 with A. Krochmal.

CHAPTER V.

THE WISE MAN'S PARTING COUNSELS.

A NEW section begins at x. 16—no ingenuity avails to establish a connection with the preceding verses. We are approaching our goal, and breathe a freer air. From the very first the ideas and images presented to us are in a healthier and more objective tone. The condemnation expressed in ver. 16 does credit to the public spirit of the writer, and, I need hardly say, is not really inconsistent (as Hitzig supposed) with the advice in ver. 20. In the words—

Even among thine acquaintance[1] curse not the king, and in thy bedchambers curse not the rich; for the birds of the heaven may carry the voice [comp. the cranes of Ibycus] and that which hath wings may report the word—

Dean Plumptre perhaps rightly sees 'the irony of indignation' which 'veils itself in the garb of a servile prudence.' There is no necessity to reduce Koheleth to the moral level of Epicurus, who is said to have deliberately preferred despotism and approved courting the monarch.

It is a still freer spirit which breathes in the remainder of the book. Let courtiers waste their time in luxury (x. 18), but throw thou thyself unhesitatingly into the swift stream of life. Be not ever forecasting, for there are some contingencies which can no more be guarded against than the falling of rain or of a tree (xi. 3, 4). Act boldly, then, like the corn-merchants, who speculate on such a grand scale,—

Send forth thy bread upon the wide waters [lit. upon the face of the waters], for thou mayst find it [i.e. obtain a good return for it] after many days (xi. 1).

---
[1] Altering the points with Klostermann.

But since fortune is capricious, do not risk thine all on a single venture. 'Ships are but boards, sailors but men' &c., as Shylock says. Divide thy merchandise, and so, if one vessel is wrecked or plundered, much may still be saved; or—another possible interpretation—store thy property in various hiding-places, so that, in case of some political revolution, thine all may not be taken from thee.—

Make seven portions, and also eight; for thou knowest not what evil shall be upon the earth (or, the land) (xi. 2).

This is not, of course, the usual explanation of these two verses, which are enigmas fairly admitting of more than one solution. Most commentators understand them as recommending beneficence, which ver. 2 requires to be of extensive range, and which ver. 1 compares to cakes of bread thrown upon the water, and gathered up no one knows by whom. So perhaps (besides Rashi, Aben Ezra, Ginsburg &c.) Goethe in the *Westöstliche Divan*

> Was willst du untersuchen
> Wohin die Milde fliesst !
> Ins Wasser wirf dein Kuchen—
> Wer weiss wer sie geniesst ! [1]

I do not think that this suits the context, which suggests activity and caution as the two good qualities recommended by Koheleth. But it is very possible that the proverb was a popular one which the author took up, giving it a fresh application.

Such is the author's parting advice to the elder part of his readers,—not very elevated, but not without a breath of courageous faith (xi. 5). Not that he has given up his advocacy of pleasure. Side by side with work, a man should cherish, even to the very last, all those sources of joy which God Himself has provided, remembering the long dark days which await him in Sheól. Then, at ver. 9, he addresses the

---

[1] But Goethe may have thought of the Turkish proverb, 'Do good, throw the loaf into the water; if the fish knows it not, the Creator does,' or the story from the life of the Caliph Mutewekyil [Mutawakkîl ?] quoted, with this proverb, from H. F. v. Diez by Dukes, *Rabbinische Blumenlese*, pp. 73-74. Comp. also the stories in the Midrash Koheleth on our passage.

young, and in measured distichs intreats them to enjoy life while they may.

> Rejoice, O young man, in thy youth,
> and let thy heart gladden thee in the flower of thine age ;
> and walk in the ways of thy heart
> and according to the sight of thine eyes ;
> And banish discontent from thy heart,
> and put away evil from thy flesh :—
> for youth and the prime of life are vanity.

Between lines 4 and 5 we find the received text burdened with a prosaic insertion, which is probably not due to an after-thought on the part of the writer, but to the anxiety of later students to rescue the orthodoxy of the book. The insertion consists of the words, Rabbinic in expression as well as in thought, ' But know that for all this God will bring thee into the judgment.'[1] It was the wisdom of true charity to insert them ; but it is our wisdom as literary students to ' banish discontent ' with the discord which they introduce by restoring the passage to its original form.

At this point Koheleth turns away from the young to those (presumably) of his own age. Again there are traces at least of a series of distichs which must once have stood here, but either the author or one of his editors, or both, have so far worked over them that the series is no longer perfect. The first suspected instance of this 'overworking' occurs at the very outset. ' Remember thy Creator in the flower of thine age,' are the opening words of Koheleth's second address. They are usually explained as taking up the idea of the last judgment expressed at the close of xi. 9. ' Since God,' to quote Dr. Ginsburg's paraphrase, ' will one day hold us accountable for all the works done in the body, we are to set the Lord always before our eyes.' The importance of this passage, when thus interpreted, is manifest. It suggests that Koheleth had struggled through his many difficulties to an assured doctrinal and practical position, and that it is not mere rejoicing, but ' rejoicing in the Lord,' that Koheleth recommends in xii. 1—

---

[1] What judgment ? Present or future (i.e. after death)? The latter gives a more forcible meaning (comp. iii. 17, xii. 14).

an edifying view of the old man's final result which every one must desire to be true if only it be consistent with the rest of the book. I fear that this is not the case. Elsewhere in the book sensuous pleasure in moderation is praised without any reference to God, and in the immediate neighbourhood of this verse the motive given for rejoicing is not the thought of God, but that of the many days of darkness (i.e. of Sheól) which are coming. Besides, the exhortation 'Remember thy Creator' does not perfectly suit the close of the verse, or indeed of the section. What is the natural inference from the fact that at an advanced age life becomes physically a burden? Surely this—that man should enjoy life while his powers are fresh. Cannot an *old man* 'remember' his Creator? (To 'remember' is to think upon; it is not a synonym for conversion.) The text therefore is almost certainly incorrect.

Has an editor, then, tampered with the text of the opening words of the exhortation? May we, for instance, follow Grätz and read, for *bōr'ěka* 'thy Creator,' *bōr'ka* 'thy fountain' (lit. thy cistern), taking this as a metaphorical expression for 'thy wife' or 'thy wedlock' (as in Prov. v. 15-18)? The objection certain to be raised is that the text when thus corrected brings the book to a lame and impotent conclusion. It may be true, as Bishop Temple has said, that chastity and monotheism are the chief legacies which the Jewish Church has bequeathed to mankind.[1] There is nothing in an exhortation to prize a pure married life unworthy of a high-minded Jewish teacher. But in this connection it is certainly to a Western reader strange, and one is sorely tempted to suppose a displacement of the words, and, following Bickell, to make the distich—

> And remember thy fountain
> in the flower of thine age—

the conclusion of the stanzas beginning at xi. 9. This, it is true, involves (1) the excision of the words 'for youth and the prime of life are vanity,' and (2) an alteration of the

---

[1] *Essays and Reviews* (1869), pp. 15-17.

construction of xii. 1, 2 (reading 'and evil days shall come' &c.) This violent change is no doubt justified by Bickell on metrical grounds, but as I cannot unreservedly adopt his metrical theory, I have not sufficient excuse for accepting his rearrangement of the text.

I wish some better remedy than that of Grätz could be devised. I would gladly close these Meditations with admiration as well as sympathy. But at the risk of being called unimaginative, I must venture to criticise the entire conclusion of the original Book of Koheleth (xii. 1–7). * Most English critics admire the poem on the evils of old age which follows on the earnest 'Remember,' and naturally think that it requires some specially sublime saying to introduce it. I do not join them in their admiration, and consequently find it easier to adopt what seems to some the 'low view' of Dr. Grätz. Observe that we have already met with an eulogy of wedded bliss side by side with a gloomy picture of death in an earlier section (ix. 9, 10).

This is the poem (if we may call it so) with which the second exhortation of Koheleth is interwoven—

Ere the evil days come, and the years approach
of which thou shalt say, I have no pleasure in them :

Ere the sun be darkened, and the light, and the moon, and the stars,
and the clouds keep returning after heavy rains [*the winter rains*, i.e. old age] :
In the day when the keepers of the house [*the hands and arms*] tremble,
and the strong men [*the feet and legs*] bow themselves,
and the grinding-maids [*the teeth*] cease because they are few,
and the (ladies) who look out at the lattice [*the eyes*] are darkened :
And the doors [*the lips*] are shut towards the street,
while the sound of the grinding is low,
And the voice riseth into a sparrow's ['*childish treble*']
and all the daughters of song [*words*] are faint.
They are afraid too of a steep place,
and terror besets every way ;

and the almond-tree is in bloom [*white hair* ¹],
and the locust drags itself along,
and the caper-berry fails [*to excite the appetite*],
For the man is on the way to his eternal home,
and the mourners go about in the street.

Ere the silver string [*the tongue*] be tied,
and the golden bowl [*the head*] break,
and the pitcher [*the heart*] be shivered at the fountain,
and the windlass [*the breathing apparatus*] break into the pit.

With a little determination the traces of development in the Biblical literature can be more or less effaced. The pious but unphilological editors of Koheleth were not deficient in this quality. After altering the introduction of the poem on old age they proceeded to furnish it with a *finale*. Not only the opening words of ver. i., but the comfortless expression 'his eternal house'² in ver. 5 gave them serious offence. One remedy would have been to transpose (with the Syriac translator) two of the letters of the Hebrew, and thus change 'home of his eternity' into 'home of his travail' (i.e. the place where 'the weary are at rest'). They preferred, however, to add two lines—

and the dust return to the earth as it was,
and the spirit return unto God who gave it.

This no doubt is a direct contradiction of iii. 21. But the ancients probably got over this, as most moderns still do, by supposing that the earlier passage did but express a sceptical suggestion which skimmed the surface of Koheleth's mind.

The excision of these words would of course not be justified in a translation intended for popular use ; but for the purposes of historical study seems almost inevitable. It hangs together with the view adopted as to the origin of xi. 9*b*, and implies the assumption that the Targum rightly paraphrases,

---

¹ Does the eastern sun blanch the 'crimson broidery' of the almond-blossom ? From the language of travellers like Thomson and Bodenstedt it would seem so.

² The Hebrew '*ōlām* here expresses perpetuity (comp. Jer. li. 39, Ps. cxliii. 51, Ezek. xxvi. 20), not (as some moderns, after Aben Ezra) long continuance It is true, that in the Targum of Isa. xlii. 11 an exit from the 'eternal house' is spoken of ; but no one doubts that the belief in the Resurrection was general in the fourth century A.D.

'and thy spirit (lit. thy breath, *nishm'thāk*) will return to stand in judgment before the Lord who gave it thee.' It ought to be mentioned, however, that some critics (accepting the clause as genuine) see in that return to God nothing more than the absorption of the human spirit into the divine (whether in a naïve popular or in a developed philosophical sense).[1] This will seem plausible at first to many readers. As a Lutheran writer says, 'Si spes, quam nos fovemus lætissimam, Ecclesiastæ adfulsisset, non obiter ipse tetigisset et verbis ambiguis notasset rem maximi momenti' (Winzer, ap. Hengstenberg). But if the Hebrew *rūakh* means, as I think it does, the personal, conscious, spiritual side of man in iii. 21,[2] I fail to see why it should not bear that meaning here.

[1] Mr. Tyler interprets it in a Stoic sense of absorption in the World-Soul.
[2] Nowack denies this meaning of *rūakh* altogether, but this seems a *Gewaltstreich*.

CHAPTER VI.

KOHELETH'S 'PORTRAIT OF OLD AGE;' THE EPILOGUE, ITS NATURE AND ORIGIN.

WE have now arrived at the conclusion of the meditations of our much-tried thinker. It is strongly poetic in colouring; but when we compare it with the grandly simple overture of the book (i. 4–8), can we help confessing to a certain degree of disappointment? It is the allegory which spoils it for modern readers, and so completely spoils it, that attempts have been sometimes made to expel the allegorical element altogether. That the first two verses are free from allegory, is admitted, and it is barely possible that the sixth verse may be so too—may be, that is, figurative rather than allegorical. Poets have delighted in these figures; how fitly does one of them adorn the lament in Woolner's *My Beautiful Lady*,—

>   Broken the golden bowl
>   Which held her hallowed soul!

The most doubtful part, then, is the description in vv. 3–5. I am not writing a commentary, and will venture to express an opinion in favour of the allegorists (it is not fair to call them satirically the anatomists).[1] It is true that there is much variety of opinion among them; this only shows that the allegory is sometimes far-fetched, not that it is a vain imagination. Can there be anything more obscure than the *canzoni*

---

[1] The title only belongs to pre-critical writers like Dr. John Smith, who, in his *Portrait of Old Age* (1666), sought to show that Solomon was thoroughly acquainted with recent anatomical discoveries. In revising my sheets, I observe that even such a fairminded student as Dean Bradley speaks of 'the long-drawn anatomical explanations of men who would replace with a dissector's report a painter's touch, a poet's melody.' But the Dean only refers to ver. 6; I understand his language, though I think him biassed by poetic associations.

in Dante's *Convito*, which we have the poet's own authority for regarding as allegorical? And if we compare the rival theories with that which they attempt to displace, can it be said that Taylor's dirge-theory,[1] or Umbreit's storm-theory,[2] or that adopted by Wright from Wetzstein[3] is more suitable to the poem than the allegorical theory? Certainly the latter is a very old, if not the oldest theory, and on a point of this sort the ancients have some claim to be deferred to. They seem to have felt instinctively that the intellectual atmosphere of Koheleth (as well as of the Chronicler) was that of the later Judaism. The following story is related in a Talmudic treatise.[4] 'The Emperor asked R. Joshua ben Hananyah, "How is it that you do not go to the house of Abidan (a place of learned discussions)?" He said to him, ": The mountain is snow (my head is white); the hoar frosts surround me (my whiskers and my beard are also hoary); its dogs do not bark (I have lost my wonted power of voice); its millers do not grind (I have no teeth); the scholars ask me whether I am looking for something I have not lost (referring probably to the old man feeling here and there)."'

Once more (see i. 2) the mournful motto, 'Vanity of vanities! saith the Koheleth; all is vanity' (xii. 8), and the book in its original form closes.[5] Did the author himself attach this motto? Surely not, if the preceding words on the return of the spirit to its God (see above, on iii. 21) are genuine, for

[1] Namely, that vv. 3-5 are cited from an authorised book of dirges (comp. 2 Chr. xxxv. 25). There seems, however, no assignable reason for separating these verses from the context. And how can the supposed mourners have sung the latter part of ver. 5?

[2] This supposes the approach of death to be described under the imagery of a gathering storm.

[3] Namely, that the evil days of the close of life are described by figures drawn from the 'seven days of death,' as the modern Syrians designate the closing days of their winter. In a native Arabic rhyme, February says to March, 'O March, O my cousin, the old women mock at me : three (days) of thine and four of mine—and we will bring the old woman to singing (another tune).' Wright, *Ecclesiastes*, p. 271 ; Delitzsch, *Hohestlied und Kohelet*, p. 447.

[4] *Shabbath*, 151b, 152b (Wright, *Ecclesiastes*, p. 262). The anecdote is given in connection with an allegoric interpretation of our poem.

[5] Dean Plumptre and Dr. Wright, however, make this the opening verse of the Epilogue. But between ver. 8 and that which follows there is no inner connection.

then 'Vanity of vanities' would be a patent misrepresentation. All is *not* 'vanity,' if there is in human nature a point connecting a man with that world, most distant and yet most near, where in the highest sense God is. If Koheleth wrote xii. 7b, he cannot have written xii. 8, any more than the author of the *Imitation* could have written *Vanitas vanitatum* both on his first page and on his last. Yet who but Koheleth can be responsible for it? For the later editors of whom I have spoken, would be far from approving such a reversal of the great charter of man's dignity in the eighth Psalm. To me, the motto simply says that all Koheleth's wanderings had but brought him back to the point from which he started. 'Grandissima vanità,' as Castelli, in his dignified Italian, puts it, 'tutto è vanità.' All that I can assign to the editors in this verse are the parenthetic words 'saith the Koheleth.' Everywhere else we find ' Koheleth ;' here alone, and perhaps vii. 17 (corrected text), 'the Koheleth.'[1]

Let us now consider the Epilogue itself.

And moreover (it should be said) that Koheleth was a wise man ; further, he taught the people wisdom, and weighed and made search, (yea) composed many proverbs. Koheleth sought to find out pleasant words, and he wrote down[2] plainly words of truth. The words of the wise are like goads, and like nails well driven in ; the members of the assemblies[3] have [in the case of Ecclesiastes] given them forth from another shepherd.[4] And as for all beyond them, my son, be warned ; of making many books there is no end, and

---

[1] The object of the article is perhaps to suggest that Koheleth is not really a proper name. In vii. 27 we should correct *ām'rāh qōheleth* to *āmar haqqōheleth*. Probably these words are an interpolation from the margin. They are nowhere else used in support of Koheleth's opinions. The author of the interpolation may have wished to indicate his disagreement with Koheleth's low opinion of women.

[2] So Aquila, Pesh., Vulg., Grätz, Renan, Klostermann (*v'kāthab*).

[3] I.e. the assemblies of 'wise men' or perhaps of Soferim. Surely *ba'alē* must refer to persons. The meaning 'assemblies' is justified by Talmudic passages quoted by Grätz, Delitzsch, and Wright.

[4] So Klostermann. 'Shepherd' must, I think, mean teacher (comp. Jer. ii. 8, iii. 15 &c.); the expression is suggested by the 'goads.' 'One shepherd' (the text-reading) might mean Solomon ; and we might go on to suppose the Solomonic origin of Proverbs as well as Ecclesiastes to be asserted in this verse. But the author of the Epilogue apparently considers Koheleth to be merely fictitiously Solomon, but really a wise man like any other. If so, he cannot have grouped it with Proverbs as a strictly Solomonic work.

much study is a weariness of the flesh.—That which the word 'all is vanity' comes to : ¹ it is understood (thus), Fear God, and keep His commandments. For this (concerns) every man. For every work shall God bring into the judgment (which shall be) upon all that is concealed and all that is manifest, whether it be good or whether it be evil.

This translation has not been reached without some emendations of the text. It seems to me that everything in this Epilogue ought to be clear. There is but one verse which contains figurative expressions ; the rest is simple prose. It is only fair, however, to give one of the current renderings of those verses in which an emendation has been attempted above.

Koheleth sought to find out pleasant words and that which was written down frankly, words of truth. Words of wise men are like goads, and like nails driven in are those which form collections [or, the well-compacted sayings, Ewald; or, the well-stored ones, Kamphausen]—they have been given by one shepherd. . . . Final result, all having been heard :—Fear God and keep His commandments, for this (concerns) every man.²

The first scholar to declare against the genuineness of the Epilogue was Döderlein (*Scholia in libros V. T. poeticos*, 1779), who was followed by Bertholdt (*Einleitung*, p. 2250 &c.), Umbreit, Knobel, and De Jong.³ It was however a Jewish scholar, Nachman Krochmal,⁴ who first developed an elaborate theory to account for the Epilogue. According to him, it

---

¹ So Klostermann, regarding this verse down to 'commandments' as an additional note on this difficult saying of Koheleth's, which was liable to give offence to orthodox readers. The word '(is) vanity' is supposed to have dropped out of the text. The object of the note is to show under what limitations it can be admitted that 'all is vanity.' Then the writer continues, ' For this (concerns) every man ; for every work' &c., to show that the limiting precept is not less universally applicable than Koheleth's melancholy formula.

² Thus Delitzsch, who takes the 'words of the wise' and the 'collections' in ver. 11 to refer at least in part, the former to the detached sayings, and the latter to the continuous passages, which together make up Ecclesiastes. The 'one shepherd' is held to be God, so that the clause involves a claim of divine inspiration.

³ De Jong's discussion of the Epilogue deserves special attention (*De Prediker*, p. 142 &c.) ; comp. however Kuenen's reply, *Onderzoek*, iii. 196 &c.)

⁴ Krochmal died in 1840, but his view on the Epilogue first saw the light in 1851 in vol. xi. of the Hebrew journal *Morè nebūkē hazzemān* (see Grätz, *Kohelet*, p. 47). His life is to be found in Zunz, *Gesammelte Schriften*, ii. 150 &c.

was added at the final settlement of the Canon at the Synod of Jamnia, A.D. 90, and was intended as a conclusion not merely for Ecclesiastes, but for the entire body of Hagiographa. He thinks (but without any historical ground) that Ecclesiastes was added at that time to close the Canon. The correctness of this view depends partly on its author's interpretation of vv. 11, 12, partly on his definition of the object of the Synod of Jamnia (see Appendix.) The two former verses are condensed thus,

The words of the wise are like ox-goads, and the members of the Sanhedrin are like firm nails, not to be moved. As for more than these, beware, my son; of making many books there is no end.

The 'wise' spoken of, thinks Krochmal, are the authors of the several books of the Hagiographa, and the warning in ver. 12 is directed against the reception of any other books into the Canon. Whether the Song of Solomon and Ecclesiastes were to be admitted, was, according to him, a subject of debate at the Synod referred to.

But there is no necessity whatever for this interpretation of vv. 11, 12. The phrase, 'the words of the wise,' is not a fit description of all the books of the Hagiographa (of Psalms, Daniel, and Chronicles for instance), and the warning in ver. 12 more probably has relation to the proverbial literature in general, such as Proverbs, Ecclesiastes, and the Wisdom of Sirach, or at least to the Book of Proverbs, to which Kleinert conjectures that Ecclesiastes once formed an appendix. There is nothing in the Epilogue to suggest a reference to the Canon. The 'many books' spoken of are probably such as did not proceed from thoroughly orthodox sources. We have absolutely no information as to Jewish literature outside the Canon. That there was a heterodox literature, has been inferred by Ewald from Jer. viii. 8, Prov. xxx. 1-4; it is also clear from several passages in the Book of Enoch. Tyler and Plumptre may possibly be right in seeing here an allusion to the incipient influence of Greek literature upon the Jews. This is at any rate more justifiable than to assume an arrangement of the Hagiographa with

Ecclesiastes for the closing book for which there is no ancient testimony.

Krochmal's ingenious theory has, however, been adopted by Jost, Grätz and Renan,[1] though Renan is willing to admit that vv. 9, 10 may be from the pen of the author himself. 'Cet épilogue complète bien la fiction qui fait la base du livre. Quel motif d'ailleurs eût amené à faire postérieurement une telle addition?'[2] I do not myself hold with Krochmal, but vv. 9-12 seem to me to hang together, and I do not think that the author himself would be at the pains to destroy his own fiction, whereas a later editor would naturally append the corrective statement that the real Koheleth was not a king, but a wise man. (Observe too that 'Koheleth' in ver. 8 has the article, but in vv. 9, 10 is without it, suggesting a change of writer.) I agree however with Renan that vv. 13, 14, which differ in tone and in form from the preceding verses, appear to be a later addition than the rest of the Epilogue. Renan, it is true, distrusts this appearance; he fears a too complicated hypothesis. But we must at least hold that vv. 13, 14 were added (whether by the Epilogist or by another) by an after-thought. The Epilogue should therefore be divided into two parts, vv. 9-12, and vv. 13, 14. In the first part, the real is distinguished from the fictitious author; his qualifications are described; the editors of his posthumous work are indicated; and a warning is given to the disciple of the Epilogist (to apply the words of M. Aurelius) 'to cast away the thirst for books.'[3] In the second part, a contradiction is given to what seemed an unworthy interpretation of a characteristic expression of Koheleth's, and the higher view of its meaning is justified—justified, that is, to those who approach the work from the practical point of view of those who have as yet no better moral 'Enchiridion.'[4]

---

[1] See Jost (*Gesch. des Judenthums*, i. 42, n. 2). Derenbourg too seems to tend in this direction (*Revue des études juives*, i. 179, note). Reuss, Bickell, and Kleinert too agree in denying that 'Koheleth' composed the Epilogue. So also apparently Geiger (*Jüd. Zeitschr.*, iv. 10, Anm.)

[2] *L'Ecclésiaste*, p. 73.   [3] *Meditations*, ii. 3.

[4] I designedly refer to the great work of Epictetus, as its adaptation by Christian hands to the use of Christian believers to some extent furnishes a parallel for the editorial adaptation of Ecclesiastes.

At what period was the Epilogue added? The consideration of its style may help us at least to a negative result. The Hebrew approaches that of the Mishna, but is yet sufficiently distinct from it to be the subject of expository paraphrase in the Talmuds.[1] It is therefore improbable that it was added long after the period of the author himself. Books like Sirach and Koheleth soon became popular, and attracted the attention of the religious authorities. Interpolation or insertion seemed the only way to counteract the spiritual danger to unsuspicious readers.

[1] Delitzsch, *Hoheslied u. Koheleth*, p. 215.

CHAPTER VII.

ECCLESIASTES AND ITS CRITICS (FROM A PHILOLOGICAL POINT OF VIEW).

By comparison with Ecclesiastes, the books which we have hitherto been studying may be called easy ; at any rate, they have not given rise to equally strange diversities of critical opinion. A chapter with the above heading seems therefore at this point specially necessary. Dr. Ginsburg's masterly sketch of the principal theories of the critics down to 1860 dispenses me, it is true, from attempting an exhaustive survey.[1] It is not the duty of every teacher of Old Testament criticism to traverse the history of his subject afresh, any more than it is that of the commentator as such to begin with a catena of the opinions of previous writers. Suffice it to call attention to two of the Jewish and two of the Christian expositors mentioned by Dr. Ginsburg, viz. Mendelssohn and Luzzatto, and Ewald and Vaihinger. MENDELSSOHN seems important not so much by his results as by his historical position. His life marks an era in Biblical study, most of all of course among the Jews, but to some extent among Christians also. His Hebrew commentary on Koheleth deserves specially to be remembered, because with it in 1770 he broke ground anew in grammatical exegesis. To him, as also to VAIHINGER, the object of Koheleth is to propound the great consolatory truth of the immortality of the soul, while EWALD, more in accordance with facts, describes it as being rather to combine

[1] For the Jewish traditions and theories, see further Schiffer, *Das Buch Koheleth nach der Auffassung der Weisen des Talmud und Midrasch und der jüdischen Erklärer des Mittelalters*, Theil I, Leipzig, 1885; and to complete Dr. Ginsburg's survey of the literature, see Zöckler's list in Lange's Commentary and the additions to this in the American edition ; also the preface to Wright's treatise on Ecclesiastes.

all that is true, however sad, and profitable, and agreeable to the will of God in a practical handbook adapted to those troublesome times. Ewald and Vaihinger both divide the book into four sections,—(1) i. 2–ii. 26, (2) iii. 1–vi. 9, (3) vi. 10–viii. 15, (4) viii. 16–xii. 8, with the Epilogue xii. 9-14. The latter, whose view is more developed than Ewald's, and whom I refer to as closing and summing up a period, maintains that each section consists of three parts which are again subdivided—for Koheleth, though you would not think it, is a literary artist—into strophes and half-strophes, and that the theme of each section is thrown out, seemingly by chance, but really with consummate art, in the preceding one. Thus the four sections interlace, and the unity of the book is established. The Epilogue, too, according to Vaihinger, can thus be proved to be the work of the author of Koheleth; for it does but ratify and develop what has already been indicated in xi. 9, and without it the connection of ideas would be incomplete.[1] I think that our experience of some interpreters of the Book of Job may predispose us to be sceptical of such ingenious subtleties, and I notice that more recent critics show a tendency to insist less on the logical distribution of the contents and to regard the book, not indeed as a mere collection of rules of conduct, but at any rate as a record of a practical and not a scholastic philosopher. This tendency is not indeed of recent origin, though it has increased in favour of late years. Prior the poet had already said that Ecclesiastes 'is not a regular and perfect treatise, but that in it great treasures are "heaped up together in a confused magnificence;"'[2] Bishop Lowth, that 'the connection of the arguments is involved in much obscurity;'[3] while Herder, in his letters to a theological student, had penned this wise though too enthusiastic sentence, which cuts at the root of all attempts at logical analysis,

Kein Buch ist mir aus dem Alterthum bekannt, welches die Summe des menschlichen Lebens, seine Abwechselungen und

[1] See Vaihinger's article in Herzog's *Realencyclopädie*, xii. 92–106. I have not seen his book on Ecclesiastes (1858).
[2] Ginsburg, *Coheleth*, p. 168.   [3] Ibid., p. 178.

Nichtigkeiten in Geschäften, Entwürfen, Speculationen und Vergnügen, zugleich mit dem was einzig in ihm wahr, daurend, fortgehend, wechselnd, lohnend ist, reicher, eindringlicher, kürzer beschriebe, als dieses.[1]

But I must retrace my steps. One of my four critics has yet to be briefly characterised—S. D. LUZZATTO of Padua, best known as the author of a Hebrew commentary on Isaiah, but also a master in later Hebrew and Aramaic scholarship. As a youth of twenty-four he wrote a deeply felt and somewhat eccentrically ingenious treatise on Koheleth, which he kept by him till 1860, when it appeared in one of the annual volumes of essays and reviews called Ozar Nechmad. In it he maintains, with profound indignation at the unworthy post-Exile writer, that the Book of Ecclesiastes denies the immortality of the soul, and recommends a life of sensuous pleasure. The writer's name, however, was, he thinks, Koheleth, and his fraud in assuming the name of Solomon was detected by the wise men of his time, who struck out the assumed name and substituted Koheleth (leaving however the words 'son of David, king in Jerusalem,' as a record of the imposture). Later students, however, were unsuspicious enough to accept the work as Solomon's, and being unable to exclude a Solomonic writing from the Canon, they inserted three qualifying half-verses of an orthodox character, viz. 'and know that for all this God will bring thee into judgment' (xi. 6*b*); 'and remember thy Creator in the days of thy youth' (xii. 1*a*); 'and the spirit shall return to God who gave it' (xii. 8*b*). This latter view, which has the doubtful support of a Talmudic passage,[2] appears to me, though from the nature of the case uncertain, and susceptible, as I think, of modification, yet in itself probable as restoring harmony to the book, and in accordance with the treatment of other Biblical texts by the Soferim (or students and editors of Scripture). Geiger may have fallen into infinite extravagances, but he has at any rate shown that the early Soferim modified many passages in the interests of orthodoxy and edification.[3] If so, they did but

---

[1] *Werke* (Suphan), x. 134.   [2] *Shabbath*, 97*a* (see Ginsburg, p. 98).
[3] See his *Urschrift und Uebersetzungen der Bibel* (1857).

carry on the process already begun by the authors of the sacred books themselves; it may be enough to remind my readers of the gradual supplementing of the original Book of Job by later writers. To the three passages of Koheleth mentioned above, must be added, as Geiger saw,[1] the two postscripts which form the Epilogue. From the close of the last century a series of writers have felt the difficulties of this section so strongly that they have assigned it to one or more later writers, and in truth, although these difficulties may be partly removed, enough remains to justify the obelising of the passage.

There is no evidence that Luzzatto ever retracted the critical view mentioned above. To the character of the author, it is true, he became more charitable in his later years. I do not think the worse of him for his original antipathy. An earnest believer himself and of fiery temperament, he could not understand the cool and cautious reflective spirit of the much-tried philosopher;[2] and as a lover of the rich, and, as the result of development, comparatively flexible Hebrew tongue, he took a dislike to a writer so wanting in facility and grace as Koheleth.[3] It was an error, but a noble one, and it shows that Luzzatto found in the study of criticism a school of moral culture as well as of literary insight.

The adoption of Luzzatto's view,[4] combined with Döderlein's as to the epilogue, removes the temptation to interpret Koheleth as the apology of any particular philosophical or theological doctrine. The author now appears, not indeed thoroughly consistent, but at least in his true light as a thinker tossed about on the sea of speculation, and without

[1] *Jüdische Zeitschrift*, iv. 9 &c.
[2] David Castelli, a cool and cautious scholar but not original, is naturally better fitted to appreciate Koheleth (see *Il libro del Kohelet*, Pisa, 1866).
[3] 'Die harte, ungefügige, tiefgesunkene Sprache des Buches entzog ihm in Luzzatto's Auge den verklärenden Lichtglanz; er blickte mit einer gewissen Missachtung auf den Schriftsteller, der sowenig Meister der edlen ihn erfüllenden Sprache war' (Geiger).
[4] Not only Geiger, but the learned and fairminded Kalisch, has made this view his own (*Bible Studies*, i. 65); among Christian scholars it has been adopted by Nöldeke and Bickell (the latter includes iii. 17 among the inserted passages, and I incline to follow him).

any fixed theoretic conclusions. Without agreeing to more than the relative lateness of the epilogue, DE JONG,[1] a Dutch scholar, recognises the true position of Koheleth, and in the psychological interest of the book sees a full compensation for the want of logical arrangement. De Jong indeed was not acquainted with the theory of Nachman Krochmal, which if sound throws such great light on the reason of the addition of the epilogue (see end of Chap. VI.) This has been accepted by Grätz and Renan, but, as I have ventured to think, upon insufficient grounds. The brevity of my reference to these two eminent exegetes must be excused by my inability to follow either of them in his main conclusions. The glossary of peculiar words and the excursus on the Greek translation given by the former (1871) possess a permanent value, and there is much of historical interest in his introduction. But I agree with Kuenen that the student who selects Grätz as his guide will have much to unlearn afterwards.[2] In order to show that Ecclesiastes is a politico-religious satire levelled against king Herod, with the special object of correcting certain evil tendencies among the Jews of that age, Grätz is compelled to have recourse to much perverse exegesis which I have no inclination to criticise.[3] Renan's present view differs widely from that given in his great unfinished history of the Semitic languages. But I shall have occasion to refer to his determination of the date of our book later.

Among recent English students, no one will refuse the palm of acuteness and originality to TYLER (1874). His strength lies not in translation and exegesis, but in the consistency with which he has applied his single key, viz. the comparison of the book with Stoic and Epicurean teaching. He is fully aware that the book has no logical divisions. Antithesis and contradiction is the fundamental characteristic of the book. Not that the author contradicts himself (comp. the quotation from Ibn Ezra in Ginsburg's *Coheleth*, p. 57), but that a faithful index of the contradictions of the two great philosophical

---

[1] *De Prediker vertaald en verklaart* door P. de Jong (Leiden, 1861).
[2] *Theologisch Tijdschrift*, 1883, p. 114.
[3] See however Kuenen's condensed criticism in *Theol. Tijdschrift*, p. 127 &c.

schools gives a greater point to his concluding warning against philosophy. It is the 'sacrificio dell' intelletto' which the author counsels. But Mr. Tyler's theory or at least his point of view demands a separate consideration. It may however be fairly said here that by general consent Mr. Tyler has done something to make the influence of Greek philosophical ideas upon Ecclesiastes a more plausible opinion.

To a subsequent chapter I must also beg to refer the reader for a notice of Gustav BICKELL'S hypothesis (1884) relative to the fortunes (or misfortunes) of the text of Koheleth. This critic is not one of those who grant that the book had from the first no logical division, and his hypothesis is one of the boldest and most plausible in the history of criticism. Its boldness is in itself no defect, but I confess I desiderate that caution which is the second indispensable requisite in a great critic. The due admixture of these two qualities nature has not yet granted. Meantime the greatest successes are perhaps attained by those who are least self-confident, least ambitious of personal distinction. Upon the whole, from the point of view of the student proper, are there more thankworthy contributions to criticism not less than to exegesis than the books of PLUMPTRE (1881), NOWACK (1883), and above all the accomplished *altmeister* Franz DELITZSCH (1875)? Whatever has been said before profitably and well, may be known by him who will consult these three accomplished though not faultless expositors. I would not be supposed to detract from other writers,[1] but I believe that the young student will not repent limiting himself, not indeed to one, but to three commentaries.

[1] Hitzig, for instance, has been passed over in spite of Nöldeke's judgment that no modern scholar has done so much for the detailed explanation of the text. This may be true, or at least be but a small exaggeration. No critic has so good a right to the name as Hitzig, who, though weak in his treatment of ideas, has the keenest perception of what is possible and impossible in interpretation. But for the larger critical questions Hitzig has not done much; the editor of the second edition of his commentary (Nowack) has therefore been obliged to rewrite the greater part of the introduction. The historical background of the book cannot be that supposed by Hitzig, nor has he hit the mark in his description of Koheleth as 'eine planmässig fortschreitende Untersuchung.' Wright fails, I venture to think, from different causes. He is slightly too timid, and deficient in literary art; and yet his scholarly work does honour to the Protestant clergy of Ireland.

R

CHAPTER VIII.

ECCLESIASTES AND ITS CRITICS (FROM A LITERARY AND PSYCHOLOGICAL POINT OF VIEW).

It is not every critic of Ecclesiastes who helps the reader to enjoy the book which is criticised. Too much criticism and too little taste have before now spoiled many excellent books on the Old Testament. Ecclesiastes needs a certain preparation of the mind and character, a certain 'elective affinity,' in order to be appreciated as it deserves. To enjoy it, we must find our own difficulties and our own moods anticipated in it. We must be able to sympathise with its author either in his world-weariness and scepticism or in his victorious struggle (if so be it was victorious) through darkness into light. We must at any rate have a taste for the development of character, and an ear for the fragments of truth which a much-tried pilgrim gathered up in his twilight wanderings. Never so much as in our own time have this taste and this ear been so largely possessed, as a recent commentary has shown in delightful detail, and I can only add to the names furnished by the writer that of one who perhaps least of all should be omitted, Miss Christina Rossetti.[1] But to prove the point in my own way, let me again select four leading critics, as representatives not so much of philology as of that subtle and variable thing—the modern spirit, viz. RENAN, GRÄTZ, STANLEY, and PLUMPTRE. The first truly is a modern of the moderns, though it is not every modern who will subscribe to his description of Ecclesiastes as 'livre charmant, le seul livre aimable qui ait été composé par un Juif.'[2]

---

[1] See especially her early sonnet 'Vanity of Vanities,' and her striking poem 'A Testimony.'   [2] *L'Antéchrist*, p. 101.

One might excuse it perhaps if in some degree dictated by a bitter grief at the misfortunes of his country; pessimism might be natural in 1872. But alas! ten years later the same view is repeated and deliberately justified, nor can the author of Koheleth be congratulated. He is now described [1] as 'le charmant écrivain qui nous a laissé cette délicieuse fantaisie philosophique, aimant la vie, tout en en voyant la vanité,' or, as a French reviewer condenses the delicate phrases of his author, 'homme du monde et de la bonne société, qui n'est, à proprement parler, ni blasé ni fatigué, mais qui sait en toutes choses garder la mesure, sans enthousiasme, sans indignation, et sans exaltation d'aucune espèce.' A speaking portrait of a Parisian *philosophe*, but does it fit the author of Ecclesiastes? No; Koheleth has had too hard a battle with his own tongue to be a 'charming writer,' and even if not exactly *blasé* (see however ii. 1–11), he is 'fatigued' enough with the oppressive burdens of Jewish life in the second century B.C. That he has no enthusiasm, and none of those visions which are the 'creators and feeders of the soul,' [2] is cause for pity, not for admiration; but that he has had no visitings of *sæva indignatio*, is an unjust inference from his acquired calmness of demeanour. He is an amiable egoïst, says M. Renan; but would Koheleth have troubled himself to write as he does, if egoïsm were the ripened fruit of his life's experience? Why does this critic give such generous sympathy to the Ecclesiastes of the Slav race,[3] and such doubtful praise to his great original? It is true, Koheleth *seems* to despair of the future, but only perhaps of the immediate future (iii. 21), and Turgenieff does this too. 'Will the right men come?' asks one of the personages of Turgenieff's *Helen*, and his friend, as the only reply, directs a questioning look into the distance. That is the Russian philosopher's last word; Koheleth has not told us his. His literary executors, no doubt, have forced a last word upon him; but we have an equal right to imagine one for ourselves. M. Renan 'likes to dream of a Paul become sceptical and dis-

---

[1] *L'Ecclésiaste*, pp. 24, 90.   [2] Mordecai in *Daniel Deronda*.
[3] See his funeral *éloge*, reprinted in *Academy*, Oct. 13, 1883, p. 248.

enchanted;'[1] his Koheleth is an only less unworthy dream. M. Renan praises Koheleth for the moderation of his philosophising; he repeatedly admits that there was an element of truth in the Utopianism of the prophets; why not 'dream' that Koheleth felt, though he either ventured not or had no time left to express it, some degree of belief in the destiny of his country?

M. Renan, in fact, seems to me at once to admire Koheleth too much, and to justify his admiration on questionable grounds. It might have been hoped that the unlikeness of this book to the other books of the Canon would have been the occasion of a worthy and a satisfying estimate from this accomplished master. A critic of narrower experience represents Koheleth partly as a cynical Hebrew Pasquin, who satirises the hated foreigner, Herod the Great, and the minions of his court, partly as an earnest opponent of a dangerous and growing school of ascetics. I refer to this theory here, not to criticise it, but to call attention to its worthier conception of Koheleth's character. The tendency of Ecclesiastes Dr. Grätz considers to be opposed to the moral and religious principles of Judaism and Christianity, but to the man as distinguished from his book he does full justice. It is a mistake when this writer's theory is represented by Dean Plumptre as making Koheleth teach 'a license like that of a St. Simonian rehabilitation of the flesh.'[2] Koheleth's choice of language is not indeed in good taste, but it was only a crude way of emphasising his opposition to a dangerous spirit of asceticism. Such at least is Dr. Grätz's view. 'Koheleth is not the slave of an egoïstic eudemonism, but merely seeks to counteract pietistic self-mortification.'[3] Dr. Grätz thinks, too, and rightly, that he can detect an old-fashioned Judaïsm in the supposed sceptical philosopher: Koheleth controverts the new tenet of immortality, but not that of the resurrection. I am anticipating again, but do so in order to contrast the sympathetic treatment of the Breslau professor with the unsympathetic or at least unsuitable portraiture of Koheleth given by the Parisian critic.

[1] *L'Antéchrist*, p. 200.   [2] *Ecclesiastes*, p. 8.   [3] Grätz, *Kohelet*, p. 33.

Of all writers known to me, however, none is so sympathetic to Koheleth as Dr. Plumptre, in whose pleasing article in Smith's Dictionary we have the germ of the most interesting commentary in the language. A still wider popularity was given to the Herder-Plumptre theory by Dr. Stanley, who eloquently describes Ecclesiastes as 'an interchange of voices, higher and lower, within a single human soul.' 'It is like,' he continues, 'the perpetual strophe and antistrophe of Pascal's *Pensées*. But it is more complicated, more entangled, than any of these, in proportion as the circumstances from which it grows are more perplexing, as the character which it represents is vaster, and grander, and more distracted.'[1] In his later work, Dr. Plumptre aptly compares the 'Two Voices' of our own poet (strictly, he remarks, there are three voices in Ecclesiastes), in which, as in Koheleth, though more decidedly, the voice of faith at last prevails over that of pessimism.[2] I fear, however, that Dr. Plumptre's generous impulse carries him farther than sober criticism can justify. The aim of writing an 'ideal biography' closing with the 'victory of faith' seems to me to have robbed his pen of that point which, though sometimes dangerous, is yet indispensable to the critic. The theory of the 'alternate voices,' of which Dr. Plumptre is, not the first,[3] but the most eloquent advocate, seems to me to be an offspring of the modern spirit. It is so very like their own case—the dual nature[4] which a series of refined critics has attributed to Koheleth, that they involuntarily invest Koheleth with the peculiar qualities of modern seekers after truth. To them, in a different sense from M. Renan's, Ecclesiastes is 'un livre aimable,' just as Marcus Aurelius and Omar Khayyám are the favourite companions of those who prefer more consistent thinking.

Certainly the author of Ecclesiastes might well be satisfied with the interest so widely felt in his very touching confidences. It is the contents, of course, which attract so many

---

[1] *Jewish Church*, ii. 256. [2] *Ecclesiastes*, pp. 53, 259.
[3] See the passage from Herder quoted in Appendix (end).
[4] Comp. Jacobi's confession (imitated by Coleridge?) that he was with the head a heathen, and with the heart a Christian.

of our contemporaries—not the form: only a student of Hebrew can appreciate the toilsome pleasure of solving philosophical enigmas. And yet M. Renan has made it possible even for an *exigeant* Parisian to enjoy, not indeed the process, but the results, of philological inquiry, in so far as they reveal the literary characteristics of this unique work; he has, indeed, in his function of artistic translator, done Koheleth even more than justice. In particular, his translations of the rhythmic passages of Koheleth which relieve the surrounding prose are real *tours de force*. These passages M. Renan, following M. Derenbourg,[1] regards as quotations from lost poetical works, reminding us that such poetical quotations are common in Arabic literature. To represent in his translation the character of the Hebrew rhythm, which is 'dancing, light, and pretentiously elegant,' M. Renan adopts the metres of Old French poetry. 'Il s'agissait de calquer en français des sentences conçues dans le ton dégagé, goguenard et prud'homme à la fois de Pibrac, de Marculfe ou de Chatonnet, de produire un saveur analogue à celle de nos quatrains de moralités ou de nos vieux proverbes en bouts-rimés.' Of the poem on old age he says that it is 'une sorte de joujou funèbre qu'on dirait ciselé par Banville ou par Théophile Gautier et que je trouve supérieur même aux quatrains de Khayyâm.'[2] I should have thought the comparison very unjust to the Persian poet. To me, I confess, the prelude or overture (i. 4-8), though not in rhythmic Hebrew, is the gem of the book. Questionable though its tendency may seem, if we look at the context, its poetry is of elemental force, and appeals to the modern reader in some of his moods more than almost anything else in the Old Testament outside the Book of Job. I cannot help alluding to Carlyle's fine application of its imagery in *Sartor Resartus*, 'Generations are as the Days of toilsome Mankind: Death and Birth are the vesper and the matin bells, that summon mankind to sleep, and to rise refreshed for new advancement.' How differently Koheleth,—

---

[1] *Revue des études juives*, i. 165-185. I do not myself see why Koheleth, who sought 'pleasant words,' should not have written poetry as well as prose.

[2] *L'Ecclésiaste*, pp. 83, 84.

One generation goeth, another cometh;
but the earth abideth for ever:
And the sun ariseth, and the sun goeth down,
and panteth unto his place where he ariseth:
It goeth to the south, and whirleth about unto the north,
the wind whirleth about continually;
and upon his circuits the wind returneth.
All streams run into the sea, and the sea is not full;
unto the place whither the streams go, thither they go again.
All things are full of weariness; no man can utter it;
the eye is not satisfied with seeing, nor the ear filled with
  hearing.

Compare with this the words, so Greek in tone, of xi. 7, as well as the constantly recurring formula 'under the sun' (e.g. i. 3, iv.'3). We can see that even Koheleth was affected by nature, but without any lightening of his load of trial. The wide-open eye of day seemed to mock him by its unfeeling serenity. He lacked that susceptibility for the whispered lessons of nature which the poet of *Job* so pre-eminently possessed; he lacked too the great modern conception of progress, embodied in that fine passage from Carlyle. He was prosaic and unimaginative, and it is partly because there is so little poetry in Ecclesiastes that there is so little Christianity. But I am already passing to another order of considerations, without which indeed we cannot estimate this singular autobiography aright. We have next to consider Koheleth from a directly religious and moral point of view.

CHAPTER IX.

ECCLESIASTES FROM A MORAL AND RELIGIOUS POINT OF VIEW.

WE have seen how large a Christian element penetrates and glorifies the bold questionings of the Book of Job. Whatever be our view on obscure problems of criticism, the character-drama which the book in its present form presents is one which it almost requires a Christian to appreciate adequately. It is different with the Book of Ecclesiastes. 'He who will allow that book to speak for itself, and does not read other meanings into almost every verse, must feel at every step that he is breathing a different atmosphere from that of the teaching of the Gospels.'[1] Still more is this the case if we claim the right of free criticism, and deny that the hints of a growing tendency to believe are due to the morbidly sceptical author of the book (if it may be called a book). Certainly the religious use of Koheleth is more directly affected by modern criticism and exegesis than that of any other Old Testament writing. The early theologians could dispense with criticism, because they so frequently allegorised or unconsciously gave a gentle twist to the literal meaning. But we, if for a religious purpose we use the book uncritically, must be well aware that we often misrepresent both the author of Koheleth himself and Christian faith. Let me only mention three texts in the use of which this misrepresentation very commonly takes place. The fixity of the spiritual state in which a man is at death may or may not be an essential Christian doctrine, but we have no right to quote either

[1] Dean Bradley, *Lectures on Ecclesiastes* (1885), p. 7.

Koheleth's despairing description of the inert life of the shades (ix. 10), or the proverbial saying on the unalterableness of the laws of nature (xi. 3), in support of this; nor is it well to adopt a phrase (descriptive of Sheól) from xii. 5, which favours the false idea expressed in the too common 'Here lieth' of the churchyard. Anticipations of really fundamental Christian doctrines are, I admit, rarely sought for in Ecclesiastes. It is well that this should be so. How completely the evangelical elements in Jewish religion had been obscured later on in this period, we have seen from the Wisdom of Sirach. It seemed in fact as if the only alternatives then for a thoughtful Jew were a more or less strict legal orthodoxy and a resigned acquiescence in things as they were, brightened only by gleams, eagerly hailed, of intellectual or sensuous pleasure. Sirach chose the former of these, Koheleth the latter. Koheleth's was not in itself the better choice. But the worse alternative needed perhaps to be stated as forcibly as possible, that men might see the rock and avoid shipwreck. Ecclesiastes, like the first part of Goethe's *Faust*, may, with the fullest justice, be called an apology for Christianity, not as containing anticipations of Christian truth—the error of Hengstenberg;[1] but inasmuch as it shows that neither wisdom, nor any other human good or human pleasure, brings permanent satisfaction to man's natural longings. It is at any rate a contribution towards the negative criticism with which such an apology must begin, just as the Book of Job is a contribution, or a series of contributions, towards a more perfect and evangelical theodicy.

There is at least one point, then, which the moral and religious critic of Ecclesiastes can adopt out of all the strangely distorted views of patristic writers, so ably summed up by Dr. Ginsburg in his Introduction, viz. that the gloomy sentence, *Vanitas vanitatum*, is perfectly accurate when applied to the life of Koheleth, but only to a life like his. Thomas à Kempis

---

[1] See *Der Prediger Salomo* (1859). Hengstenberg misses, it is true, any direct reference to the Christian hope, but finds the idea of chastisement as a proof of divine love in iii. 18, vii. 2–4, an emphatic affirmation of eternal life in iii. 21, and the resignation of a faith like Job's in iii. 11, vii. 24, viii. 17, xi. 5. Koheleth's questionings are therefore according to him 'eine heilige Philosophie.'

could prelude with two verses from Koheleth (i. 2, 8), but he could only prelude. A life of true service—one whose centre is outside self or family or even nation—is not vanity nor vexation of spirit: Koheleth might have added this as the burden of a second part of his book. But did he not actually append it as his epilogue? Did he not 'faintly trust' the hope of immortality (xii. 7)? Did he not work his way back to a living faith, like 'Asaph' in Ps. lxxiii.? There is no question that the book was admitted into the Canon on the assumption that he did. As a great Jewish preacher says, the book [in its present form] opens with Nothingness, but closes with the fear of God.[1] It is parallel in this respect to many Jewish lives, like that of Heine, which may be described as the prodigal son's quest of his long-lost father. Accepting this view, we may join with another Jewish writer in his admiration of the influences of Jewish theism, which were then at least so strong that a consistent Jewish sceptic was an impossibility. 'It is this,' he remarks, 'that gives the peculiar charm to this little book.'[2] It is impossible to give a conclusive refutation of this view, which I should like to believe true, but which seems to me to labour under exegetical difficulties. To me, Koheleth is not a theist in any vital sense in his philosophic meditations, and his so-called 'last word' seems forced upon him by later scribes, just as Sirach's orthodoxy was at any rate heightened in colour by subsequent editors. To me, Derenbourg's view is a dream, though an edifying one. It may be that the author did return to the simple faith of his childhood. He certainly never lost his theism, though pale and cheerless it was indeed, and utterly unable to stand against the assaults of doubt and despondency. It may be that history, neglected history, taught him at last to believe in the divine guidance of the fortunes of Israel. I would fain imagine this retracing of the weary pilgrim's steps; but other and less pleasing dreams to a Christian are equally possible and I do not venture to accept the return of the prodigal as a well-authenticated fact.

---

[1] Preface to vol. iii. of S. Holdheim's *Predigten*.
[2] J. Derenbourg, *Revue des études juives*, No. 2, Oct. 1880.

We must remember too that the troubled wanderer had not really so many steps to retrace. Much that both Christians and Jews now regard as essential to faith was not, in the time of Koheleth, commonly so regarded. I am well aware of the great intuitions of some of the psalmists at certain sublime moments, and admit that they seem to us to lead naturally on to our own orthodoxy. But these intuitions could not and did not possess the force of dogmas. The great doctrines of the Resurrection and of Immortality had long to wait for a moderate degree of acceptance (they were not held, for instance, by Sirach), and longer still before they coalesced in a new and greater doctrine of the future life. Koheleth's dissatisfaction with the doctrine of present retribution (the central point both of his heterodoxy and of Job's) might have helped him to accept the former of these. His acquaintance with non-Jewish philosophical literature, if we may venture to assume this as a fact, might have led him, as it led the author of the Wisdom of Solomon, to embrace the hope of immortality. But though there probably is an allusion to this hope as well-founded in xii. 7*b*, we have seen reason to doubt whether the words came from Koheleth himself; at any rate, they are isolated, and many do not admit the allusion. Either of these doctrines would have saved Koheleth from despondency had he accepted it. From our present point of view, we must blame him for not accepting one refuge or the other, or even that simpler belief in the imperishableness of the Jewish race which Sirach had, and which has preserved so many Israelitish hearts in trials as severe as Koheleth's. There must have been a strange weakness in his moral fibre; how else can we account either for his want of Jewish feeling or, I would now add, using the word in its looser sense, for his pessimism? As Huber has well observed,[1] none of the ancient peoples was naturally less inclined to pessimism than the Jews, so that a work like Ecclesiastes is a portent in the Old Testament, and alien to the spirit of true Judaism. I cannot wonder that both Jews and Christians have now and again been repelled by this

---

[1] *Der Pessimismus*, 1876, p. 8. Schopenhauer too calls the Jews the most optimistic race in history.

strange book¹ and denied its title to canonicity, partly for its pessimism, partly for its supposed Epicureanism, or that the author of the Book of Wisdom before them should have given Koheleth the most scathing of condemnations by putting almost its very language into the mouth of the ungodly.² The true student may no doubt be equally severe upon Koheleth for his despair of wisdom and depreciation of its delights (i. 17, 18, ii. 15, 16), which are hardly redeemed by the utilitarian sayings in vii. 11, 12.

I cannot justify Koheleth, but I can plead for a mitigation of these censures, and altogether defend the admission of the Book (not, of course, as Solomonic) into the sacred Canon. Whether Jewish or not, the pessimistic theory of life has a sound kernel. 'Our sadness,' as Thoreau says, 'is not sad, but our cheap joys. Let us be sad about all we see and are, for so we demand and pray for better. It is the constant prayer [of the good] and whole Christian religion.'³ This too is the burden of E. von Hartmann's criticism of a crudely optimistic Christianity; and need we reject the truth for the extravagances of the teacher? Next, as to the preference of sensuous enjoyment to philosophic pursuits in Koheleth. I would not seek to weaken passages like ii. 24, viii. 15, by putting them down to the irony of a *sæva indignatio*. But as for the depreciation of intellectual pleasure, may it not be excused by the author's want of a sure prospect of the 'age to come' such as we find in those lines of Davenant,⁴

> Before by death you nearer knowledge gain
> (For to increase your knowledge you must die),
> Tell me if all that knowledge be not vain,
> On which we proudly in this life rely.

And as to the commendations of sensuous pleasure, have they not a relative justification?⁵ The legalism of the 'righteous

---

¹ See Appendix.
² Wisd. ii. 6; comp. Plumptre, *Ecclesiastes*, p. 71 &c., Wright, *Koheleth*, pp. 69, 70.   ³ *Letters to Various Persons*, p. 25.
⁴ See the extracts in Trench's *Household Book of English Poetry*, p. 405.
⁵ I do not of course assent to the form in which Grätz puts this, to serve his hypothesis as to the age of Koheleth. See Appendix.

overmuch' threatened already perhaps to make life an intolerable burden. And though Koheleth erred in the form of his teaching, yet he did well to teach the 'duty of delight' (Ruskin) and to oppose an orthodoxy which sought, not merely to transform, but to kill nature. It is to his credit that he touches on the relations of the sexes with such studious reserve.[1] As a rule, the enjoyments which he recommends are those of the table, which in Sirach's time (Ecclus. xxxii. 3-5) and perhaps also in Koheleth's included music and singing,—in short, festive but refined society. His praise of festive mirth is at any rate more excusable morally than Omar Khayyâm's impassioned commendations of the winecup.[2] As Jeremy Taylor says, 'It was the best thing that was then commonly known that they should seize upon the present with a temperate use of permitted pleasures.'[3] Lastly, the admission of the book into the Canon is (perhaps we may say) not less providential than that of the Song of Songs. The latter shows us human nature in simple and healthy relations of life; the former, a human nature in a morbid state and in depressed and artificial circumstances. How to return at least to inward simplicity and health, the latter part (not the Epilogue) of the Book of Job beautifully shows us.

Our great idealist poet Shelley, who so admired Job, disliked Ecclesiastes for the same reason as the ancient heretics already mentioned. One greater than he, our 'sage and serious' Milton, justifies the sacred Scripture for the variety of its contents on the same ground that he advocates 'unlicensed printing.' Both are 'for the trial of virtue and the exercise of truth.' We need not, then, he says, be surprised if the Bible 'brings in holiest men passionately murmuring

[1] Once Koheleth appears as a sharp critic of the female sex (vii. 26-29).

[2] Lagarde describes Omar as 'ein schlemmer, der die angst des irdischen daseins und die öde langeweile seiner noch in den anfängen stehenden wissenschaft hinwegzuschwelgen suchte' (*Symmicta*, 1877, p. 9). Too hard a judgment perhaps on this changeful and impressionable nature. See Bodenstedt's version as well as Fitzgerald's.

[3] *The Rule and Exercises of Holy Dying*, chap. i., sect. 3. Parts of this chapter remind us strongly of Koheleth, and are strange indeed in a book of Christian devotion.

against Providence through all the arguments of Epicurus.'[1] The Bible, according to Milton, is perfect not in spite but because of its variety; it is like the rugged 'mountains of God,' not like the symmetrical works of human art. But Milton has also reminded us that a fool may misuse even sacred Scripture.

[1] *Prose Works*, ed. Bohn, ii. 69.

CHAPTER X.

DATE AND PLACE OF COMPOSITION.

JEWISH tradition, while admitting a Hezekian or post-Hezekian redaction of the book, assigns the original authorship of Ecclesiastes to Solomon. The Song of Songs it regards as the monument of this king's early manhood, the Book of Proverbs of his middle age, and the semi-philosophical meditations before us as the work of his old age. The tradition was connected by the Aggada with the favourite legend[1] of the discrowned Solomon, but is based upon the book itself, the passages due to the literary fiction of Solomon's authorship (which Bickell indeed attributes to an interpolator) having been misunderstood. Would that the author of the *Lectures on the Jewish Church* had given the weight of his name to the true explanation of these passages! The reticence of the lines devoted in the second volume of the *Lectures* to Ecclesiastes has led some critics to imagine that according to Dean Stanley, this book, like much of Proverbs, might possibly be the work of the 'wisest' of Israel's kings. Little had the author profited by Ewald if he really allowed such an absolute legend the smallest standing-ground among reasonable hypotheses! Whichever way we look, whether to the social picture, or to the language, or to the ideas of the book, its recent origin forces itself upon us. The social picture and the ideas need not detain us here. Either Solomon was transported in prophetic ecstasy to far distant times (the Targum on Koheleth frequently describes him as a prophet), or the writer is a child of the dawning modern age of Judaism. The former alternative is plainly impossible. Political servitude, and a generally depressed state of

[1] See the *Midrasch Kohelet* (ed. Wünsche, 1880), or Ginsburg, p. 38.

society (exceptional cases of prosperity notwithstanding), mark the book as the work of a dark post-Exile period. The absence of any national feeling equally distinguishes it from the monuments of the earlier humanistic movement (even from Job). The germs of philosophic thought, which cannot be explained away, supply, if this be possible, a still more convincing argument. We shall return to these later on : at present, let us confine ourselves to the linguistic evidence, which has been set forth with such accuracy and completeness by Delitzsch [1] and after him by Dr. Wright of Dublin.

The Hebrew language has no history if Ecclesiastes belongs to the classical period ; indeed, the Hebrew name of the book may seem of itself to stamp it as of post-Exile origin (see note on Koheleth in Appendix). The student would do well, however, to examine all the peculiar words or forms in Delitzsch's glossary, and to classify them for himself, under two principal heads, (1) those which occur elsewhere but in distinctively late-Hebrew books, (2) those only found in Koheleth, with four subdivisions, viz., (*a*) words which can be explained from Biblical Hebrew usage, (*b*) those which belong to the vocabulary of the Mishna, (*c*) those of Aramaic origin and affinities, (*d*) those borrowed from non-Semitic languages. The student should also notice the striking grammatical peculiarities of Koheleth, especially the fact that the ordinary historic tense (the imperfect with Waw consecutive) is hardly ever used. The scholar's instinct but three times reveals itself in the adoption of this old literary idiom (i. 17, iv. 1, 7), but elsewhere the usage of the Mishna is already law. Almost equally important is the fact that the Hebrew mood-distinctions are so little used in Koheleth (on which point see Delitzsch's introduction) ; indeed, we may say upon the whole that that which gives a characteristic flavour to the old Hebrew style is ' ready to vanish away.' The Mishnic peculiarities of the book are especially interesting, as confirming our view of its origin. The author is very different in his opinions from the doctors of the Mishna, but he resembles them in his questioning and reflective spirit, and helped to

---

[1] Comp. the glossary at the end of Grätz's commentary.

form the linguistic instrument which they required. Less important, but not to be ignored, are the Aramaic elements. Even Dr. Adam Clarke, untrained scholar as he was, pronounced that the attempts which had as yet been made to overthrow the evidence, were 'often trifling and generally ineffectual.'[1] The Aramaisms of Koheleth are irreconcileable with a pre-Exile date; they can only be paralleled and explained from the Aramaic portions of the books of Ezra and Daniel. That they are comparatively few, only proves that the force of the Aramaising movement has abated, and that the Hebrew language, at any rate in the hands of some of its chief cultivators, is passing into a new phase (the Mishnic). The judgment of Ewald, as already expressed in 1837, appears to me on the whole satisfactory: 'One might easily imagine Koheleth to be the very latest book in the Old Testament. A premature conclusion, since Aramaic influence extended very gradually and secretly, so that one writer might easily be more Aramaic in the colouring of his style than another. But though not [even if not] the latest, it cannot have been written till long after Aramaic had begun powerfully to influence Hebrew, and therefore *not before* the last century of the Persian rule.'[2]

For the sake of my argument, it is hardly necessary to refer to the words of non-Semitic origin, which are (as most critics rightly hold) but two in number; 1 פַּרְדֵּס (ii. 5, plur.) undoubtedly a Hebraised Persian word, on which I lay no stress here, because it occurs, not only in Neh. ii. 8, but also in Cant. iv. 13, where many critics deny that it militates against a pre-Exile date, and 2 פִּתְגָם (viii. 11), which occurs in the Aramaic parts of Ezra and Daniel, and also in Esth. i. 20, and while used in the Targums and in Syriac, did not become naturalised in Talmudic. This word, too, is commonly regarded as Hebraised Persian, but, following Zirkel, the eminent Jewish scholar Heinrich Grätz declares it to be the Hebraised form of a Greek word. Is this possible or probable? Are there any genuine Græcisms of language, and

---

[1] Quoted by Ginsburg, *Koheleth*, p. 197.
Die poetischen Bücher des Alten Bundes, Theil iv.

consequently also of thought, in the Book of Koheleth? An important question, to which we will return.

The date suggested by Ewald, and accepted by Knobel, Herzfeld, Vaihinger, Delitzsch, and Ginsburg, suits the political circumstances implied in Koheleth. The Jews had long since lost the feelings of trust and gratitude with which in 'better days' (vii. 10) they regarded the court of Persia; the desecration of the temple by Bagoses or Bagoes (Jos. *Ant.* xi. 7) is but one of the calamities which befel Judæa in the last century of the Persian rule. It is a conjecture of Delitzsch that iv. 3 contains a reminiscence of Artaxerxes II. Mnemon (died about 360), who was ninety-four years old, and according to Justin (x. 1), had 115 sons, and of his murdered successor Artaxerxes III. Ochus. Probably, if we knew more of this period, we should be able to produce other plausible illustrations. Certainly the state of society suits the date proposed. As Delitzsch remarks, 'The unrighteous judgment, iii. 16; the despotic depression, iv. 1, viii. 9, v. 8; the riotous court-life, x. 16-19; the raising of mean men to the highest dignities, x. 5-7; the inexorable severity of the law of military service, viii. 8; the prudence required by the organised system of espionage,—all these things were characteristic of this period.' Probably an advocate of a different theory would interpret these passages otherwise; but as yet no conclusive argument has been offered for supposing allusions to circumstances of the Greek period.

Let me frankly admit, in conclusion, that the evidence of the Hebrew favours a later date than that proposed by Ewald —favours, but does not actually require it. It seems, however, that if the book be of the Greek period, we have a right to expect some definite traces of Greek influence. This will supply the subject of the next chapter.

At any rate, the author addresses himself to Palestinian readers. He lives, not (I should suppose) in the country, as Ewald thought, but near the temple, or at least has opportunities of frequenting it (v. 1,[1] viii. 10). Some recent scholars

---

[1] The 'house of God' must, I think, mean the temple of Jerusalem. That of Onias IV. was not built till 160 B.C. The synagogues would not be called 'houses of God' (on Ps. lxxiv. 8, see Hitzig).

place him in Alexandria; but the reference to the corn trade in xi. 1 does not prove this to be correct; indeed, the very same section contains a reference to *rain* (so xii. 2). Sharpe[1] is alone in preferring Antioch, the capital of the Greek kingdom of Syria. Kleinert's remark that 'king in Jerusalem' (i. 12) implies a foreign abode is met by the remark that Jerusalem was in the writer's time no longer a royal city. The author may have travelled, and like Sirach have had personal acquaintance with the dangers of court-life (either at Susa or at Alexandria). The references to the king do not perhaps compel this supposition; 'are not my princes altogether kings?' (Isa. x. 8) could be said of Persian satraps.

[1] *History of the Hebrew Nation and its Literature* (ed. 2), p. 344.

CHAPTER XI.

DOES KOHELETH CONTAIN GREEK WORDS OR IDEAS?

WE now begin the consideration of the question, Are there any well-ascertained Græcisms in the language and in the thought of this obviously exceptional book? That there are many Greek loan-words in Targumic and Talmudic, is undeniable, though Levy in his lexicon has no doubt exaggerated their number. G. Zirkel, a Roman Catholic scholar, was the first who answered in the affirmative, confining himself to the linguistic side of the argument. His principal work,[1] *Untersuchungen über den Prediger* (Würzburg, 1792), is not in the Bodleian Library, but Eichhorn's review in his *Allgemeine Bibliothek*, vol. iv. (1792), contains a summary of Zirkel's evidence from which I select the following.

(*a*) יָפֶה, in sense of καλός 'becoming' (iii. 11, v. 17). This is one of the Græcisms which commend themselves the most to Grätz and Kleinert. The former points especially to v. 17, where he takes טוב אשר יפה together as representing καλὸν κἀγαθόν (comp. Plumptre on v. 18). The construction, however, is mistaken (see Delitzsch). The second אשר indicates that יפה is a synonym of וטב 'excellent.' The notion of the beautiful can b developed in various ways. The sense 'becoming,' characteristic of later Hebrew, is more distinctly required in iii. 11.

(*b*) 'In the clause לָמָּה חָכַמְתִּי אֲנִי אָז יֹתֵר (ii. 15) the words אָז יֹתֵר must signify ἔτι μᾶλλον: quid mihi prodest majorem adhuc sapientiæ operam dare?' But the demonstrative particle אז means, not ἔτι, but 'in these circumstances' (Jer. xxii. 15). Its position and connection with יתר are for emphasis. The fact of experience mentioned makes any special care for wisdom unreasonable.

(*c*) 'עֲשׂוֹת טוֹב (iii. 12) is a literal translation of εὖ πράττειν.' This

---

[1] He also published *Der Prediger Salomon; ein Lesebuch für den jungen Weltbürger; übersetzt und erklärt* (1792). The very title bears the mark of the century.

CHAP. XI.   DOES KOHELETH CONTAIN GREEK WORDS ?   261

is accepted by Kleinert and also by Tyler. The very next verse
seems to explain this phrase by ראה טוב (comp. v. 17) ; certainly the
ethical meaning is against the analogy of ii. 24, iii. 22, and similar
passages. But should we not, with Grätz and Nowack, correct
רְאוֹת טוב in iii. 12?

(*d*) 'כִּי הָאֱלֹהִים וגו' (v. 19) must mean, God gives him joy of heart.
ענה "respondere" seems to have borrowed the meaning "remunerari"
from ἀμείβεσθαι, which has both senses. The ancient writer of the
book thought thus in Greek, ὅτι θεὸς ἀμείβεται (αὐτὸν) εὐφροσύνῃ τῆς
καρδίας.' Zirkel forgets Ps. lxv. 6. See however Delitzsch.

(*e*) הֲלָךְ־נָפֶשׁ (vi. 9) = ὁρμὴ τῆς ψυχῆς [M. Aurelius iii. 15]. But
the phrase is idiomatic Hebrew for 'roving of the desire.'

(*f*) יֵצֵא אֶת־כֻּלָּם (vii. 18). 'The Hebrew writer found no other
equivalent for μέσην βαδίζειν.' But unless he borrowed the idea
(that of cultivating the mean in moral practice), why should he have
tried to express the technical term?

(*g*) כִּי־זֶה כָּל־הָאָדָם (xii. 13). 'A pure Græcism, τοῦτο παντὸς
ἀνθρώπου.' But how otherwise could the idea of the universal obli-
gation to fear God have been expressed? Comp. the opening words
of iii. 19.

To these may be added (*h*) ביום טובה (vii. 14) = εὐημερία (see
however xii. 1) ; (*i*) the 'technical term' תור (i. 13, ii. 3, vii. 25) =
σκέπτεσθαι [but good Hebrew for 'to explore'] ; (*k*) פתגם (viii. 11) =
φθέγμα ; (*l*) פרדס (ii. 15) = παράδεισος (see above).

No one in our day would dream of accepting these
'Græcisms' in a mass.

Zirkel tried to prove too much, as Grätz himself truly
observes. Any peculiar word or construction he set down as
un-Hebraic and hurried to explain it by some Greek parallel,
ignoring the capacity of development inherent in the Hebrew
language. His attempt failed in his own generation. Three
recent scholars however (Grätz, Kleinert, and Tyler), have been
more or less captivated by his idea, and have proposed some
new and some old 'Græcisms' for the acceptance of scholars.
To me it seems that, their three or four very disputable words
and phrases are not enough. If the author of Koheleth really
thought half in Greek, the Greek colouring of the language
would surely not have been confined to such a few expressions. If מה־שהיה (vii. 24) were really derived from τὸ τί ἐστιν,
as Kleinert supposes, should we not meet with it oftener?

But the phrase most naturally means, not 'the essence of things,' but 'that which hath come into existence;' phenomena are not easily understood in their ultimate causes, is the simple meaning of the sentence. I have said nothing as yet of the supposed Græcism in the epilogue—the last place where we should have expected one (considering ver. 12). But Mr. Tyler's proposal to explain הַכֹּל (xii. 13) by τὸ καθόλου or τὸ ὅλον (a formula introducing a general conclusion), falls to the ground, when the true explanation of the passage has been stated (see p. 232).

There are therefore no Græcisms in the language of the book. Of course *ideas* may have been derived from a Greek source notwithstanding. The book, as we have seen already, is conspicuous by its want of a native Jewish background, nor does it show any affinity to Babylonian or Persian theology. It obviously stands at the close of the great Jewish humanistic movement, and gives an entirely new colour to the traditional humanism by its sceptical tone and its commendations of sensuous pleasure. It is not surprising that St. Jerome should remark on ix. 7-9, that the author appears to be reproducing the low ideas of some Greek philosophers, though, as this Father supposes, only to refute them.

'Et hæc inquit, aliquis loquatur Epicurus, et Aristippus et Cyrenaici et cæteræ pecudes Philosophorum. Ego autem, mecum diligenter retractans, invenio'[1] &c.

Few besides Prof. Salmon would accept the view that Eccles. ix. 7-9 and similar passages are the utterances of an infidel objector (see Bishop Ellicott's Commentary); but it is perfectly possible to hold that there are distinctively Epicurean doctrines in the Koheleth. The later history of Jewish thought may well seem to render this opinion probable. How dangerously fascinating Epicureanism must have been when the word 'Epicuros' became a synonym in Rabbinic Hebrew for infidel or even atheist.[2] It is indeed no mere

---

[1] *Opera*, ii. (1699), 765 (*Comm. in Ecclesiasten*). Comp. the use made of Koheleth's phraseology by the author of Wisdom (ii. 6-10).

[2] See *Sanhedrin*, x. 1:— אלו שאין להם חלק לעולם הבא האומר אין תחית המתים מן התורה ואין תורה מן שמים ואפיקורוס.—Comp. *Aboth*, ii. 14 (10 Taylor), and *Genesis Rabbah*, 19 ('the serpent was Epicuros').

fancy that just as Pharisaism had affinities with Stoicism, so Sadducæism had with Epicureanism. As Harnack well says, 'No intellectual movement could withdraw itself from the influences which proceeded from the victory of the Greeks over the Eastern world.'[1] Mr. Tyler,[2] however, and his ally Dean Plumptre, have scarcely made the best of their case, the Epicurean affinities which they discover in Koheleth being by no means striking. Much use is made of the *De Rerum Naturâ* of Lucretius—a somewhat late authority! But if points of contact with Lucretius are to be hunted for, ought we not also to mention the discrepancies between the 'wise man' and the poet? If Lucr. i. 113-116 may be used to illustrate Eccles. iii. 21, must we not equally emphasise the difference between the festive mirth recommended by Koheleth (ix. 7, 8 &c.) and the simple pleasures so beautifully sung by Lucretius (ii. 20-33), and which remind us rather of the charming naturalness of the Hebrew Song of Songs?[3] The number of vague analogies between Koheleth and Epicureanism might perhaps have been even increased, but I can find no passage in the former which distinctly expresses any scholastic doctrine of Epicureanism. For instance the doctrine of Atomism assumed for illustration by Dean Plumptre,[4] cannot be found there by even the keenest exegesis; the plurality of worlds is not even distantly alluded to, and the denial of the spirit, if implied in iii. 21 (see p. 212), is only implied in the primitive Hebrew sense, familiar to us from Job and the Psalter. The recommendation of ἀταραξία (to use the Epicurean term), coupled with sensuous pleasure (v. 18-20), requires no philosophic basis, and is simply the expression of a *pococurante* mood, only too natural in one debarred from a

[1] *Lehrbuch der Dogmengeschichte*, p. 46.
[2] See his *Ecclesiastes, a Contribution to its Interpretation*, &c. (1874). The main results of this work were accepted by Prof. Siegfried, who reviewed it in the *Zeitschrift f. wissenschaftl. Theologie*, 1875, pp. 284-291.
[3] This discrepancy I had noted down before observing that Dean Plumptre had quoted the very same passage of Lucretius as a parallel to Eccles. ii. 24. For my own view of Koheleth's recommendations, see p. 253. Lucretius seems to me, in this strain, to soar higher than Koheleth; Omar Khayyâm to fall below him.
[4] *Ecclesiastes*, p. 47.

career of fruitful activity. Lastly, there is nothing in the phraseology either of the Hebrew or of the Septuagint to suggest an acquaintance with Epicureanism.

A stronger case can be made for the influence of Stoicism. The undoubted Oriental affinities of this system and its moral and theological spirit would, as Mr. Tyler observes, naturally commend it to a Jewish writer. We know that, at a somewhat later day, Stoicism exercised a strong fascination on some of the noblest Jewish minds. Philo,[1] the Book of Wisdom, and the so-called Fourth Book of Maccabees, have undeniable allusions to it; and more or less probable vestiges of Stoicism have been found in the oldest Jewish Sibyl[2] (about B.C. 140) and in the Targum of Onkelos.[3] But how does the case stand with Koheleth? First of all, are there any traces of Stoic terminology? That terminology varied no doubt within certain limits, and could not be accurately reproduced in Hebrew. Still even under the contorted forms of expression to which a Hebrew-writing Stoic or semi-Stoic might be driven we could hardly fail to recognise the familiar Stoic expressions, εἱμαρμένη, πρόνοια, φαντασία, φύσις, φρόνησις, ἀρετή. The Septuagint version ought to help us here. But among the twenty words almost or entirely peculiar to the Greek of Ecclesiastes, the only two technical philosophic terms are σοφία and γνῶσις.

Next, can we detect references to distinctive Stoic doctrines? Mr. Tyler lays great stress in his reply on the Catalogue of Times and Seasons (iii. 1–8), which he regards as an expansion of the Stoic ὁμολογουμένως ζῆν. But the idea that there is an appointed order of things, and that every action has its place in it, is much more a corollary of the doctrine of Destiny than of the doctrine of Duty. The essence of the latter doctrine is that men were meant to conform and ought to conform to the Universal Order, acquiesc-

---

[1] Philo alludes, e.g., to the Stoic doctrine of revolutions (which some have found in Koheleth) and remarks that the Stoics think of God as of a boy who builds up sandhills, and then throws them down again.
[2] Hilgenfeld, *Jüdische Apokalyptik*, p. 51, &c.
[3] See Deut. viii. 18, and especially Gen. ii. 7 (Neubürger in Grätz's *Monatsschrift*, 1873, p. 566).

ing in that which is inevitable, shaping in the best way that which is possible to be moulded. Upon this the practical ethics of Stoicism depend. But this is the very point which is absent in Ecclesiastes. The Catalogue of Times and Seasons ends not with the Stoic exhortation ἐκπλήρου τὴν χώραν, 'Fulfil thy appointed part,' but with the despondent reflection of the Fatalist, 'What profit hath he that worketh in that wherein he toileth?' (iii. 9.) A second argument is that the idea 'There is no new thing under the sun' (i. 9) is a phase of the Stoic doctrine of cyclical revolutions. But all that which gave form and colour to the Stoic doctrine is entirely absent—especially, as Mr. Tyler himself admits, the idea of ἐκπύρωσις. The idea, as it is found in Ecclesiastes, has nothing Stoic or even philosophical about it. It is simply an old man's observation that human actions, like natural phenomena, tend to repeat themselves in successive generations.[1]

That there are analogies between Stoicism and the ideas of Koheleth need not be denied; Dr. Kalisch has collected some of them in his very interesting philosophico-religious dialogue.[2] Prominent among these is the peculiar use of the terms 'madness' and 'folly.' 'From the followers of Zeno,' remarks Dean Plumptre,[3] 'he learned also to look upon virtue and vice in their intellectual aspects. The common weaknesses and follies of mankind were to him, as to them, only so many different forms and degrees of absolute insanity (i. 17, ii. 12, vii. 25, ix. 3).' But this division of mankind into wise men and fools is common to the Stoa with the ancient Hebrew sages who 'sat in the gate.' When the great populariser of Stoicism says, 'Sapientia perfectum bonum est mentis humanæ,'[4] he almost translates more than one of the proverbs which we have studied already. Another point of contact with Stoicism is undoubtedly the Determinism of the

---

[1] For this criticism upon Mr. Tyler's view of iii. 1-8, I am indebted to Dr. Hatch.
[2] *Path and Goal*, p. 116. But see p. 92.
[3] *Ecclesiastes*, p. 45.
[4] Seneca, *Ep.* 89, quoted by Bruch, *Weisheitslehre der Hebräer*, p. 253, with reference to the teaching of Proverbs.

book, which, as Prof. Kleinert observes, leaves no room for freedom of the will, and fuses the conceptions of εἱμαρμένη and πρόνοια (see especially chap. iii.). But such Determinism need not have been learned in the school of Zeno. It is genuinely Semitic (did not Zeno come from the Semitic Citium?) What is the religion of Islam but a grandiose system of Determinism? Indeed, where is virtual Determinism more forcibly expressed than in the Old Testament itself (e.g., Isa. lxiii. 17)?

Those who adopt the view which I am controverting are apt to appeal to somewhat late philosophic authorities. I cannot here discuss the parallelisms which have been found in the Meditations or Self-communings (Τὰ εἰς ἑαυτόν) of the great Stoic emperor. Some, for instance, consider the ῥύσεις καὶ ἀλλοιώσεις which 'renew the world continually' (*M. A.* vi. 15) and the περιοδικὴ παλιγγενεσία τῶν ὅλων (*M. A.* xi. 1) to be alluded to in Eccles. i. 5–9. More genuine are some at least of the other parallelisms, e.g. Eccles. i. 9, *M. A.* vi. 37, vii. 1, x. 27, xii. 26; Eccles. ii. 25, *M. A.* ii. 3 (*ad init.*); Eccles. iii. 11, *M. A.* iv. 23 (*ad init.*); Eccles. vi. 9, *M. A.* iv. 26; Eccles. xi. 5, *M. A.* x. 26. I admit that there is a certain vague affinity between the two thinkers; both are earnest, both despair of reforming society, both have left but a fragmentary record of their meditations. But the 'humanest of the Roman race'[1] stands out, upon the whole, far above the less cultured and more severely tried Israelite. Alike in intellectual powers and in moral elevation the soul of the Roman is of a truly imperial order. He is not, like Koheleth, a 'malist' (see pp. 201–202); he boldly denies evil, and his strong faith in Providence cannot be disturbed by apparent irregularities in the order of things. It is true that this does but make the sadness of his golden and almost Christian book the more depressing. But the book *is* 'golden.'[2] Koheleth and M. Aurelius alike call forth our pity and admiration, but in what different proportions!

---

[1] R. H. Stoddard, *The Morals of M. Aurelius.*
[2] Comp. Niebuhr, *Lectures on the History of Rome*, iii. 247.

If, then, there are points of agreement between Koheleth and M. Aurelius, there must also of necessity be points of disagreement. Every page of their writings would, I think, supply them. Suffice it to put side by side the saying of Koheleth, 'God is in heaven, and thou upon earth' (v. 2), and M. Aurelius' invocation of the world as the 'city of God' (iv. 23). The comparison suggests one of the greatest discrepancies between Koheleth and the Stoics—the doctrine of God. Such faith as the former still retains is faith in a transcendent and not an immanent Deity. The germs of a doctrine of Immanence which the older Wisdom-literature contains (Kleinert quotes Ps. civ. 30, Job xxvi. 13), have found no lodgment in the mind of our author, who is more affected by the legal and extreme supernaturalistic [1] point of view than he is perhaps aware.

Mr. Tyler's introduction to his *Ecclesiastes* is a work of great acuteness and originality, and seeks to provide against all reasonable objections; I cannot do justice to it here. One part of his theory, however, is too remarkable to be passed over (see above, pp. 240, 241). He supposes that Stoic and Epicurean doctrines were deliberately set over against each other by the wise man who wrote our book, in order by the clash of opposites to deter the reader from dangerous and unsatisfying investigations. The goal of the author's philosophising thus becomes the negation of all philosophy, and this 'sacrificio dell' intelletto' he insinuatingly commends by the subtlest use of artifice. Such a theory may have occurred to one or another early writer (see Ginsburg), but seems out of harmony with the character of the author as revealed in his book. He is not such a weak-kneed wrestler for truth. You may fancy him sometimes a Stoic, sometimes an Epicurean; but he always speaks like a man in earnest, however his opinions may change through the fluctuations of his moods. Mr. Tyler's theory confounds Koheleth's point of view with that of a far inferior thinker, the author of Ecclesiasticus (see above, p. 199).

---

[1] The phrase is objectionably modern, but in this connection could not be avoided.

I cannot, therefore, be persuaded to explain this enigmatical book by a supposed contact with Greek philosophy such as we do really find in the Book of Wisdom. I have no prejudice against the supposition in itself. It would help me to understand the Hellenising movement at a later day if Stoic and (still more) Epicurean ideas had already filtered into the minds of the Jewish aristocracy. The denunciations in the Book of Enoch (xciv. 5, xcviii. 15, civ. 10) not impossibly refer to a heretical philosophical literature (see p. 233); the only question is, To a native or to a half foreign literature? I see no sufficient reason at present for adopting the latter alternative. Koheleth is really a native Hebrew philosopher, the first Jew who, however awkwardly and ineffectually, 'gave his mind to seek and explore by wisdom concerning all things that are done under heaven' (i. 13). Very touching in this light are the memoranda which he has left us. They are incomplete enough; Koheleth is but the forerunner of more systematic philosophisers. His ideas are nothing less than scholastic; how could we expect anything different, his first object being in all probability to soothe the pain of an inward struggle by giving it literary expression? If, however, I was compelled to suggest a secondary reference to any foreign system, I could most easily suppose one to the pessimistic teaching of Hegesias Peisithanatos, who, after Ptolemy Soter and Philadelphus had made Alexandria the seat of the world's commerce and the centre of Greek literature and culture, was seized with the thought of the vanity of all things, of the preponderance of evil, and of the impossibility of happiness.[1] Koheleth's teaching would be a safeguard to any Jew who might be tempted by this too popular philosopher. He admits ματαιότης ματαιοτήτων, but insists that, granting all drawbacks, 'the light is sweet' (xi. 7), the living are better off than the dead (ix. 4-6), and sensuous pleasure, used in moderation, is at least a relative good (ii. 24); also that it is futile to inquire 'why the former days (of the earlier Ptolemies?) were better than these' (vii. 10), and, if a later view of his meaning may be trusted,

[1] Zeller, *Philosophie der Griechen*, ii. 1, p. 278.

he sought to displace the many dangerous books which were current by words which were at once pleasantly written and objectively true (xii. 10, 12).

Koheleth is a native Hebrew philosopher. The philosophy of an eastern sage is not to be tied up in the rigid formulæ of the West. Easterns may indeed take kindly to Western doctrines; but where they think independently, they eschew system. Koheleth's seeming Stoicism is, as we have seen, of primitive Hebrew affinities; his seeming Epicureanism, if it be not sufficiently explained as a mental reaction against the gloom of the times, may perhaps be connected more or less closely, not with the schools of Greek philosophers, but with the banquet-halls of Egypt. The Hebrew writer's invitations to enjoy life remind us of the call to 'drink and be happy,' which accompanied the grim symbolic 'coffin,' or mummy, at Egyptian feasts (probably they were funeral-feasts), according to Herodotus (ii. 78), and of the festal dirges translated by Goodwin and Stern.[1] A stanza in one of the latter may be given here. It is from the song supposed to be sung by the harper at an anniversary funeral feast in honour of Neferhotep, a royal scribe, and still to be seen cut in the stone at Abd-el-Gurna, in the Theban necropolis. As Ebers has remarked,[2] the song 'shows how a certain fresh delight in life mingled with the feelings about death that were prevalent among the ancient Egyptians, who celebrated their festivals more boisterously than most other peoples.' By a poetic fiction, the dead man is supposed to be present, and to listen to the song.

> Make a good day, O holy father!
> Let odours and oils stand before thy nostril.
> Wreaths of lotus are on the arms and the bosom of thy sister,
> Dwelling in thy heart, sitting beside thee.
> Let song and music be before thy face,
> And leave behind thee all evil cares!
> Mind thee of joy, till cometh the day of pilgrimage,
> When we draw near the land which loveth silence.

---

[1] *Records of the Past*, iv. 115-118; vi. 127-130.
[2] 'Cairo, the Old in the New,' *Contemp. Rev.*, xliii. 852.

We have seen that the Wisdom of Sirach betrays a taste for Egyptian festivity (p. 191). May we not suppose that Koheleth too had travelled to Alexandria? This view commends itself to Kleinert, and I have no objection to it with due limitations. Koheleth may have envied and sought to copy the light-hearted gaiety of the valley of the Nile. But we ought not to conceal the fact that the lines quoted above are followed by others which have no parallel in Koheleth.

> Good for thee then will have been (an honest life),
> Therefore be just and hate transgressions,
> For he who loveth justice (will be blest).
> (They in the shades) are sitting on the bank of the river,
> Thy soul is among them, drinking its sacred water.
> . . . . (woe to the bad one !)
> He shall sit miserable in the heat of infernal fires.

There is a wide difference between a people who believed in a happy Amenti where Osiris himself dwelt and the Jew who doubted much but believed firmly in Sheól. I admit then the probability that the latter had travelled, and was not unaffected by the brightness of Egyptian society, but I see no reason to suppose that he knew and was influenced by the expressions of Egyptian songs. The resemblances adduced are to me as fortuitous as those between the love-poems of the Nile valley and the Hebrew Song of Songs, or (we may add) as that striking one between Eccles. i. 4 and some of the opening lines of the 'Song of the Harper,'—

> Men pass away since the time of Ra [the sun of day]
> And the youths come in their stead.
> Like as Ra reappears every morning,
> And Tum [the sun of night] sets in the horizon,
> Men are begetting,
> And women are conceiving.[1]

I make no excuse for the length of this inquiry. If we could trace Greek influences, linguistic or philosophical, in

---

[1] *Records of the Past*, vi. 127.

CHAP. XI.   DOES KOHELETH CONTAIN GREEK WORDS ?   271

the strange book before us, its date would be decided. Taking into account the circumstances of the writer, we might assign it to the reign of Ptolemy IV. Philopator, when the Egyptian rule began to be calamitous for Judæa. Kleinert would place it rather in one of the early, fortunate reigns (*Herzog-Plitt*, xii. 173); but he forms perhaps too favourable a view of the social picture in Koheleth. Hitzig, who gives a very restricted range to Greek philosophical influence upon our book, and accepts none of Zirkel's Græcisms, fixes the date in the first year of Ptolemy V. Epiphanes. Geiger, Nöldeke, Kuenen, Tyler, and Plumptre, on various grounds, think this the most probable period,[1] and the view is endorsed by Zeller, the historian of Greek philosophy.

A Maccabæan and still more a Herodian date seem to me absolutely excluded, though Zirkel and Renan have advocated the one, and Heinrich Grätz (see p. 240) the other. The book is certainly pre-Maccabæan, not merely because of a Talmudic anecdote,[2] but because of its want of religious fervour (comp. Esther) and its cosmopolitanism. The germs of the Jewish parties may be there, but only the germs. To me Hitzig's is the latest possible date ; but if we *must* admit a vague and indirect Greek influence, should we not place the book a little earlier as suggested above? But I do not see that we *must* admit even a vague Greek influence. The inquiring spirit was present in the class of 'wise men' even before the Exile, and the circumstances of the later Jews were, from the Exile onwards, well fitted to exercise and develope it. Hellenic teaching was in no way necessary to an ardent but unsystematic thinker like Koheleth. *The date proposed by Ewald and Delitzsch is on this and other grounds probable, and on linguistic grounds not impossible.*

There are two recent treatises on the philosophical affinities of Koheleth which may be mentioned here, though

[1] Geiger, *Urschrift*, pp. 60, 61 ; Nöldeke, *Die alttestamentliche Literatur.*, p. 175; Kuenen, *Hist.-krit. Onderzoek.*, iii. 188, *Theologisch. Tijdschrift*, 1883, p. 143.
[2] See reference, p. 280.

only the first is known to me. Paul Kleinert, who has long made a special study of Koheleth (see his *Prediger Salomo*, 1864), contributed to the *Theolog. Studien und Kritiken*, 1883, p. 761, &c., a striking paper called 'Sind im Buche Koheleth ausserhebräische Einflüsse anzuerkennen,' and August Palm in 1885 published a *programme* entitled '*Qohelet und die nacharistotelische Philosophie*' (Mannheim).

CHAPTER XII.

TEXTUAL PROBLEMS OF KOHELETH.

I.

ACCORDING to Delitzsch, the Song of Solomon is the most difficult book in the Old Testament. If so, Ecclesiastes comes next in order. None of the attempts to discover a logical plan having been successful, Gustav Bickell's new hypothesis (1884) deserves a respectful hearing, since it endeavours to solve the enigma in a most original way, connecting it with the problem of the text. This critic starts from the observation that continuous passages of some extent are suddenly closed by an abrupt transition, and that such passages are pretty equal in length. His explanation of this is a purely mechanical one. The troubles of the commentators have arisen principally from an accident which happened to a standard MS., called by Bickell, 'die Unfallshandschrift' (the Accident-manuscript). This MS. seems to have consisted of 21 or 22 leaves, with an average of 518 to 535 letters to a leaf. To speak more precisely, it was composed of fasciculi of four double leaves each; the book began on the sixth leaf of the first fasciculus, and ended on the second, or more probably on the third leaf of the fourth. Through a loosening of the two middle fasciculi, a dislocation took place, and an almost entirely new order arose, though with one exception the leaves which had been placed in pairs remained together. But the story of the fortunes of Ecclesiastes has not yet been told. Three hands, besides the original writer, have worked on this ill-fated book. One of these is considered to have been a downright 'enemy' who

T

tampered with the text before the dislocation had taken place. From him proceed 'the protests against Koheleth's principles on the obedience due to the king in viii. 1, 5a as well as the offensive expressions in xi. 5, xii. 4, 5, by which he sought to make the book ridiculous and contemptible.' Subsequently to him, and after the leaves had been thrown into confusion, another writer made 'well-meaning additions,' and so brought the book into nearly its present form; among these additions was the Epilogue. His aim was 'to brighten Koheleth's gloomy view of the world, partly by emphasising the doctrine of a present retribution, but still more by pointing to a future judgment in which inequalities should be rectified.' The third hand is that of the so-called pseudo-Solomonic interpolator. He must have gone to work after the Epilogist, for the latter simply knows Koheleth as a wise man skilled in proverbial composition. Bickell also claims to make transpositions on a small scale, and offers many emendations sometimes based on the Septuagint. 'Habent sua fata libelli.'

I have said that Bickell's explanation of the want of order in Ecclesiastes is a purely mechanical one. It is not on that account to be rejected. A German reviewer [1] has mentioned a case within his own experience in which the double leaves of one of the fasciculi of an Oriental MS. had been disarranged in the binding, a circumstance which had led to various additions and alterations. It may indeed be urged as an objection that the Septuagint text differs in no very material respect from the Massoretic. But a work like Ecclesiastes had at first in all probability but a very slight circulation, so that an accident to a single MS. would naturally involve unusually serious consequences. Still from the possibility to the actuality of the 'accident' is a long step. Apart from other difficulties in the theory, the number and arbitrariness of the transpositions, additions, and alterations are reason enough to make one hesitate to accept it; and when we pass from the very plausible arrangement of the contents (Bickell, pp. 53, 54) to the translation of the text, it is often only

[1] In the *Theologisches Literaturblatt*, Sept. 19, 1884.

possible to make them tally by a violent and imaginative exegesis.

Among the transpositions (to which I have no theoretic objection [1]) are the following:

    v. 9–16 placed after ii. 11,
    viii. 9–14 ,, ,, iii. 8,
    vi. 8–12 ,, ,, x. 1,
    iv. 9–16 ,, ,, vii. 20,
    x. 16–xi. 6 ,, ,, v. 8,
    xi. 6   ,, ,, xi. 3.

Bickell's theory that the passages which assert or suggest Solomonic authorship in i. 1, 12, 16, ii. 7, 8, 9, [12], are due to an interpolator,[2] is plausible; it throws a new light on the statement of the Epilogue (xii. 9) that 'Koheleth was a wise man,' and a motive for the interpolation can be readily imagined —the desire to obtain ecclesiastical sanction for the book. It is, however, incapable of proof.

II.

There are in fact few books on Ecclesiastes so stimulating as Bickell's, though it needs to be read with discrimination [3] (comp. p. 241). Putting aside the author's peculiar theory, it must be owned that he has enabled us to realise the inherent difficulties of the text as it stands, and contributed some very happy corrections. All critics will admit the need of such emendations. The text of Koheleth is even more faulty than that of Job, Psalms, or Proverbs. We cannot wonder at this. Meditations often so fragmentary on such a difficult subject were foredoomed to suffer greatly at the hands of copyists. A minute study of the various readings and of the corrections which have been proposed would lead us too far, interesting as it would be (compare Renan's remarks, *L'Ecclésiaste*, p. 53). Cappellus (Louis

---

[1] Van der Palm first conjectured that passages had been misplaced, and Grätz has adopted the idea (*Kohélet*, pp. 40–43).

[2] Comp. Rashbam's interpolation theory (Ginsburg, *Coheleth*, p. 42).

[3] See Budde's review of Bickell's work in the *Theologische Literaturzeitung*, Feb. 7, 1885.

Cappel) has done most for the text among the earlier critics (see his *Critica Sacra*, Par. 1650); Grätz has also made useful suggestions based upon the versions. Renan, and (as we have seen) Bickell, have corrected the text on a larger scale; occasional emendations of great value are due to Hitzig, Delitzsch, Klostermann, and Krochmal. The notes in the expected new edition of Eyre and Spottiswoode's *Variorum Bible* will indicate the most important various readings and corrections; to these I would refer the reader. The corrections of Bickell are those least known to most students. In considering them, we must distinguish between those which arise out of his peculiar critical theory and those which are simply the outcome of his singular and brilliant insight. Of the latter, I will here only mention two. One occurs in iii. 11, where for אֶת־הָעֹלָם (or אֶת־הָעוֹלָם the Oriental or Babylonian reading), he gives (see below, p. 299) לְבַקֵּשׁ אֶת־בְּלִי־הָעֹלָם, remarking that בְּלִי survived in the text translated in the Septuagint. The fact is, however, that though Cod. Vat. does read σύμπαντα τὸν αἰῶνα, Cod. Alex., Cod. Sin., and the Complutensian ed. all read σὺν τὸν αἰῶνα, and as the verse begins Τὰ σύμπαντα (v. l. Σύμπαντα) it is probable enough that σύμπαντα was written the second time in Cod. Vat. by mistake. At any rate, copyists both of the Greek and of the Hebrew were sometimes inclined to insert or omit 'all' at haphazard; thus, in iv. 2, Cod. Vat. inserts 'all,' which is omitted in Cod. Alex. and Cod. Sin.

Another, adopted above at p. 220, is in viii. 10. Read וּבָאוּ. בְּבָרִים (נִקְבָּרִים) (or וּבִמְקוֹם קָדוֹשׁ יְהַלֵּכוּ is a fragment of the correct reading וּבִמְקוֹם which stood side by side with the alternative reading וּמִמְּקוֹם.

On the question of interpolations, enough has been said already. Probably Cornill's book on Ezekiel will dispose many critics to look more favourably on attempts to purify Biblical texts from glosses and other interpolations. Grätz's conclusion certainly cannot be maintained, 'Sämmtliche Sentenzen gehören streng zu ihrer nachbarlichen Gedankengruppe, führen den Gedanken weiter oder spitzen ihn zu.'

I have still to speak of the Septuagint version. Its importance for textual criticism is great; indeed, we may say with Klostermann that the Massoretic text and this translation are virtually two copies of one and the same archetype. It is distinguished from the Septuagint versions of the Books of Job, Proverbs, and even Psalms by its fidelity. Those versions approximate more or less closely to the elegant manner of Symmachus, but the Greek style of the Septuagint Koheleth is most peculiar, admitting such words as ἀντίρρησις, ἔγκοπος, ἐκκλησιαστής, ἐντρύφημα, ἐπικοσμεῖν, παραφορά, περιουσιασμός περιφέρεια, περισπασμός, προαίρεσις (in special sense, ii. 17) ἐξουσιάζειν (not less than eleven times), and such abnormal phrases as ὑπὸ τὸν ἥλιον (i. 3 and often), and especially σὺν as an equivalent of את when distinctive of the accusative (ii. 17, iii. 10, iv. 3, vii. 15, and nine other passages; elsewhere σύμπαντα or the like). The last-named peculiarity reminds us strongly of Aquila [1] (comp. [God created] σὺν τὸν οὐρανὸν καὶ σὺν τὴν γῆν, Aquila's rendering of Gen. i. 1); but it must be also mentioned that in more than half the passages in which את of the accusative occurs in the original, this characteristic rendering of Aquila is *not* found. This fact militates against the theory of Grätz,[2] that the Septuagint version of Ecclesiastes is really the second improved edition of Aquila, and against that of Salzberger,[3] who argues that the fragments given as from Aquila in Origen's Hexapla are not really Aquila's at all, the one and only true edition of Aquila's Ecclesiastes being that now extant in the Septuagint (comp. the case of Theodotion's Daniel). It seems clear that the Septuagint version, as it stands, is a composite one, but it is possible, as Montfaucon long ago pointed out,[4] that an early version once existed, independent of Aquila.

[1] On Aquila and his theory of interpretation, comp. Renan, *L'Ecclésiaste*, p. 54; and on his artificial vocabulary, Field's remarks, *Hexapla*, Prolegomena, p. xxii.

[2] *Kohélet*, Anhang. Before Grätz, Frankel was already inclined to think that the Septuagint version might be really Aquila's (*Vorstudien*, p. 238, note *w*). So more positively Freudenthal. Renan inclines to agree with Grätz.

[3] Grätz's *Monatsschrift*, 1873, pp. 168-174

[4] *Hexapla* (1713), i., Præliminaria, p. 42. Montfaucon indicates vii. 23*a* as manifestly made up of a genuine version, and one interpolated from Aquila. Comp. Clericus' note on Eccles iv. 1.

The question of the origin of this version is of some critical importance, for if the work of Aquila, the Septuagint Ecclesiastes cannot be earlier than 130 A.D. Supposing this to be the first Greek version of the book, we obtain an argument in favour of the Herodian date of Ecclesiastes advocated by Grätz. Upon the whole, however, there seems no sufficient reason for doubting that there was a Septuagint version of the book distinct from Aquila's, as indeed Origen's Hexapla and St. Jerome in the preface to his commentary attest, and that this version in its original form goes back, like the versions of Job and Proverbs, to one of the last centuries before Christ.

On the Peshitto version of Koheleth and Ruth there is a monograph by G. Janichs, *Animadversiones criticæ* &c. (Breslau, 1871), with which compare Nöldeke's review, *Lit. Centralblatt*, 1871, No. 49. For the text of the *Græcus Venetus*, see Gebhardt's edition (Leipz. 1874). Ginsburg's well-known work (1861) contains sections on the versions.

CHAPTER XIII.

THE CANONICITY OF ECCLESIASTES AND ECCLESIASTICUS.

I.

IT is not surprising that these strange Meditations should have had great difficulty in penetrating into the Canon. There is sufficient evidence (see the works of Plumptre and Wright)[1] that the so-called Wisdom of Solomon is in part a deliberate contradiction of sentiments expressed in our book. The most striking instance of this antagonism is in Wisd. ii. 6–10 (cf. Eccles. ix. 7–9), where the words of Koheleth are actually put into the mouth of the ungodly libertines of Alexandria. The date of Wisdom is disputed, but cannot be earlier than the reign of Ptolemy VII. Physcon (B.C. 145–117). The attitude of the writer towards Koheleth may perhaps be compared with that of the Palestinian teachers who relegated the book among the apocrypha on this among other grounds, that it contained heretical statements, e.g. 'Rejoice, O young man, in thy youth' &c. (xi. 9). Nothing is more certain than that the Book of Koheleth was an Antilegomenon in Palestine in the first century before Christ. And yet it certainly had its friends and supporters both then and later. Simeon ben Shetach and his brother-in-law, King Alexander Jannæus (B.C. 105–79),

---

[1] Plumptre, *Ecclesiastes*, pp. 71–74; Wright, *Koheleth*, pp. 67–70. It is plainly impossible in the light of the history of dogma to place Wisdom before Ecclesiastes. Yet Hitzig has done this. Nachtigal took a sounder view in 1799 when he published a book on Wisdom regarded *als Gegenstück des Koheleth*. It forms vol. ii. of a singular work called *Die Versammlung der Weisen*, of which Koheleth forms vol. i.

were as familiar with Koheleth as the young men of Alexandria, and Simeon, according to the Talmudic story[1] (*Bereshith Rabba*, c. 91), quoted Eccles. vii. 12*a* with a prefix (דכתיב 'as it is written ') proper to a Biblical quotation. From another Talmudic narrative (*Baba bathra*, 4*a*) it would seem that Koheleth was cited in the time of Herod the Great as of equal authority with the Pentateuch, and from a third (*Shabbath*, 30*b*) that St. Paul's teacher, Gamaliel, permitted quotations from our book equally with those from canonical Scriptures. Like the Song of Songs, however, it called forth a lively opposition from severe judges. The schools of Hillel and Shammai were divided on the merits of these books. At first the Shammaites, who were adverse to them, carried a majority of the votes of the Jewish doctors. But when, after the destruction of Jerusalem, Jewish learning reorganised itself at Jamnia (4½ leagues south of Jaffa), the opposite view (viz. that the Song and Koheleth 'defile the hands'—i.e. are holy Scriptures) was again brought forward in a synod held about A.D. 90, and finally sanctioned in a second synod held A.D. 118. The arguments urged on both sides were such as belong to an uncritical age. No attempt was made to penetrate into the spirit and object of Koheleth, but test passages were singled out. The heretically sounding words in xi. 9*a* were at first held by some to be decisive against the claim of canonicity, but—we are told—when the 'wise men' took the close of the verse into consideration (' but know that for all this God will bring thee into the judgment '), they exclaimed יפה אמר שלמה, ' Solomon has spoken appropriately.'[2]

This first synod or sanhedrin of Jamnia has played an important part in recent arguments. According to Krochmal, Grätz, and Renan, one object of the Jewish doctors was to decide whether the Song and Koheleth ought to be admitted into the Canon. It seems, however, to have been satisfactorily

---

[1] See Schiffer, *Das Buch Kohelet nach der Auffassung der Weisen*, part i., pp. 100-102.

[2] *Midrasch Koheleth*, § 1, 3; comp. *Pesikta* of *R. Kahana*, § 8 (Schiffer, pp. 6, 7).

shown [1] that their uncertainty was not as to whether these books ought to be admitted, but whether they had been rightly admitted. It is true that there was, even as late as A.D. 90, a chance for any struggling book (e.g. Sirach) to find its way into the Canon. But in the case of the Song and Koheleth a preliminary canonisation had taken place; it only remained to set at rest all lingering doubts in the minds of those who disputed the earlier decision. Another matter was also considered, according to Krochmal, at the synod of A.D. 90, viz. how to indicate that with the admission of Ecclesiastes the Canon of the Hagiographa was closed. I have already referred to this scholar's view of the Epilogue (p. 232 &c.), and need only add that, if we may trust the statement of the Talmud, the canonicity of Koheleth was finally carried in deference to an argument which presupposes that xii. 13, 14 was already an integral part of Koheleth. The Talmudic passage is well known; it runs thus—

'The wise men' [i.e. the school of Shammai] 'sought to "hide" the Book of Koheleth because of its contradictory sayings. And why did they not "hide" it? Because the beginning and the close of it consist of words of Tōra' [i.e. are in harmony with revealed truth [2]]. By the 'beginning' the Jewish doctors meant Koheleth's assertion that 'all a man's toil which he toileth *under the sun* (i.e. all earthly, unspiritual toil) is unprofitable (i. 3), and by the 'close' the emphatic injunction and dogmatic declaration of the epilogist in xii. 13, 14. The Talmudic statement agrees, as is well known, with the note of St. Jerome on these verses. 'Aiunt Hebræi quum inter cætera scripta Salomonis quæ antiquata sunt, nec in memoriâ duraverunt, et hic liber obliterandus videretur, eo quòd vanas Dei assereret creaturas, et totum putaret esse pro nihilo, et cibum, et potum, et delitias transeuntes præferret omnibus; ex hoc uno capitulo meruisse auctoritatem, ut in divinorum voluminum numero poneretur,

---

[1] By Delitzsch'; see Wright's *Koheleth*, p. 471, and comp. Strack, art. 'Kanon des A. T.' in *Herzog-Plitt*, vol. vii.

[2] I quote the characteristic closing words, תחילתו דברי תורה וסופו דברי תורה (*Shabbath*, c. 30b).

quòd totam disputationem suam, et omnem catalogum hâc quasi ἀνακεφαλαιώσει coarctaverit, et dixerit finem sermonum auditu esse promtissimum, nec aliquid in se habere difficile: ut scilicet Deum timeamus, et ejus præcepta faciamus' (*Opera*, ii. 787).

The canonicity of Ecclesiastes was rarely disputed in the ancient Church. The fifth œcumenical council at Constantinople pronounced decisively in its favour. On the Christian heretics in the fourth century who rejected it, see Ginsburg, *Coheleth*, p. 103.

Let me refer again, in conclusion, to the story in which that remarkable man—'the restorer of the Law'—Simeon ben Shetach plays a chief part. It not only shows that Koheleth was a religious authority at the end of the second or beginning of the first century B.C., but implies that at this period the book was already comparatively old, and, one may fairly say, pre-Maccabæan. I presume too that the addition of the Epilogue (see pp. 234–5) with the all-important 13th and 14th verses had been made before Simeon's time.

II.

It was remarked above that as late as A.D. 90 there was a chance for any struggling book to gain admission into the Canon. Now for at least 180 years the Wisdom of Ben Sira had been struggling for recognition as canonical. In spite of the fact that it did not claim the authorship of any ancient sage, and that, like Koheleth, it contained some questionable passages, it was certainly in high favour both in Alexandria and in Palestine. As Delitzsch points out, 'the oldest Palestinian authorities (Simeon ben Shetach, the brother of Queen Salome, about B.C. 90, seems to be the earliest) quote it as canonical, and the censures of Babylonian teachers only refer to the Aramaic Targum, not to the original work. The latter was driven out of the field by the Aramaic version, which, though very much interpolated, was more accessible to the people.'[1] Simeon ben Shetach was counted among

[1] *Gesch. der jüdischen Poesie*, p. 20.

CHAP. XIII.   THE CANONICITY OF ECCLESIASTES   283

the Jewish 'fathers,' and a saying of his is given in *Pirke Aboth*, i. 10. It is remarkable that the very same passage of *Bereshith Rabba* (c. 91) which contains this wise man's quotations from Koheleth (see above) also contains one from Sirach introduced with the formula בספרא דבן סירא כתיב, 'in the book of Ben Sira it is written.' The quotation is, 'Exalt her, and she shall set thee between princes'—apparently a genuine saying of Ben Sira (Sirach), though not found in our Ecclesiasticus. The first word ('Exalt her') comes, it is true, from Prov. iv. 8, but, as Dr. Wright remarks,[1] Ben Sira 'was fond of tacking on new endings to old proverbs.' At a much later period, a quotation from Ben Sira (Sir. vii. 10?) is made by Rab (about 165-247 A.D.) introduced with the formula משום שנאמר, 'because it is said,' *Erubin*, c. 65a. Strack indeed supposes that Rab meant to quote from canonical Scripture, but by a slip quoted from Ben Sira instead; but this is too bold a conjecture. Lastly, Rabba (about 270-330 A.D.) quotes a saying of our book (Sir. xiii. 15; xxvii. 9) as 'repeated a third time in the Kethubhim (the Hagiographa)'—משולש בכתובים, *Baba Kamma*, c. 92b.

It is quite true that, according to the Talmudic passage referred to on p. 196, the Book of Ben Sira stands on the border-line between the canonical and the non-canonical literature: the words are, 'The Books of Ben Sira, and all books which were written thenceforward, do not defile the hands.' But taking this in connection with the vehement declaration of Rabbi Akiba that the man who reads Ben Sira and other 'extraneous' books has no portion in the world to come,[2] we may safely assume that the Book of Ben Sira had a position of exceptional authority with not a few Jewish readers. It is equally certain, as the above quotations show, that even down to the beginning of the fourth century A.D. sayings of Sirach were invested with the authority of Scripture. Whatever, then, may have been the theory (and no one pretends that the Synods of Jamnia placed Sirach

---

[1] *Koheleth*, p. 46.
[2] See the passage from *Sanhedrin* (Jer. Talm.), x. 28a, quoted at length in Wright's *Koheleth*, pp. 467-468.

on a level with Koheleth), the practice of some Jewish teachers was to treat Sirach as virtually canonical, which reminds us of the similar practice of some Christian Fathers. St. Augustine says (but he retracted it afterwards) of the two books of Wisdom, 'qui quoniam in auctoritatem recipi meruerunt, inter propheticos numerandi sunt' (*De doctr. Christianâ*, ii. 8), and both Origen and Cyprian quote Sirach as sacred scripture. Probably, as Fritzsche remarks, Sirach first became known to Christian teachers at Alexandria at the end of the second century.

AIDS TO THE STUDENT

THE literature upon Koheleth is unusually large. Some of the most important books and articles have been referred to already, and the student will naturally have at hand Dr. Wright's list in *The Book of Koheleth* (1883), Introd., pp. xiv.–xvii. It may suffice to add among the less known books, J. G. Herder, *Briefe das Studium der Theologie betreffend*, erster Theil (xi.), *Werke*, ed. Suphan, Bd. x.; Theodore Preston, *Ecclesiastes, Hebrew Text and a Latin Version, with original notes, and a translation of the Comm. of Mendelssohn* (1845); E. Böhl, *Dissertationes de aramaismis libri Koheleth* (Erlangen, 1860); Bernh. Schäfer, *Neue Untersuchungen über das Buch Koheleth* (Freiburg in Breisgau, 1870); J. S. Bloch, *Ursprung und Entstehungszeit des Buches Kohelet* (Bamberg, 1872); *Studien zur Gesch. der Sammlung der althebr. Literatur* (Breslau, 1876); C. Taylor, *The Dirge of Coheleth in Eccl.* xii., *discussed and literally translated* (1874); J. J. S. Perowne, articles on Ecclesiastes in *Expositor*, begun 1879; M. M. Kalisch, *Path and Goal* (contains translation of our book and much illustrative matter), 1880; A. Kuenen, *Religion of Israel* (1875), iii. 153 &c., also *Onderzoek* (1873), vol. iii., and article in *Theologisch Tijdschrift*, 1883, p. 113, &c.; S. Schiffer, *Das Buch Kohelet nach der Auffassung der Weisen des Talmud und Midrasch und der jüd. Erklärer des Mittelalters*, Theil i. (Leipz. 1885); Engelhardt, 'Ueber den Epilog des Koheleth' in *Studien und Kritiken*, 1875; Klostermann, article on Wright's *Koheleth*, in same periodical, 1885. See also Pusey's *Daniel the Prophet*, ed. 2, pp. 327-8, and the introduction to Prof. Salmon's commentary in Ellicott. [Prof. A. Palm's bibliographical monograph, *Die Qohelet-Literatur, ein Beitrag zur Geschichte der Exegese des Alten Testaments*, 1886, appeared too late to be of use.]

APPENDIX

IN WHICH VARIOUS POINTS IN THE BOOK ARE ILLUSTRATED OR MORE FULLY TREATED.

1. Pfleiderer on St. Paul (p. 3).
2. The word Kenotic; Phil. ii. 7 (p. 7).
3. Kleinert on Job vi. 25 (p. 21).
4. On Job xix. 25-27 (pp. 33-35).
5. Job's repudiation of sins (p. 39).
6. On Job xxxviii. 31, 32 (p. 52).
7. Source of story of Job (pp. 60-63).
8. Corrected text of Deut. xxxii. 8, 9 (p. 81).
9. The style of Elihu (p. 92).
10. The Aramaisms and Arabisms of Job (p. 99).
11. Herder on Job (pp. 106-111).
12. Septuagint of Job (pp. 113, 114).
13. Hārūn ar-Rashíd and Solomon (p. 131).
14. On Prov. xxvii. 6 (p. 148).
15. Eternity of Korán (p. 192).
16. Text of Proverbs (p. 173).
17. Religious value of Proverbs (p. 176, 177).
18. Aids to the Student (p. 178).
19. Date of Jesus son of Sirach (p. 180).
20. On Sirach xxi. 27 (p. 189).
21. Sirach's Hymn of Praise (p. 193).
22. Ancient versions of Sirach (p. 195).
23. Aids to the Student (p. 198).
24. On the Title Koheleth (p. 207).
25. On Eccles. iii. 11 (p. 210).
26. On Eccles. vii. 28 (p. 219).
27. On Eccles. xi. 9-xii. 7 (pp. 223-227).
28. On Eccles. xii. 9 &c. (p. 232).
29. Grätz on Koheleth's opposition to asceticism (p. 244).
30. Herder on the alternate voices in Koheleth (p. 245).

1. *Page* 3.—Pfleiderer, in the spirit of Lagarde, accounts for the Pauline view of the atonement by the 'stereotyped legal Jewish' doctrine of the atoning merit of the death of holy men (*Hibbert Lectures*, pp. 60-62). But was not this idea familiar and in some sense presumably real to Jesus? And why speak of a 'stereotyped' formula? Examples of a self-devotion designed to 'merit' good for the community, or even for an individual, abound in Judaism.

2. *Page* 7, *note* 2.—The word Kenotic is conveniently descriptive of a theory, and does not bind one who uses it to any particular expo-

sition of the difficult Greek of Phil. ii. 7. I need not decide, therefore, whether we should render ἐν μορφῇ θεοῦ בדמות האלהים with Delitzsch, or בדמות אלהים with Salkinson. To the names of eminent exegetes mentioned on page 7, add that of Godet.

3. *Page* 21 (on Job vi. 25).—Kleinert (*Theol. Studien u. Kritiken*, 1886, pp. 285-86) improves the parallelism by translating 'Wie so gar nicht verletzend sind Worte der Rechtschaffenheit, aber wie so gar nichts rügt die Rechtsrüge von euch.' He thinks that מה here, as occasionally elsewhere, and *mā* often in Arabic, has the sense of 'not' (see Ewald, *Lehrbuch*, § 325*b*); comp. ix. 2, xvi. 6, xxxi. 1, and the characteristic כַּמָּה 'how seldom,' xxi. 19. Without entering into his doubtful justification of 'verletzend,' it is possible to render 'How far from grievous are straightforward speeches, but how little is proved by the reproof from you!'

4. *Pages* 33-35 (Job xix. 25-27).—First, as to the sense of Goel (A.V. and R.V. 'redeemer'). The sense seems determined by xvi. 18 (see above, p. 31). It is vengeance for his blood that Job demands, and hence in xix. 29 he warns his false friends to beware of the *sword* of divine justice. The 'friends' have identified themselves with that unjust Deity against whom Job appeals to the 'witness in heaven' (xvi. 20)—the moral God of whom he has a dim but growing intuition. The whole plan of the book, as Kleinert remarks, calls for a definite legal meaning. But as no direct reference to Job's blood occurs in xix. 25-27, 'my vindicator' will be a sufficiently exact rendering (as in Isa. xliv. 6). I cannot however follow Kleinert in his recognition of the hope of immortality in this passage.

Next as to the text. Bickell's recension of it, when pointed in the ordinary manner, is as follows:—

²⁵ וַאֲנִי יָדַעְתִּי גֹּאֲלִי חָי
וְאַחֲרוֹן עַל־עָפָר יָקוּם:
²⁶ וְאַחַר עֵדִי נִקְּפָה זֹאת
וּמִשַּׁדַּי אֶחֱזֶה אֱלָהּ:
²⁷ אֲשֶׁר אֲנִי אֶחֱזֶה־לִּי
וְעֵינַי רָאוּ וְלֹא־זָר
כָּלוּ כִלְיֹתַי בְּחֻקִּי:

Bickell does not attempt to make easy Hebrew; the passage *ought not* in such a connection to be too easy. He renders ver. 26*a*, 'Et postea, his præsentibus absolutis, veniet testis meus' (God, his witness, as xvi. 19), comparing for the sense of נקפה Isa. xxix. 1. Certainly we seem to require in ver. 26 some further development of the idea suggested by the appearance of the Goel on the dust of Job's burial-place, and such a development is not supplied by the received text. We must not look at any corrupt passage by itself, but take it with the context. Those who defend the text of ver. 26 as it stands have on their side the parallelism of עוֹרִי and בְּשָׂרִי (comp. ver. 20); but this parallelism is counterbalanced by the want of correspondence between נִקְּפוּ־זֹאת and אֶחֱזֶה אֱלוֹהַּ. Dr. C. Taylor suggests an aposiopesis, and gives the sense intended by the writer thus, 'When they have penetrated my skin, and of my flesh have had their fill' (comp. ver. 22*b*). Is it not more likely that וּמִבְּשָׂרִי came into the text *through a reminiscence* of ver. 22*b*? 'I shall see these things from Shaddai' will be, on Bickell's view, equivalent to 'I shall see these things *attested* by Shaddai.' As yet, the sufferer exclaims, I can recognise this, viz. my innocence, for myself alone; mine eyes have seen it, but not another's (Prov. xxvii. 2). The connexion is in every way improved. Job first of all desired an inscribed testimony to his innocence, but now he aspires to something better.

Bickell's is the most natural reconstruction of the passage as yet proposed ; so far as ver. 26*b* is concerned, it is supported in the main by the Septuagint. More violent corrections are offered by Dr. A. Neubauer, *Athenæum*, June 27, 1885.—As a rendering of *the text as it stands*, I think R.V. is justified in giving 'from my flesh' (with marg., '*Or*, without '); 'mine eyes shall see' (= 'will have seen ') certainly suggests that Job will be clothed with some body when he sees God (Dillmann's reply is not adequate). 'Without my flesh ' (so Amer. Revisers) is in itself justifiable (see especially xi. 15); in the use of the privative ‍ן became more and more frequent in the later periods (comp. the Talmudic מְאוֹר עֵינַיִם = 'blind ').

5. *Page* 39.—Job's catalogue of the sins which he repudiates. The parallel suggested between Job and an Egyptian formulary may be illustrated by a passage in the life of the great Stoic Emperor. A learned Bishop, popular in his day, reminds us of 'that golden Table of Ptolomy (*sic*) Arsacides, which the Emperour Marcus Aurelius found at Thebes, which for the worthiness thereof that worthy Emperour caused every night to be laid at his bed's head, and at his death gave it as a singular treasure to his sonne Commodus. The Table was written in Greeke characters, and contained in it these protestations : "I never exalted the proud rich man, neither hated the poor just man: I never denied justice to the poor for his poverty neither pardoned the wealthy for his riches. . . . I alwaies favoured the poor that was able to do little, and God, who was able to do much, alwaies favoured me."' (*The Practice of Quietnesse*, by George Webbe, D.D., 1699 ?)

6. *Page* 52 (On Job xxxviii. 31, 32, ix. 9).—(1) I admit that the identification of כִּימָה and the Pleiades is uncertain. Still it is plausible, especially when we compare Ar. *kumat* 'heap.' And even if it should be shown that *kimtu* was not the Babylonian name for the Pleiades, this would not be decisive against the identification proposed. The Babylonians did not give the name *kisiluv* to Orion, yet Stern's argument (*Jüdische Zeitschrift*, 1865, Heft 4 ; comp. Nöldeke, Schenkel's *Bibel-Lexikon*, iv. 369, 370) in favour of equating *k'sil* and Orion remains valid. (2) As to מַעֲדַנּוֹת 'sweet influences' is fortunate enough to exist by sufferance in the margin of R.V. It is sometimes defended by comparing 1 Sam. xv. 32. But the only possible renderings there are 'in bonds' or 'trembling' (see *Variorum Bible ad loc.*). Dr. Driver has shown that 'sweet influences' is a legacy from Sebastian Münster (1535). (3) מַזָּרוֹת is probably not to be identified with מַזָּלוֹת (2 Kings xxiii. 5), in spite of the authority of the Sept. and the Targum (see Dillmann's note). In this I agree with G. Hoffmann, whose adventurous interpretations of the astronomical names in Amos and Job do not however as yet seem to me acceptable. According to him, *kima* = Sirius, *k'sil* = Orion, Mazzaroth = the Hyades and Aldebaran, 'Ayish' = the Pleiades (Stade's *Zeitschrift*, 1883, Heft 1). Mazzaroth = Ass. *mazarati* ; Mazzaloth (i.e. the zodiacal signs) seems to be the plural of *mazzāla* = Ass. *manzaltu* station.[1]

7. *Pages* 60–63.—That the story of Job is an embellished folk-tale is probable, though still unproved. The delightful humour which in the Prologue (see pp. 14, 110), as in the myths of Plato, stands side by side with the most impressive solemnity of itself points to this view. No one has expressed this better than Wellhausen, in a review of Dillmann's *Hiob*, *Jahrbücher für deutsche Theologie*, xvi. 552 &c. : ' Den launigen und doch mürrischen Ton, den der nonchalante Satan Gott gegenüber anschlägt, so ganz auf Du und Du, würde schwerlich der Dichter des Hiob gewagt haben ; schwerlich auch würde es ihm gelungen sein, mit so merkwürdig einfachen Mitteln so wunderbar plastische Figuren zu entwerfen.' He also points out the inconsistencies of the story, precisely such as we might expect in a folk-tale, and concludes (a little hastily) that the Prologue is *altogether* a folk-story and had no didactic object. Eichhorn, too, in a review of Michaelis on Job (*Allgemeine Bibliothek*, i. 430 &c.), well points out that the illusion of the poem is much impaired by not admitting an element in the plot derived from tradition. Of course this view of *Job* as based on a folk-tale is quite reconcileable with the view that the hero is a personification.

[1] On Mazzaloth, see Friedrich Delitzsch, *Prolegomena* &c. (1886), p. 142.

The latter is much older than the last century; it explains the Jewish saying (p. 60) that 'Job was a parable,' and the fascination which the book possessed for the age preceding the final dispersion of the Jews.[1]

8. *Page* 81 (further correction of text of Deut. xxxii. 8, 9).—The passage becomes more rhythmical if with Bickell we reproduce the Septuagint Hebrew text at the close of ver. 8 as בני אלהים and continue (ver. 9),

ויחלק יהוה יעקב [or עמו]
חבל נחלתו ישראל :

The correction of the last couplet is important as a supplement of the explanation of ver. 8 given in the text. To other nations God gave protective angels, but He reserved Israel for Himself. (See Bickell, *Zeitschrift f. kathol. Theologie*, 1885, pp. 718–19, and comp. his *Carmina V. T. metricè*, 1882, p. 192, where he adheres in both verses to the received text.)

The Style of Elihu.

9. *Page* 92.—No student of the Hebrew of *Job* will overlook the admirable 'studies' on the style of Elihu by J. G. Stickel (*Das Buch Hiob*, 1842, pp. 248–262) and Carl Budde (*Beiträge zur Kritik des Buches Hiob*, 1876, pp. 65–160). The former succeeded in obtaining the admission of such an eminent critical analyst as Kuenen, that style by itself would be scarcely sufficient to prove the later origin of the Elihu speeches. It also, no doubt, assisted Delitzsch to recognise in Elihu the same 'Hebræoarabic' impress as in the rest of the book. In spite of this effective 'study,' Dillmann's brief treatment of the same subject in 1869 made it clear that the subject had not yet by any means been threshed out, and perhaps no more powerful argument against chaps. xxxii.–xxxvii. has been produced than that contained in a single closely-printed page (289) of his commentary. There was therefore a good chance for a *Privatdocent* to win himself a name by a renewed attempt to state the linguistic facts more thoroughly and impartially than before. This indeed fairly expresses Budde's object, which is not at all to offer a direct proof that the disputed chapters belong to the original poem, but merely to show that the opposite view cannot be demonstrated on stylistic grounds. His method is to collect, first of all, points of resemblance and then points of difference between 'Elihu' and the rest of the book. Last among the latter appear the Aramaisms and Arabisms. Budde

---

[1] See Rosenthal, *Vier apokryphische Bücher aus der Zeit und Schule Akiba's* (1885), pp. 6–12.

rejects the view, adopted from Stickel (see p. 92) by Canon F. C. Cook, that the deeper colouring of Aramaic is only the poet's way of indicating the Aramæan origin of Elihu. He denies that there is any such greater amount of Aramaism as can form a real distinction between 'Elihu' and the undisputed chapters. I will not inquire whether the subjectivity of a writer may impress itself on his statistics, and willingly grant that the Aramaic colouring in 'Elihu' may perhaps affect the reader more owing to the faults of style to which Budde himself alludes on p. 157, and which, to me, indicate an age or at least a writer of less taste and talent than the original author. The Aramaisms may be thrown into stronger relief by these infirmities, and so the colouring may seem deeper than it is. I am not however sure that there *is* an illusion in the matter. Among the counter-instances of Aramaism given by Budde from the speeches of Eliphaz, there are at least two which have no right to figure there, viz. מִנָּם, xv. 29, and אַ֥י for אַיִן, xxii. 30, both which forms are probably corrupt readings. Until Dillmann has published his second edition I venture to retain the statement on p. 92. There is a stronger Aramaising element in Elihu, which, with other marks of a peculiar and *inferior*[1] style, warrants us in assigning the section to a later writer. This is, of course, not precluded by the numerous Hebraistic *points of contact* with the main part of the book, which Carl Budde has so abundantly collected (*Beiträge*, pp. 92-123). No one can doubt that the original poem very early became an absorbing study in the circles of 'wise men.'

As to the words and phrases (of pure Hebrew origin) in which Elihu *differs* from the body of the work, I may remark that it is sometimes difficult to realise their full significance from Budde's catalogue. Kleinert has thrown much light on some of them in a recent essay. He has, for instance,[2] shown the bearings of the fact that the disputed chapters persistently avoid the juristic sense of צָדַק (Kal), except in a quotation from speeches of Job (xxxiv. 5), Elihu himself only using the word of correctness in statement (xxxiii. 12), or of moral righteousness (xxxv. 7), and that הִרְשִׁיעַ has the sense of 'acting wickedly' only in a passage of Elihu (xxxiv. 12). The use of צֶדֶק, צַדִּיק, and צְדָקָה in xxxii. 1, xxxiii. 26, xxxv. 8, xxxvi. 3, is also dwelt upon in this connexion. It is true that Budde does not conceal these points; he tabulates them correctly, but does not indicate

---

[1] 'Ist's denkbar, dass ein solcher Dichter demjenigen Redner, dem er die Hauptrolle zugedacht, die Charakteristik jenes *inferioren* Redetypus zugewiesen haben könnte?' Kleinert.

[2] Das spezifisch-hebräische im Buch Iliob, *Theol. Studien und Kritiken*, 1886, pp. 299-300.

the point of view from which they can be understood. Kleinert supplies this omission. The body of the poem, he remarks, is juristic in spirit; the speeches of Elihu ethical and hortatory. This brings with it a different mode of regarding the problem of Job's sufferings. 'Die Reden Elihu's haben zu dem gerichtlichen Aufriss der Buchanlage nur das alleräusserlichste Verhältniss. Sie verlassen die scharfgezogenen Grundlinien der rechtlichen Auseinandersetzung, um in eine ethisch-paränetische, rein chokmatisch-didaktische Erörterung der Frage überzulenken.' Kleinert also notes one peculiar word of Elihu's which I have not met with in Budde, but which, from Kleinert's point of view, is important—בֹּפֶר, 'a ransom' (xxxiii. 24, xxxvi. 18). Why did not the juristic theologians of the Colloquies use it? Evidently the speeches of Elihu are later compositions.

The Aramaisms and Arabisms of Job (excepting the Elihu portion).

10. *Page* 99.—The critic, no less than the prophet, is still with too many a favourite subject of ironical remark; 'they say of him, Doth he not speak in riddles'?[1] The origin of *Job*, upon the linguistic as well as the theological side, may be a riddle, but the interest of the book is such that we cannot give up the riddle. We may not all agree upon the solution; the riddle may be one that admits of different answers. All that this proves is the injudiciousness of dogmatism, which specially needs emphasising with respect to the bearings of the linguistic data. To say, with Nöldeke,[2] 'We have no ground for regarding the language of *Job* as anything but a very pure Hebrew' seems to me as extreme as to assert with G. H. Bernstein (the well-known Syriac scholar) that the amount of Aramaic colouring would of itself bring the book into the post-Exile period. Bernstein carried to a dangerous extreme a tendency already combated by Michaelis and Eichhorn;[3] but his research is thoroughgoing and systematic. Those who, like the present writer, have no access to it, may be referred to L. Bertholdt's *Historisch-kritische Einleitung*[4] (Erlangen, 1812-1819), where it is carefully examined, and its arguments, as it would seem, reduced to something like their just proportions. Bertholdt does not scruple to admit that distinctively Aramaising constructions are wanting in *Job*, and that words

---

[1] Ezek. xx. 49.
[2] *Die alttestamentliche Literatur*, p. 192.
[3] See Eichhorn's notice of Michaelis in vol. i. of his *Allgemeine Bibliothek der biblischen Literatur*.
[4] Pp. 2076, 2077. Bernstein's title is, *Ueber das Alter, den Inhalt, den Zweck und die gegenwärtige Gestalt des Buches Hiob* (in Keil and Tzschirner's *Analekten*, 1813, pp. 1-137).

with Aramaic affinities may have existed in Hebrew before the Exile. Still he decides that though part of the argument falls to pieces, yet for most there is a real foundation. This too, is substantially the judgment of Carl Budde. 'Despite all deductions from Bernstein's list it remains true that just the Book of Job is specially rich in words which principally belong to the Aramaic dialects.'[1] Dillmann, too, who takes pains to emphasise the comparative scarcity of Aramaisms in the strictest sense of the word, yet finds in the body of the work (excluding the Elihu portion) Aramaising and Arabising words enough to suggest that the author lived hard by Aramaic- and Arabic-speaking peoples.[2] By taking this view, Dillmann (whose philological caution and accuracy give weight to his opinion) separates himself from those who, like Eichhorn and more recently the Jewish scholar Kaempf,[3] confidently maintain that the peculiar words in *Job* are genuine Hebrew 'Sprachgut.' To make this probable, we ought to be able to show that they have more affinities with northern than with southern Semitic (see p. 99), a task as yet unaccomplished. Dillmann, too, would certainly dissent from Canon Cook's opinion that the Aramaisms of Job are only 'such as characterise the antique and highly poetic style.' According to him, they are equally unfavourable to a very early and to a very late date.

Various lists of Aramaising words have been given since Bernstein's. I give here that of Dr. Lee in his *Book of the Patriarch Job* (p. 50), which has the merit of having been constructed from his own reading of *Job*. It refers to the whole book :—

נהרה (iii. 4) ; מנהו (iv. 12) ; לאויל (v. 2) ; אדרש (ib. 8), occur in the Aramaic, not the Hebrew sense ; תמלל (viii. 2) ; ישׂנה (ib. 7) ; מנהם (xi. 20) ; עמם (xii. 2) ; מלין (ib. 11) ; משׂניא (ib. 23) ; מלתי ואחותי (xiii. 17) ; אחוך (xv. 17) ; וזה for ואשר (ib.) ; שלהבת (ib. 31) ; נלרי (xvi. 15) ; חמרמרה (ib. 16) ; קנצי (xviii. 2) ; יגעל ... עבר (xxi. 10) ; בחיי (xxiv. 22) ; בחבי (xxxi. 33) ; אחוה (xxxii. 10, 18) ; פדע (xxxiii. 24) ; אאלפך (ib. 33) ; כתר (xxxvi. 2) ; בחרת (ib. 21) ; גבר (xxxviii. 3) ; נחיר (xli. 12). I will not criticise this list, which no doubt contains some questionable items. We might, however, insert other words in exchange, e.g. טושׂ (ix. 26) ; שׂחר (xvi. 19) ; כפים (xxx. 6) ; and כפן (v. 22, xxx. 3) ; and perhaps רקב (xiii. 28), which Geiger plausibly compares with Syr. *rakbo* 'wineskin' (so the tradition represented by the Septuagint, the Peshitto, and Barhebræus). Some supposed Arabisms may also in all probability be transferred to the list of Aramaisms ; but the Arabisms which remain will abundantly justify

---

[1] *Beiträge zur Kritik des Buches Hiob* (1876), p. 140.
[2] *Hiob* (1869), Einleitung, pp. xxvii. xxix.
[3] *Die Grabschrift Eschmunazar's* (1874), p. 8.

what has been stated in the section on *Job*. I have not attempted to decide precisely where the poet heard both Arabic and Aramaic. Dillmann accepts the view mentioned on p. 75. But Gilead, too, was at all times inhabited by Arab tribes, both nomad and settled,[1] and the region itself was called Arabia.[2]

11. *Pages* 106-111.—Herder (to whom I gladly refer the student) is perhaps the best representative of the modern literary point of view. Whatever he says on the Hebrew Scriptures is worth reading, even when his remarks need correction. No one felt the poetry of *Job* more deeply than Herder; to the religious ideas of the poem his eyes were not equally open. Indeed, it must have been hard to discern and appreciate these adequately in the eighteenth century; the newly-discovered sacred books of the East, with their deep though obscure metaphysical conceptions, for a time almost overshadowed the far more sobre Hebrew Scriptures. Like Carlyle (who is to some extent his echo) Herder underrates the specifically Hebrew element in the book, which is of course not very visible on a hasty perusal. One point, however, that he sees very clearly, though he does not use the expression, is that *Job* is a character-drama. He denies that the speeches are monotonous.

'So eintönig für uns alle Reden klingen, so sind sie mit Licht und Schatten angelegt und der Faden, oder vielmehr die Verwirrung der Materie, nimmt zu von Rede zu Rede, bis Hiob sich selbst fasset und seine Behauptungen lindert. Wer diesen Faden nicht verfolgt und insonderheit nicht bemerkt, wie Hiob seinem Gegner immer den eigenen Pfeil aus der Hand windet; entweder das besser sagt, was jener sagte, oder die Gründe jenes eben für sich braucht—der hat das Lebendige, Wachsende, kurz die Seele des Buchs verfehlet' (*Hiob als Composition betrachtet, Werke*, Suphan, ii. 318).

He has also clearly perceived the poet's keen sympathy with mythology, and this, combined with the (supposed) few imitations of *Job* in the Old Testament, confirmed him in the erroneous view that the original writer of *Job* was an Edomitish Emeer. On the limited influence of *Job* he has some vigorous sentences, the edge of which, however, is turned by more recent criticism. It is of the prophets he is chiefly thinking, when he finds so few traces of acquaintance with Job in the Scriptures, and of the pre-Exile prophets. 'Wie drängen und drücken sich die Propheten! wie borgen sie von einander Bilder in einem ziemlich engen Kreise und führen sie nur, jeder nach seiner Art, aus! Diese alte ehrwürdige

---

[1] Blau, *Zeitschr. der deutsch. morgenl. Ges.*, xxv. 540.
[2] Wetzstein in Delitzsch's *Job*, p. 528.

Pyramide steht im Ganzen unnachgeahmt da und ist vielleicht unnachahmbar.' This passage occurs in the fifth conversation in his *Geist der Ebräischen Poesie* (*Werke*, ed. Suphan, xi. 310). The student of *Job* will not neglect this and also the two preceding very attractive chapters. The description of Elihu is not the least interesting passage. Herder does his best to account for the presence of this unexpected fifth speaker, but really shows how unaccountable it is except on the theory of later addition. Prof. Briggs's theory (p. 93) that the poor speeches of Elihu are intended 'as a literary foil' was suggested by Herder. 'Bemerken Sie aber, dass er nur als Schatte dasteht, dies Gottes-Orakel zu erheben' (*Werke*, xi. 284).

12. *Pages* 113, 114.—The latest study on the original Septuagint text of the Book of Job is by Bickell in the *Zeitschrift für katholische Theologie*, 1886, pp. 557-564. As to the date of the Alexandrine version, Hody's remark, *De Bibliorum Textibus*, p. 196, deserves attention, viz. that Philo already quotes from it,—Τίς γάρ, ὡς ὁ Ἰώβ φησι, καθαρὸς ἀπὸ ῥύπου, καὶ ἂν μία ἡμέρα ἐστὶν ἡ ζωή (Sept. of Job xiv. 4 ὁ βίος); *De Mutatione Nominum*, § 6 (i. 585).

13. *Page* 131.—The character of Harūn ar-Rashíd, in fact, became almost as distorted by legend as that of Solomon. Neither of them were models of civil justice (Weil, *Geschichte der Chalifen*, ii. 127).

14. *Page* 148 (Prov. xxvii. 6).—Consult, however, the Septuagint, which seems to have read 'מ at the beginning of the second line ('More faithful . . . . than' &c.). See Cornill on Ezek. xxxv. 13.

15. *Page* 162, *note* 1.—The Mo'tazilites ('the Protestants of Islam') denied the eternity of the Korán because it implied the existence of two eternal beings (Weil, *Gesch. der Chalifen*, ii. 262).

16. *Page* 173.— Text of Proverbs. Among the minor additions in Sept., note the μή in Prov. v. 16 (so Vatican and, originally, Sinaitic MS.), if we may follow Lagarde and Field. The Alexandrine MS., however, and the Complutensian edition, omit μή, which is also wanting in Aquila. Comp. Field's *Hexapla ad loc.*

17. *Pages* 176, 177 (Religious Value of Proverbs).—To appreciate the religious spirit of this fine book, we require some imaginative sympathy with past ages. The 'staid, quiet, "douce," orderly burgher of the Book of Proverbs, who is regular in his attendance at the Temple, diligent in his business, prosperous in his affairs, of repute among the elders, with daughters doing virtuously, and a wife that has his house decked with coverings of tapestry, while her own clothing is silk and purple' (Mr. Binney's words in *Is it possible to make the best of both worlds?*), is not the noblest type of man, and therefore not the model Christian even of our own day.

18. *Page* 178 (*Aids to the Student*).—Add, *Les sentences et proverbes du Talmud et du Midrasch.* Par Moïse Schuhl. Par. 1878.

19. *Page* 180.—On the date of Jesus son of Sirach, comp. Hody, *De Bibliorum Textibus Originalibus* (Oxon., 1705), pp. 192–194.

20. *Page* 189, *note* 1 (Sirach xxi. 27).—Fritzsche weakens the proverb by taking 'Satan' as equivalent to 'accuser' (Ps. cix. 6, Zech. iii. 1). The wise man says that it is no use for the ungodly man to disclaim responsibility for his sin. 'The Satan' either means the depraved will (comp. Dukes, *Rabbin. Blumenlese*, p. 108) or the great evil spirit. In the latter case the wise man says that for all practical purposes the tempter called Satan may be identified with the inborn tempter of the heart. Comp. Ps. xxxvi. 2, 'The ungodly man hath an oracle of transgression within his heart.'

21. *Page* 193 (The Hymn of Praise).—Frankel suspected xliv. 16 to be an interpolation, on the ground that the view of Enoch as an example of μετάνοια is Philonian (*Palästinische Exegese*, p. 44). Against this see Fritzsche, who explains the passage as a characteristically uncritical inference from Gen. v. 22. Enoch was a pattern of μετάνοια because he walked with God after begetting Methuselah.

22. *Page* 195 (Ancient Versions of Sirach).—The Peshitto version deviates, one may venture to assume, in many points from the original Sirach. Geiger has pointed out some remarkable instances of this (*Zeitschr. der deutschen morgenl. Ges.* xii. 536 &c.), and if the Greek version is to be regarded as absolutely authoritative, the number of deviations must be extremely great. Fritzsche goes so far as to say that in the latter part of the Syriac Sirach (from about chap. xxx.) the original is only hazily traceable ('durchschimmert'). He describes this version as really no version, but 'eine ziemlich leichtfertig hingeschriebene Paraphrase' ('a rather careless paraphrase'). This, as fairer judges of the Syriac are agreed, is not an accurate statement of the case. It can be readily disproved by referring to some of the passages in which the Greek translator has manifestly misrendered the original (e.g. xxiv. 27; see above, p. 196). Dr. Edersheim, who is working upon both versions, agrees with Bickell that the Syriac often enables us to restore the Hebrew, where the Greek text is wrong. This is not placing the Syriac in a superior position to the Greek, but giving it the subsidiary importance which it deserves. Doubtless, the Hebrew text which the Syriac translator employed was in many places corrupt.—The best edition of the Peshitto, I may add, is in Lagarde's *Libri Vet. Test. Apocryphi Syriaci* (1861). It is from Walton's Polyglot, but 'codicum nitriensium ope et coniecturis meis hic illic emendatiorem' [one sixth-century MS. of Ecclesiasticus is used].

The Old Latin has many peculiarities; its inaccuracies are no proof of arbitrariness; the translator means to be faithful to his *Greek* original. Many verses are transposed; others misplaced. For instances of the former, Fritzsche refers to iii. 27, iv. 31, 32, vi. 9, 10, ix. 14, 16, xii. 5, 7; for the latter, to xvi. 24, 25, xix. 5, 6, xlix. 17. Sometimes a double text is translated, e.g. xix. 3, xx. 24. It is to be used with great caution, but its age makes it valuable for determining the Greek text. For the text of Ecclesiasticus in the Codex Amiatinus, see Lagarde's *Mittheilungen*.

23. *Page* 198 (*Aids to the Student*).—To the works mentioned add Bruch, *Weisheitslehre* (1851), p. 283 &c., and especially Jehuda ben Seeb's little known work *The Wisdom of Joshua ben Sira rendered into Hebrew and German, and paraphrased in Syriac with the Biur*, Breslau, 1798 (translated title), and Geiger, 'Warum gehört das Buch Sirach zu den Apocryphen?' in *Zeitschr. d. deutschen morgenl. Gesellschaft*, xii. 536 &c.

The Title Qoheleth (*twice, see below,* '*the Qoheleth* ').

24. *Page* 207, *note* 2.—The name is undoubtedly an enigma, and M. Renan thinks that ordinary philological methods are inadequate to its solution. Even Aquila leaves it untranslated (κωλέθ). Without stopping here to criticise M. Renan's theory that Q H L T H were the initials of words (comp. Rambam, Rashi) in some way descriptive of Solomon,[1] let me frankly admit that none of the older explanations is absolutely certain, because neither *Qōhēl* nor *Qohēleth* occurs elsewhere in the Old Testament literature. Two views however are specially prevalent, and I will first mention that which seems to me (with Gesenius, Delitzsch, Nowack &c.) to deserve the preference. In one respect indeed it harmonises with the rival explanation, viz. in supposing Qal to have adopted the signification of Hifil (the Hifil of Q H L *is* found in the Old Testament), so that *Qōhēl* will mean 'one who calls together an assembly.' The adoption thus supposed is found especially in proper names (e.g. רחביה). But how to explain the feminine form *Qohéleth*? By a tendency of later Hebrew to use fem. participles with a masc. sense.[2] In Talmudic Hebrew, e.g., we find לָקְחוֹת, 'buyers,' נְקוּרוֹת, 'stonemasons,' לְעוּזוֹת, 'foreigners' (passive participles in this stage of the language tend to adopt an active sense). But even earlier we find the same tendency among *proper names*. Take for instance Sophereth (*hassophereth* in Ezra ii. 55; *sophereth* in Neh. vii. 57), Pokereth (Ezra ii. 57). Why should not the name Qoheleth have been

---
[1] On this, see Wright, *Ecclesiastes* &c. p. 127.
[2] Strack, *Lehrbuch der neuhebr. Sprache*, p. 54.

given to the great Teacher of the book before us, just as the name Sophereth was given apparently to a scribe? Delitzsch [1] reminds us that in Arabic the fem. termination serves sometimes to intensify the meaning, or, as Ewald puts it, 'ut abstracto is innuatur in quo tota hæc virtus vel alia proprietas consummatissima sit, ut ejus exemplum haberi queat.'[2] Thus Qoheleth might mean 'the ideal teacher,' and this no doubt would be a title which would well describe the later view of Solomon. It is simpler, however, to take the fem. termination as expressing action or office; thus in Arabic *khalifa* means 1, succession or the dignity of the successor, 2, the successor or representative himself, the 'caliph,' and in Hebrew and Assyrian *pekhāh, pakhatu* 'viceroy.' Comp. ἡ ἐξουσία, 'die Obrigkeit.'

The alternative is, with Ewald, Hitzig, Ginsburg, Kuenen, Kleinert, to explain Qoheleth as in apposition to חָכְמָה, Wisdom being represented in Prov. i. 20, 21, viii. 1-4, as addressing men in the places of concourse (Klostermann eccentrically explains ἡ συλλογίζουσα or συλλογιστική). Solomon, according to this view, is regarded by the author as the impersonation of Wisdom (as Protagoras was called Σοφία). It is most unlikely, however, that Solomon should have been thus regarded, considering the strange discipline which the author describes Qoheleth as having passed through, and how different is the language of Wisdom when, as in Prov. i.-ix., she is represented as addressing an assembly! A reference to vii. 27, where Qoheleth seems to be spoken of in the fem., is invalid, as we should undoubtedly correct *haqqohéleth* in accordance with xii. 8 [3] (comp. *hassofereth*, Ezra ii. 55).

The Sept. rendering ἐκκλησιαστής, whence the 'concionator' of Vulg., is therefore to be preferred to the singular Greek rend. ἡ ἐκκλησιάστρια of Græcus Venetus.

25. *Page* 210.—Eccles. iii. 11. Might we render, 'Also he hath put (the knowledge of) that which is secret into their mind, except that,' &c., i.e. 'though God has enabled man to find out many secrets, yet human science is of very limited extent'? This implies Bickell's pointing עֹלָם.

26. *Page* 219.—Eccles. vii. 28. The misogyny of the writer was doubtless produced by some sad personal experience. Its evil effect upon himself was mitigated by his discovery of another Jonathan with a love 'passing the love of women.' This reminds us of the

---

[1] *Hoheslied und Koheleth*, pp. 212-3.
[2] *Grammatica arabica*, § 284 (i. 167). Comp. Wright, *Arabic Grammar*, i. 157 (§ 233).
[3] The mistake was caused by the rarity of קֹהֶלֶת with the article.

author of the celebrated mediæval 'Romance of the Rose.'[1] 'What is Love?' asks the lover, and Reason answers, 'It is a mere sickness of the thought, a sport of the fancy. If thou scape at last from Love's snares, I hold it but a grace. Many a one has lost body and soul in his service' (comp. Eccles. vii. 26). And then he continues, 'There is a kind of love which lawful is and good, as noble as it is rare,—the friendship of men.' To quote Chaucer's translation,

> And certeyn he is wel bigone
> Among a thousand that findeth oon.
> For ther may be no richesse
> Ageyns frendshippe of worthynesse.

The allusion to Eccles. vii. 29 is obvious. Thus the same varieties of character recur in all ages. This point of view is very different from that of the Agadic writers who borrow from Eccles. vii. 26 a weapon against 'heresy' (*mīnūth*), a term which includes the Jewish Christian faith. All are agreed that the 'bitter woman' is heresy, and one of them declares that the closing words of the verse refer to 'the men of Capernaum' (see Matt. ix. 8). Delitzsch, *Ein Tag in Kapernaum*, 1886, p. 48; comp. Wünsche, *Midrasch Koheleth*, p. 110.

27. *Pages* 223-227.—Eccles. xi. 9-xii.-7. The key to the whole passage is xi. 8. 'For, if a man lives many years, let him rejoice in them all, and let him remember the days of darkness, that they shall be many.' I cannot accept the ingenious conjecture of Dr. C. Taylor, which might (see Chap. X.) have been supported by a reference to Egypt, that xii. 3-5 are cited from an authorised book of dirges. Not only these verses but xii. 1*b*-6 form a poem on the evils of old age, the whole effect of which is lost without some prefix, such as 'Rejoice in thy youth.' Döderlein supplies this prefix in xii. 6 ; but this is not enough. If we hesitate, with Luzzatto, Geiger, and Nöldeke to cancel xii. 1*a* as a later addition for purposes of edification, we must, with Grätz and Bickell, read either אֶת־בּוֹרְךָ or אֶת־בְּאֵרְךָ. These two readings seem to have existed side by side, and to an ingenious moralist this fact apparently suggested a new and edifying reading אֶת־בּוֹרְאֶךָ. Hence Akabia ben Mahalallel,[2] one of the earliest of the Jewish 'fathers,' and probably a contemporary of Gamaliel I., advises considering these three points as a safeguard against sin, 'Whence thou comest, whither thou goest, and before whom thou wilt have to give an account.' 'Whence thou comest,'

---

[1] Comp. *British Quarterly Review*, Oct. 1871.

[2] *Aboth*, iii. 1 (ed. Strack); comp. Schiffer, *Das Buch Kohelet nach der Auffassung der Weisen*, part i., p. 49.

implying בְּאֵרֶךָ, 'thy fountain;' 'whither thou goest,' בּוֹרֶךָ, 'thy pit, or grave;' 'before whom thou wilt stand,' בּוֹרְאֶךָ, 'thy creator.'

28. *Page* 232.—Döderlein (in a popular work on Ecclesiastes, p. 119) describes xii. 9 &c. as the epilogue, 'perhaps, of a larger collection of writings and of the earlier Hebrew canon.' Herder, too, thinks that the close of the book suggests a collection of sayings of several wise men (*Werke*, ed. Suphan, x. 134).

29. *Page* 244.—According to Grätz, Koheleth is not to be taken in earnest when he writes as if in a sombre and pessimistic mood. Such passages Grätz tries to explain away. Koheleth, he thinks, is the enemy of those who cultivate such a mood, and who, like the school of Shammai, combine with it an extravagant and unnatural asceticism (comp. vii. 16, 17). The present, Koheleth knows, is far from ideal, but he would fain reconcile young men to inevitable evils by pointing them to the relative goods still open to them. This attitude of the author enables Grätz to account for Koheleth's denial of the doctrine of Immortality. This doctrine, he remarks, was not of native Jewish origin, but imported from Alexandria, and was the source of the ascetic gloom opposed by Koheleth. Koheleth's denial of the Immortality of the Soul does not, according to Grätz, involve the denial of the Resurrection of the Body, the Resurrection being regarded in early Judaism as a new creative act.[1] It is not clear to me, however, that Koheleth accepts the Resurrection doctrine, even if he does not expressly controvert it.

30. *Page* 245, *note* 3.—Herder says with insight, though with some exaggeration, that most of Koheleth consists of isolated observations on the course of the world and the experience of the writer. No artistic connection need be sought for. But if we must seek for one (*so that Herder is not convinced of the soundness of the theory*), it is strange that no one has observed the twofold voice in the book, 'da ein Grübler Wahrheit sucht, und in dem Ton seines Ichs meistens damit, "dass alles eitel sey," endet; eine andre Stimme aber, im Ton des Du, ihn oft unterbricht, ihm das Verwegne seiner Untersuchungen vorhält und meistens damit endet, "was zuletzt das Resultat des ganzen Lebens bleibe?" Es ist nicht völlig Frag' und Antwort, Zweifel und Auflösung, aber doch aus Einem und demselben Munde etwas, das beyden gleicht, und sich durch Abbrüche und Fortsetzungen unterscheidet.' *Briefe das Studium der Theologie betreffend*, erster Theil (*Werke*, Suphan, x. 135–136).

[1] *Kohelet*, p. 29. Certainly this is not the view of Talmudic Judaism, at least not in the sense described by Dr. Grätz. See Weber, *Altsynagogale Theologie*, p. 323.

INDEX.

AARON, celebrated by Sirach, 193
Achamoth, Gnostic myth of, 161 *n*.
Adam, occurrence of the word in 'Proverbs,' 119
Addison, 145
Age, ascribed to Job, 71; description of, 229 *sq*.
Agur, 154, 170 *sq*.
Ahriman, 80
Akabia ben Mahalallel, 300
Akiba, Rabbi, 283
Alexandria, importance of, to Jews, 181
Allegorical view of 'Job,' 65; of Koheleth's portrait of old age, 229 *sq*.
Alphabet of Ben Sira, 195 *sq*.
Amenemhat I., 156
Amos, parallels to 'Job' in, 87
Amos iv. 13, v. 8, perhaps interpolations, 52 *n*.
Angels, doctrine of, 44 *sq*. *See also* Spirits
Apap, the serpent, 76
Apocrypha, value of the, 179
Aquila, versions of, 277
Arabian theory of angels, 44 *n*.
Arabic Literature, euphuism in, 206
Arabic Poets, subjectivity, 64; parallels to 'Job' in, 100
Arabic Proverbs compared with Hebrew, 134; one quoted, 64
Arabisms, in 'Job,' 99, 291 *sq*.; in Proverbs, 172
Aramaisms, in 'Job,' 15 *n*., 92, 97, 99, 291 *sq*., 294; in 'Proverbs,' 154, 168, 172; in Koheleth, 257
Aristeas, the fragment of, 96
Aristotle, definition of Virtue, 28
Arnold, Matthew, 122
Artaxerxes II. and III., 258
Ashmedai, 80

Assyrian, Discoveries, 5 *sq*.; Policy of uprooting nations, 73; Theory of Angels, 44 *n*.
Atomism, doctrine of, 263
Atonement, doctrine of the, 3, 287, 45
Augustine, Saint, quoted, 147, 284
Aurelius, Marcus, mentioned, 289; quoted, 234; compared with Koheleth, 245, 266 *sq*.

BABYLONIAN, animal fables, 126; physical theology, 52
Bacon, Lord, the *New Atlantis*, 132; *Adv. of Learning*, 210
Bagoses, 258
Bede, the Ven., on 'Job,' 90
Bedouin prayer, 52
Behemoth, 56
Ben Abuyah, 150
Bereshith Rabba, quoted, 188
Bernstein, on 'Job,' 293
Bertholdt, on 'Job,' 293
Bible, Milton's view of the, 253
Biblical criticism, 1 *sq*.
Bickell, as a critic, 241; on Job (xix. 25-27), 35, 288; on Prov. (xxii. 19-21), 138; on Sirach, 195; on Koheleth (iv. 13-16), 213, (iii. 11) 276, (viii. 10) 220, 276; list of poetical passages in Koheleth, 206; on the text of Koheleth, 273; and *passim*
Bildad, his home, 15; the advocate of tradition, 17, 23
Binney, Mr., 296
Birthday, Job's curse of his, 16
Blake, William, quoted, 54; his illustrations to 'Job,' 19, 45 *n*., 50, 56, 59, 65, 106 *sq*.
Book of the Dead, parallels with 'Job,' 39, 76

BÖT

Böttcher, on 'Job,' 68
Bradley, Dean, 215, 229 *n.*, 248
Breton legend of St. Ives, 140
Briggs, Prof., on Elihu's speeches, 93, 296
Budde, on Aramaisms in 'Job,' 291 *sqq.*
Buddha, 218
Buddhist sayings, 128
Budge, Mr., on Tiamat, 78
Bullinger, on Sirach, 197
Bunsen, quoted, 108 *n.*
Bunyan, 109

CAMERARIUS, edition of Sirach, 197
Canon, the, final settlement, 233, 281
Carlyle, quoted, 112, 144 *n.*, 246
Ceremonial system, value of, 119 *sq.*; approved by Sirach, 190
Chabas, M., quoted, 57
Chaldæans, 73; their philosophy known to Job, 51
Chateaubriand, quoted, 65
Chinese proverbs, 129
Christ, never used directly anti-sacrificial language, 3 *sq.*; Kenotic view of His person, 7; whether Job a type of, 102 *sq.*; foregleams of, in Prov. viii., 176
Christian doctrine in Koheleth, 248 *sq.*
Church of England, attitude to Biblical criticism, 1 *sq.*
Cicero, dialogues, 207
Clement, of Rome, 176
Coleridge, quoted, 108
Constantinople, Councils at, 107, 282
Cosmos, conception of the world as, 52, 161
Cox, Dr., quoted, 46

DANIEL, plural authorship of the Book of, 8
Dante, allusions to, 28, 51, 66, 76, 159, 194, 230; quotations from, 45, 54, 130; comparison of the *Divina Commedia* to 'Job,' 111
Davenant, quoted, 252
David, idealisation of, 131 *sqq.*
Davidson, on Job (xix. 25-27), 34
Dawn, personified, 77
De Jong, on Koheleth, 240
Delitzsch, on the Praise of Wisdom, 163; on the date of Proverbs,

ELE

170; on the period of Koheleth, 258; his Hebrew New Testament, 288; and *passim*
Derenbourg, quoted, 100
De Sanctis, quoted, viii.
Determinism, in Koheleth, 265 *sqq.*
Deuteronomy, in the reign of Josiah, 6; points of contact with Job, 86; influence on the Praise of Wisdom, 168 *sq.*; (xxxii. 8) explained, 81 *n.*, 291
De Vere, Aubrey, quoted, 105
Dillmann, on style of Job, 294
Din Ibrahim, morality of the, 98
Dragon Myth, 16, 24, 76
Dramatic character of 'Job,' 107
Drunkenness, 140, 156

EBERS, Prof., 40, 269
Ecclesiastes, the Book of—
(*a*) Canonicity, 279 *sqq.*; title, 207 *n.*, 298; date and place of composition, 255 *sqq.*, 271, 278; break in its composition, 204; language, 256; style, 203, 207, 246; how far autobiographical, 209; comparison with Job, 203; with Sirach, 279; its standpoint, 200 *sqq.*; its pessimism, 215, 251 *sq.*, 301; its relation to Epicureanism, 215, 222, 252, 262 *sq.*; to Stoicism, 264
(*b*) *Passages explained or emended*: (iii. 11, 12) 210, 260, 276, 299; (iii. 17-21) 211; (iv. 13-16) 213; (v. 17) 260; (v. 19) 261; (vi. 9) 261; (vii. 1) 215; (vii. 18) 261; (vii. 27) 219; (viii. 10) 220, 276; (viii. 12) 220; (x. 20) 222; (xi. 9-xii. 7) 300; (xii. 1-7) 226; (xii. 8-14) 229 *sqq.*, 261, 301
Transpositions, 273 *sq.*; Interpolations, 275, and 211, 213, 224 *sq.*, 226, 229 *sq.*
Ecclesiasticus, *see* Sirach
Edwards, Sutherland, on Mephistopheles, 110
Egypt, theory that 'Job' was composed in, 75
Egyptian, animal fables, 126 *n.*; discoveries, 5; incantations, 16; proverbs, 129; influence on Koheleth, 269 *sq.*
Egyptian-Jewish literature, 181
Elephantiasis, Job's disease, 22

INDEX

ELE

Elephants, 57
Elihu, genealogy, 42 *n*; speeches of, 68, 90 *sqq*.; their date, 42, 92; their style, 47, 92, 291
Eliphaz, his home, 15; the 'depositary of a revelation,' 17
Elohim, the sons of the, 14, 79, 81, 82, 151
Emerson, quoted, 160
Enoch, 297; Book of, 268
Epictetus, 234 *n*.
Epicureanism, in Koheleth, 240 *sq*., 252, 262 *sq*.
Epicurus, 222
Ethics, practical, relation to Hebrew Wisdom, 118 *sq*.; of the Proverbs, 135 *sq*.
Euergetes II. Physkon, 180
Ewald, his division of the Book of Proverbs, 134; of the Praise of Wisdom, 162; on the date of Proverbs, 190; on Koheleth, 236 *sqq*.; and *passim*
Ezekiel (xiv. 14), 60
Ezra, why not mentioned in Sirach, 193 *sq*.

FAMILY life, in Proverbs, 136
Farmers, Israelitish goodwill to, 136, 214
Faust, the Hebrew, 150
Fees, whether paid to the 'Wise Men,' 124 *n*.
Fénelon, 67
Friends, Job's, Emeers, 15; representatives of orthodoxy, 17; their narrowness, 30
Froude, J. A., quoted on Job xxvii., 95 *n*.

GAMALIEL, 280
Geiger, on Koheleth, 238 *sq*.
Genesis, no protest against Idolatry in, 71; opening chapters of, 6; (xiv. 19-22) 160
Gilchrist, Life of Blake, 107
Ginsburg, Dr., on 'proportionate retribution' in Job, 69; on Koheleth, 236; on Eccles. (iii. 12), 210 *n*.; and *passim*
Gnostic myth of Achamoth, 161
God, name of, in Koheleth, 201, 217
Godet, 288
Grätz, on Koheleth, 244, 301
Grave, Job's, 60
Greek influence on Koheleth, 202, 241, 260 *sqq*.

ISR

Green, Prof., of Princeton, on Job, (xix. 25-27) 33, 34 *n*.; (xxvii.-xxviii.) 94
Gregory the Great, on 'Job,' 90

HAI GAON, Rabbi, on 'Job,' 61
Harischandra compared to Job, 63
Harnack, quoted, 263
Harūn ar-Rashīd, 131, 296
Hegesias Peisithanatos, 268
Heine, on 'Job,' 104
Hellenic movement in Palestine, 181
Hengstenberg, on 'Job,' 61; on Koheleth, 249 *n*.
Herder, on 'Job,' 295; on Koheleth, 301
Hezekiah, the Song of, 88; his supposed authorship of Proverbs xxv.-xxix., 142 *sq*.; his views on medical science, 191
Hillel, Rabbi, a copious fabulist, 128; the School of, on Koheleth, 280
Hitopadesa, quoted, 153
Hitzig, as a critic, 241 *n*.; on the arrangement of the Praise of Wisdom, 163; and *passim*
Hooker, 161, 162, 216 *sq*.
Hosea, parallels to 'Job' in, 87
Humboldt, A. von, 46
Humour, touches of, in 'Job,' 13, 14, 49, 109, 290; in Proverbs, 148 *n*.; in Koheleth, 200, 216
Husbandmen, Israelite goodwill to, 136, 214

IBN EZRA, opinion that 'Job' was a translation, 96
Ibycus, the cranes of, 222
Idealism, of the Prophets, 119
Immortality, the hope of, in Proverbs, 122 *sq*.; attitude of Koheleth to, 216, 251, 301
Inconsistencies in the Canonical Scriptures, 204
Indian, animal fables, 126 *n*.; proverbs, 129
Inspiration, view of, broadened by literary criticism, 7
Irving, Edward, 162
Isaiah, mythological allusions in, 78; parallels to 'Job' in, 84, 87; xxviii. 14, 120 *n*.
Israel, Job a type of, 58; the word not in Proverbs, 119; Koheleth indifferent to its religious primacy, 199

X

INDEX

ISR

Israelites, low religious position before the Exile, 6; their sympathy with husbandmen, 136, 214
Italian moralists, their use of 'Job,' viii.
Ives, Saint, Breton legend of, 140

JAMNIA, Synod of, 233, 280
Jehovah, the name, 71, 72 *n.*; consistency of the speeches of, in 'Job,' 48, 94
Jeremiah, parallels to 'Job' in, 86
Jerome, Saint, on metrical character of 'Job,' 12 *n.*; on Epicureanism in Koheleth, 262, 281
Jewish nation, like Job, a byword, 32

Job, the Book of—
  (*a*) Proposed title for, 12; divisions of, 12 *sq.*; perhaps a translation, 96 *sq.*; probable stages of the growth of, 66 *sqq.*; date of, 67 *sqq.*, 88, 157; place of composition, 75; effect of removing the interpolations in, 70; Aramaic colouring of, 15 *n.*, 92; whether historical, 60 *sq.*, 183, 290; whether autobiographical, 63; whether a drama, 107; polemical aim of, 65; religious teaching of, 102 *sqq.*; feeling for nature in, 51; humour in, 13 *sq.*, 49, 109, 290; influence of, on other writers, viii. 83 *sq.*
  (*b*) **Author**, the greatest master of Hebrew Wisdom, 11; circumstances of his age reflected in xvii. 6-9, 32; a traveller, 75, 97; looks beyond Israel, 65; place of writing, 75
  (*c*) **Hero**, his name, 62; title given him by the Syrians, 65; his nationality, 13, 59, 117, 170; whether historical, 60 *sqq.*, 103; great age ascribed to him, 71; his grave, 60; dual aspect of, 32; a type, 17, 21, 22, 28, 31, 32, 58, 65
  (*d*) **Text**. (i.) *Passages explained or emended*: (vi. 25) 288; (xi. 6) 26; (xiii. 15) 28; (xv. 7) 167; (xvi. 2) 31; (xix. 25-27) 33 *sqq.*, 288 *sq.*; (xxxiii. 13) 44; (xxxviii. 41) 52 *n.*; (xxxix. 10) 53 *n.*

LUT

  (ii.) *Passages misplaced*, list of, 114; also 38, 39 *n.*, 40 *n.*, 41, 50, 68, 94, 115
  (iii.) *Passages interpolated*, 55 *sq.*, 68 *sq.*, 94, &c.
Joel ii. 17 explained, 32
Joseph, the tax farmer, 182, 191, 213
Josephus, quoted, 190
Joshua ben Hananyah, Rabbi, 230

KALISCH, Dr., on Eccles. iii. 12, 210 *n.*; his *Path and Goal*, 265
Kant, on Job's friends, 37
Kenotic view of Christ's person, 7, 287
Khîda, a riddle, 125
Kings, First Book of, (iv. 32) 132, (xix. 12) 19
Kleinert, on Job (vi. 25), 288; on the style of Elihu, 293
Klostermann, translation of Eccles. vii. 21, 219
Koheleth, the name, 207, 231; his personality partly fused with Solomon, 208; his originality, 205, 268 *sq.* *See also* Ecclesiastes
Koheleth, the Book of, *see* Ecclesiastes
Koran, quoted, &c., 31, 62 *n.*, 63, 79 *n.*
Krochmal, N., on Epilogue to Koheleth, 232 *sq.*
K'sil, = Orion, 77
Kuenen, on the Levitical Law, 3

LAGARDE, on the use of 'Eloah,' 72 *n.*
Lamentations, parallels to 'Job' in, 86
Landed property, accumulation of, 146
Law, the Levitical, authorship of, 3 *sqq.*; not enforced in pre-Exile period, 6; identification of, with personified wisdom, 162, 192; Koheleth's attitude to, 218
Lee, Prof. S., on 'Job,' 97, 294
Lemuel, 154, 170 *sq.*
Letteris, Max, 150
Leviathan, 56
Love for one's enemies, 147
Lowth, Bp., 16, 61, 107, 186, 237
Lucretius, quoted, 201, 205; compared with Koheleth, 263
Luther, on Job, 61; on Sirach, 197; on Koheleth, 205

INDEX

LUZ

Luzzatto, on the 'God of Job,' 104; on Koheleth, 238 sq.

MAL'AK YAHVÈ, 80
Mal'akim, 79, 80, 82
Marduk, the god, 77
Mariolatry, 162 n.
Marvell, Andrew, quoted, 144
Māshāl, 125 sq., 132, 163
Maspero, quoted, 76
Massa, in the Hauran, Israelite colony at, 171
Medical Science, attitudes of Sirach and Hezekiah to, 190 sq.
Meir, Rabbi, the writer of animal fables, 128
Mendelssohn, on Koheleth, 236
Mephistopheles, 110 n.
Merodach, the god, 77
Merx, view of Job, 62, 113
Messianic hope, 119, 188
Midrash, proverbs in, 128
Milton, allusions to, 53, 62, 107, 108, 112, 162, 253; quotations from, 19, 41, 107, 160, 162
Mishnic peculiarities in Koheleth, 256
M'liça, a dark saying, 125
Mohammed, delight of, in 'Job,' 63; religion of, 98
Mommsen, quoted, 181
Monarchy, view of, in Proverbs, 145; in Koheleth, 222
Monogamy, in Proverbs, 136
Monotheism, of Job, 74; in Proverbs, 130
Morality, of the Proverbs, 135 sq., 177
Moses, authorship of the Law, 3; nature of his work, 6
Mo'tazilites, 98, 162 n., 296
Mozley, quoted, 103
Mussaph prayer, 193
Mythology, in 'Job,' 76

NARRATIVE poetry, alien to Hebrew genius, 13
Nature, feeling for, in 'Job,' 51; in Sirach, 193
Nebuchadnezzar, 73
Neferhotep, stanzas in honour of, 269
Neubauer, Dr. A., 289
New Testament, attitude to Proverbs, 177
Nowack, on Eccles. (iii. 12), 210 n.
Numerical Proverbs, 153

PRO

OLD TESTAMENT, general remarks on the criticism of, 1 sqq.; need to distinguish between the parts of, 7; critical problems of, not prominent in Christ's time, 7
Omar Khayyam, 200, 245, 246, 253, 263
Onias, the High Priest, 213
Onkelos, Targum of, 264
Oort, Dr., on proverbs, 127
Orion, 77

PALMER, Major, 52
Parables, in the Old Testament, 126
Paradise, tradition of, 123
Patriarchal Age, whether delineated in Job, 13, 71 sqq.
Paul, Saint, doctrine of the Atonement, 3, 287
Pentateuch, the literary analysis of it, 5 sq.
Peshitto translation of Proverbs, 174
Philo, 151, 161 n., 264
Pisa, Job frescoes at, 106
Pleiades, 52, 290
Plumptre, Dean, 122, 158, 207 n., 212, 245, 263, 265; and passim
Prior, the poet, on Koheleth, 237
Prophetical books, plural authorship in, 8
Prophets, their antisacrificial language, 4; their horizon that of their own times, 8; their relations to the 'Wise Men,' 119 sqq., 182 sq.
Proverbs, different names for, 125; no collection of popular, 125; some originally current as riddles, 127
Proverbs, the Book of—
(a) The division of, 134; repetitions in, 133, 143; no subject arrangement, 134; the tone of the different parts of, 135, 146, 167, 177; their dates, 130, 133, 145, 149, 152, 165 sqq.; their authorship, 130 sqq., 142, 135, 165 sq.; their form and style, 133, 139, 143, 149, 154, 168; interpolations in, 173 sqq.; transpositions in, 174
(b) *Passages explained or emended*: (v. 16) 296; (viii. 22) 160; (xiv. 32) 122; (xviii. 24) 137; (xix. 1) 135 n.; (xix. 7) 134; (xxii. 19-21) 138; (xxiii. 18) 123; (xxvii. 6) 148, 296; (xxx. 1-5) 149 sq.,

170; (xxx. 15-16) 153; (xxx. 31) 175; (xxxi. 1) 170
Psalms, relations of, to 'Job,' 84, 88; Psalm viii. 5 parodied in 'Job' (vii. 17, 18), 22
Ptahhotep, Proverbs of, 121
Ptolemy Arsacides, Golden Table, 289
Pusey, Dr. quoted, 1

Q'DŌSHĪM, 80, 149 *n*.
Quinet quoted, 105

RA, the sun god, 76
Rahab, the helpers of, 24, 76
Raven (in Job xxxviii. 41), 52 *n*.
Realism of the 'Wise Men,' 119
Renan, on the style of Elihu, 47; on Koheleth, 206, 234, 242 *sq*., 246, 298; and *passim*
Resh Lakish, Rabbi, quoted, 60
Resurrection, hope of, 34, 75, 188 *sq*., 251, 301
Retribution, proportionate, 23, 35, 58, 73, 98, 121, 140, 167, 189, 190 *n*., 200, 219, 251
Riddles, proverbs originally current as, 127
Rig Veda, quoted, 78, 152
Romans, vii. 20 adopted from Proverbs (xxiv. 17, 18), 147
Romaunt of the Rose, quoted, 300
Rossetti, Miss C., 242

SACRIFICIAL system, importance of, in post-Exile period, 4; relations of Job to, 71. *See also* Law
Salmon, Prof., on Eccles. (ix. 7-9), 262
Samaritans, 194
Sammael, 80
Sandys', George, translation of 'Job,' 106
Satan, the, 14, 79, 80, 109, 188 *sq*., 297
Schiller, 12
Schultens, Albert, quoted, 61, 97, 99
Sea Life, familiar, 140; cf. 133
Seneca, quoted, 57, 265
Septuagint version, of 'Job,' 113, 114, 296; of Proverbs, 173; of Koheleth, 277
Seven Wise Men, of Greece, 119, 124
Shammaites, on Koheleth, 280 *sq*.
Shedim, 80

Shelley, delight in Job, 112, 253; dislike of Koheleth, 253
Sibyl, the oldest Jewish, 264
Simeon ben Shetach, 282 *sq*.
Simon II., 180, 181 *sq*.
Sirach, parentage, 180; early life, 182; a true 'scribe,' 185; unacquainted with Greek philosophy, 190; interested in nature and history, 193
Sirach, the Book of—
(a) Canonicity, 279 *sq*., 282 *sq*.; the name Ecclesiasticus, 197; written in Hebrew, 194, 196; ancient versions of, 297; its date, 180 *sqq*.; subject arrangement, 183; style, 185; whether autobiographical, 186; parallelisms in, to Proverbs, 184; no philosophical thought in, 182; imperfect moral teaching in, 187; conception of the divine nature, 188
(b) *Passages emended or explained*: (xi. 16) 188; (xxi. 27) 189 *n*.; (xxiv. 27) 196; (xxv. 15) 196; (xlvi. 18) 196; (xlviii. 11) 189, 193; (l. 1) 193; (l. 26) 193
Soferim, 238. *See also* 'Wise Men'
Solar Myths, 16, 22, 24, 76, 77
Solomon, secular turn of, 72; reputed authorship of Proverbs, 130 *sqq*., 165, 170; Koheleth's representative of humanity, 202, 207; reputed authorship of Koheleth, 255, 275
Sophia, Gnostic myth of, 161 *n*.
Sophocles, 107, 220
Spanheim, quoted, 97
Spenser, the poet, 12
Spinoza, on Job, 61
Spirits, classes of, 44 *sq*.
Stanley, Dean, on Koheleth, 245, 255
Star worship, 71, 82
Steersmanship, the term, 133
Stickel, quoted, 102
Stoicism, in Koheleth, 240 *sq*., 264
Swift, 15
Swinburne, quoted, 212
Syrian title for Job, 65

TALMUD, on Job, 64; proverbs in the, 128; Sirach cited in, 196; comparison of Koheleth with, 205; on Koheleth, 281

Tasso, 109 *n.*
Taylor, C., on Job (xix. 26), 289
Taylor, Jeremy, 253
Temple, Bishop, 225
Tennyson, quoted, 212
Theism, argument for, early based on tradition, 23; of the Praise of Wisdom, 167
Theodore of Mopsuestia, 107
Thirlwall, Bishop, quoted, 2
Thomas à Kempis, 231, 249
Thomson, the poet, quoted, 21
Thoreau, quoted, 106, 252
Tiamat, 77
Trades, disparaged in Sirach, 186
Turgenieff, 243
Turner, Studies Biblical and Oriental, quoted, 46
Tyler, on Koheleth, 240, 263 *sq.*

Unicorn, in Job (xxxix. 10), 53 *n.*
Utilitarianism of the Wise Men, 121, 137
Uz, locality of, 13 *n.*

Vaihinger, on Koheleth, 236 *sq.*
Varuna, Vedic hymn to, 154

Vatke, on date of Proverbs, 1
Vedic hymns, 77, 154. *See also* Rig Veda
Virtue, Koheleth's 'theory of,' 218

Webbe, George, quoted, 113
Wellhausen, on Levitical Law, 3 *sqq.*; on Job, 290
Wisdom, the Hebrew, nature of, 117 *sq.*; personification of, 162, 192
Wise Men, the, 118, 123, 148, 182 *sqq.*
Women, in Proverbs, 135, 154; in Sirach, 187; in Koheleth, 219, 299
Woolner, quoted, 229
Wordsworth, 162
Wright, Bateson, on Job, 113

Zeno, 265 *sq.*
Zirkel, on Græcisms in Job, 260 *sq.*
Zophar, home of, 15; the 'man of common sense,' 17
Zwischenschriften, 180

www.ingramcontent.com/pod-product-compliance
Lightning Source LLC
Chambersburg PA
CBHW030747230426
43667CB00007B/869